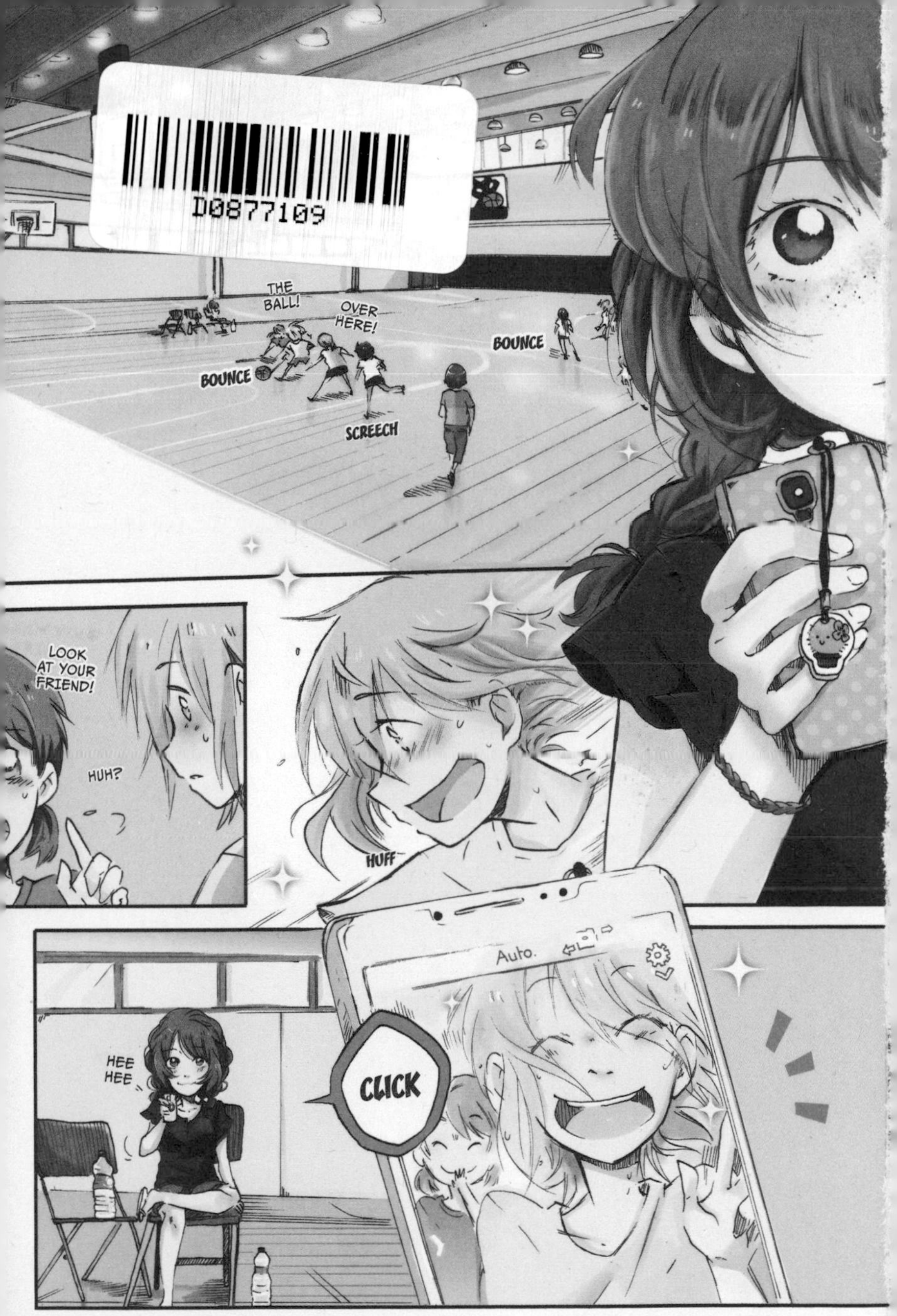
OVER HERE!
THE BALL!
BOUNCE
BOUNCE
SCREECH
HUFF
LOOK AT YOUR FRIEND!
HUH?
Auto.
CLICK
HEE HEE

Table of Contents

Chapter 10
Distance

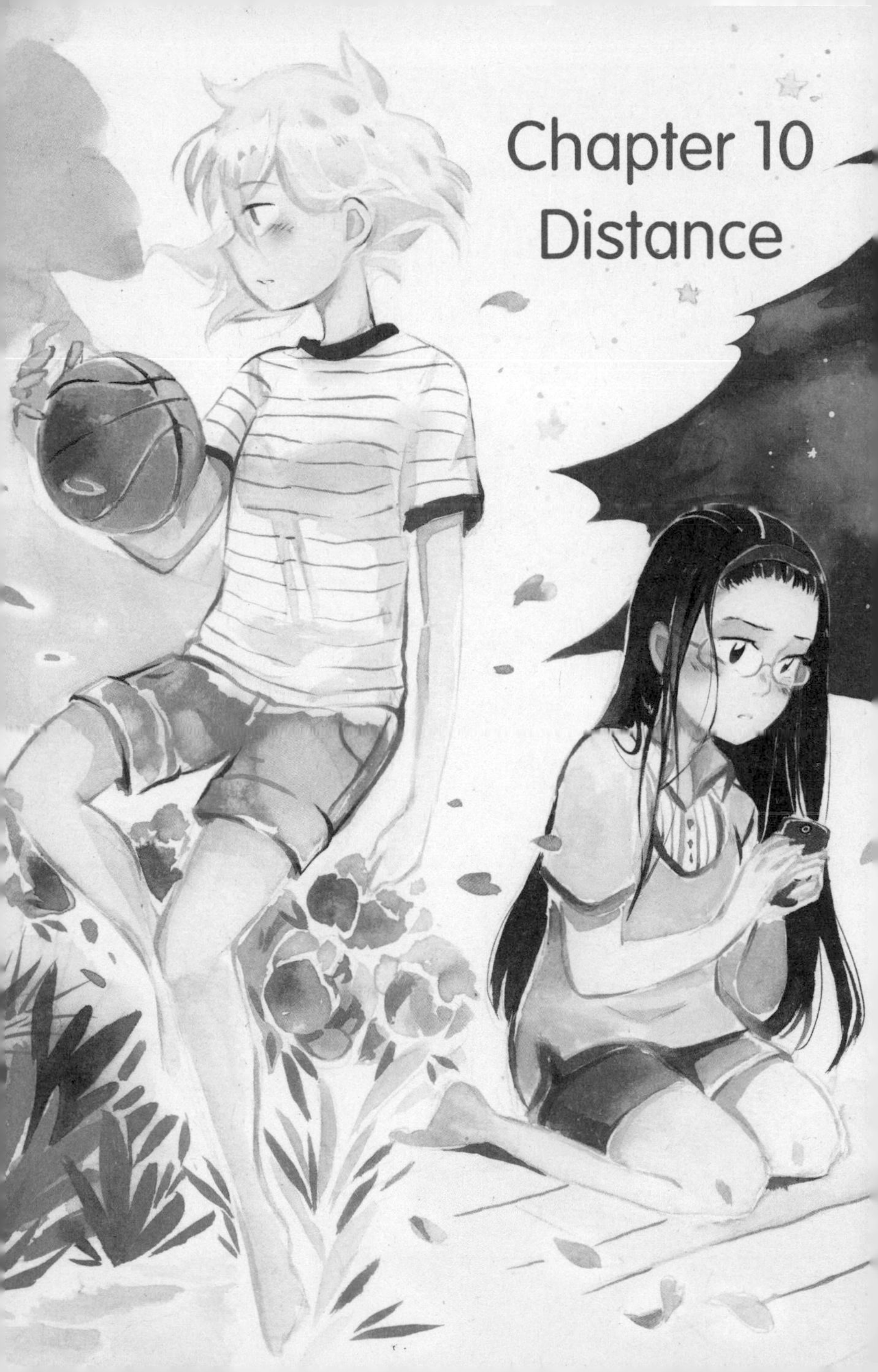

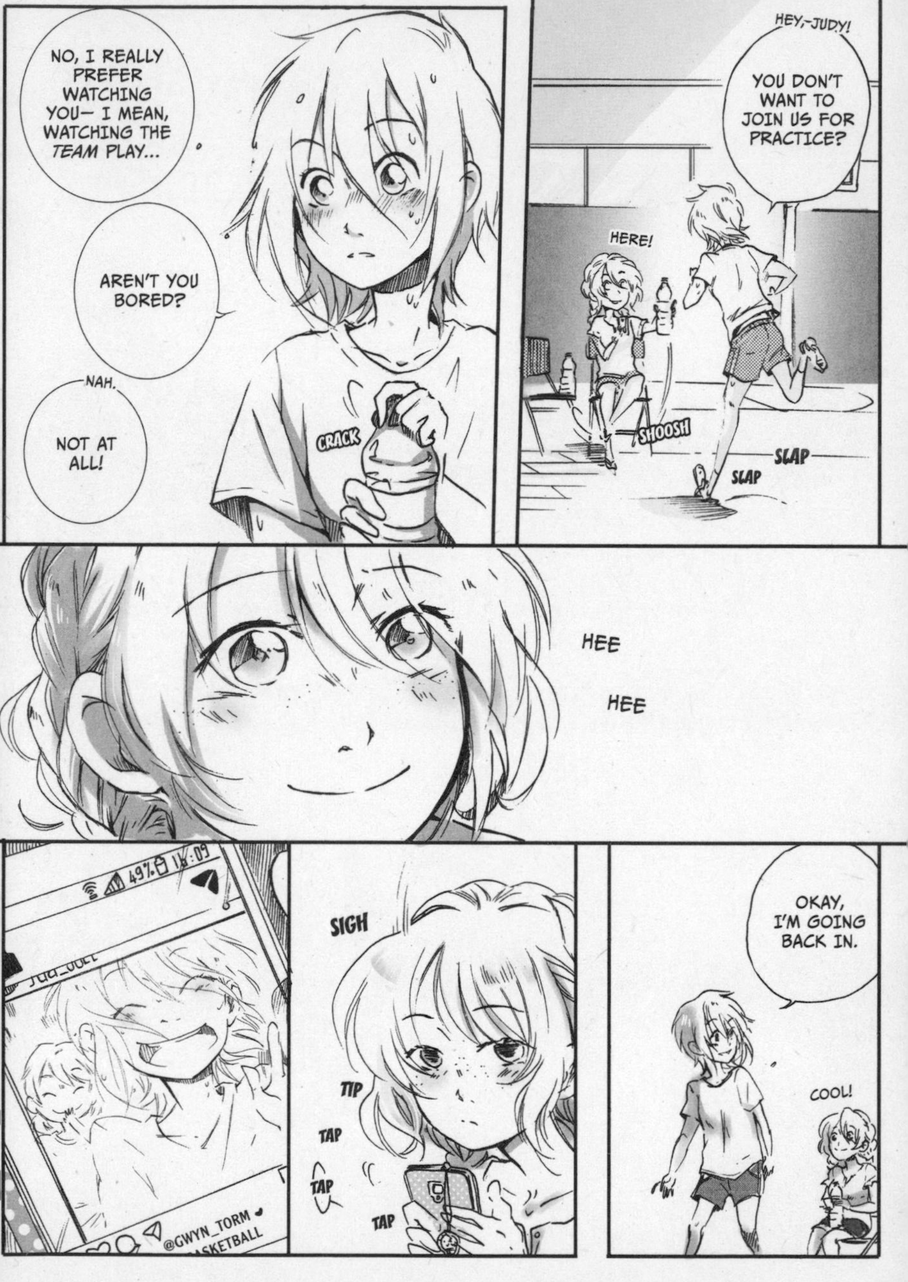
HEY, JUDY!
YOU DON'T WANT TO JOIN US FOR PRACTICE?
HERE!
SHOOSH
SLAP
SLAP
NO, I REALLY PREFER WATCHING YOU— I MEAN, WATCHING THE *TEAM* PLAY...
AREN'T YOU BORED?
NAH.
NOT AT ALL!
CRACK
HEE
HEE
OKAY, I'M GOING BACK IN.
COOL!
SIGH
TIP
TAP
TAP
TAP
49%
@GWYN_TORM

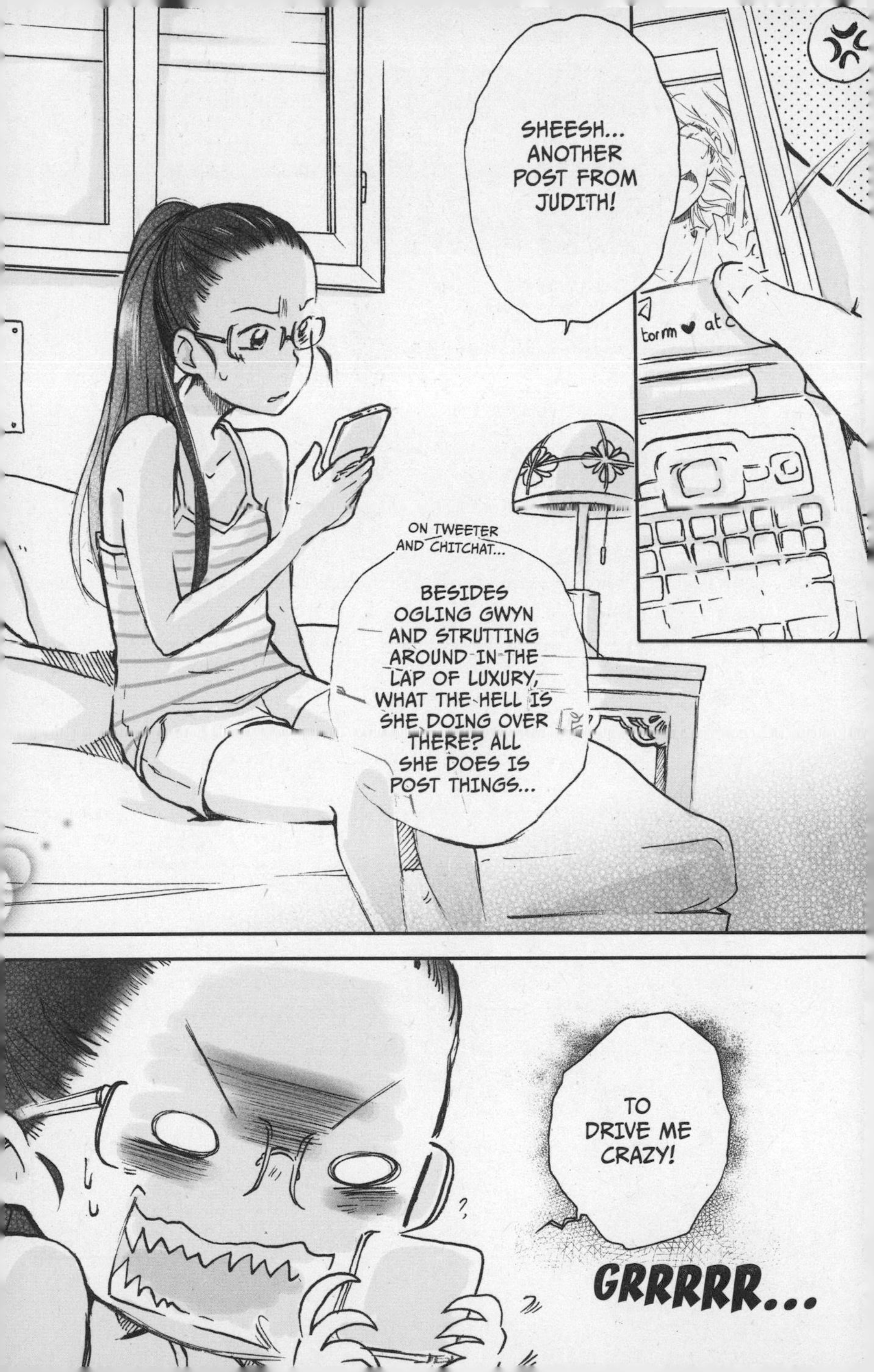
SHEESH... ANOTHER POST FROM JUDITH!
ON TWEETER AND CHITCHAT...
BESIDES OGLING GWYN AND STRUTTING AROUND IN THE LAP OF LUXURY, WHAT THE HELL IS SHE DOING OVER THERE? ALL SHE DOES IS POST THINGS...
TO DRIVE ME CRAZY!
GRRRRR...

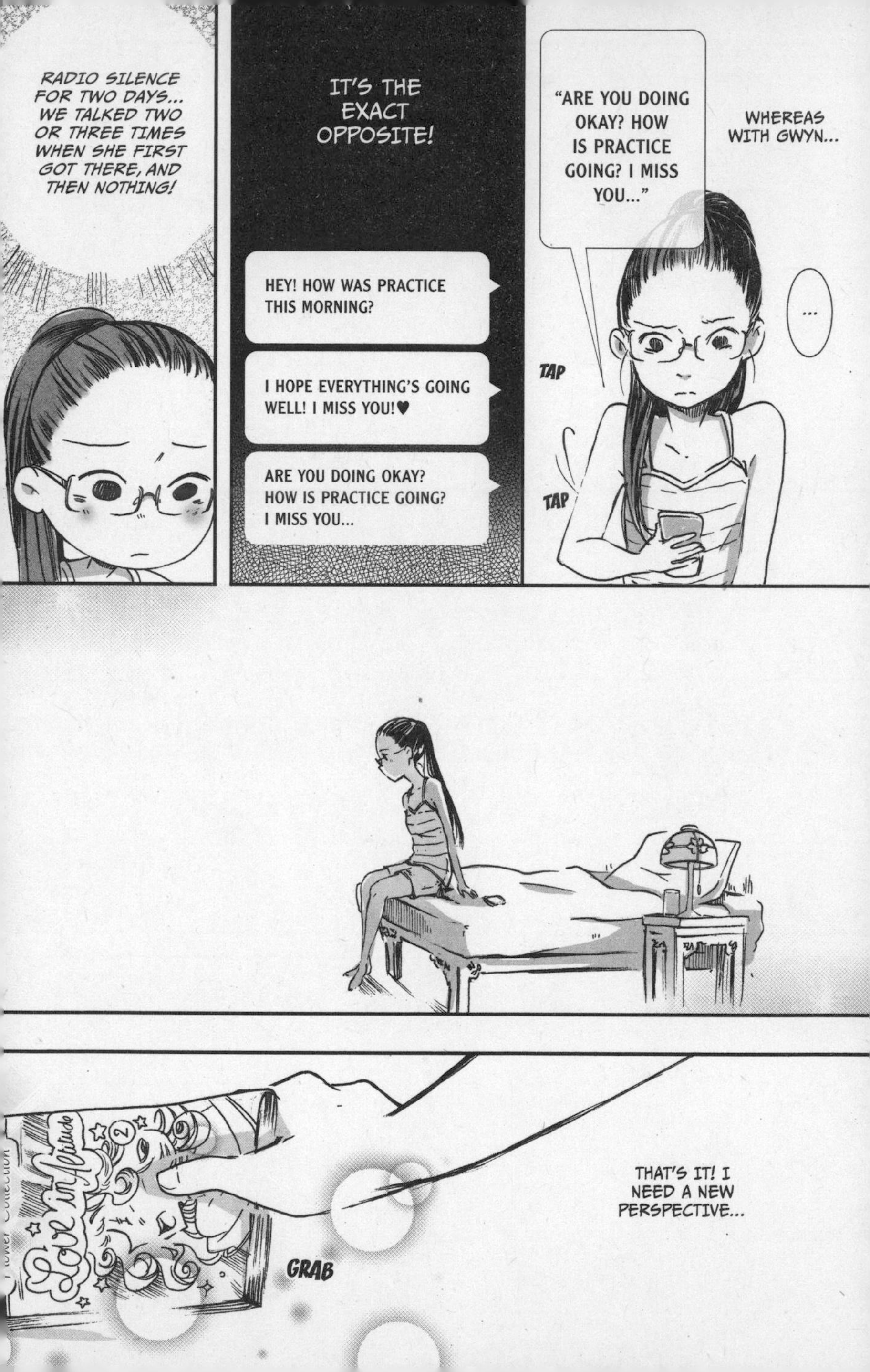
WHEREAS WITH GWYN...
"ARE YOU DOING OKAY? HOW IS PRACTICE GOING? I MISS YOU..."
...
TAP
TAP
IT'S THE EXACT OPPOSITE!
HEY! HOW WAS PRACTICE THIS MORNING?
I HOPE EVERYTHING'S GOING WELL! I MISS YOU!♥
ARE YOU DOING OKAY? HOW IS PRACTICE GOING? I MISS YOU...
RADIO SILENCE FOR TWO DAYS... WE TALKED TWO OR THREE TIMES WHEN SHE FIRST GOT THERE, AND THEN NOTHING!
THAT'S IT! I NEED A NEW PERSPECTIVE...
Love in Altitude
2
GRAB

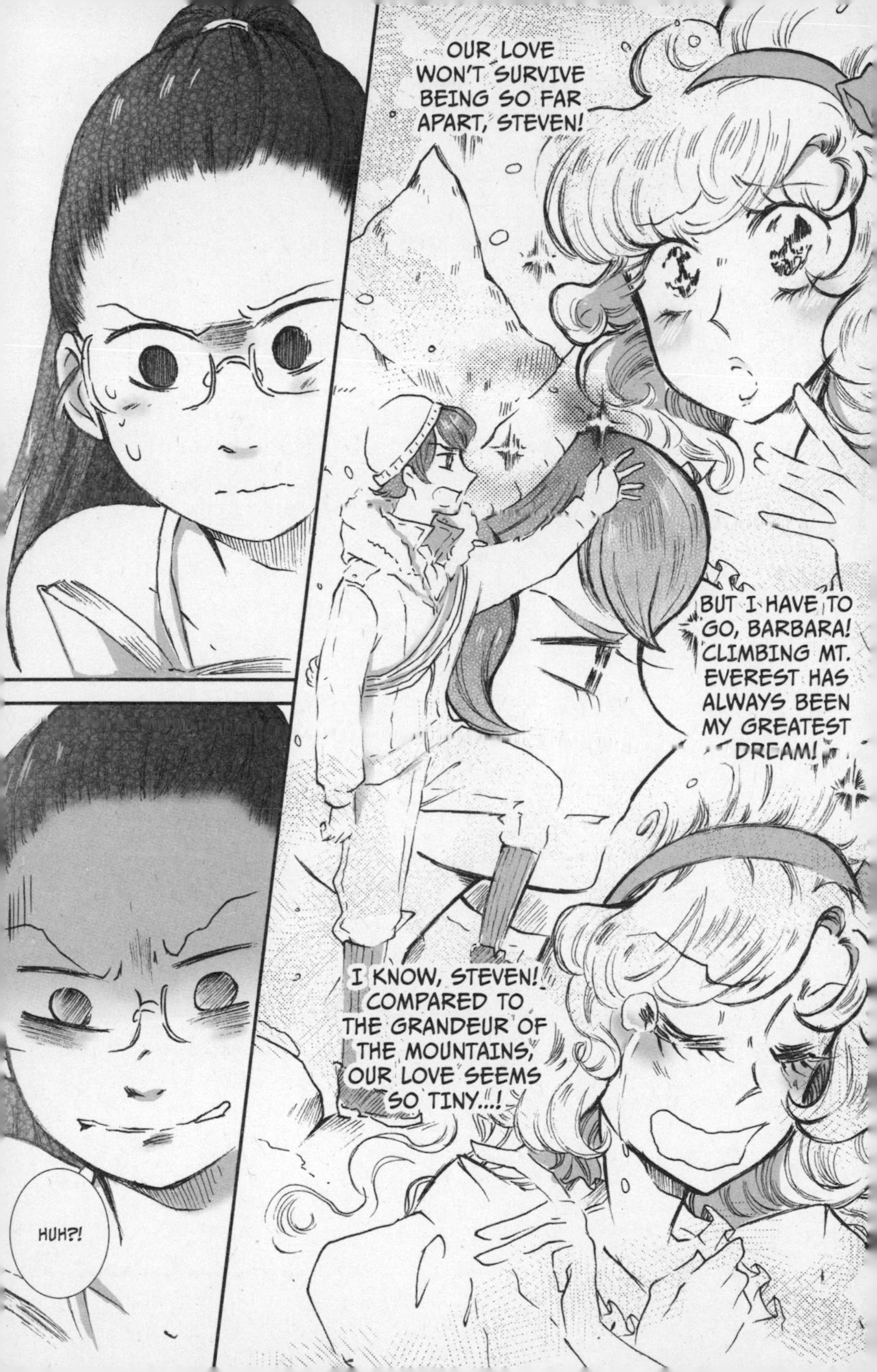
OUR LOVE WON'T SURVIVE BEING SO FAR APART, STEVEN!
BUT I HAVE TO GO, BARBARA! CLIMBING MT. EVEREST HAS ALWAYS BEEN MY GREATEST DREAM!
I KNOW, STEVEN! COMPARED TO THE GRANDEUR OF THE MOUNTAINS, OUR LOVE SEEMS SO TINY...!
HUH?!

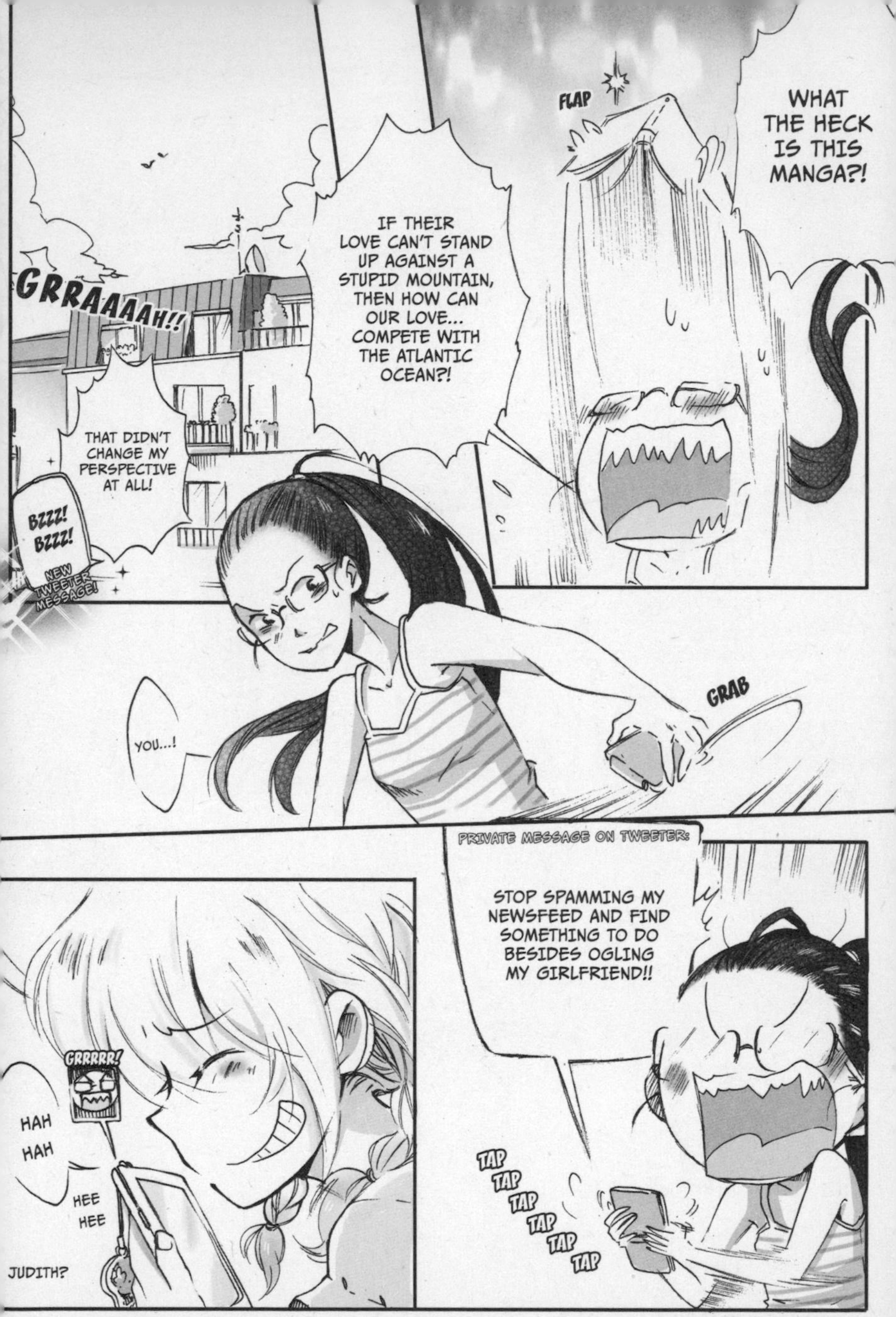
FLAP
WHAT THE HECK IS THIS MANGA?!
IF THEIR LOVE CAN'T STAND UP AGAINST A STUPID MOUNTAIN, THEN HOW CAN OUR LOVE... COMPETE WITH THE ATLANTIC OCEAN?!
GRRAAAAAH!!
THAT DIDN'T CHANGE MY PERSPECTIVE AT ALL!
BZZZ! BZZZ!
NEW TWEETER MESSAGE!
GRAB
YOU...!
PRIVATE MESSAGE ON TWEETER:
STOP SPAMMING MY NEWSFEED AND FIND SOMETHING TO DO BESIDES OGLING MY GIRLFRIEND!!
TAP TAP TAP TAP TAP TAP
GRRRRR!
HAH HAH
HEE HEE
JUDITH?

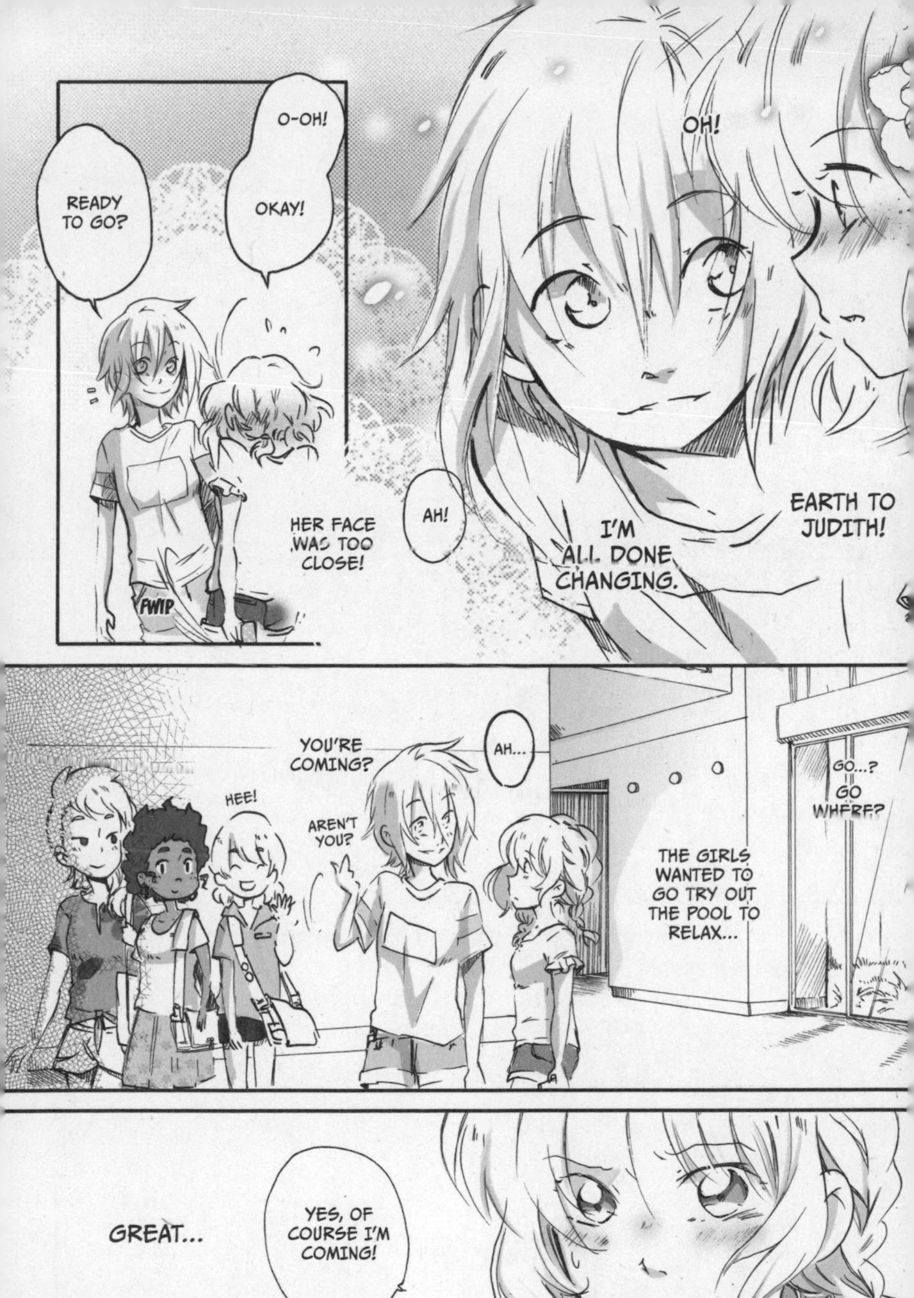
OH!
EARTH TO JUDITH!
I'M ALL DONE CHANGING.
AH!
HER FACE WAS TOO CLOSE!
O-OH!
OKAY!
READY TO GO?
FWIP
GO...?
GO WHERE?
THE GIRLS WANTED TO GO TRY OUT THE POOL TO RELAX...
AH...
YOU'RE COMING?
AREN'T YOU?
HEE!
YES, OF COURSE I'M COMING!
GREAT...

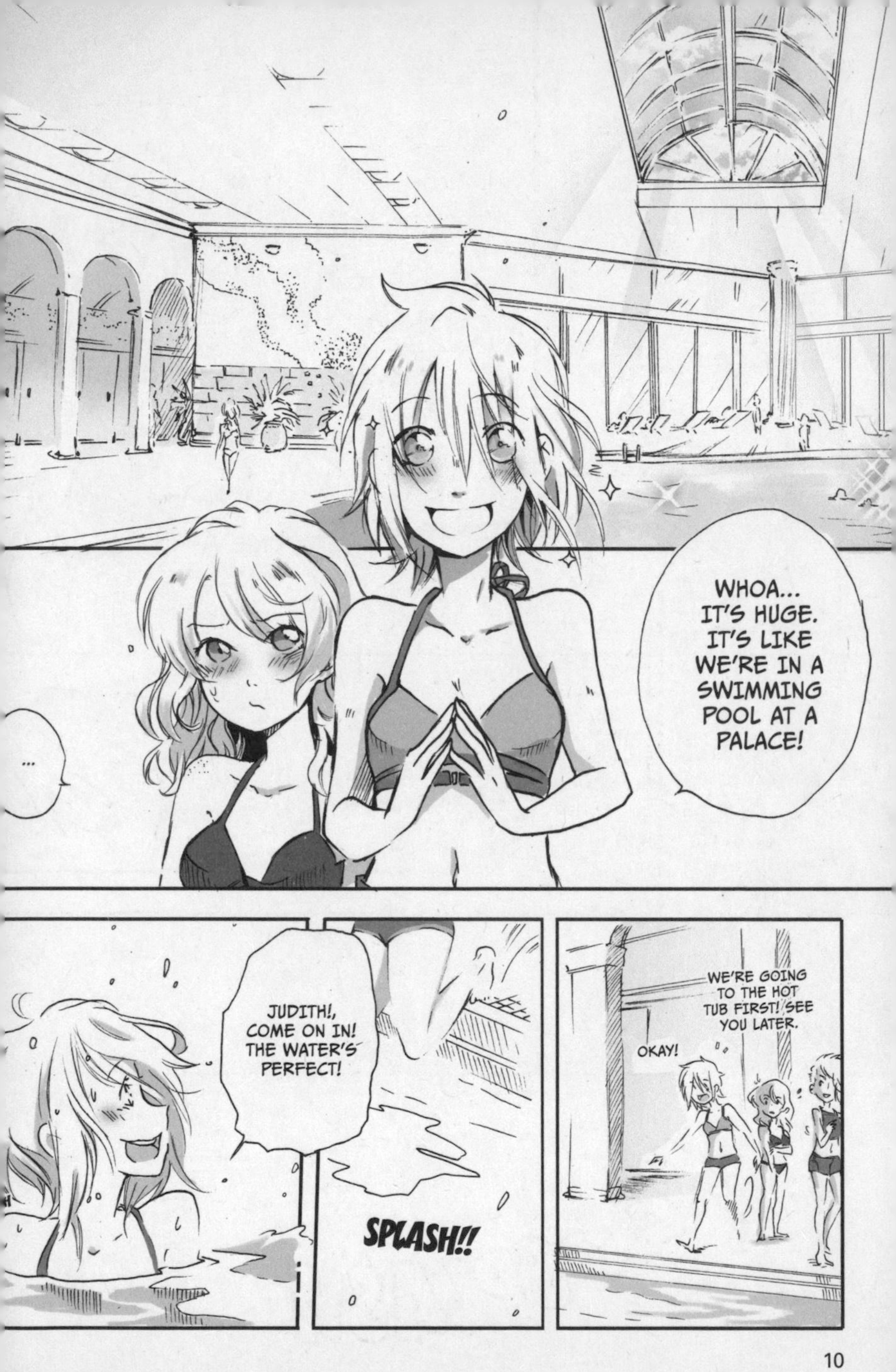
WHOA... IT'S HUGE. IT'S LIKE WE'RE IN A SWIMMING POOL AT A PALACE!
...
WE'RE GOING TO THE HOT TUB FIRST! SEE YOU LATER.
OKAY!
SPLASH!!
JUDITH!, COME ON IN! THE WATER'S PERFECT!

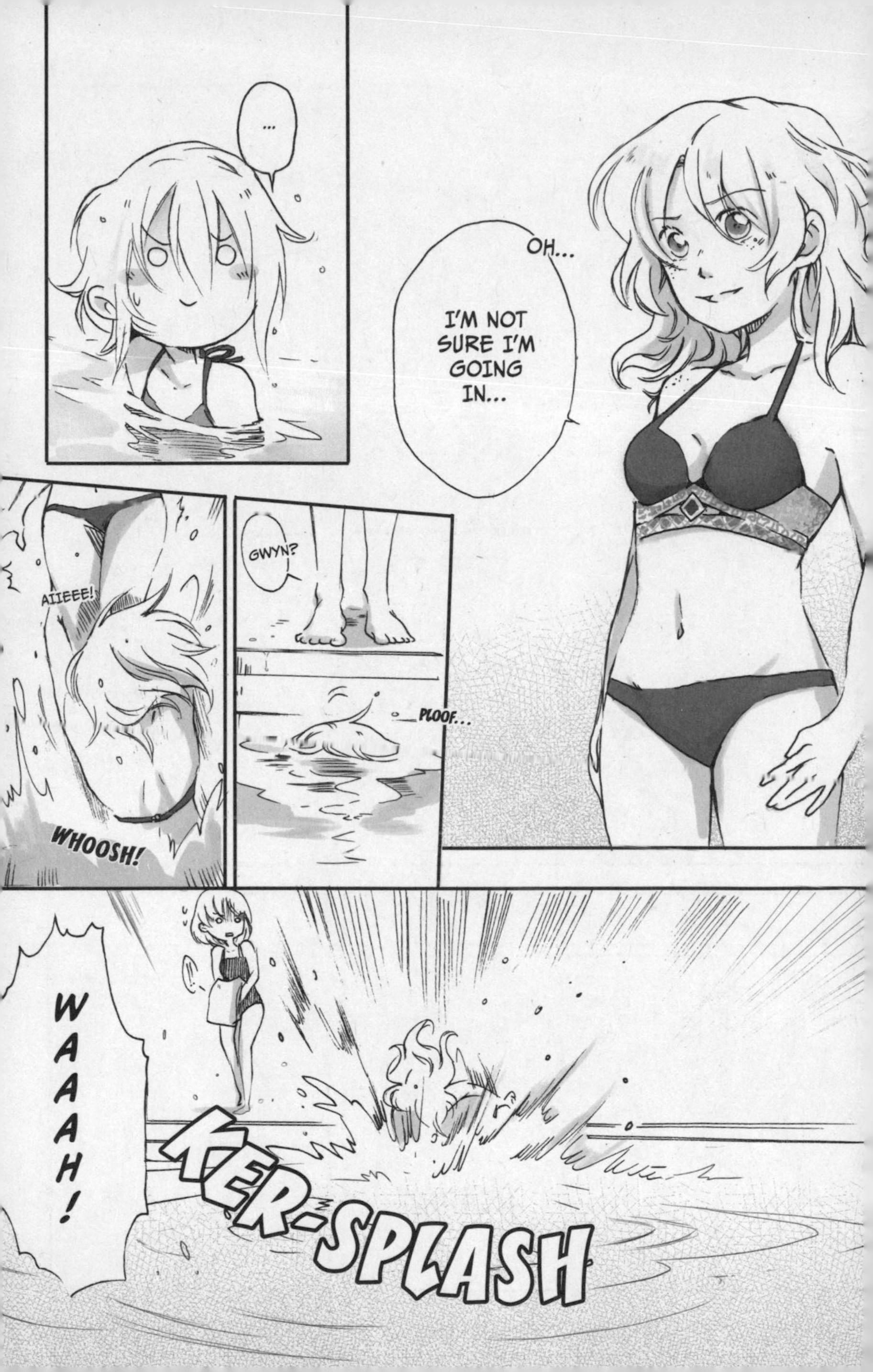
OH...
I'M NOT SURE I'M GOING IN...
...
GWYN?
PLOOF...
AIIEEE!
WHOOSH!
WAAAAH!
KER-SPLASH

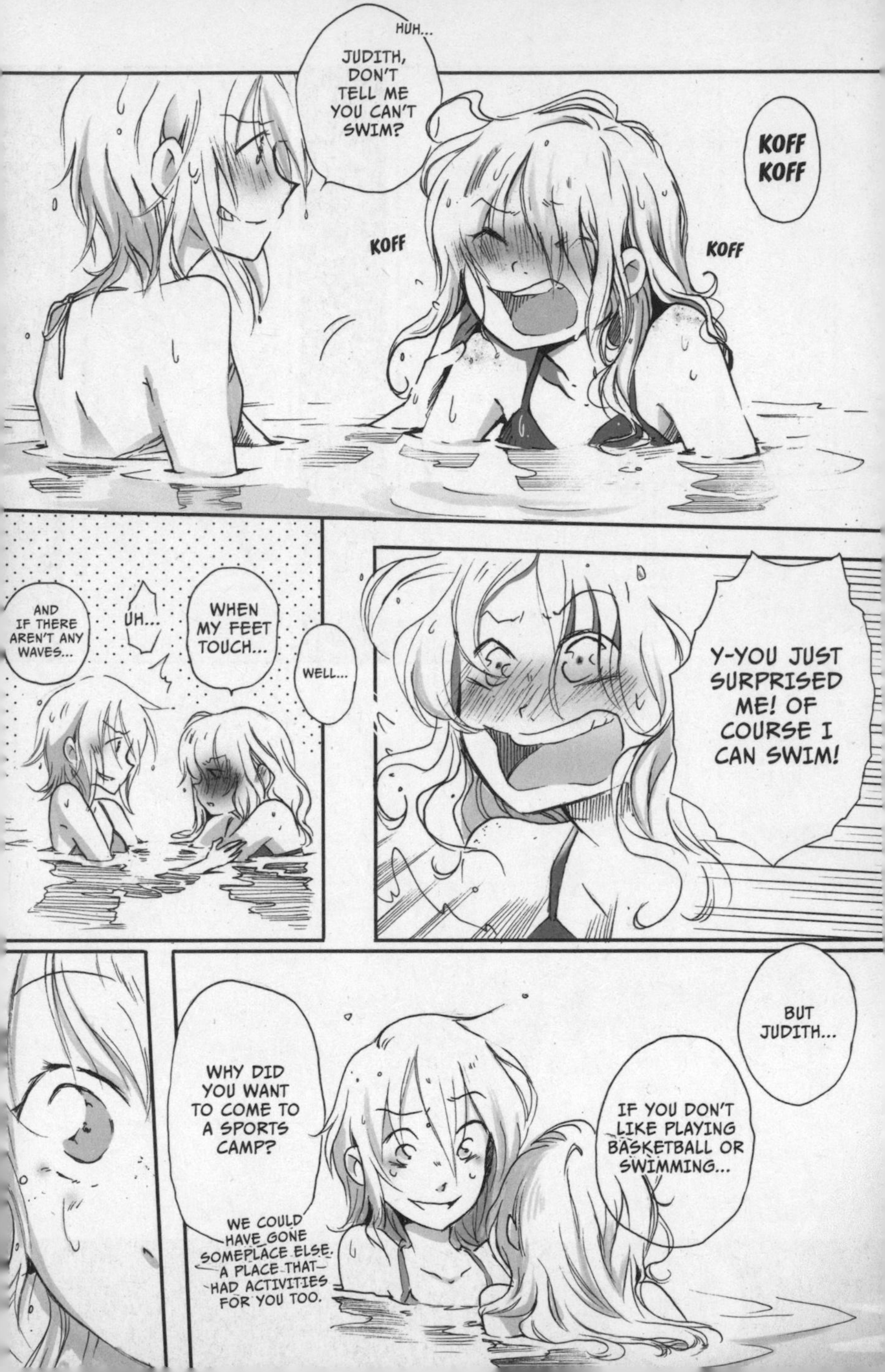
KOFF KOFF
HUH...
JUDITH, DON'T TELL ME YOU CAN'T SWIM?
KOFF
KOFF
Y-YOU JUST SURPRISED ME! OF COURSE I CAN SWIM!
WELL...
WHEN MY FEET TOUCH...
UH...
AND IF THERE AREN'T ANY WAVES...
BUT JUDITH...
IF YOU DON'T LIKE PLAYING BASKETBALL OR SWIMMING...
WHY DID YOU WANT TO COME TO A SPORTS CAMP?
WE COULD HAVE GONE SOMEPLACE ELSE. A PLACE THAT HAD ACTIVITIES FOR YOU TOO.

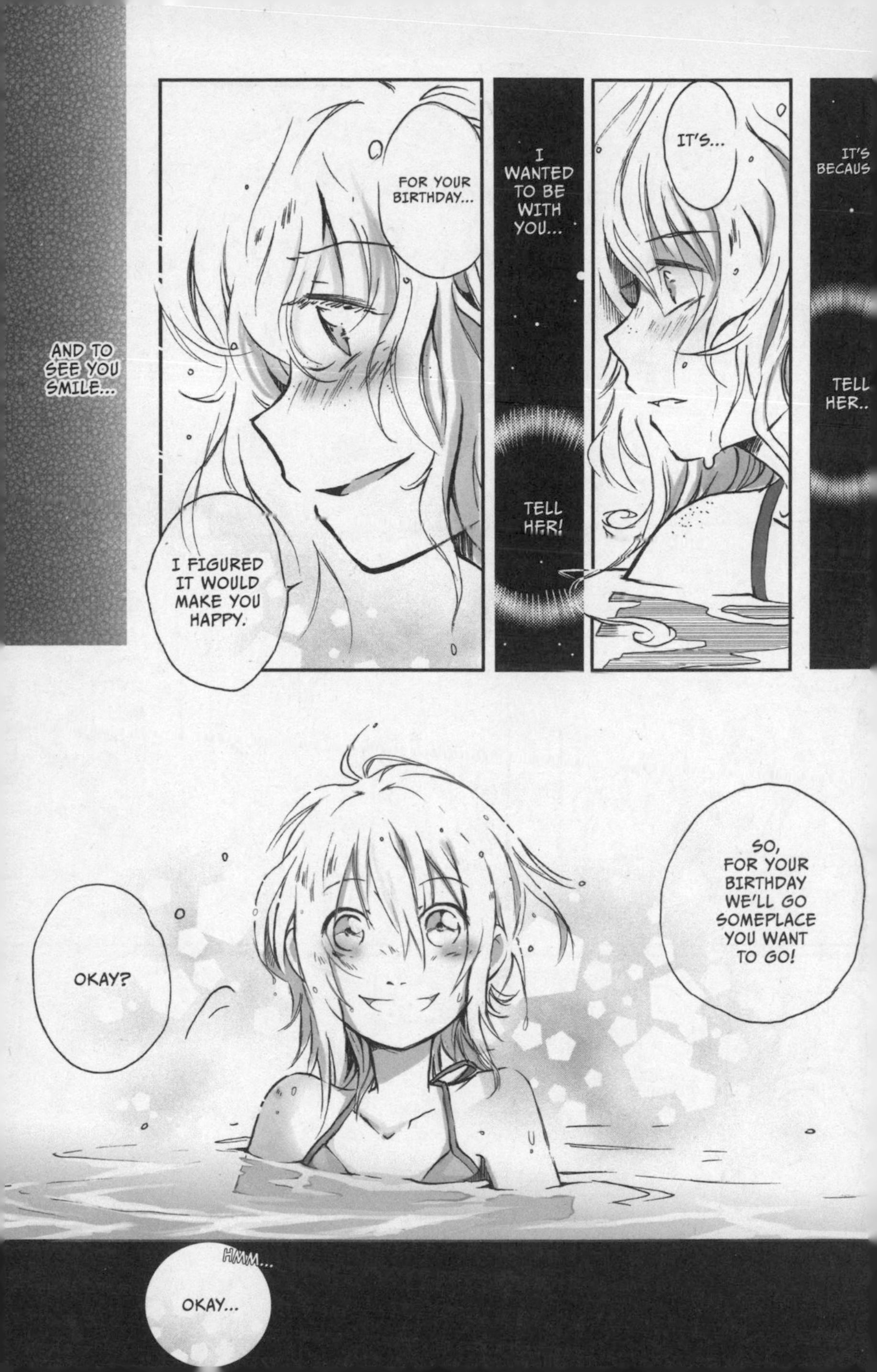
IT'S BECAUS
TELL HER..
IT'S...
I WANTED TO BE WITH YOU...
TELL HER!
FOR YOUR BIRTHDAY...
I FIGURED IT WOULD MAKE YOU HAPPY.
AND TO SEE YOU SMILE...
SO, FOR YOUR BIRTHDAY WE'LL GO SOMEPLACE YOU WANT TO GO!
OKAY?
HMM...
OKAY...

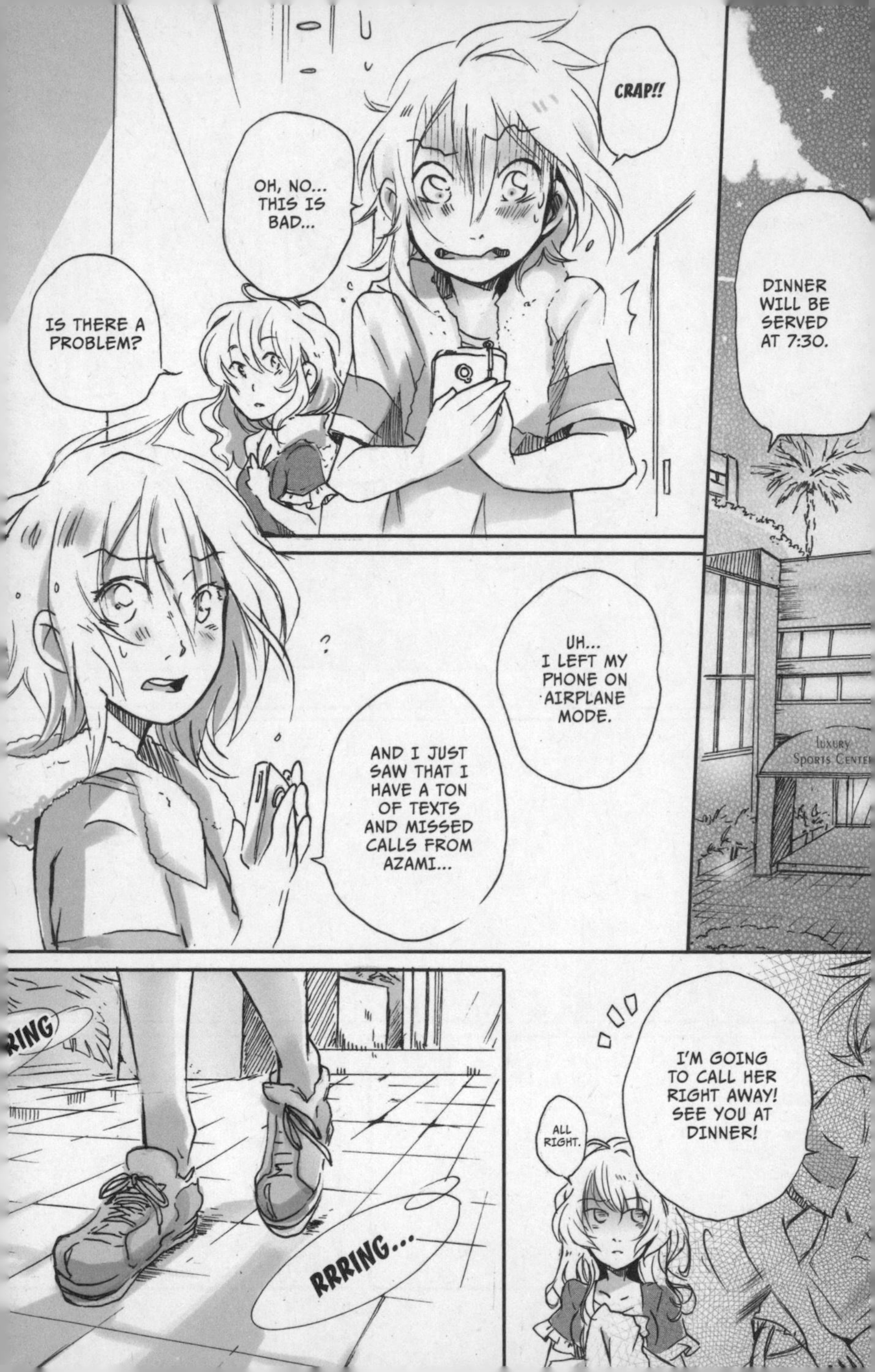
DINNER WILL BE SERVED AT 7:30.
Luxury Sports Center
CRAP!!
OH, NO... THIS IS BAD...
IS THERE A PROBLEM?
UH... I LEFT MY PHONE ON AIRPLANE MODE.
AND I JUST SAW THAT I HAVE A TON OF TEXTS AND MISSED CALLS FROM AZAMI...
I'M GOING TO CALL HER RIGHT AWAY! SEE YOU AT DINNER!
ALL RIGHT.
RRING
RRRING...

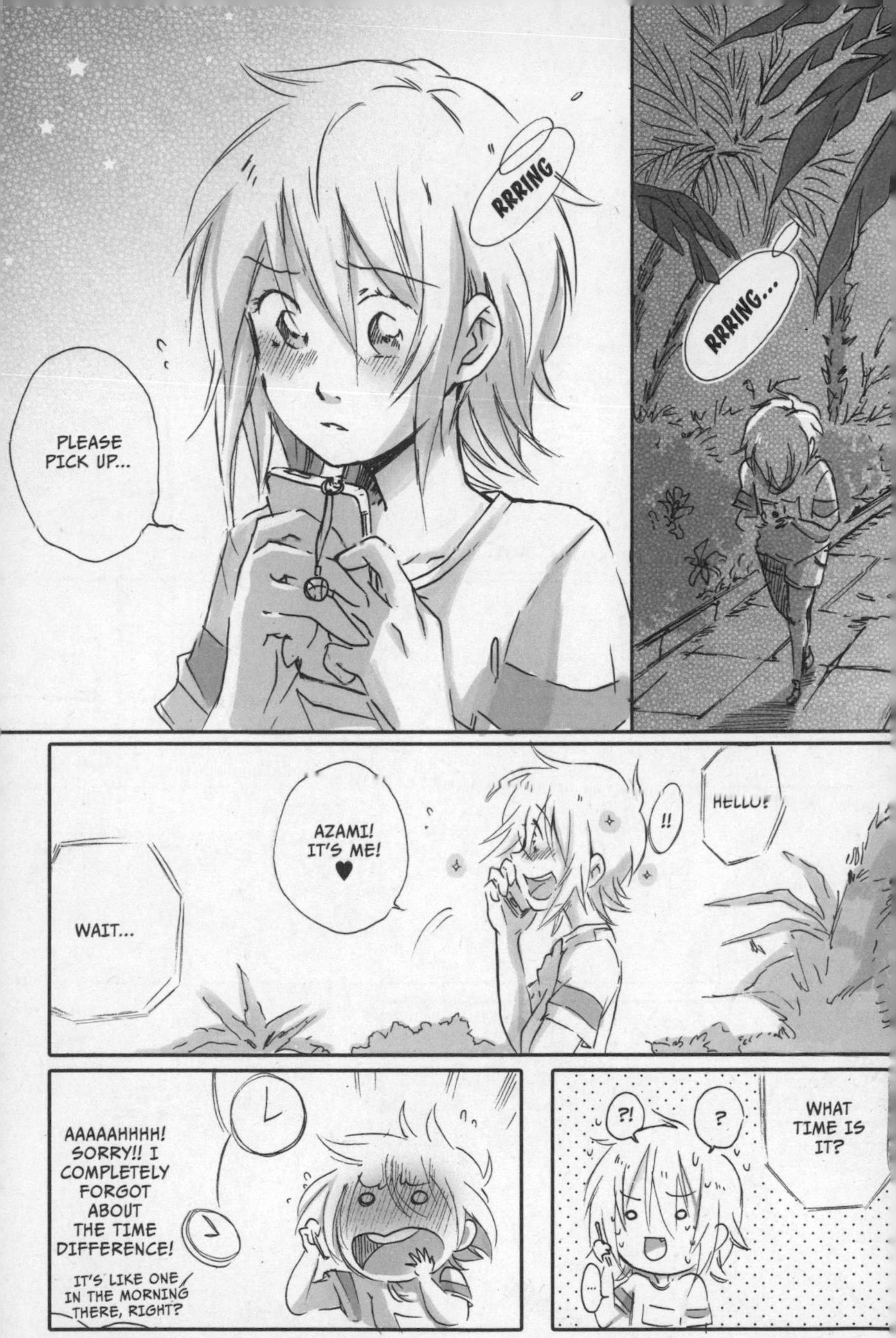
RRRING...
RRRING
PLEASE PICK UP...
HELLO!
!!
AZAMI! IT'S ME! ♥
WAIT...
WHAT TIME IS IT?
?
?!
...
AAAAAHHHH! SORRY!! I COMPLETELY FORGOT ABOUT THE TIME DIFFERENCE!
IT'S LIKE ONE IN THE MORNING THERE, RIGHT?

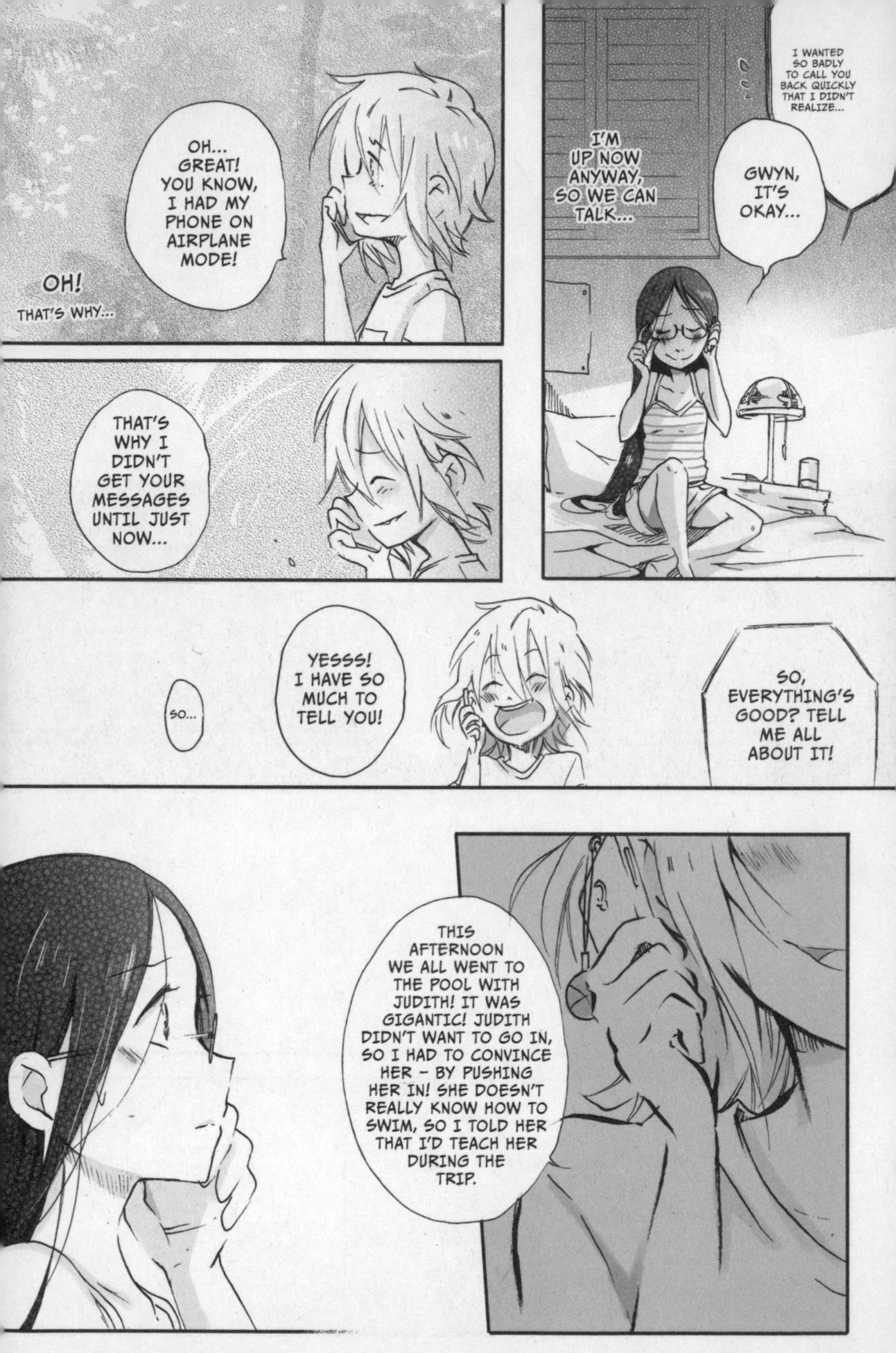

I WANTED SO BADLY TO CALL YOU BACK QUICKLY THAT I DIDN'T REALIZE...
GWYN, IT'S OKAY...
I'M UP NOW ANYWAY, SO WE CAN TALK...
OH... GREAT! YOU KNOW, I HAD MY PHONE ON AIRPLANE MODE!
OH!
THAT'S WHY...
THAT'S WHY I DIDN'T GET YOUR MESSAGES UNTIL JUST NOW...
SO, EVERYTHING'S GOOD? TELL ME ALL ABOUT IT!
YESSS! I HAVE SO MUCH TO TELL YOU!
SO...
THIS AFTERNOON WE ALL WENT TO THE POOL WITH JUDITH! IT WAS GIGANTIC! JUDITH DIDN'T WANT TO GO IN, SO I HAD TO CONVINCE HER – BY PUSHING HER IN! SHE DOESN'T REALLY KNOW HOW TO SWIM, SO I TOLD HER THAT I'D TEACH HER DURING THE TRIP.

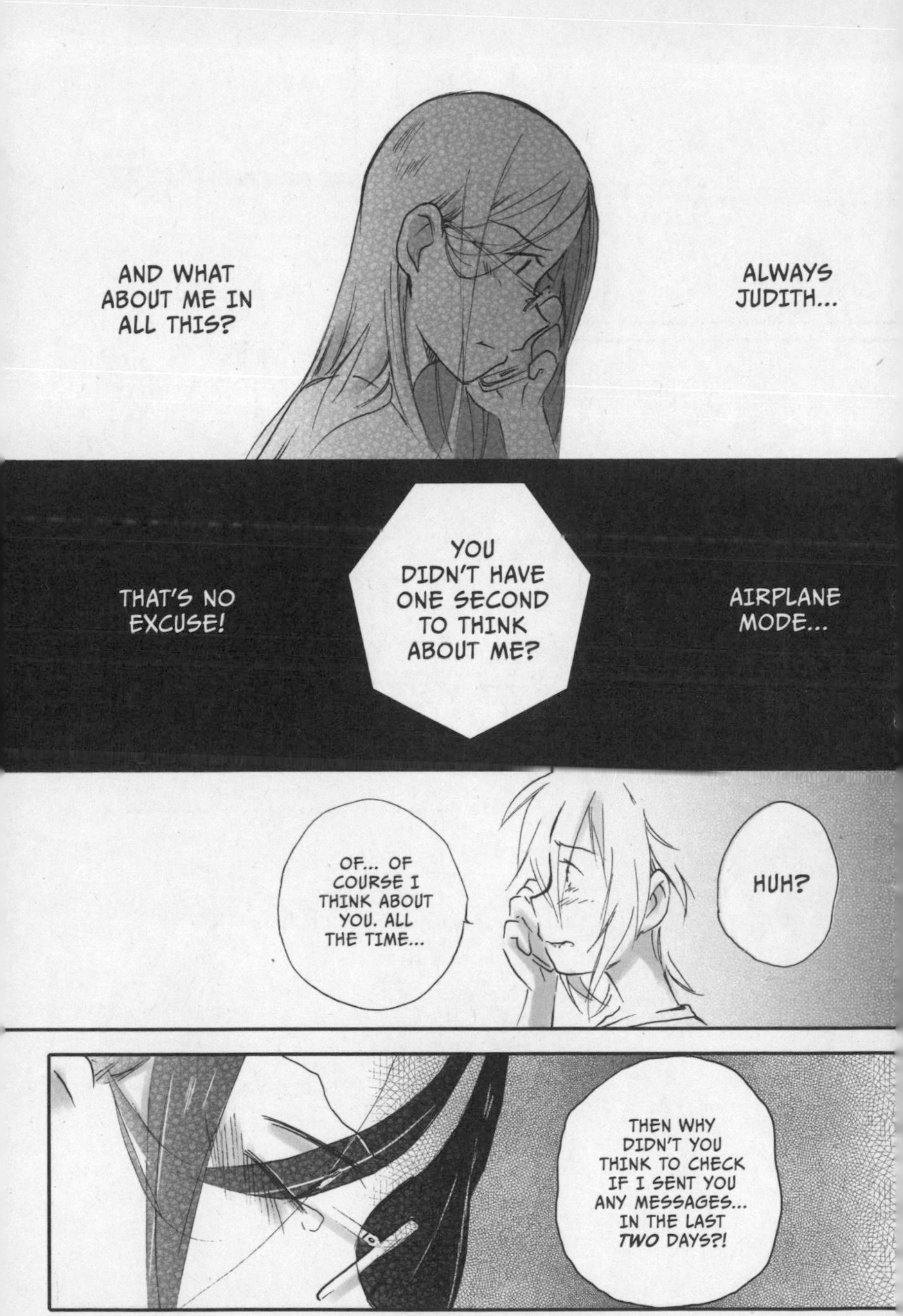
ALWAYS JUDITH...
AND WHAT ABOUT ME IN ALL THIS?
AIRPLANE MODE...
YOU DIDN'T HAVE ONE SECOND TO THINK ABOUT ME?
THAT'S NO EXCUSE!
HUH?
OF... OF COURSE I THINK ABOUT YOU. ALL THE TIME...
THEN WHY DIDN'T YOU THINK TO CHECK IF I SENT YOU ANY MESSAGES... IN THE LAST *TWO* DAYS?!

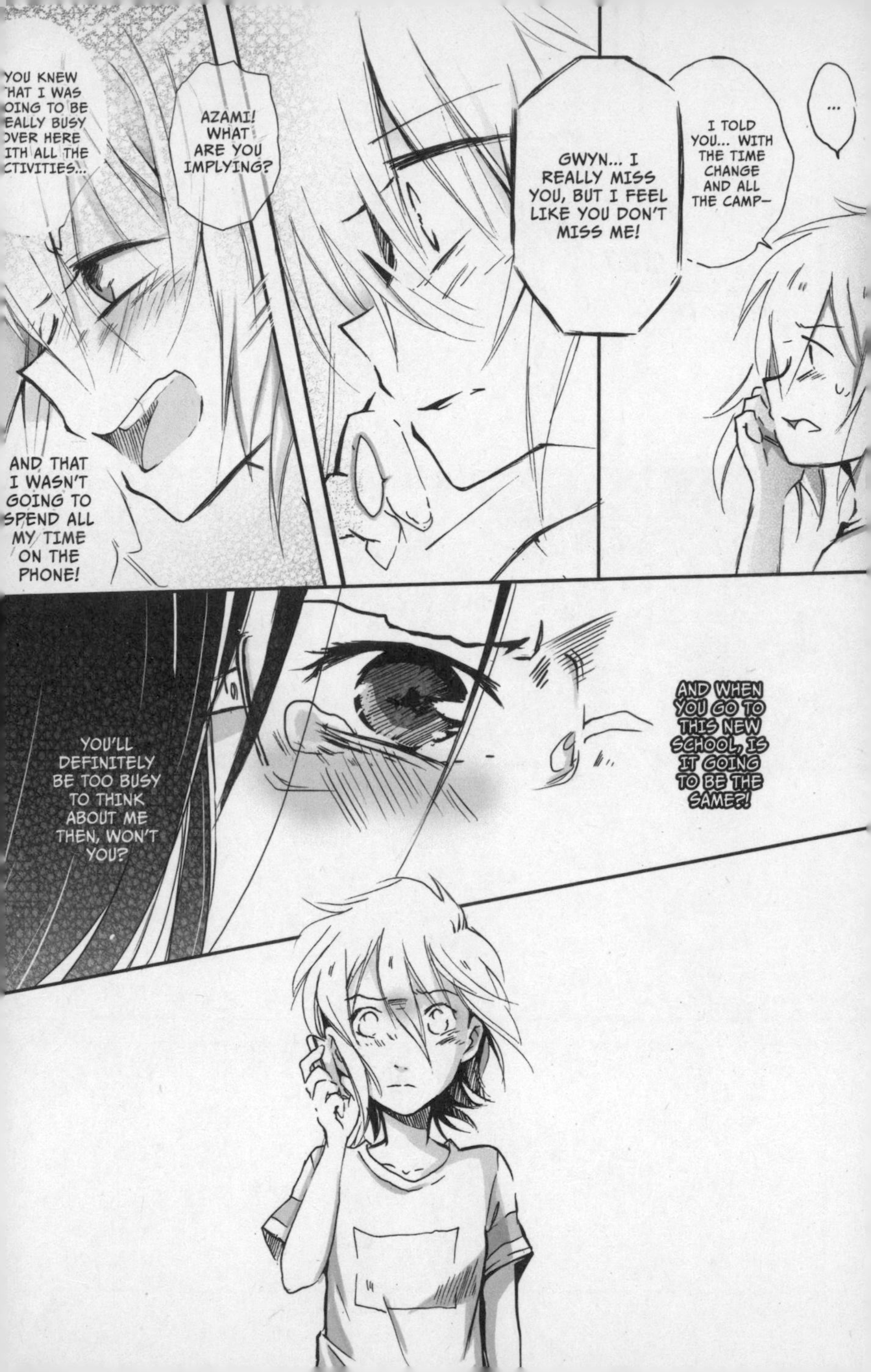
...
I TOLD YOU... WITH THE TIME CHANGE AND ALL THE CAMP–
GWYN... I REALLY MISS YOU, BUT I FEEL LIKE YOU DON'T MISS ME!
AZAMI! WHAT ARE YOU IMPLYING?
YOU KNEW THAT I WAS OING TO BE EALLY BUSY OVER HERE ITH ALL THE CTIVITIES...
AND THAT I WASN'T GOING TO SPEND ALL MY TIME ON THE PHONE!
AND WHEN YOU GO TO THIS NEW SCHOOL, IS IT GOING TO BE THE SAME?!
YOU'LL DEFINITELY BE TOO BUSY TO THINK ABOUT ME THEN, WON'T YOU?

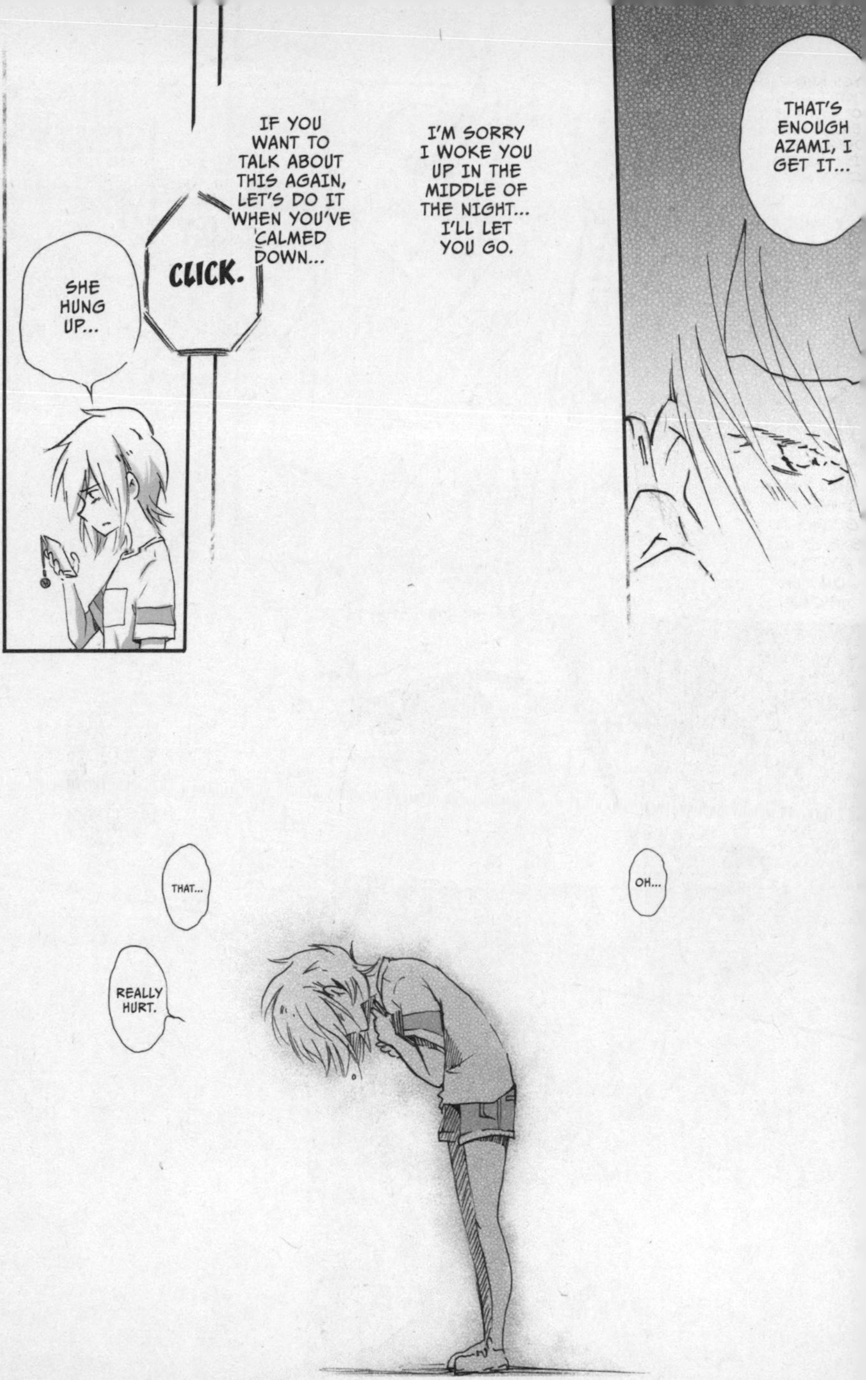
THAT'S ENOUGH AZAMI, I GET IT...
I'M SORRY I WOKE YOU UP IN THE MIDDLE OF THE NIGHT... I'LL LET YOU GO.
IF YOU WANT TO TALK ABOUT THIS AGAIN, LET'S DO IT WHEN YOU'VE CALMED DOWN...
CLICK.
SHE HUNG UP...
OH...
THAT...
REALLY HURT.

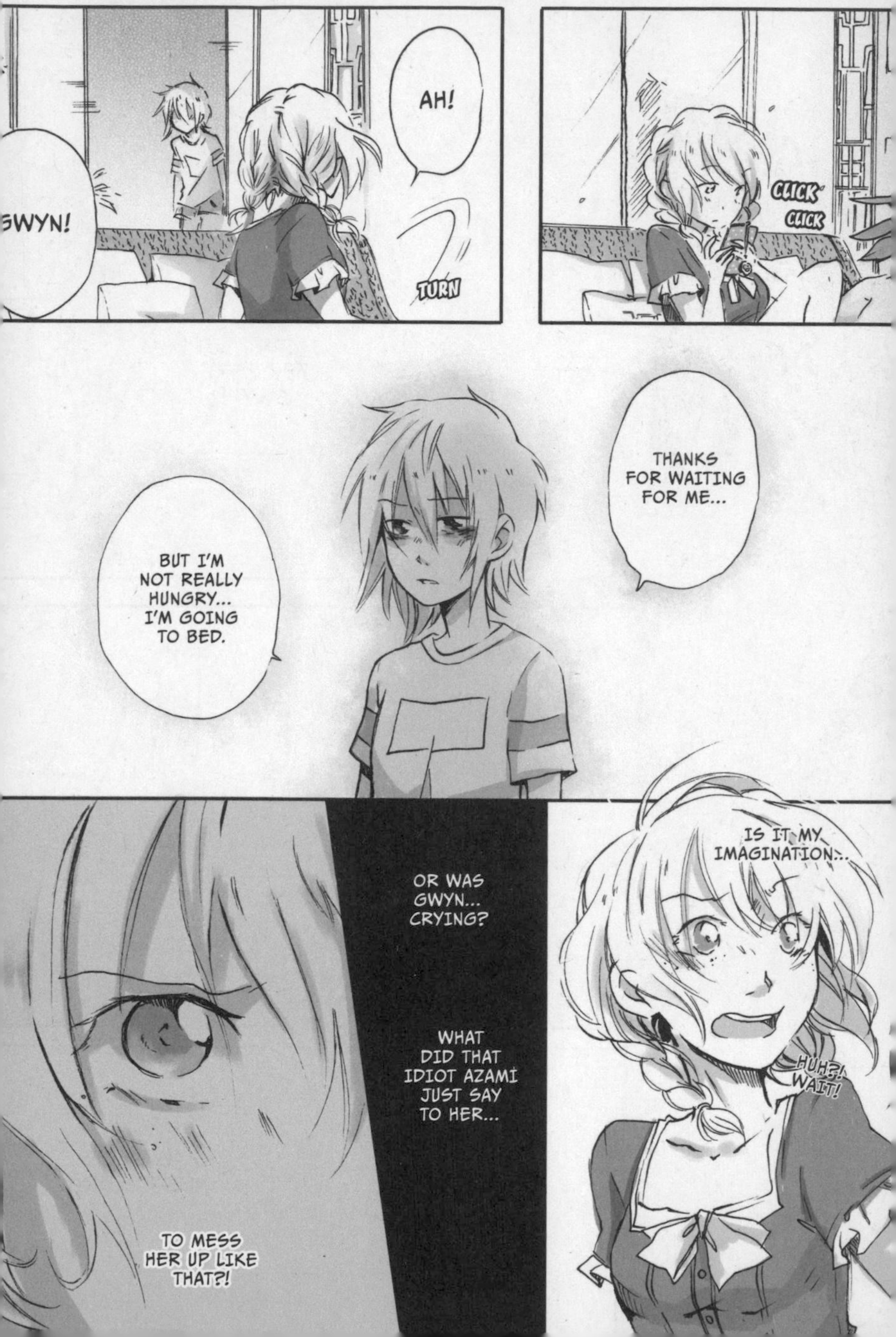
CLICK
CLICK
AH!
GWYN!
TURN
THANKS FOR WAITING FOR ME...
BUT I'M NOT REALLY HUNGRY... I'M GOING TO BED.
IS IT MY IMAGINATION...
HUH?! WAIT!
OR WAS GWYN... CRYING?
WHAT DID THAT IDIOT AZAMI JUST SAY TO HER...
TO MESS HER UP LIKE THAT?!

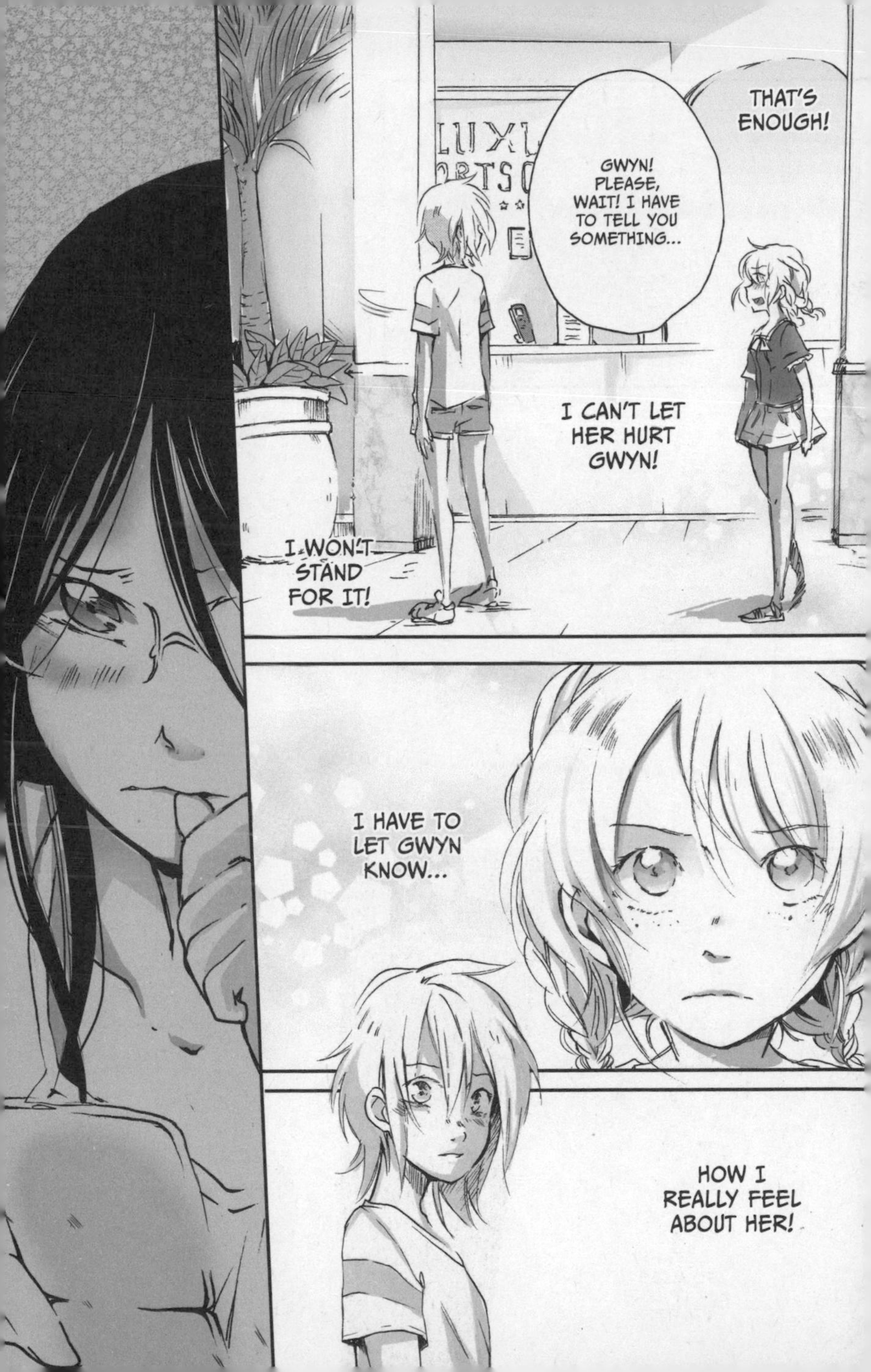
THAT'S ENOUGH!
GWYN! PLEASE, WAIT! I HAVE TO TELL YOU SOMETHING...
I CAN'T LET HER HURT GWYN!
I WON'T STAND FOR IT!
I HAVE TO LET GWYN KNOW...
HOW I REALLY FEEL ABOUT HER!

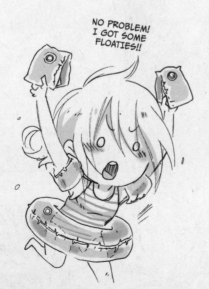

GWYN, I KEPT MEANING TO TELL YOU I CAN'T SWIM...
NO PROBLEM! I GOT SOME FLOATIES!!

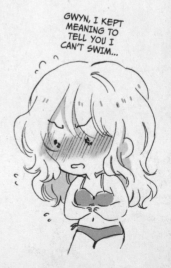

Chapter 11 Declaration of love

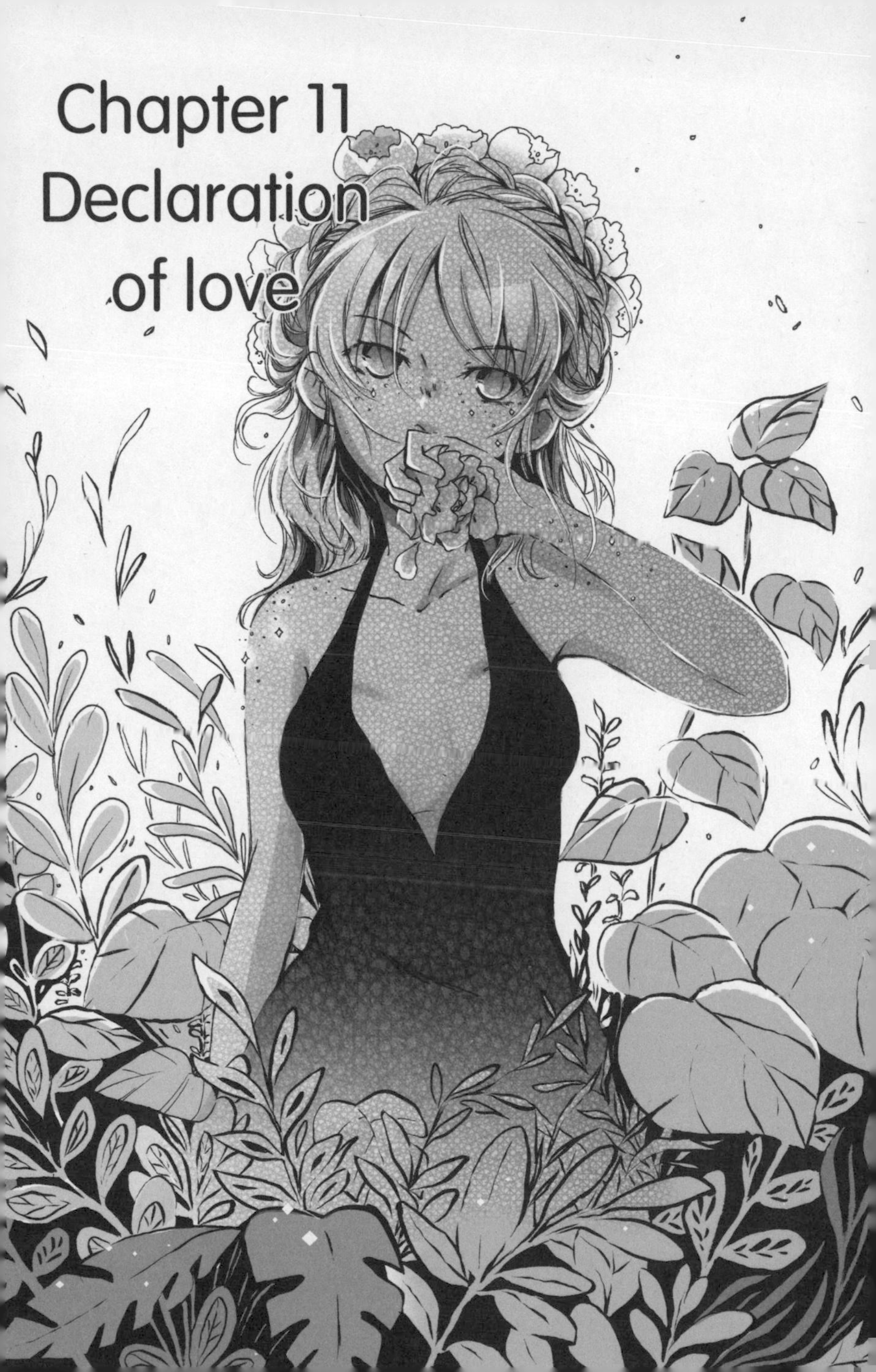

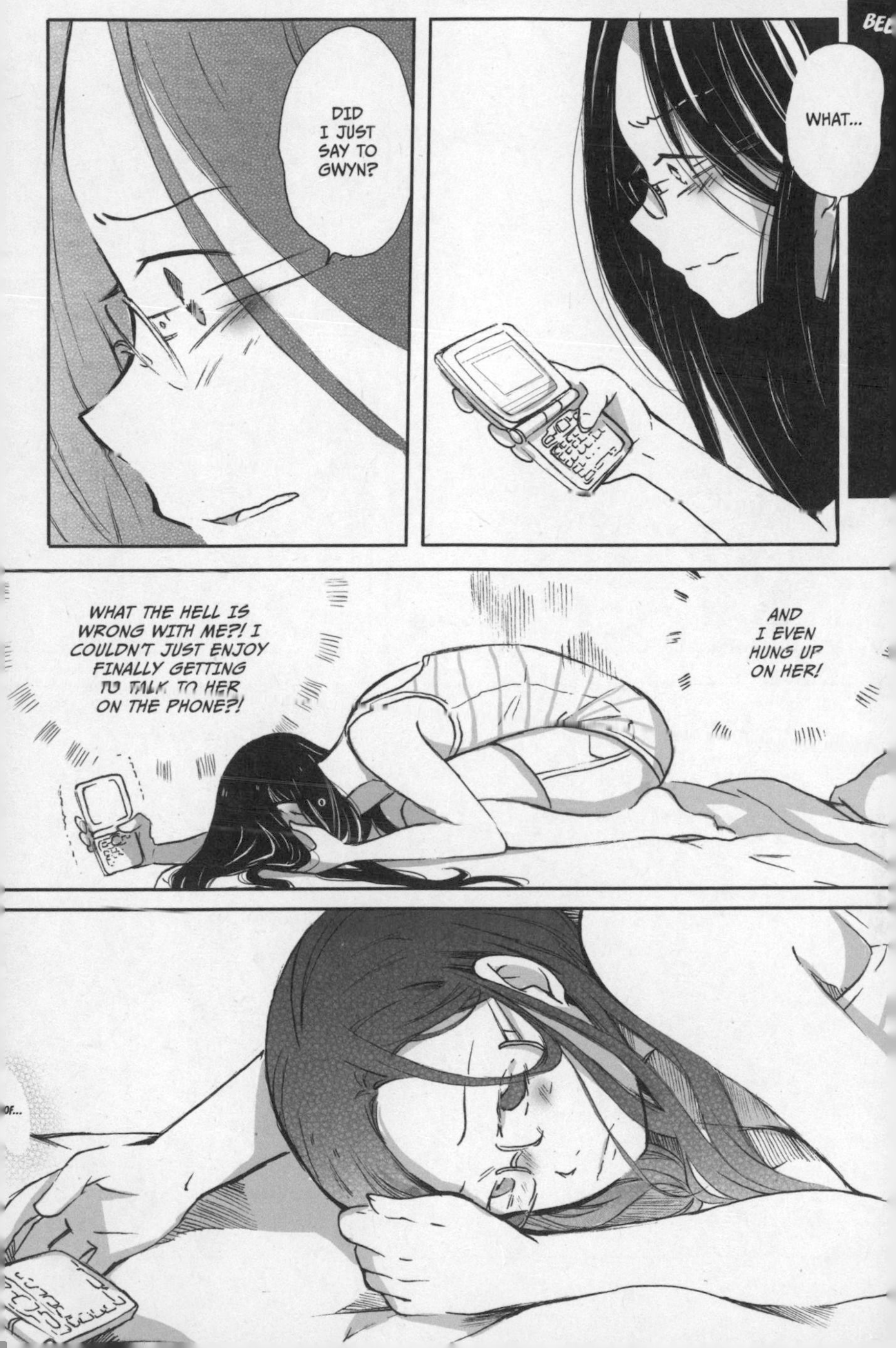
WHAT...
DID I JUST SAY TO GWYN?
AND I EVEN HUNG UP ON HER!
WHAT THE HELL IS WRONG WITH ME?! I COULDN'T JUST ENJOY FINALLY GETTING TO TALK TO HER ON THE PHONE?!

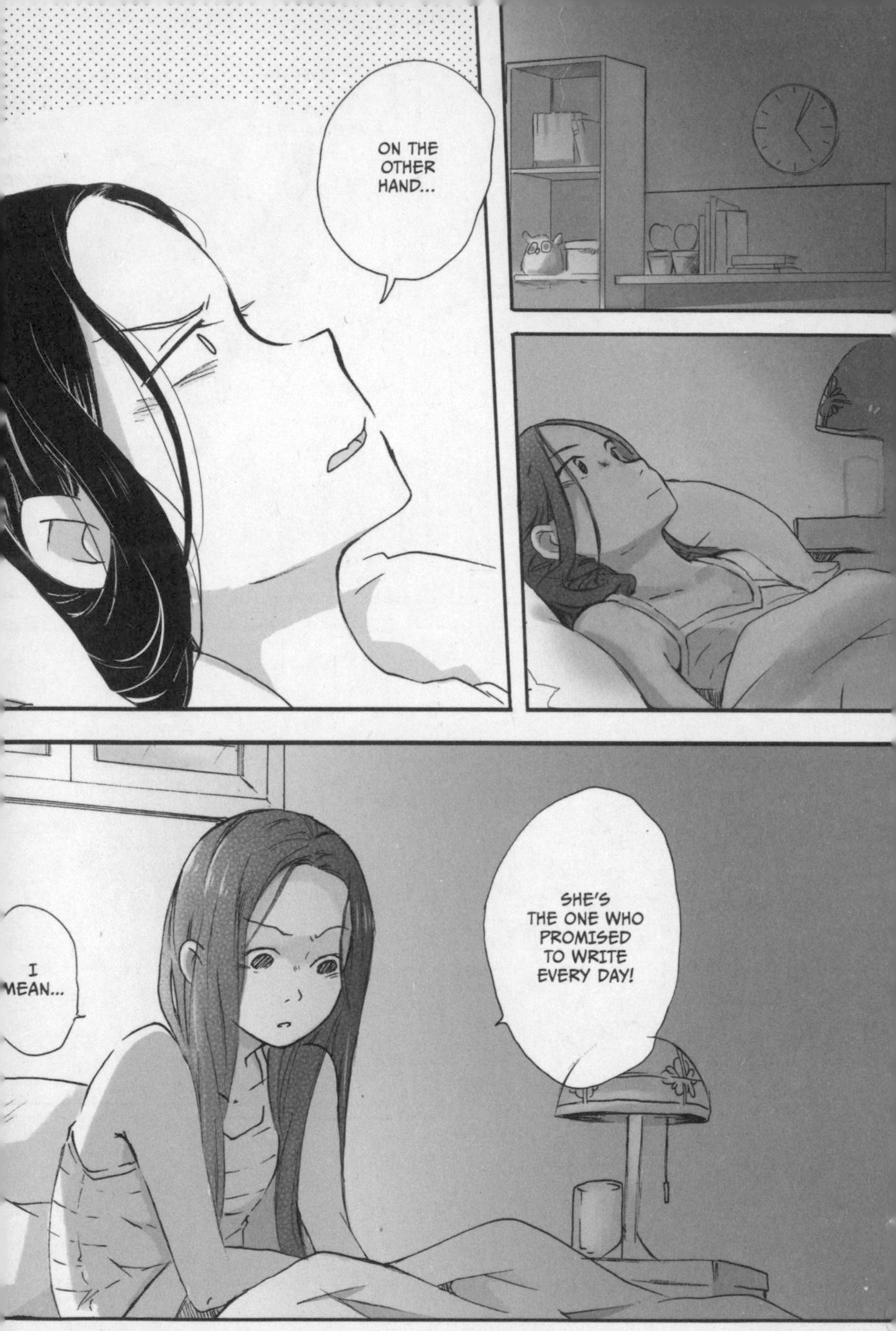
ON THE OTHER HAND...
SHE'S THE ONE WHO PROMISED TO WRITE EVERY DAY!
I MEAN...

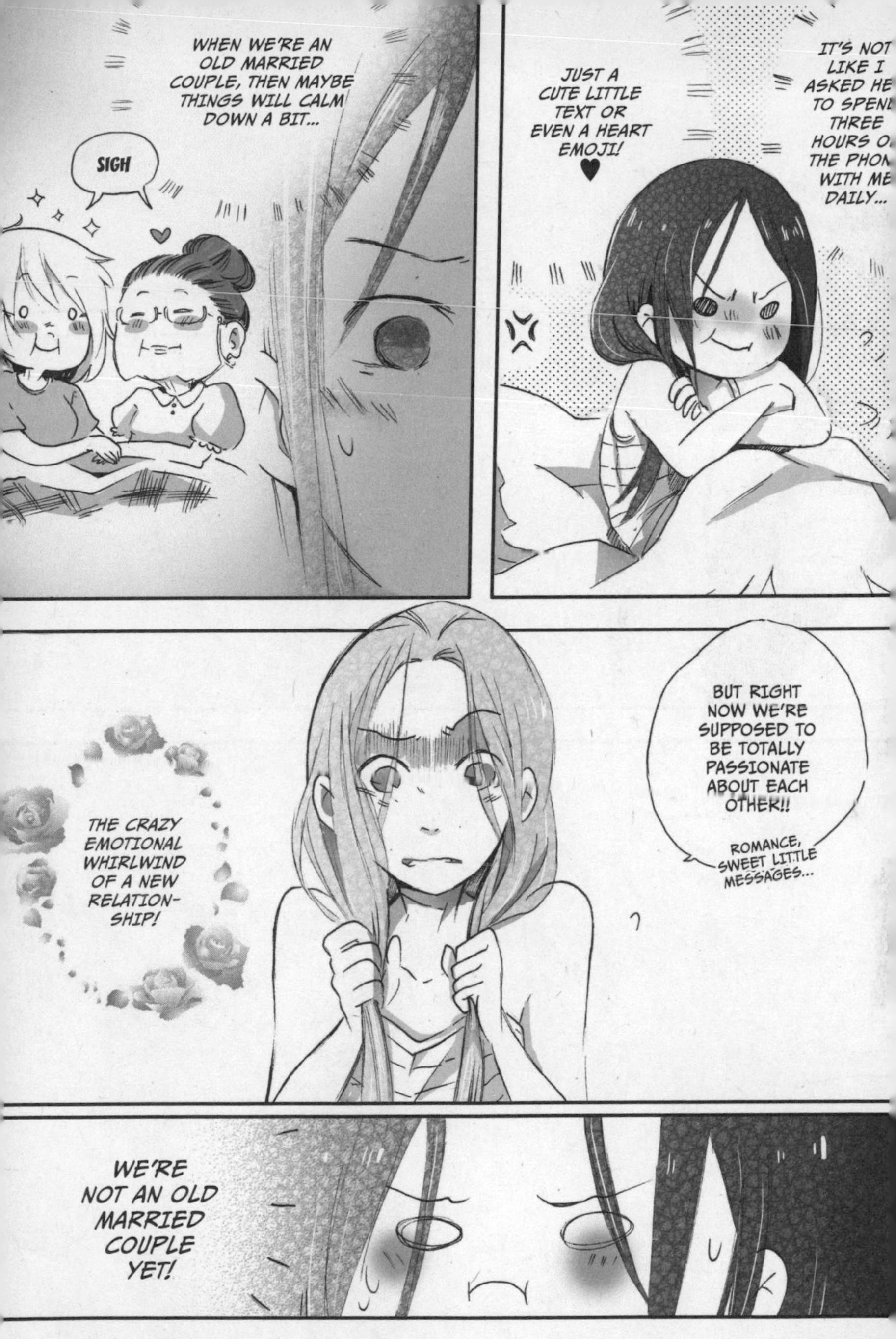
IT'S NOT LIKE I ASKED HE TO SPEN THREE HOURS O THE PHON WITH ME DAILY...
JUST A CUTE LITTLE TEXT OR EVEN A HEART EMOJI! ♥
WHEN WE'RE AN OLD MARRIED COUPLE, THEN MAYBE THINGS WILL CALM DOWN A BIT...
SIGH
BUT RIGHT NOW WE'RE SUPPOSED TO BE TOTALLY PASSIONATE ABOUT EACH OTHER!!
ROMANCE, SWEET LITTLE MESSAGES...
THE CRAZY EMOTIONAL WHIRLWIND OF A NEW RELATION-SHIP!
WE'RE NOT AN OLD MARRIED COUPLE YET!

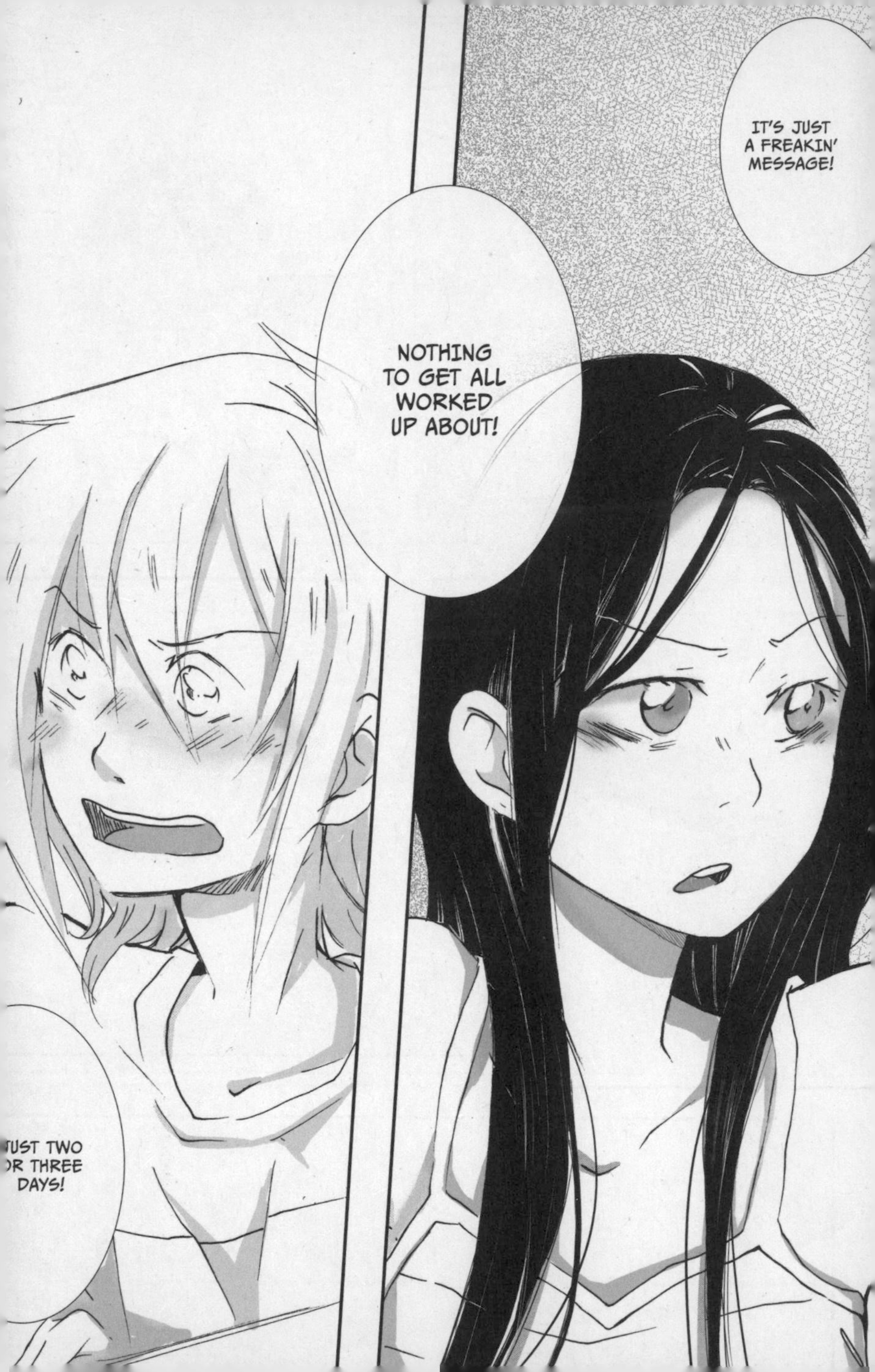
IT'S JUST A FREAKIN' MESSAGE!
NOTHING TO GET ALL WORKED UP ABOUT!
UST TWO R THREE DAYS!

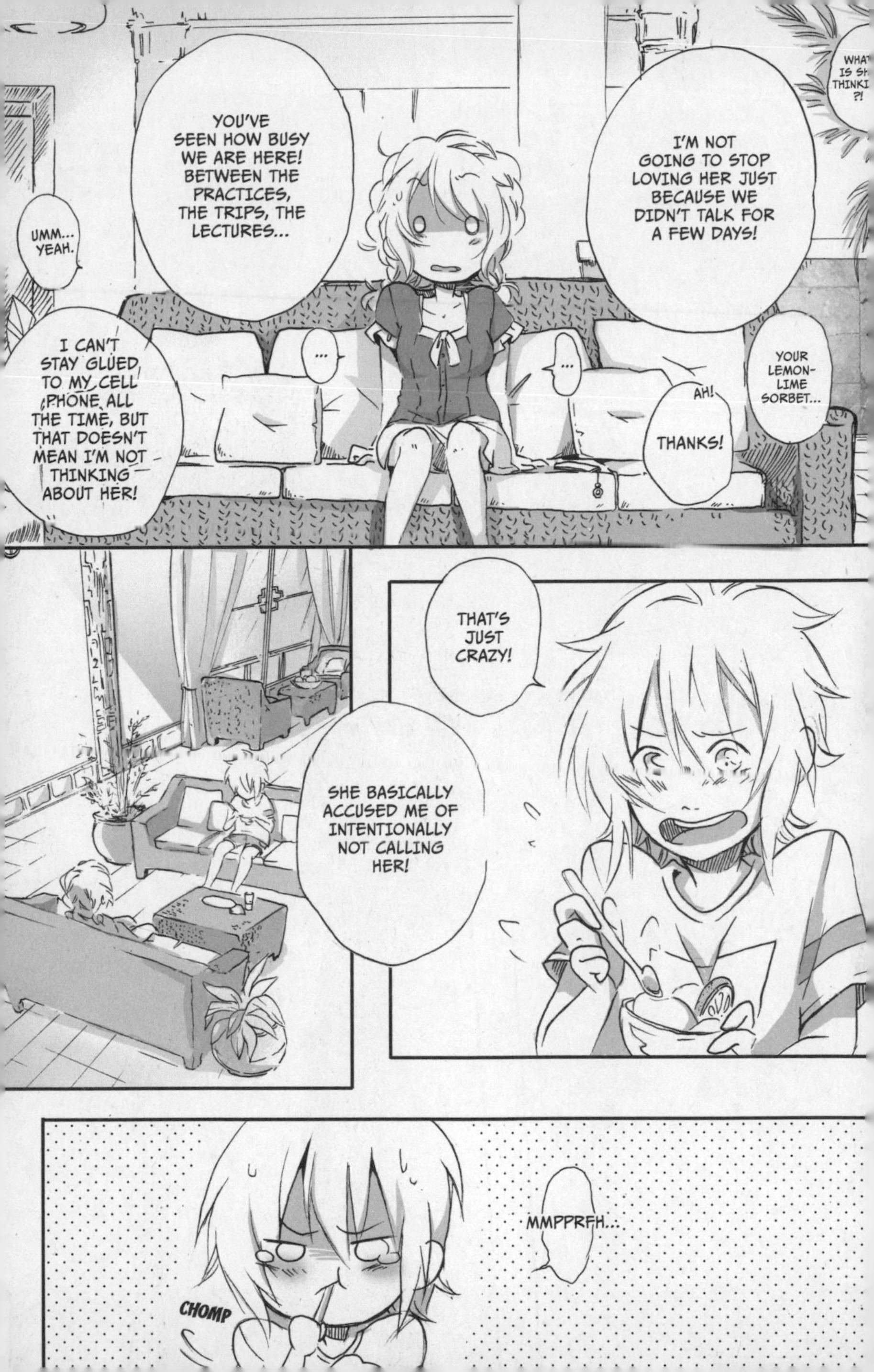
WHAT IS SH THINKI ?!
I'M NOT GOING TO STOP LOVING HER JUST BECAUSE WE DIDN'T TALK FOR A FEW DAYS!
YOUR LEMON-LIME SORBET...
AH!
THANKS!
...
YOU'VE SEEN HOW BUSY WE ARE HERE! BETWEEN THE PRACTICES, THE TRIPS, THE LECTURES...
...
UMM... YEAH.
I CAN'T STAY GLUED TO MY CELL PHONE ALL THE TIME, BUT THAT DOESN'T MEAN I'M NOT THINKING ABOUT HER!
THAT'S JUST CRAZY!
SHE BASICALLY ACCUSED ME OF INTENTIONALLY NOT CALLING HER!
MMPPRFH...
CHOMP

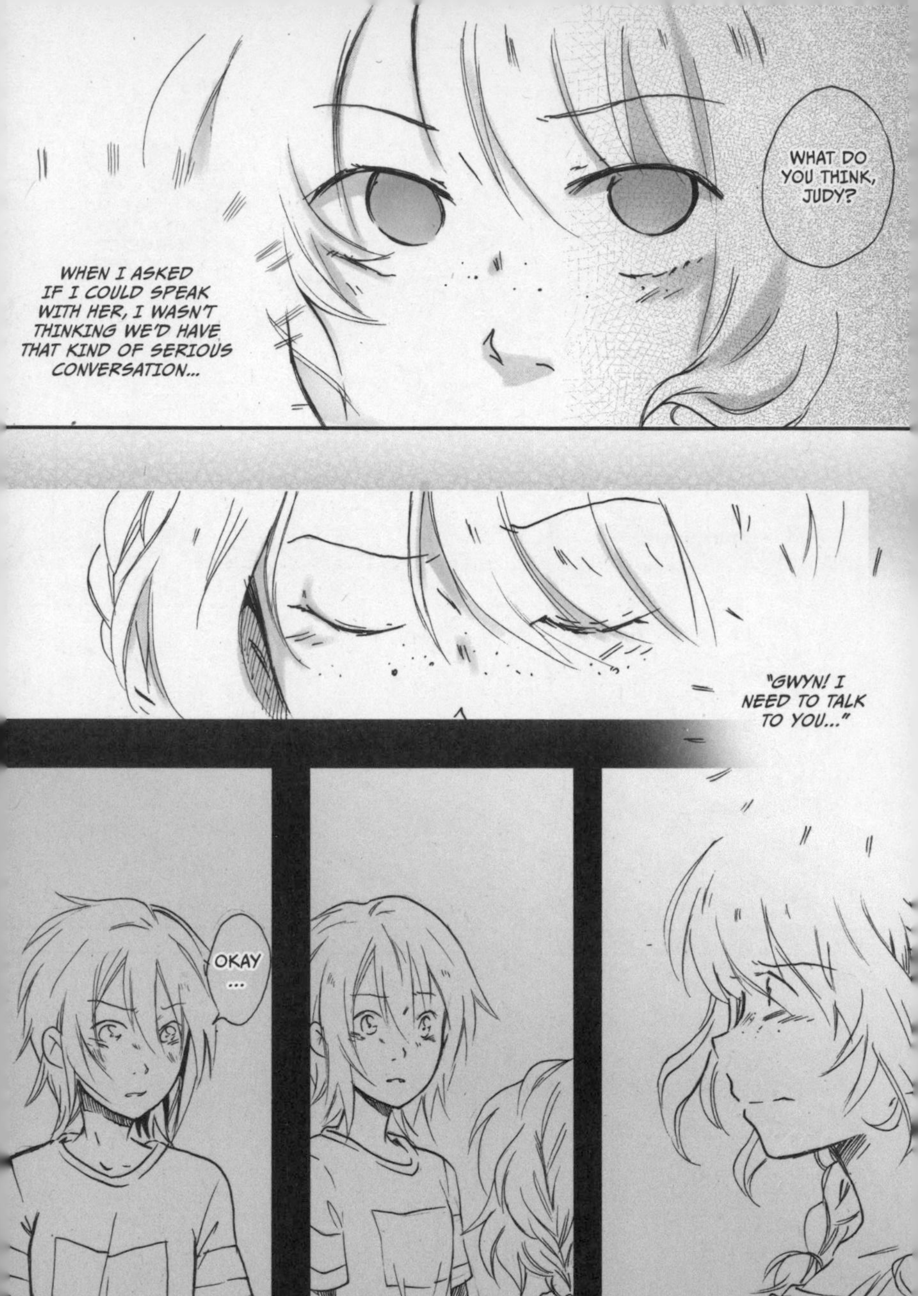
WHAT DO YOU THINK, JUDY?
WHEN I ASKED IF I COULD SPEAK WITH HER, I WASN'T THINKING WE'D HAVE THAT KIND OF SERIOUS CONVERSATION...
"GWYN! I NEED TO TALK TO YOU..."
OKAY ...

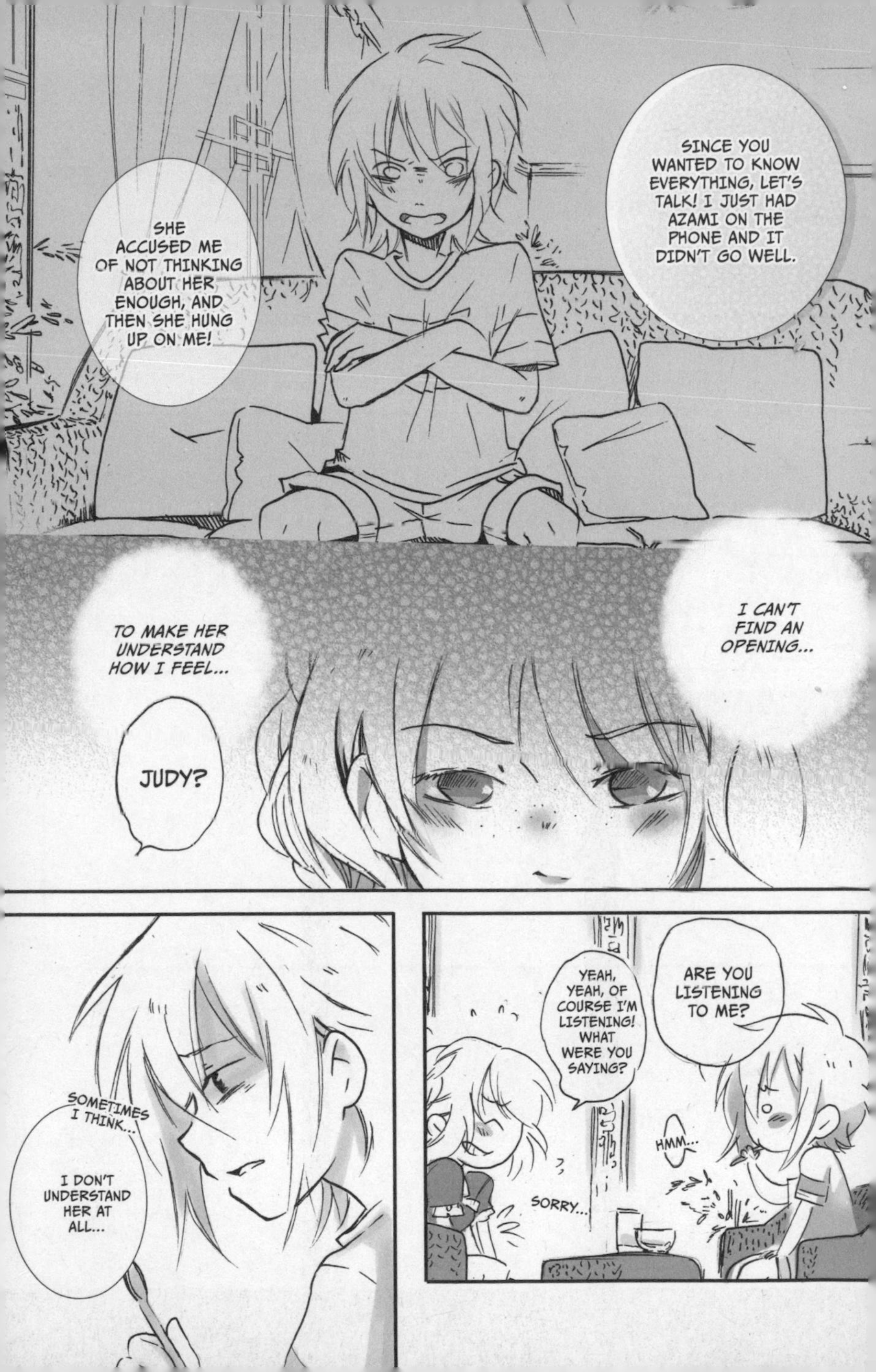
SINCE YOU WANTED TO KNOW EVERYTHING, LET'S TALK! I JUST HAD AZAMI ON THE PHONE AND IT DIDN'T GO WELL.
SHE ACCUSED ME OF NOT THINKING ABOUT HER ENOUGH, AND THEN SHE HUNG UP ON ME!
I CAN'T FIND AN OPENING...
TO MAKE HER UNDERSTAND HOW I FEEL...
JUDY?
ARE YOU LISTENING TO ME?
YEAH, YEAH, OF COURSE I'M LISTENING! WHAT WERE YOU SAYING?
HMM...
SORRY...
SOMETIMES I THINK...
I DON'T UNDERSTAND HER AT ALL...

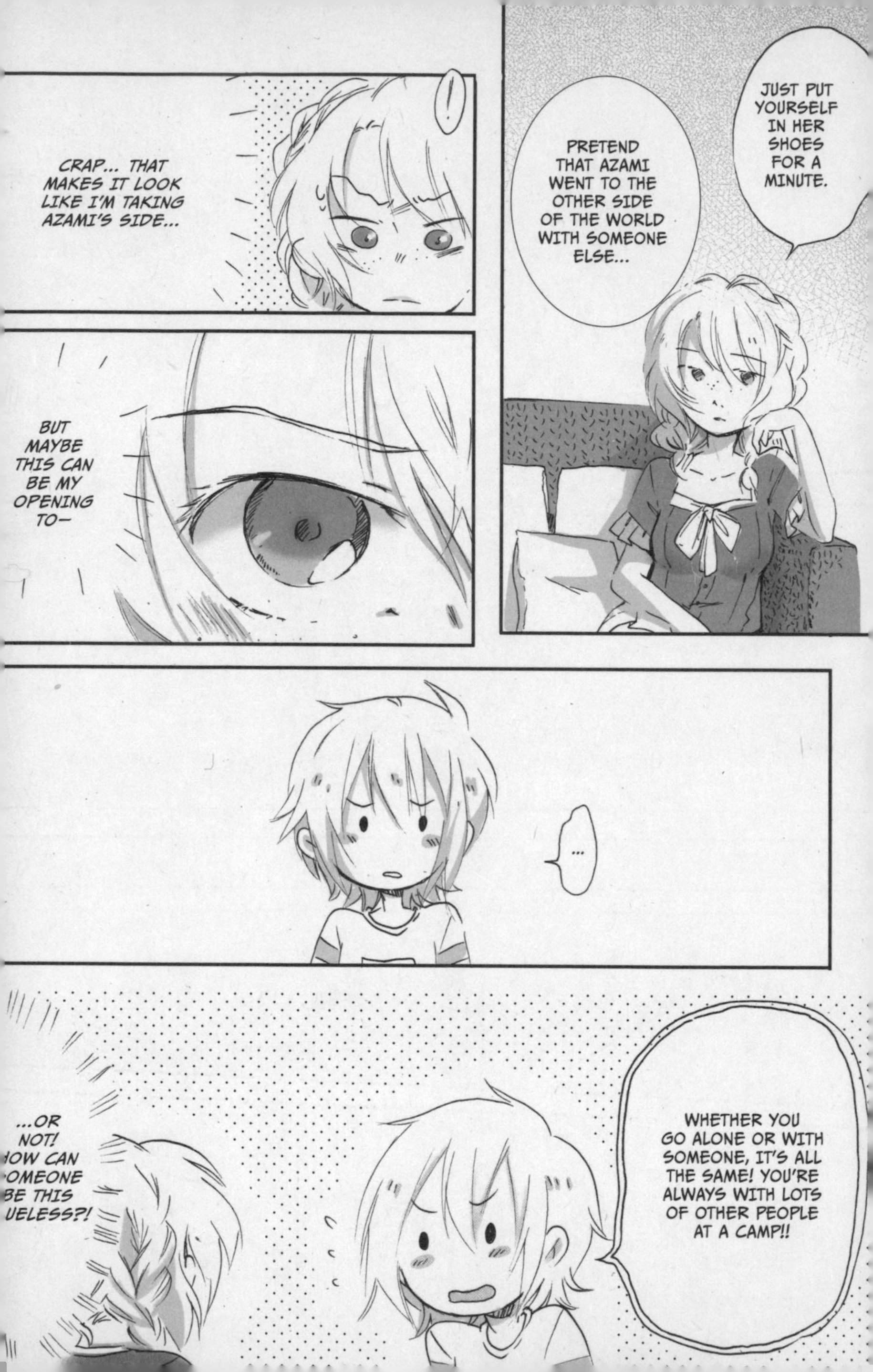
JUST PUT YOURSELF IN HER SHOES FOR A MINUTE.
PRETEND THAT AZAMI WENT TO THE OTHER SIDE OF THE WORLD WITH SOMEONE ELSE...
!
CRAP... THAT MAKES IT LOOK LIKE I'M TAKING AZAMI'S SIDE...
BUT MAYBE THIS CAN BE MY OPENING TO—
...
WHETHER YOU GO ALONE OR WITH SOMEONE, IT'S ALL THE SAME! YOU'RE ALWAYS WITH LOTS OF OTHER PEOPLE AT A CAMP!!
...OR NOT! OW CAN OMEONE BE THIS UELESS?!

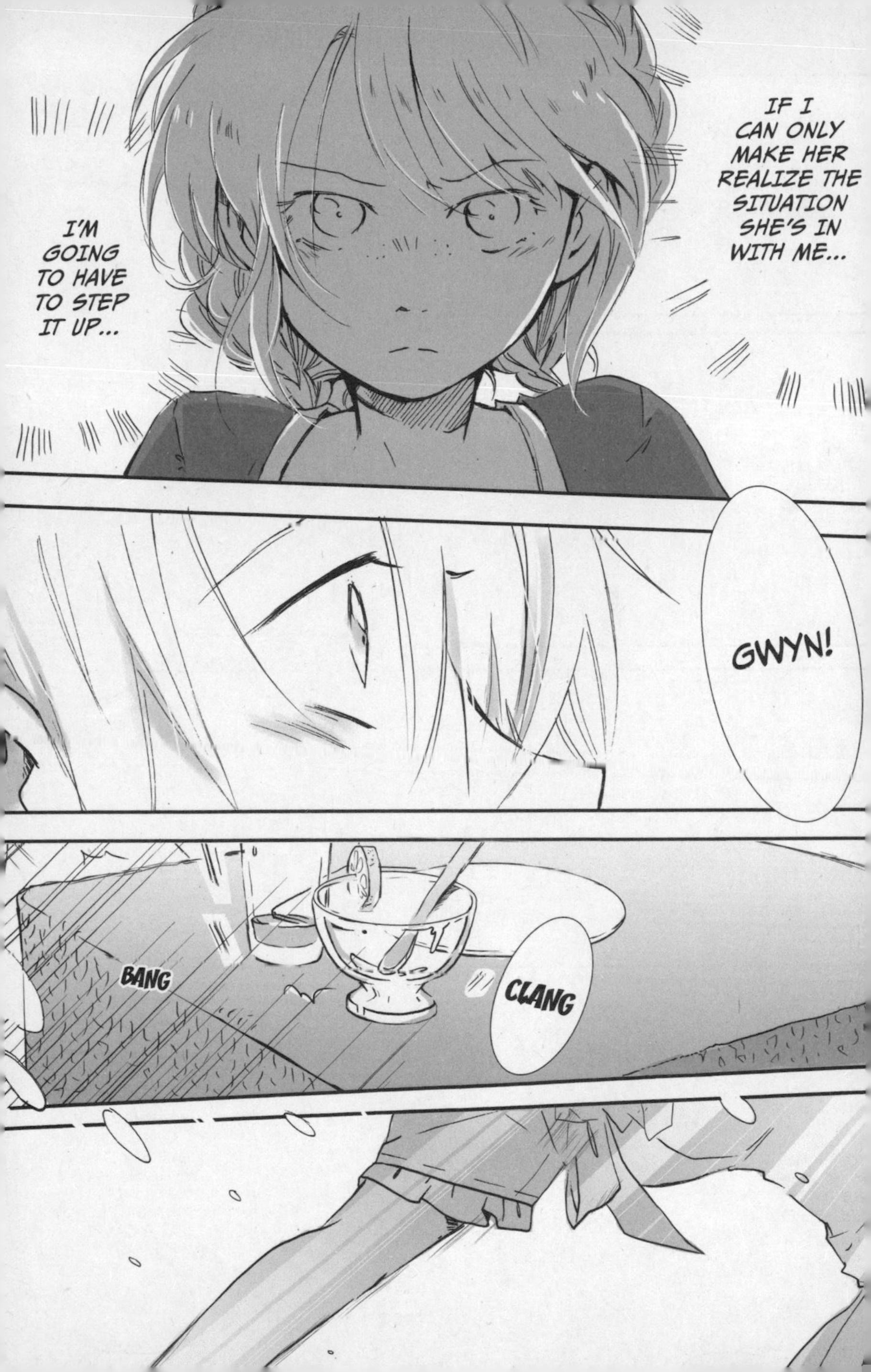
IF I CAN ONLY MAKE HER REALIZE THE SITUATION SHE'S IN WITH ME...
I'M GOING TO HAVE TO STEP IT UP...
GWYN!
CLANG
BANG

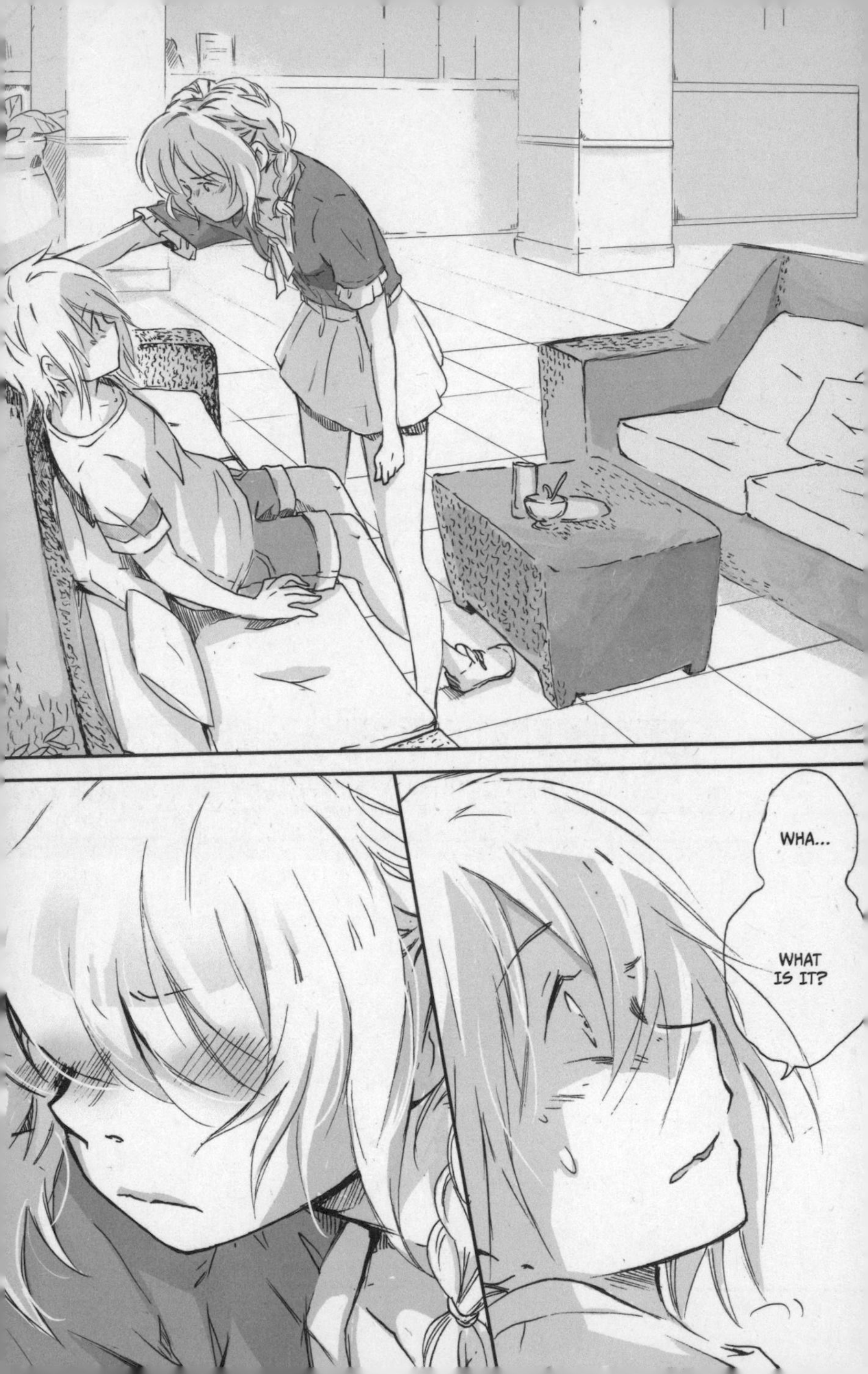
WHA...
WHAT IS IT?

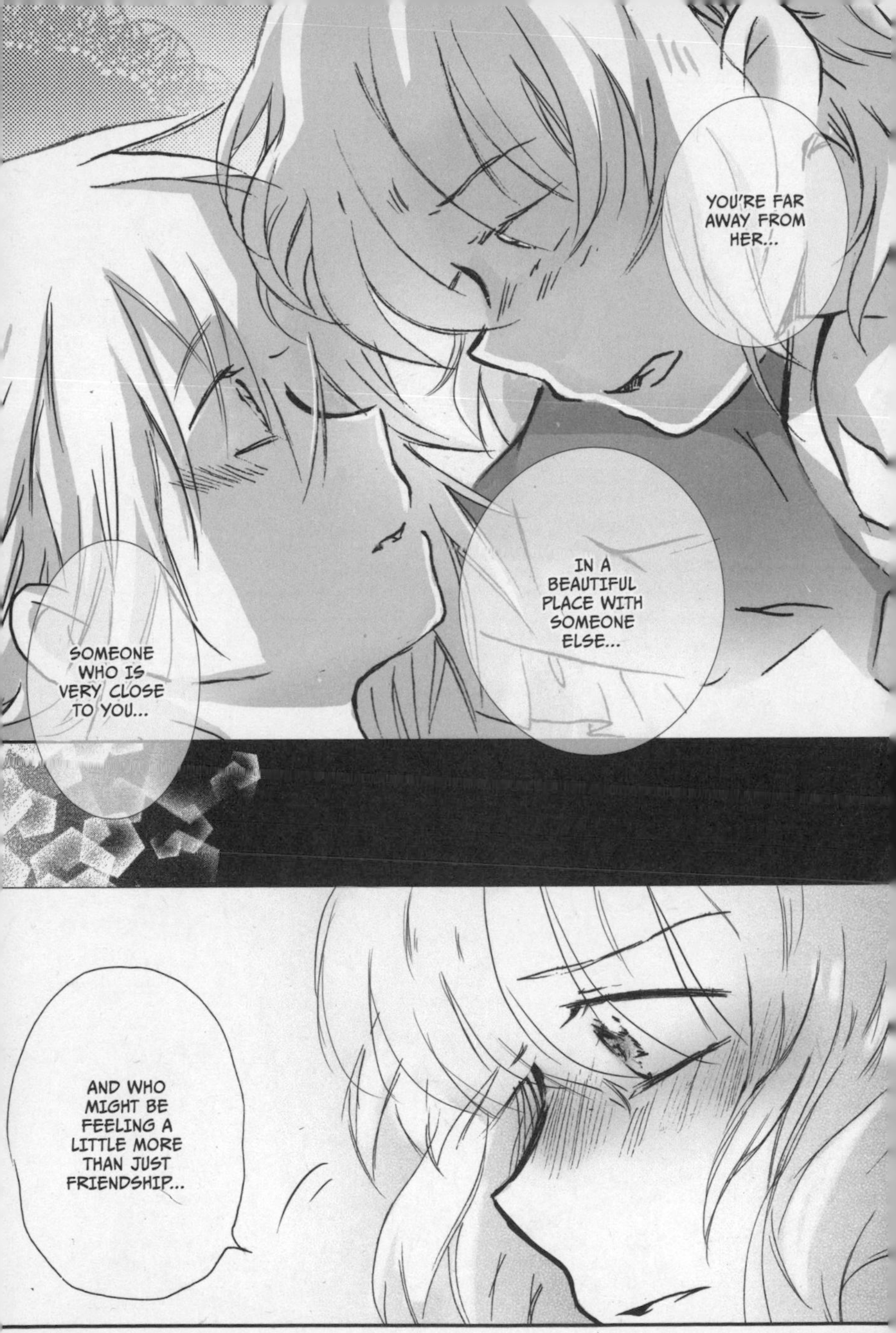
YOU'RE FAR AWAY FROM HER...
IN A BEAUTIFUL PLACE WITH SOMEONE ELSE...
SOMEONE WHO IS VERY CLOSE TO YOU...
AND WHO MIGHT BE FEELING A LITTLE MORE THAN JUST FRIENDSHIP...

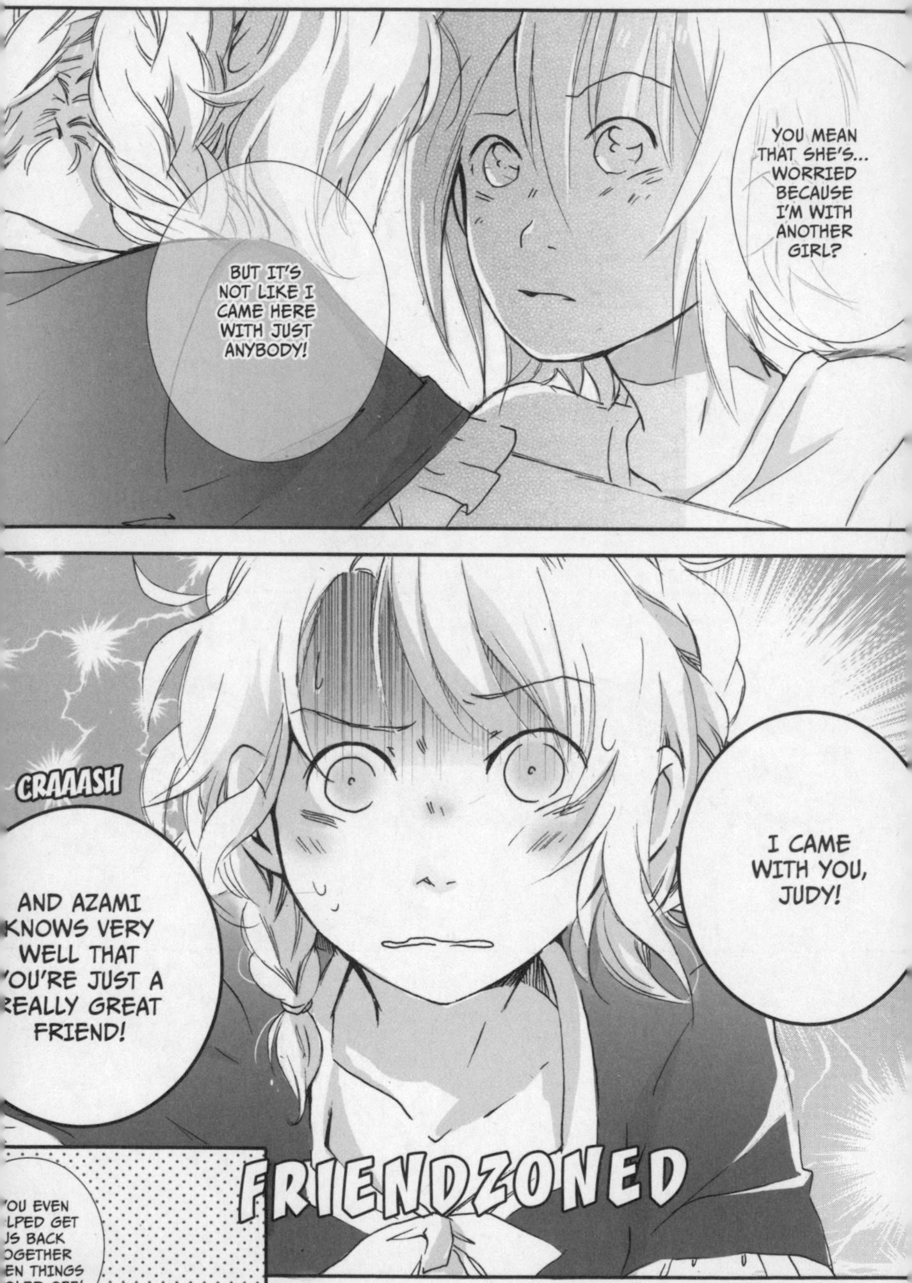
YOU MEAN THAT SHE'S... WORRIED BECAUSE I'M WITH ANOTHER GIRL?
BUT IT'S NOT LIKE I CAME HERE WITH JUST ANYBODY!
I CAME WITH YOU, JUDY!
CRAAASH
AND AZAMI KNOWS VERY WELL THAT OU'RE JUST A EALLY GREAT FRIEND!
FRIENDZONED
OU EVEN LPED GET S BACK OGETHER EN THINGS OLED OFF!

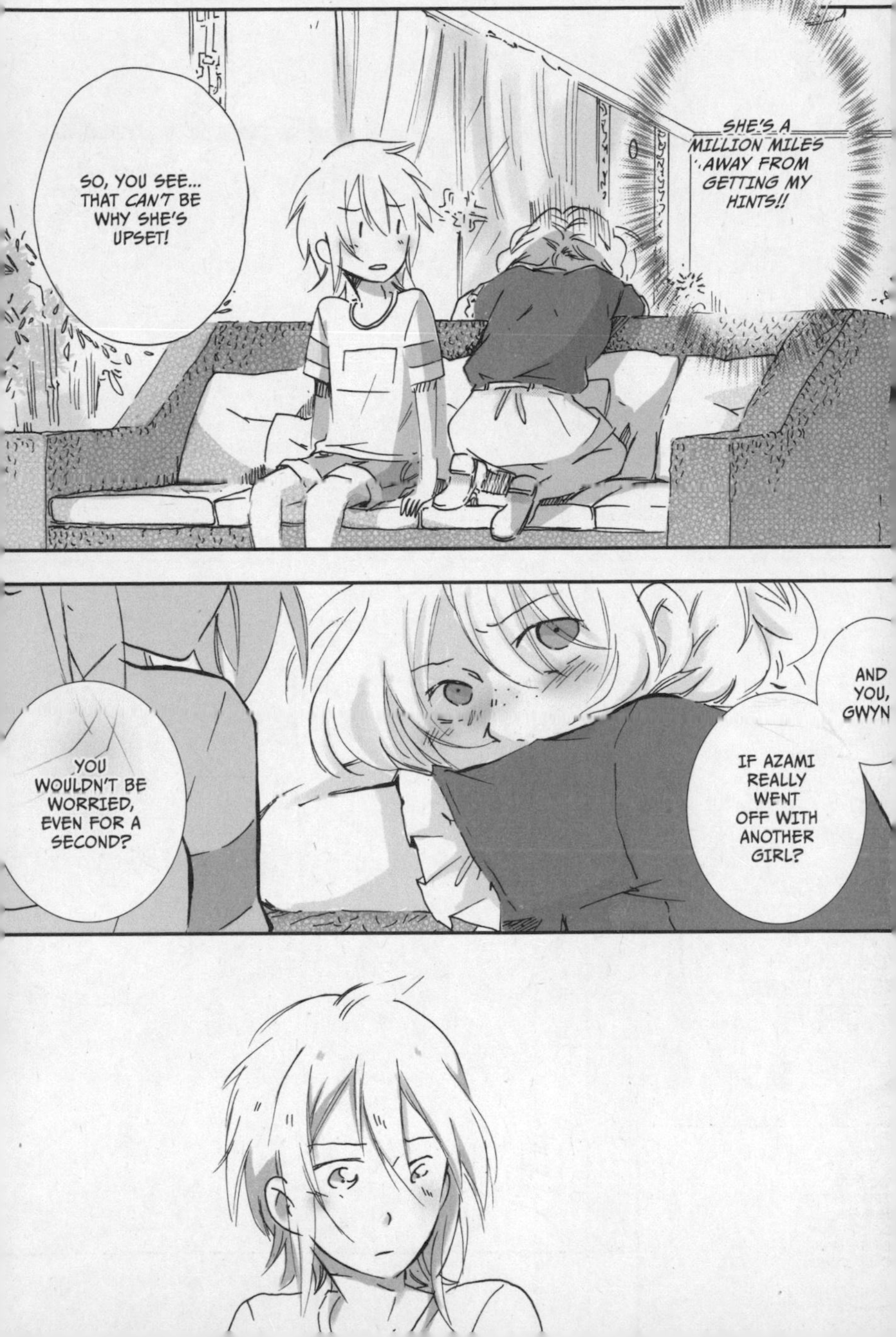
SHE'S A MILLION MILES AWAY FROM GETTING MY HINTS!!
SO, YOU SEE... THAT *CAN'T* BE WHY SHE'S UPSET!
AND YOU, GWYN
IF AZAMI REALLY WENT OFF WITH ANOTHER GIRL?
YOU WOULDN'T BE WORRIED, EVEN FOR A SECOND?

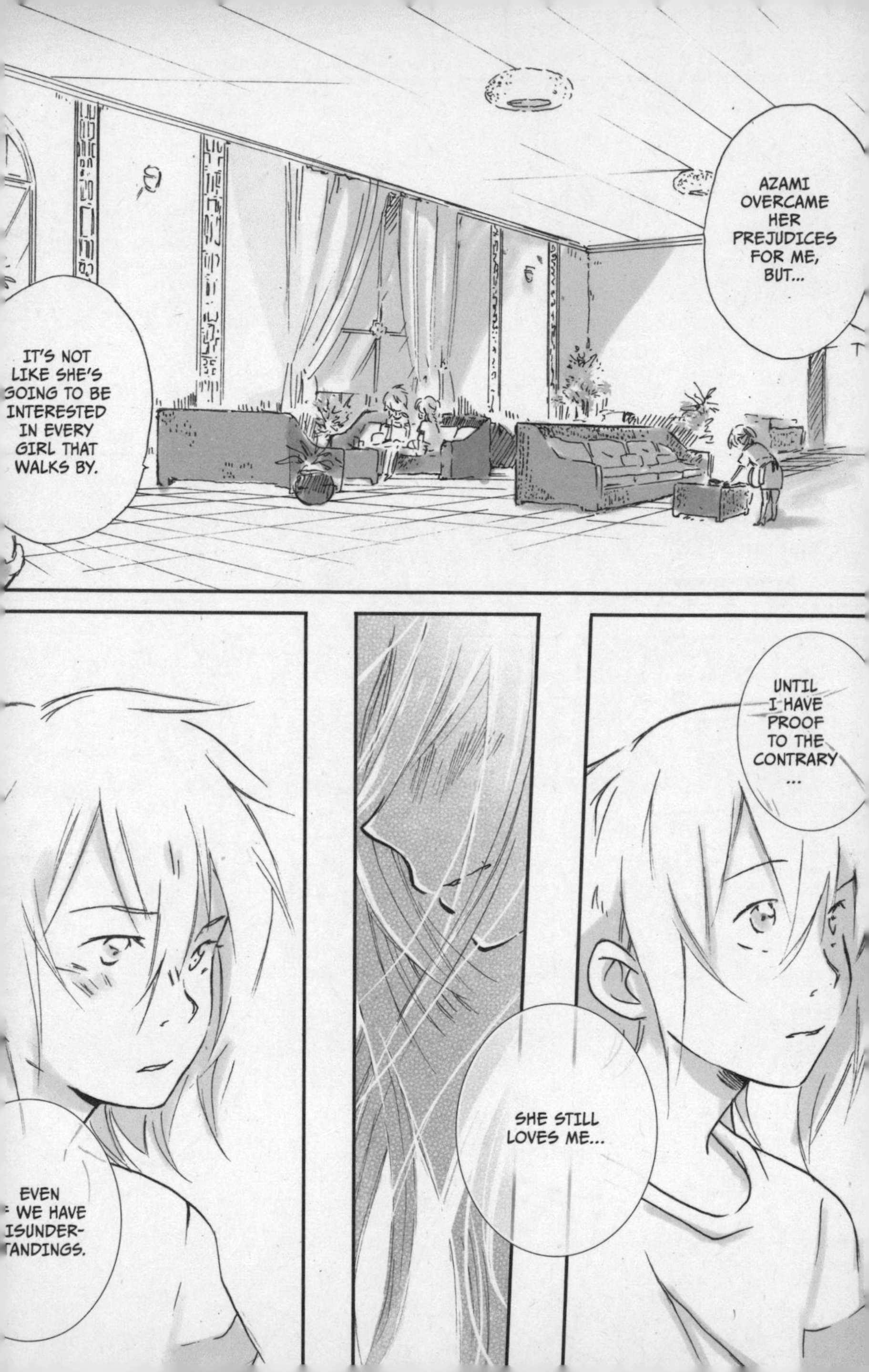
AZAMI OVERCAME HER PREJUDICES FOR ME, BUT...
IT'S NOT LIKE SHE'S GOING TO BE INTERESTED IN EVERY GIRL THAT WALKS BY.
UNTIL I HAVE PROOF TO THE CONTRARY...
SHE STILL LOVES ME...
EVEN WE HAVE ISUNDER-TANDINGS.

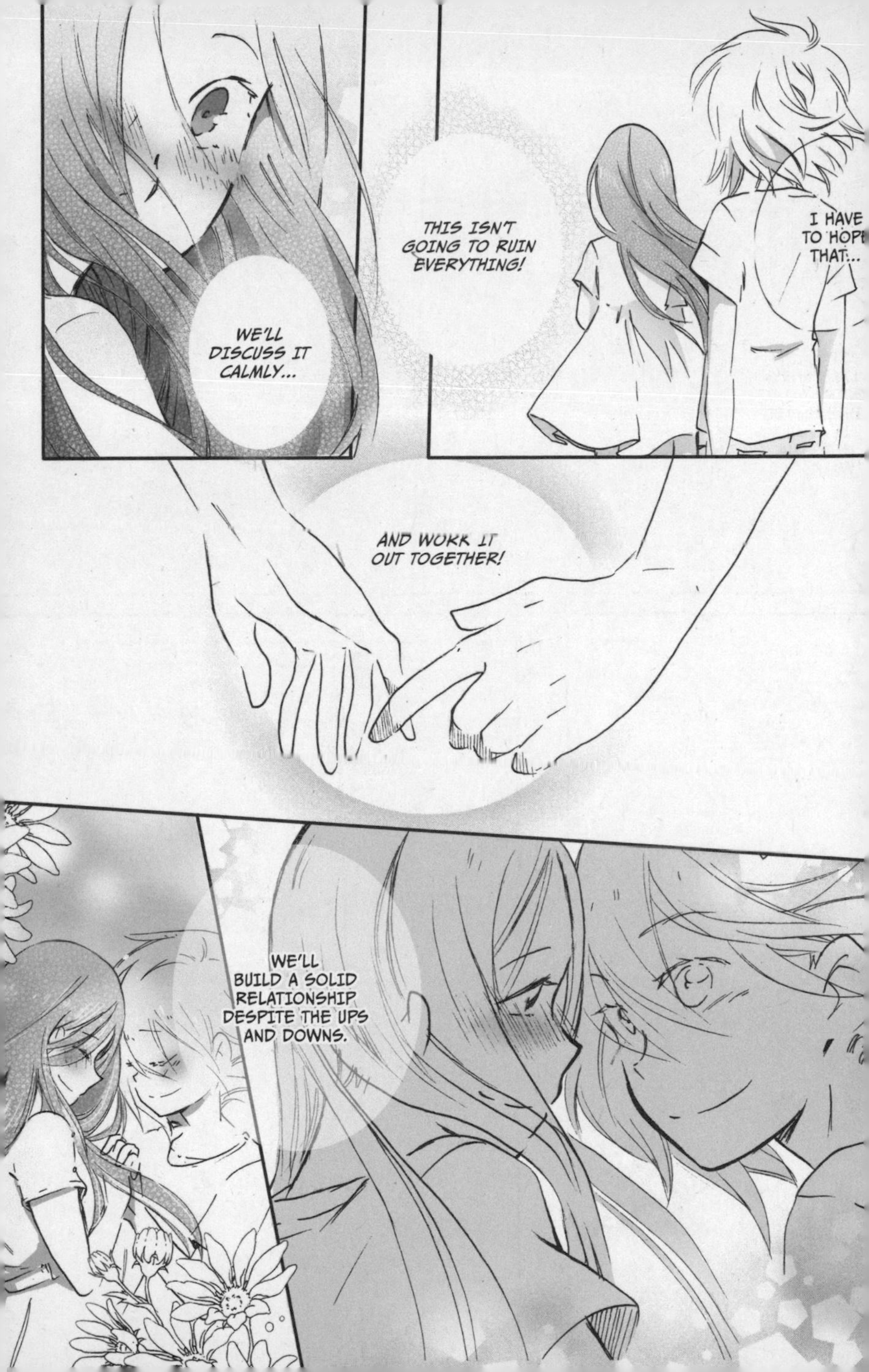
I HAVE TO HOPE THAT...
THIS ISN'T GOING TO RUIN EVERYTHING!
WE'LL DISCUSS IT CALMLY...
AND WORK IT OUT TOGETHER!
WE'LL BUILD A SOLID RELATIONSHIP DESPITE THE UPS AND DOWNS.

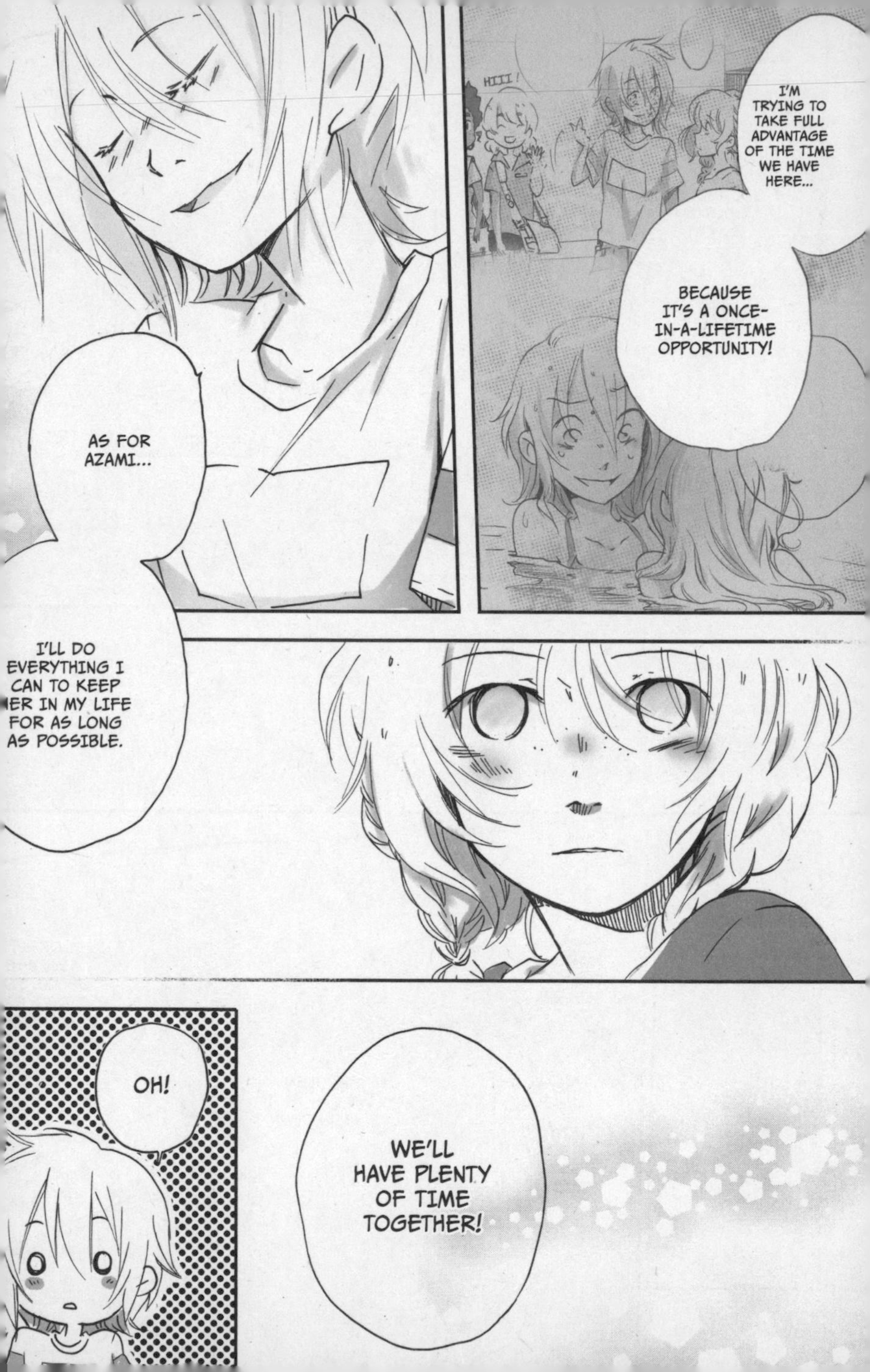
I'M TRYING TO TAKE FULL ADVANTAGE OF THE TIME WE HAVE HERE...
HIII!
BECAUSE IT'S A ONCE-IN-A-LIFETIME OPPORTUNITY!
AS FOR AZAMI...
I'LL DO EVERYTHING I CAN TO KEEP HER IN MY LIFE FOR AS LONG AS POSSIBLE.
WE'LL HAVE PLENTY OF TIME TOGETHER!
OH!

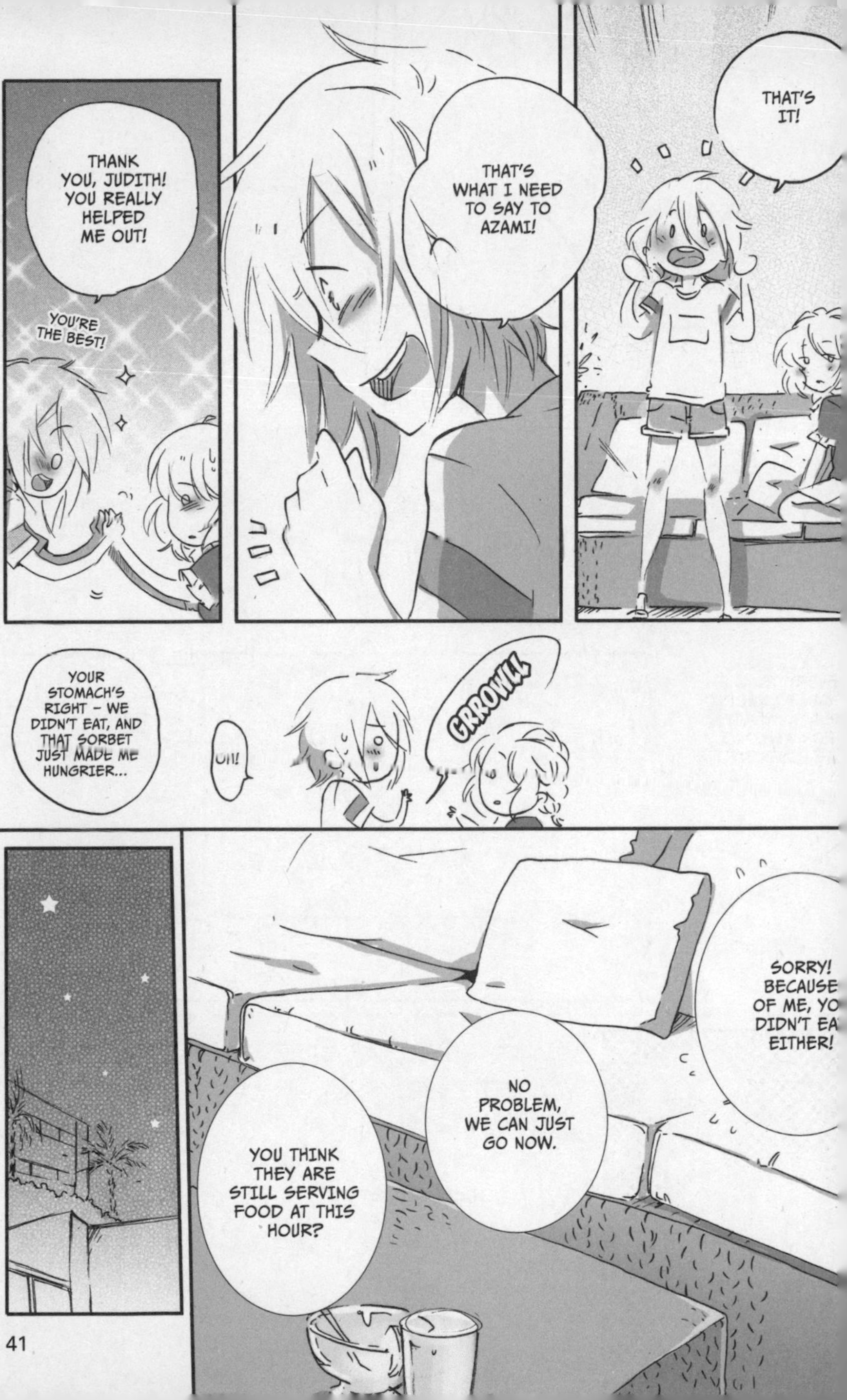
THAT'S IT!
THAT'S WHAT I NEED TO SAY TO AZAMI!
THANK YOU, JUDITH! YOU REALLY HELPED ME OUT!
YOU'RE THE BEST!
GRROWLL
UH!
YOUR STOMACH'S RIGHT – WE DIDN'T EAT, AND THAT SORBET JUST MADE ME HUNGRIER...
SORRY! BECAUSE OF ME, YO DIDN'T EA EITHER!
NO PROBLEM, WE CAN JUST GO NOW.
YOU THINK THEY ARE STILL SERVING FOOD AT THIS HOUR?

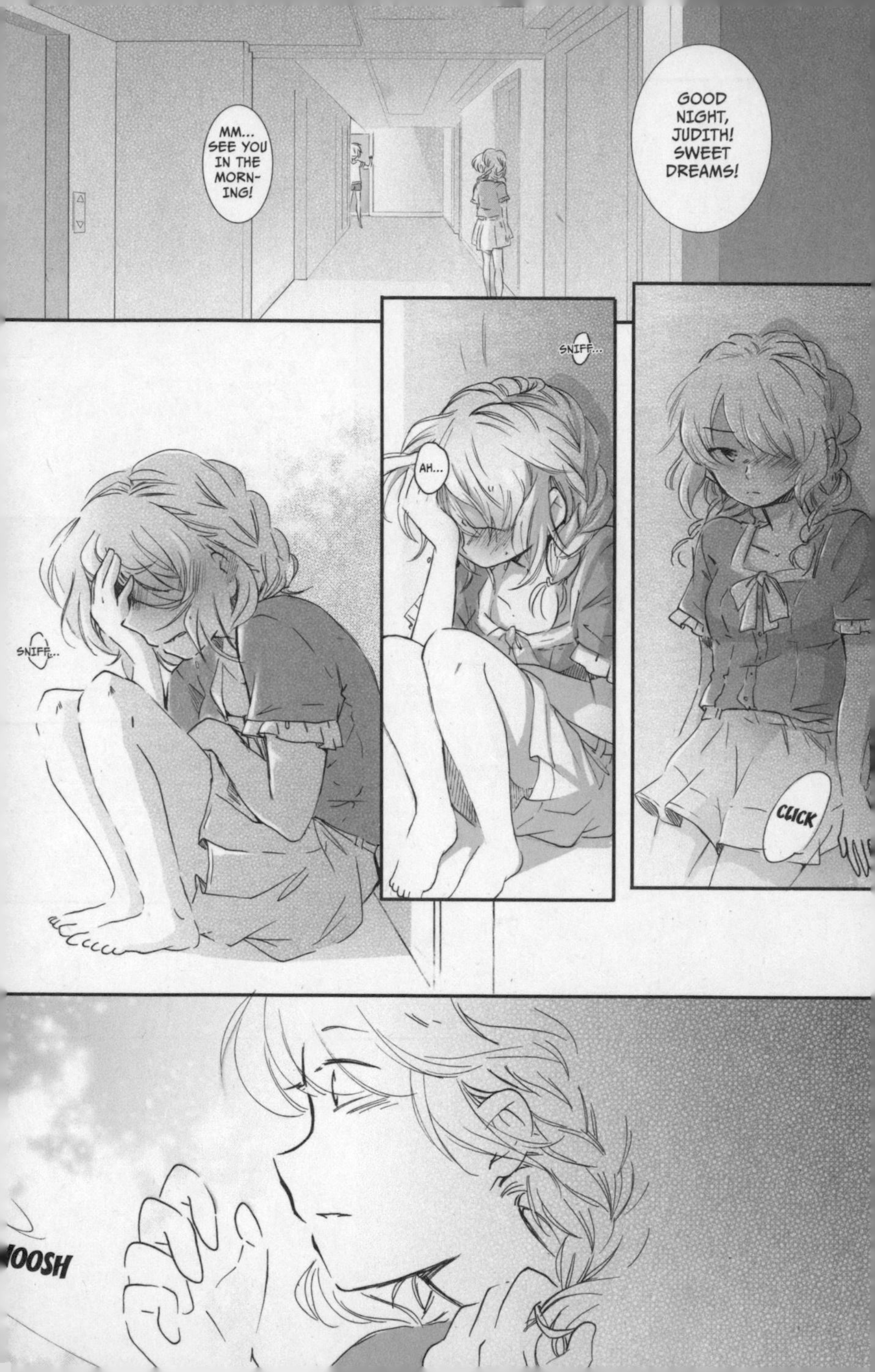
GOOD NIGHT, JUDITH! SWEET DREAMS!
MM... SEE YOU IN THE MORNING!
CLICK
SNIFF...
AH...
SNIFF...
OOSH

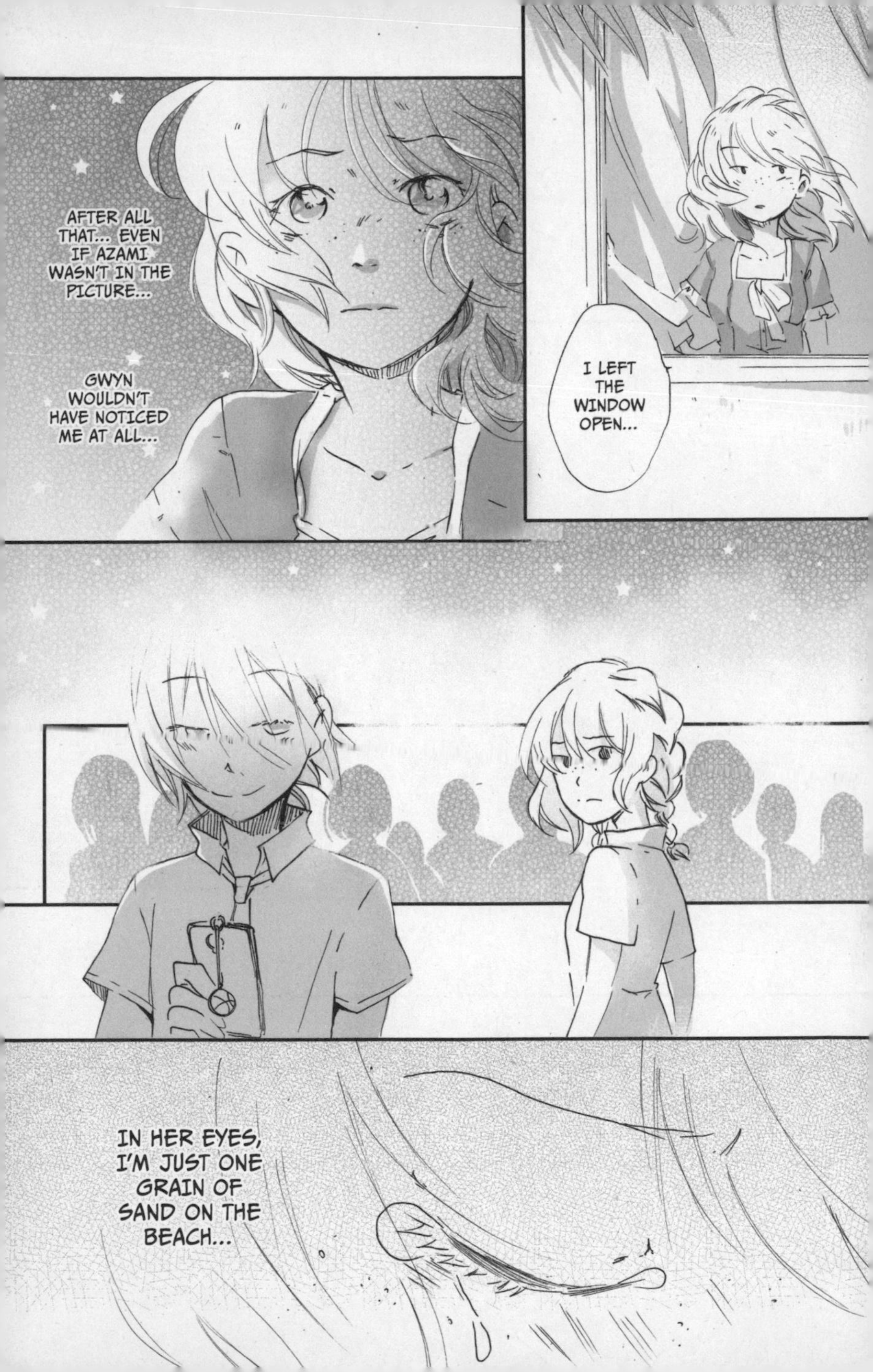
I LEFT THE WINDOW OPEN...
AFTER ALL THAT... EVEN IF AZAMI WASN'T IN THE PICTURE...
GWYN WOULDN'T HAVE NOTICED ME AT ALL...
IN HER EYES, I'M JUST ONE GRAIN OF SAND ON THE BEACH...

Chapter 12
Before the End of the Summer

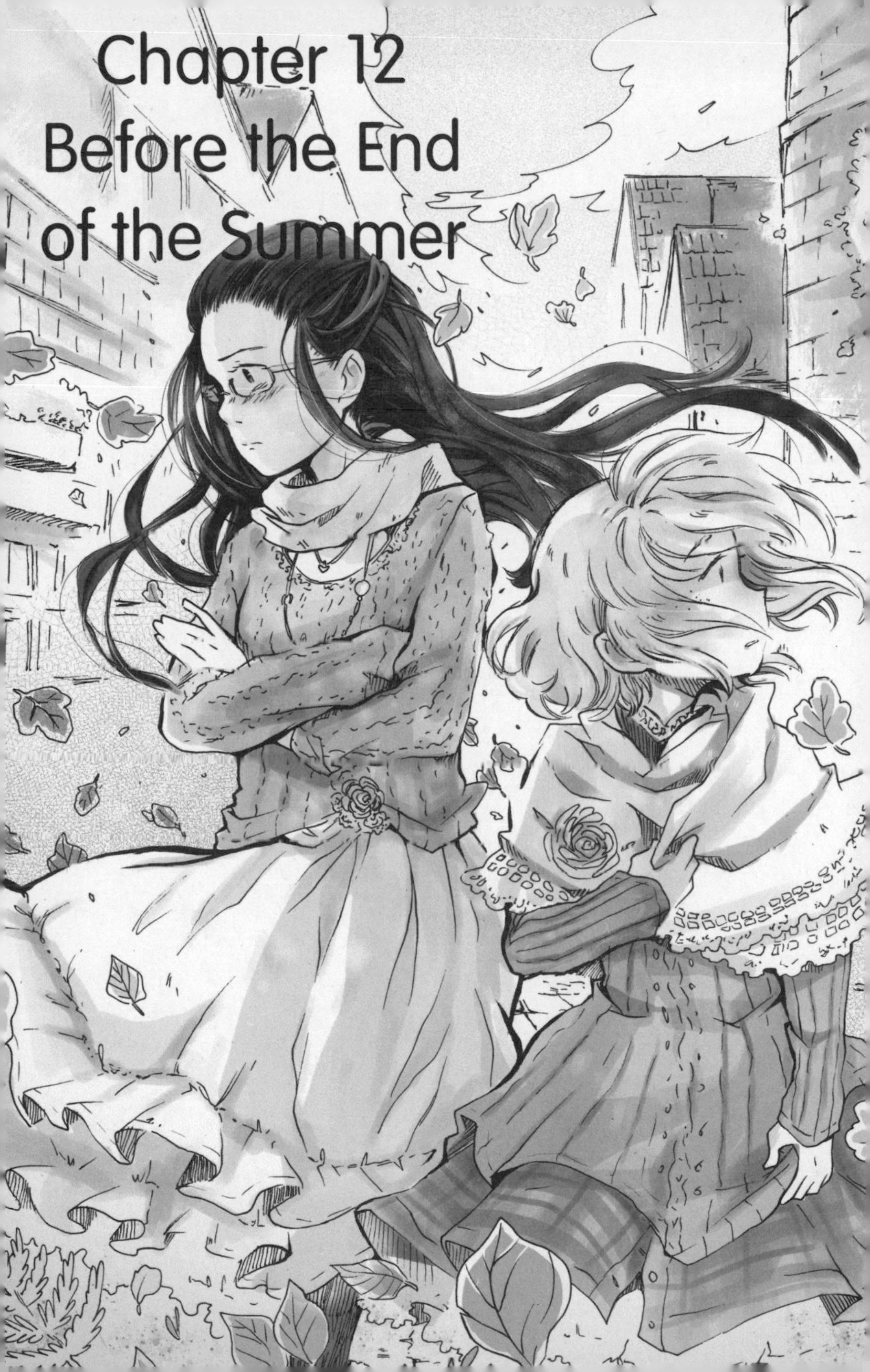

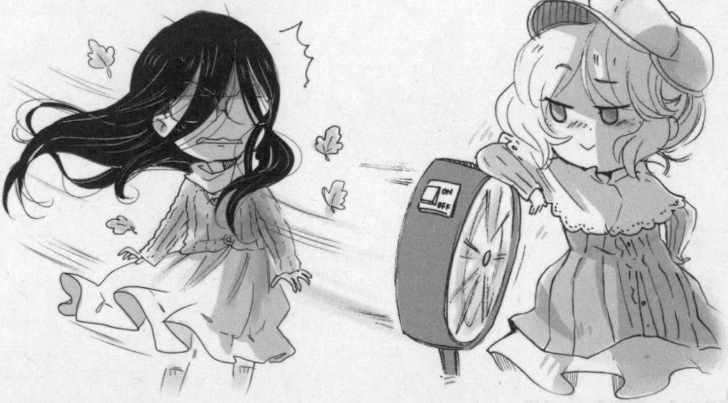
ON
OFF

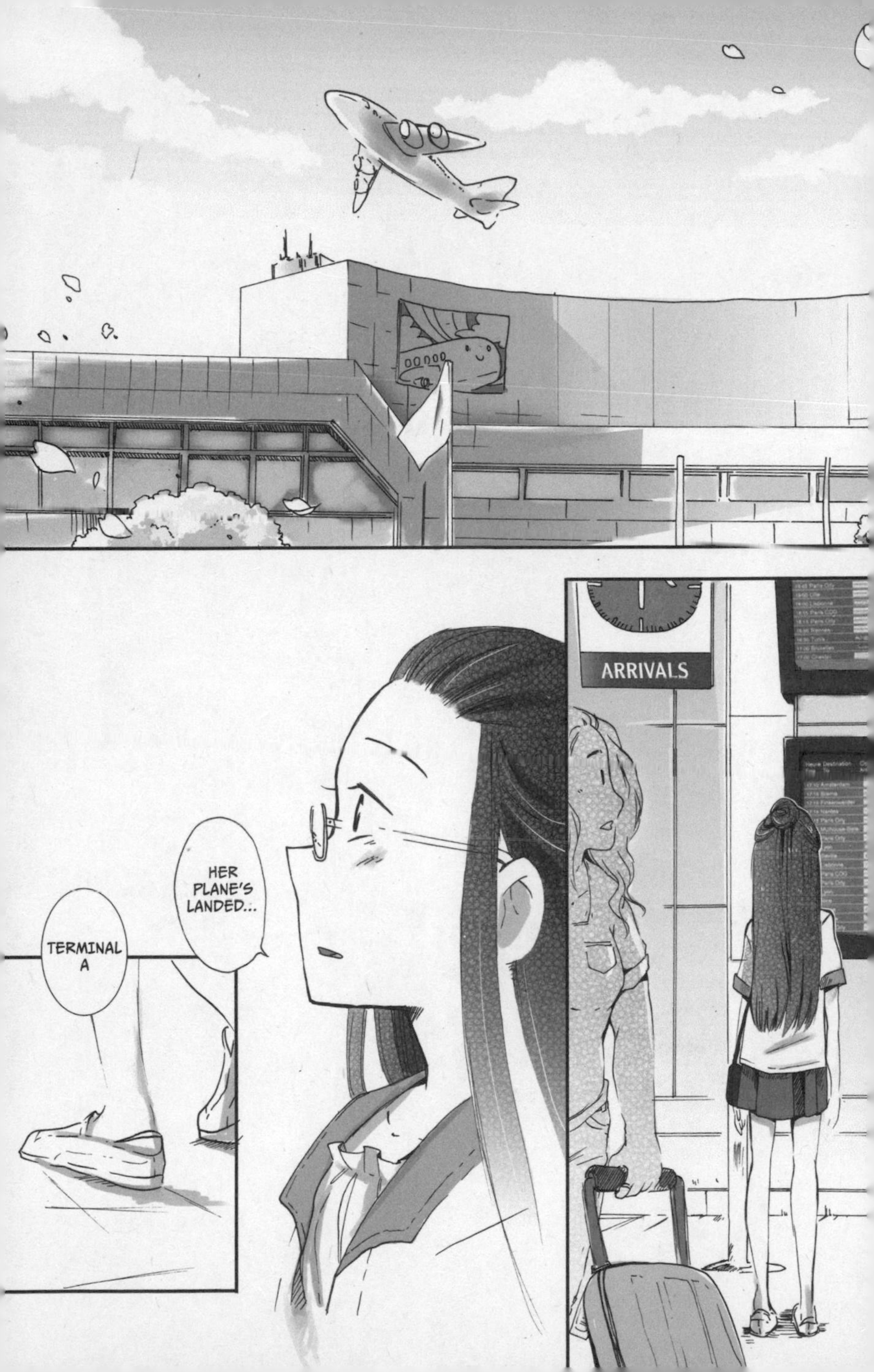
ARRIVALS
HER PLANE'S LANDED...
TERMINAL A

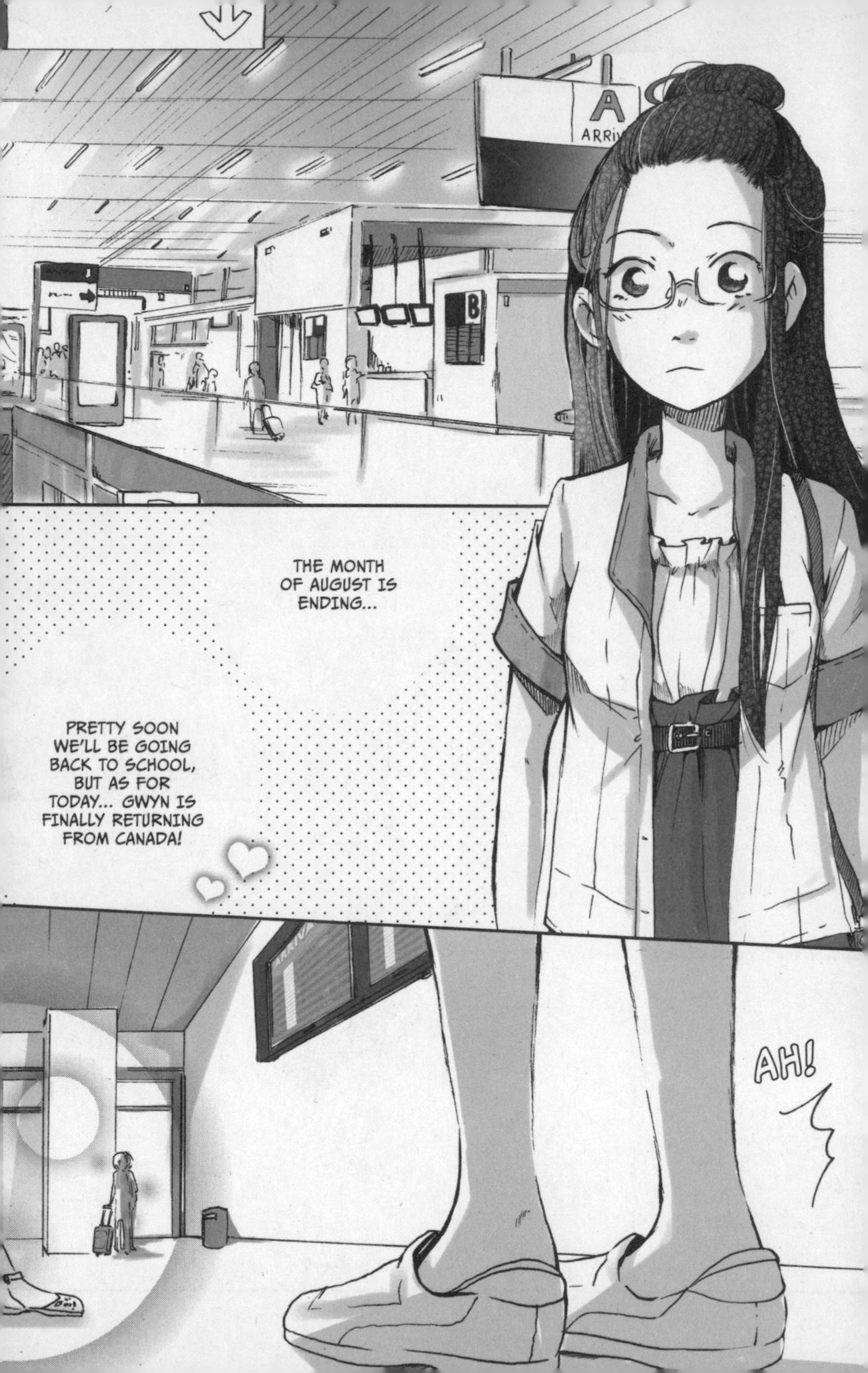
THE MONTH OF AUGUST IS ENDING...
PRETTY SOON WE'LL BE GOING BACK TO SCHOOL, BUT AS FOR TODAY... GWYN IS FINALLY RETURNING FROM CANADA!
AH!

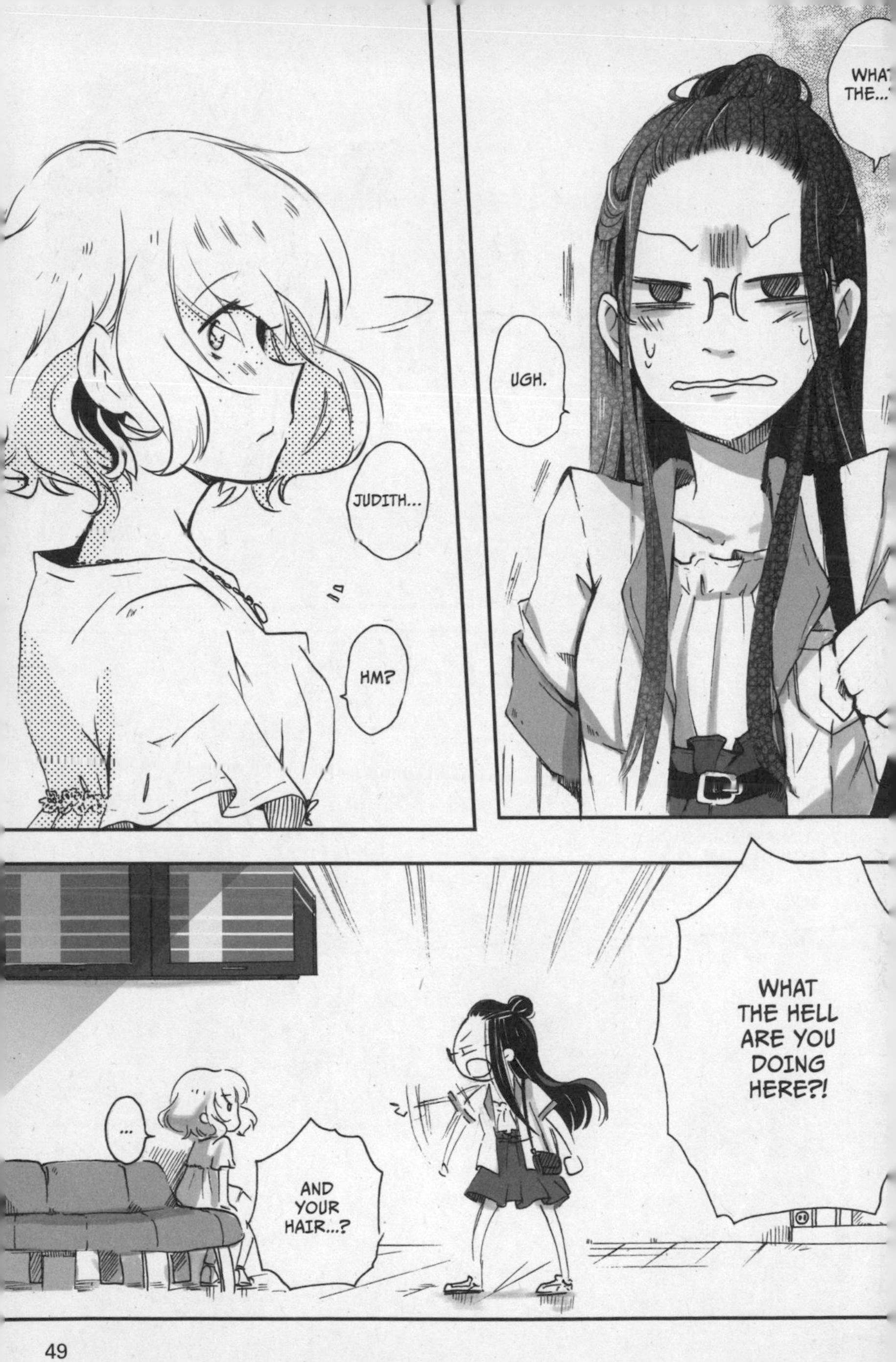
WHAT THE...
UGH.
JUDITH...
HM?
WHAT THE HELL ARE YOU DOING HERE?!
AND YOUR HAIR...?
...

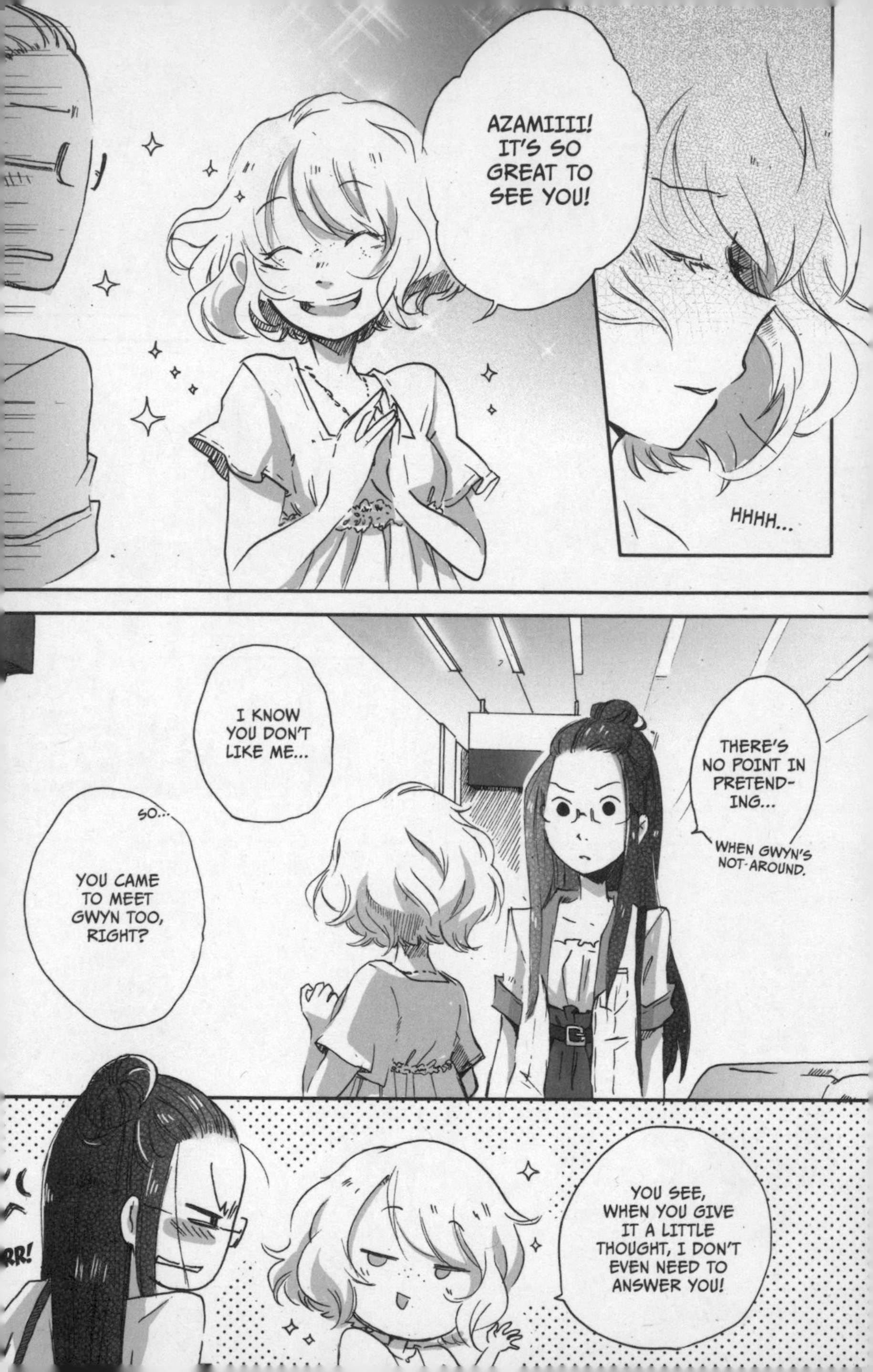
AZAMIIII! IT'S SO GREAT TO SEE YOU!
HHHH...
THERE'S NO POINT IN PRETEND-ING...
WHEN GWYN'S NOT-AROUND.
I KNOW YOU DON'T LIKE ME...
SO...
YOU CAME TO MEET GWYN TOO, RIGHT?
YOU SEE, WHEN YOU GIVE IT A LITTLE THOUGHT, I DON'T EVEN NEED TO ANSWER YOU!

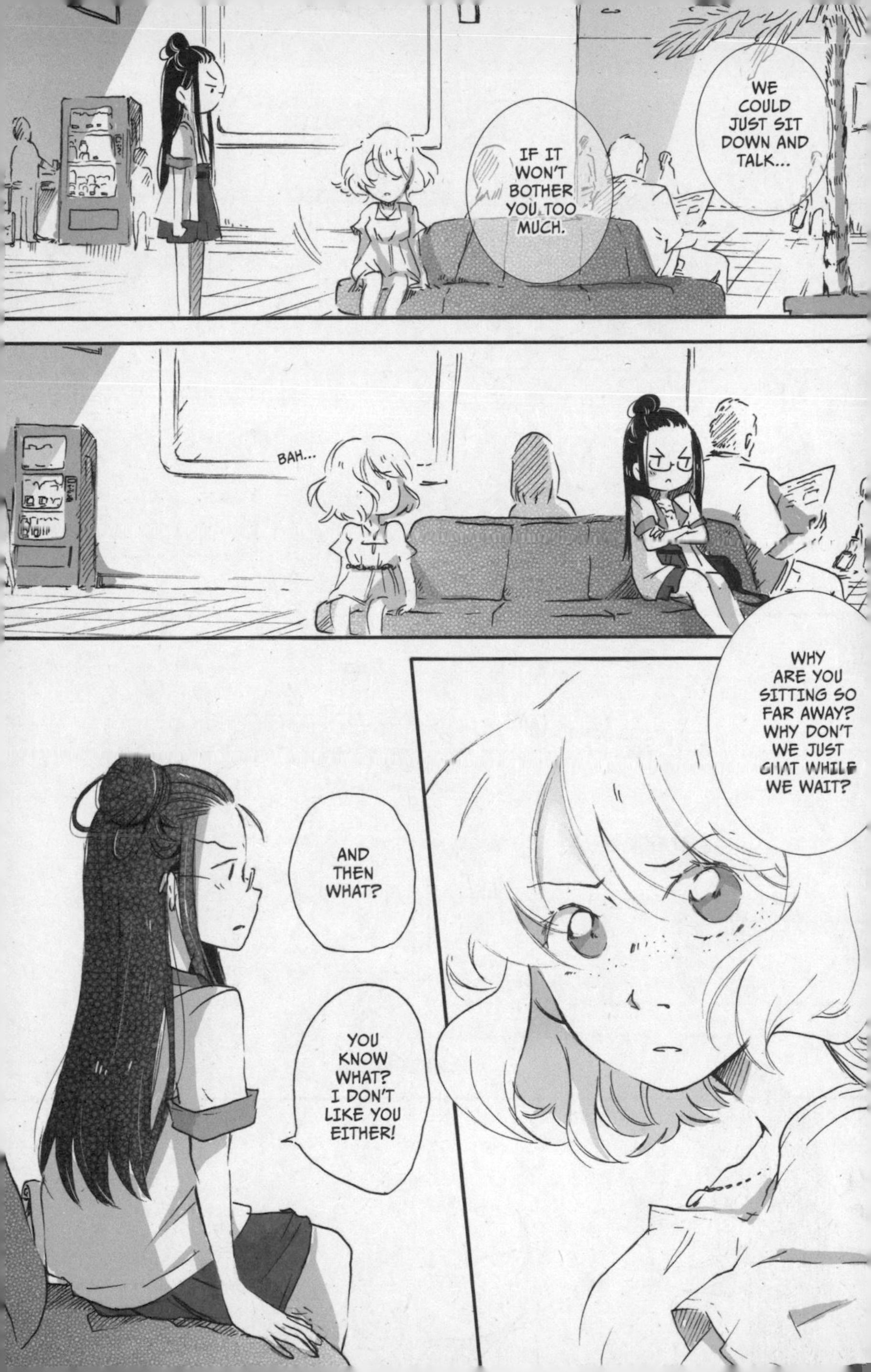
WE COULD JUST SIT DOWN AND TALK...
IF IT WON'T BOTHER YOU TOO MUCH.
BAH...
WHY ARE YOU SITTING SO FAR AWAY? WHY DON'T WE JUST CHAT WHILE WE WAIT?
AND THEN WHAT?
YOU KNOW WHAT? I DON'T LIKE YOU EITHER!

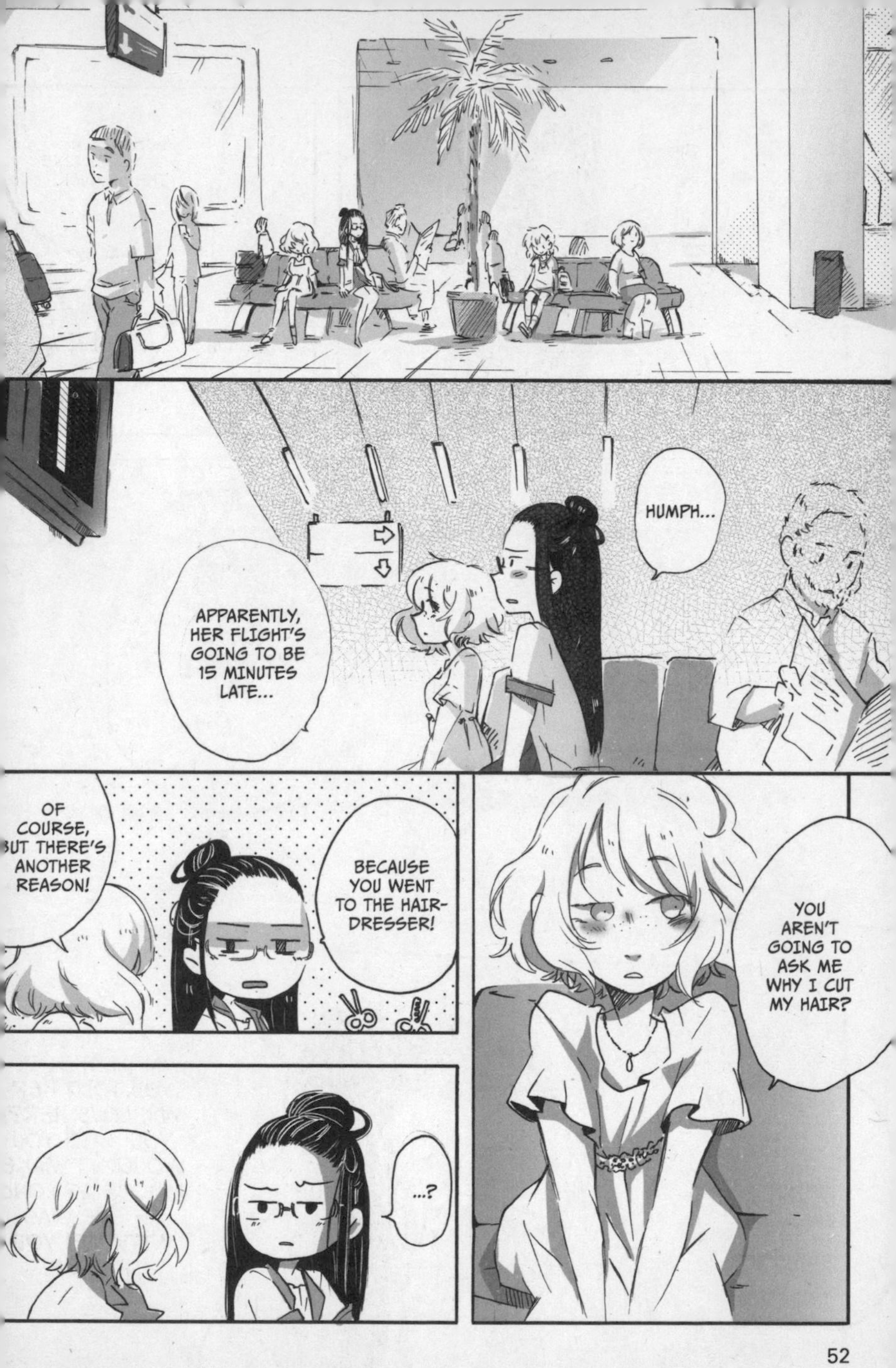
HUMPH...
APPARENTLY, HER FLIGHT'S GOING TO BE 15 MINUTES LATE...
YOU AREN'T GOING TO ASK ME WHY I CUT MY HAIR?
BECAUSE YOU WENT TO THE HAIR-DRESSER!
OF COURSE, BUT THERE'S ANOTHER REASON!
...?

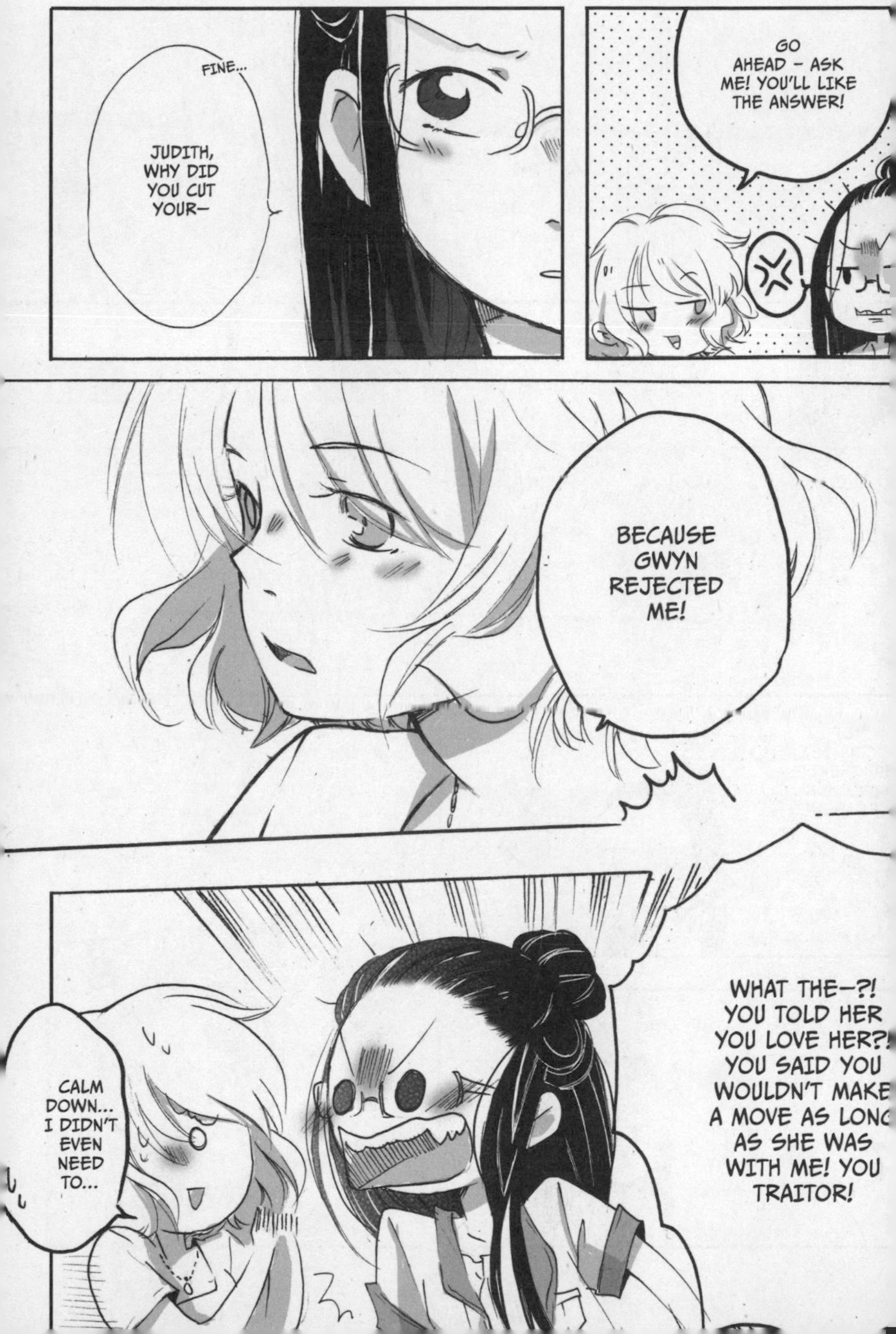
GO AHEAD – ASK ME! YOU'LL LIKE THE ANSWER!
FINE...
JUDITH, WHY DID YOU CUT YOUR–
BECAUSE GWYN REJECTED ME!
WHAT THE–?! YOU TOLD HER YOU LOVE HER?! YOU SAID YOU WOULDN'T MAKE A MOVE AS LONG AS SHE WAS WITH ME! YOU TRAITOR!
CALM DOWN... I DIDN'T EVEN NEED TO...

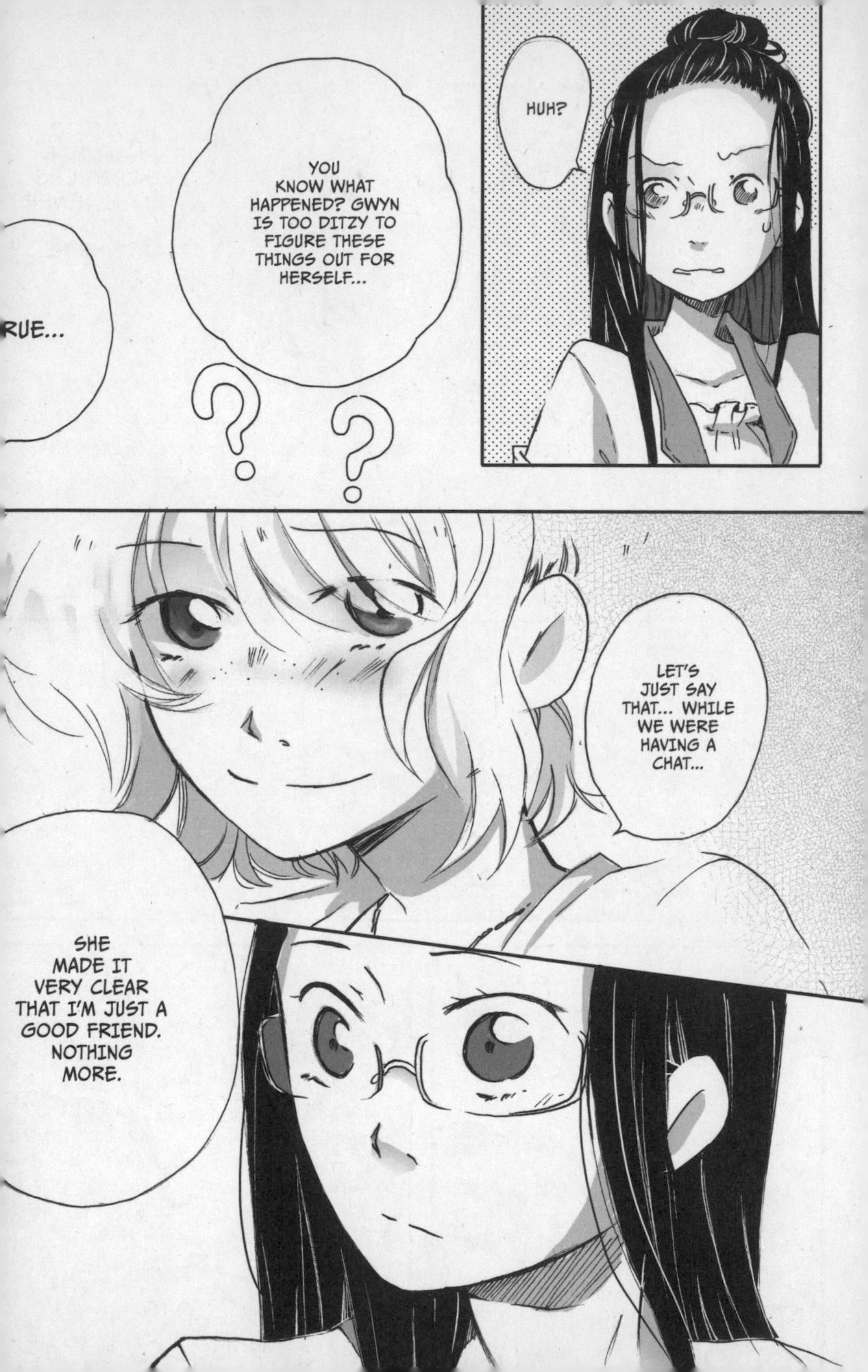
HUH?
YOU KNOW WHAT HAPPENED? GWYN IS TOO DITZY TO FIGURE THESE THINGS OUT FOR HERSELF...
RUE...
LET'S JUST SAY THAT... WHILE WE WERE HAVING A CHAT...
SHE MADE IT VERY CLEAR THAT I'M JUST A GOOD FRIEND. NOTHING MORE.

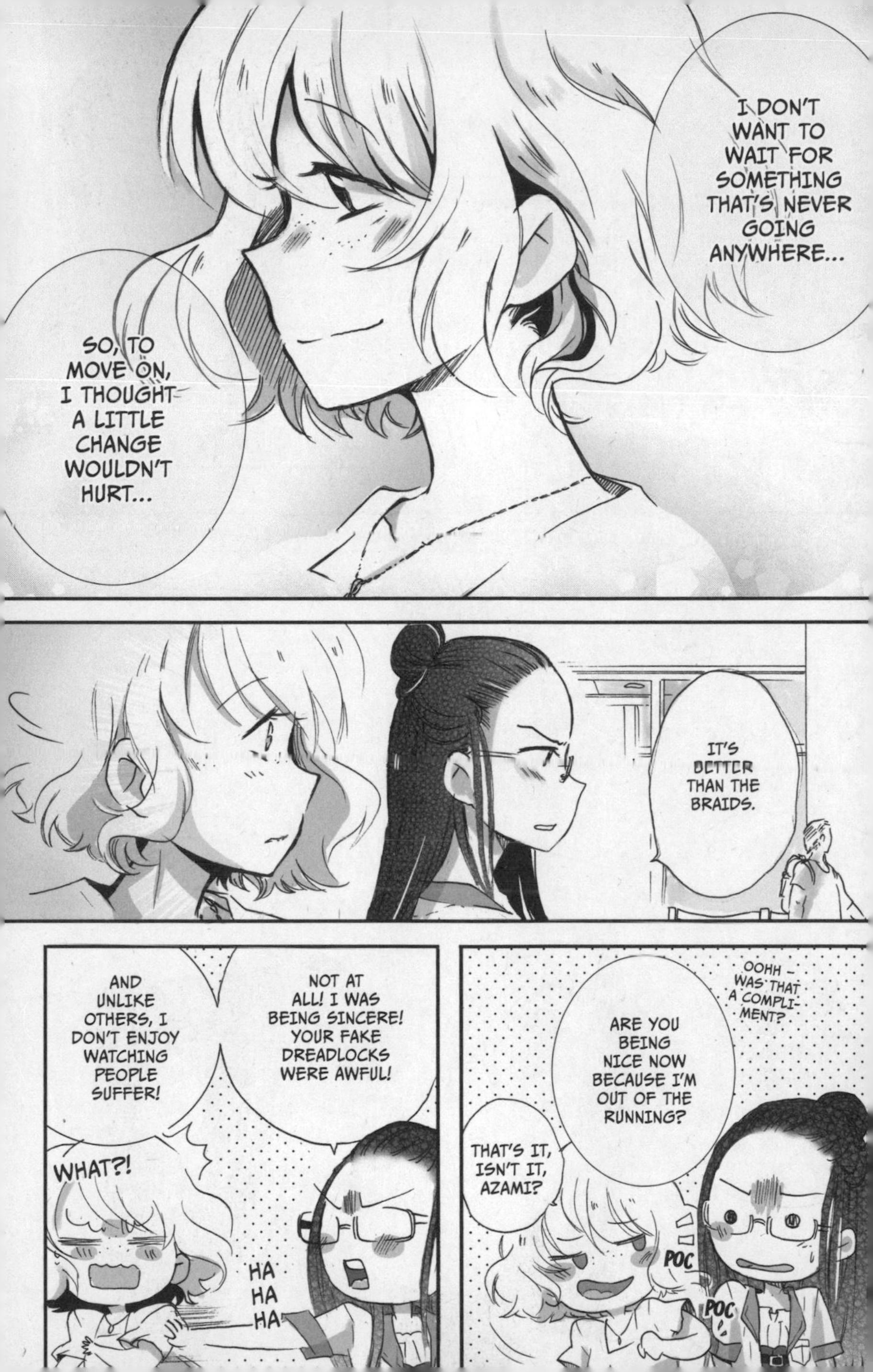
I DON'T WANT TO WAIT FOR SOMETHING THAT'S NEVER GOING ANYWHERE...
SO, TO MOVE ON, I THOUGHT A LITTLE CHANGE WOULDN'T HURT...
IT'S BETTER THAN THE BRAIDS.
OOHH – WAS THAT A COMPLIMENT?
ARE YOU BEING NICE NOW BECAUSE I'M OUT OF THE RUNNING?
THAT'S IT, ISN'T IT, AZAMI?
POC
POC
NOT AT ALL! I WAS BEING SINCERE! YOUR FAKE DREADLOCKS WERE AWFUL!
AND UNLIKE OTHERS, I DON'T ENJOY WATCHING PEOPLE SUFFER!
WHAT?!
HA HA HA

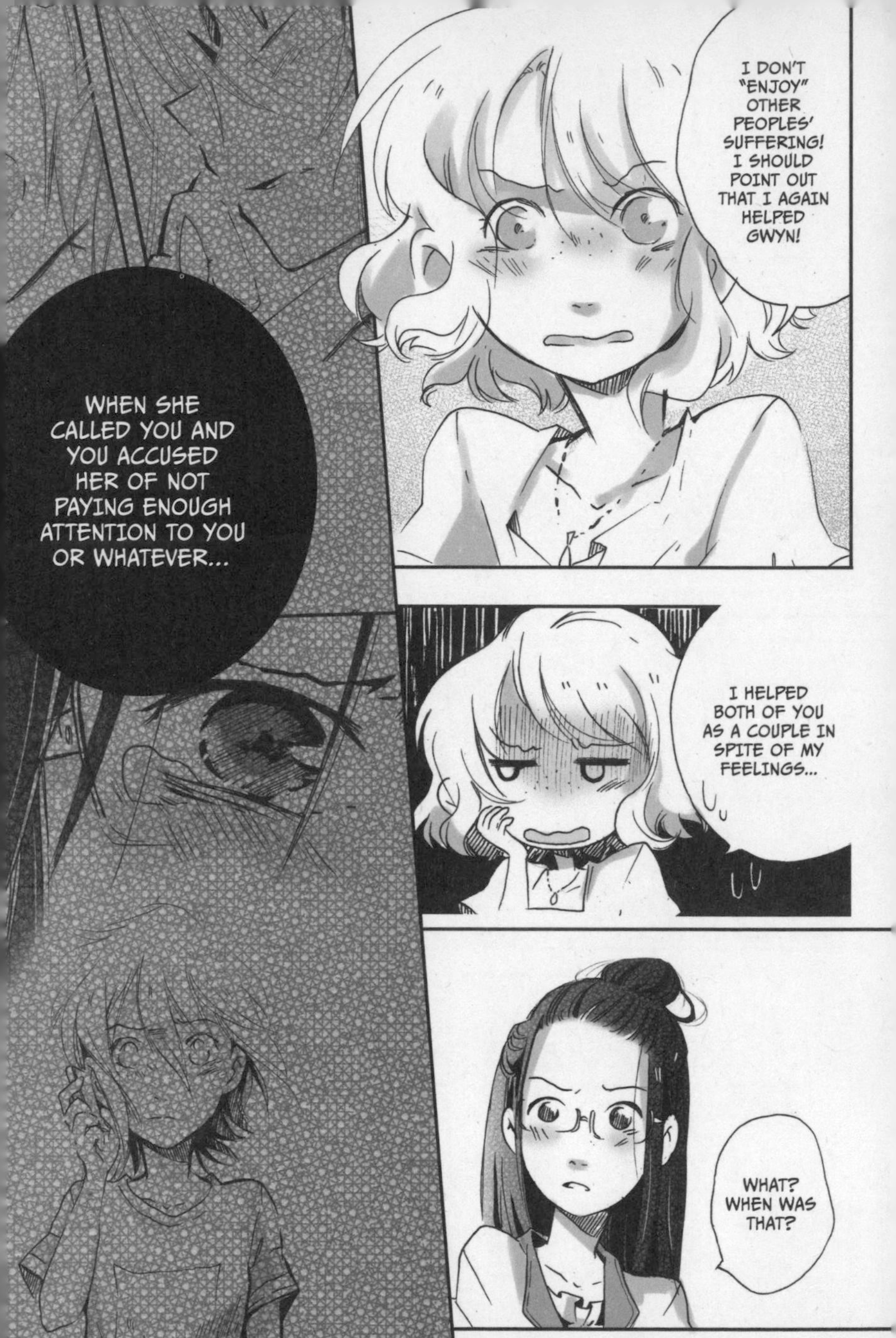
I DON'T "ENJOY" OTHER PEOPLES' SUFFERING! I SHOULD POINT OUT THAT I AGAIN HELPED GWYN!
I HELPED BOTH OF YOU AS A COUPLE IN SPITE OF MY FEELINGS...
WHAT? WHEN WAS THAT?
WHEN SHE CALLED YOU AND YOU ACCUSED HER OF NOT PAYING ENOUGH ATTENTION TO YOU OR WHATEVER...

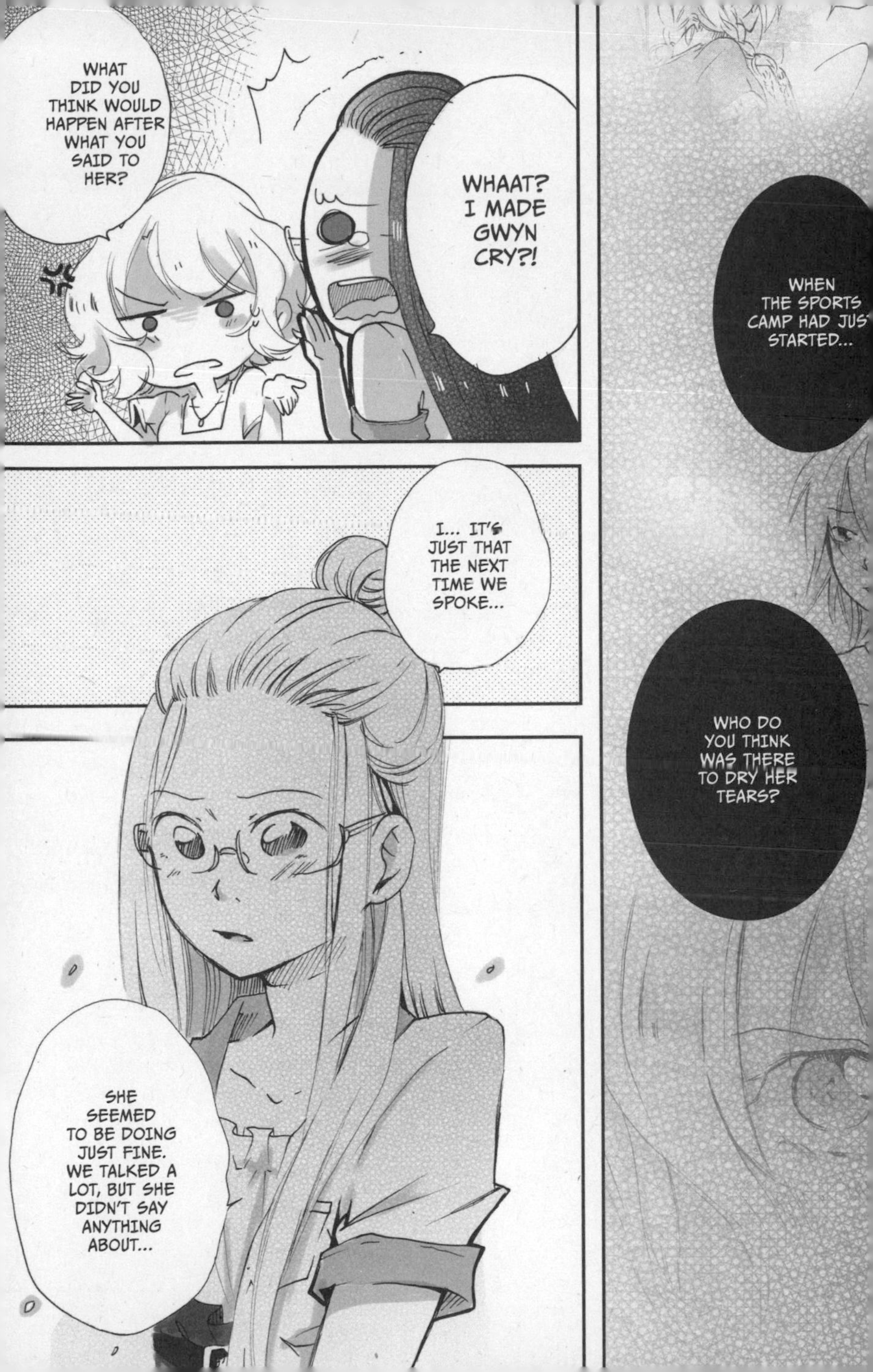
WHEN THE SPORTS CAMP HAD JUST STARTED...
WHO DO YOU THINK WAS THERE TO DRY HER TEARS?
WHAAT? I MADE GWYN CRY?!
WHAT DID YOU THINK WOULD HAPPEN AFTER WHAT YOU SAID TO HER?
I... IT'S JUST THAT THE NEXT TIME WE SPOKE...
SHE SEEMED TO BE DOING JUST FINE. WE TALKED A LOT, BUT SHE DIDN'T SAY ANYTHING ABOUT...

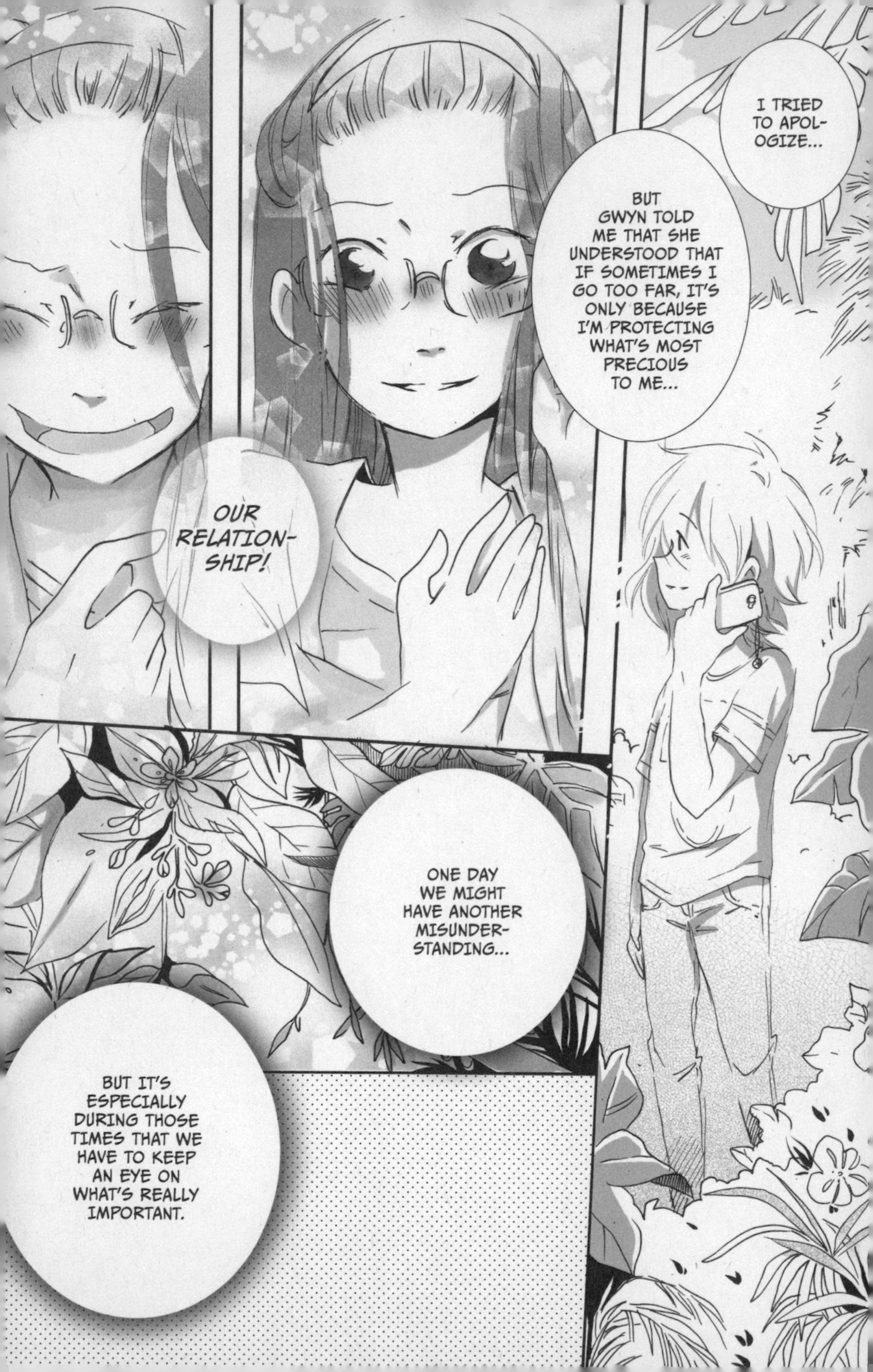
I TRIED TO APOLOGIZE...
BUT GWYN TOLD ME THAT SHE UNDERSTOOD THAT IF SOMETIMES I GO TOO FAR, IT'S ONLY BECAUSE I'M PROTECTING WHAT'S MOST PRECIOUS TO ME...
OUR RELATIONSHIP!
ONE DAY WE MIGHT HAVE ANOTHER MISUNDERSTANDING...
BUT IT'S ESPECIALLY DURING THOSE TIMES THAT WE HAVE TO KEEP AN EYE ON WHAT'S REALLY IMPORTANT.

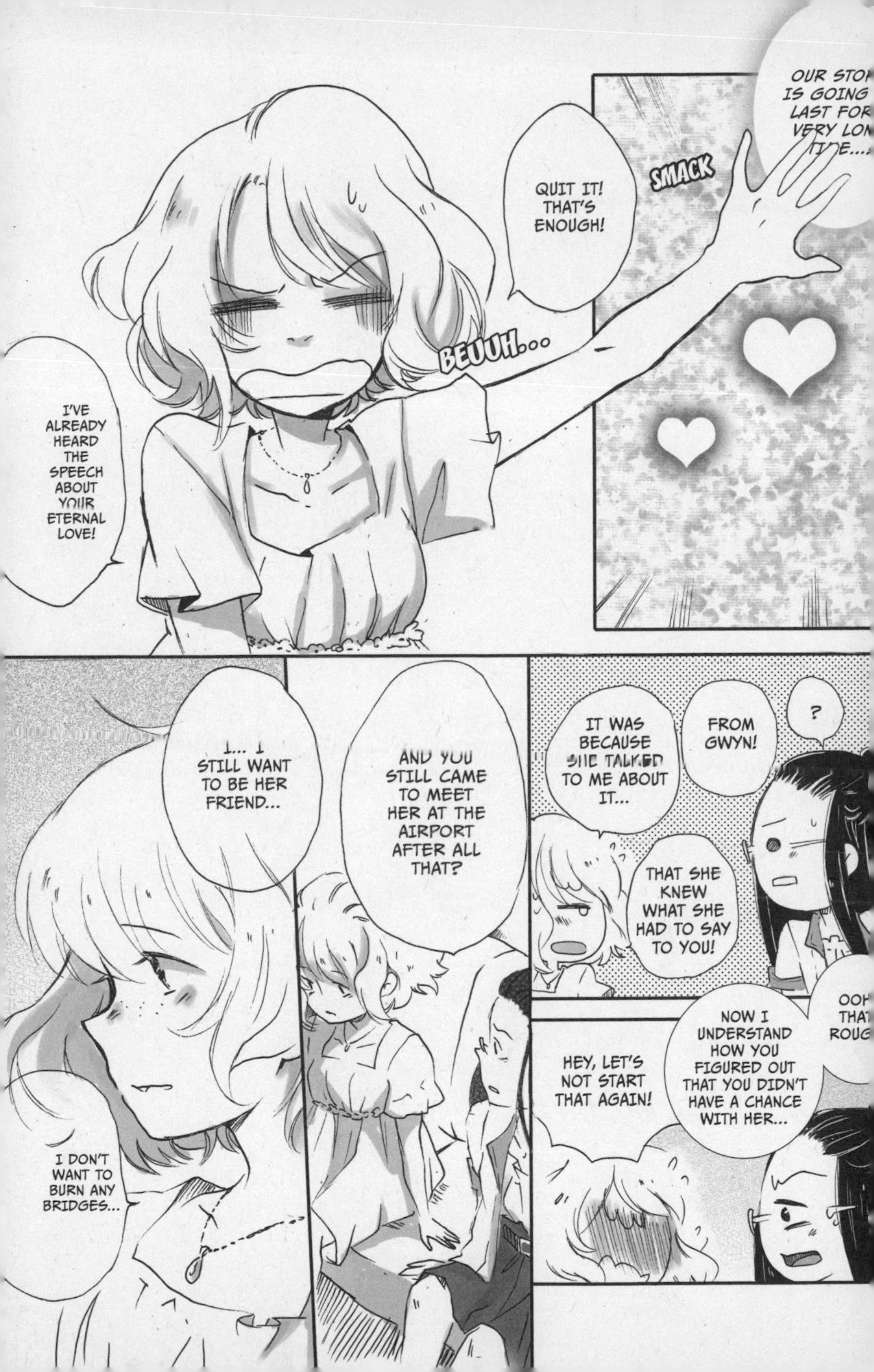
OUR STO IS GOING LAST FOR VERY LON
SMACK
QUIT IT! THAT'S ENOUGH!
BEUUH...
I'VE ALREADY HEARD THE SPEECH ABOUT YOUR ETERNAL LOVE!
?
FROM GWYN!
IT WAS BECAUSE SHE TALKED TO ME ABOUT IT...
THAT SHE KNEW WHAT SHE HAD TO SAY TO YOU!
OOH THAT ROUG
NOW I UNDERSTAND HOW YOU FIGURED OUT THAT YOU DIDN'T HAVE A CHANCE WITH HER...
HEY, LET'S NOT START THAT AGAIN!
AND YOU STILL CAME TO MEET HER AT THE AIRPORT AFTER ALL THAT?
I... I STILL WANT TO BE HER FRIEND...
I DON'T WANT TO BURN ANY BRIDGES...

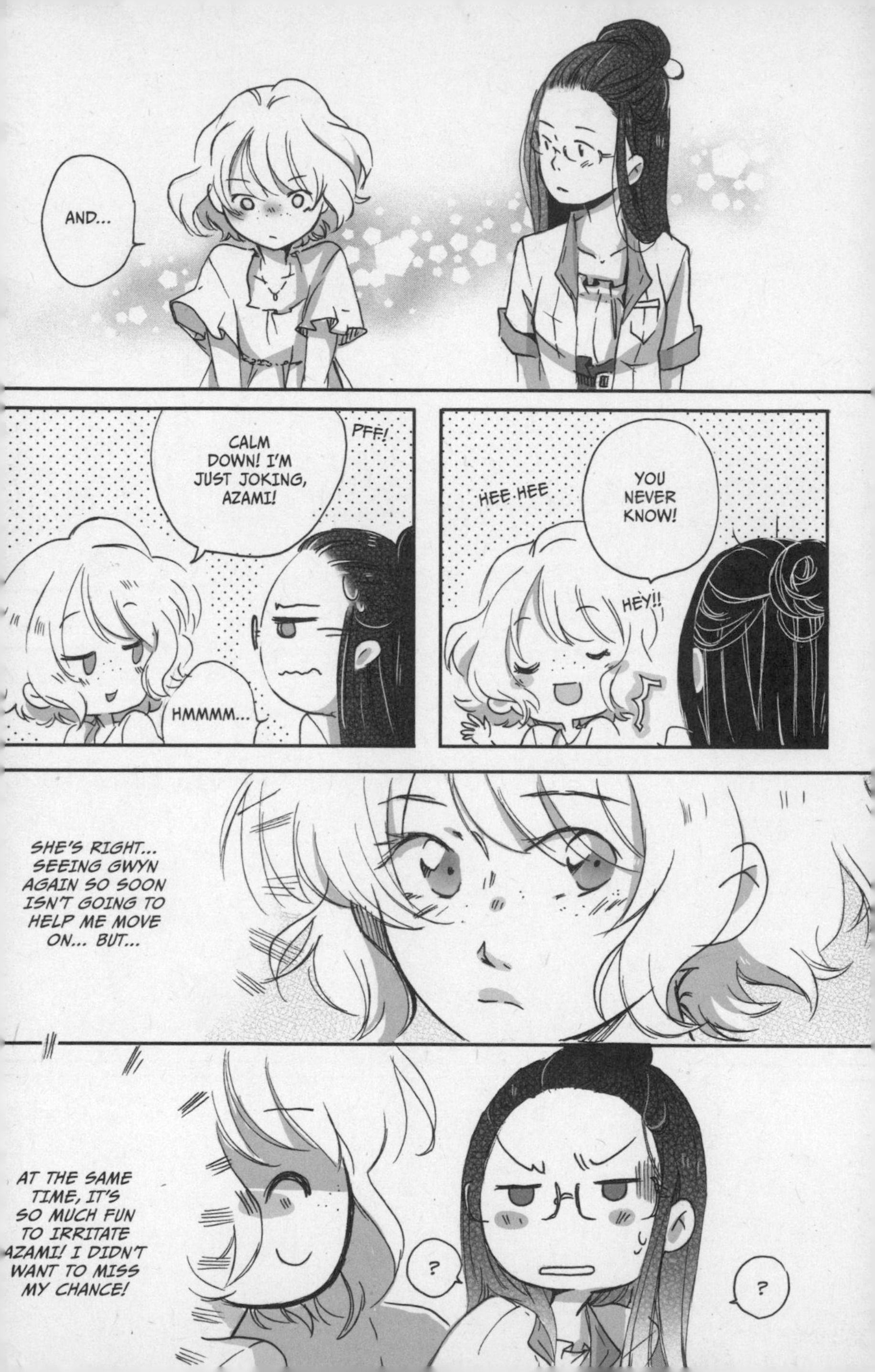
AND...
YOU NEVER KNOW!
HEE HEE
HEY!!
PFF!
CALM DOWN! I'M JUST JOKING, AZAMI!
HMMMM...
SHE'S RIGHT... SEEING GWYN AGAIN SO SOON ISN'T GOING TO HELP ME MOVE ON... BUT...
?
?
AT THE SAME TIME, IT'S SO MUCH FUN TO IRRITATE AZAMI! I DIDN'T WANT TO MISS MY CHANCE!

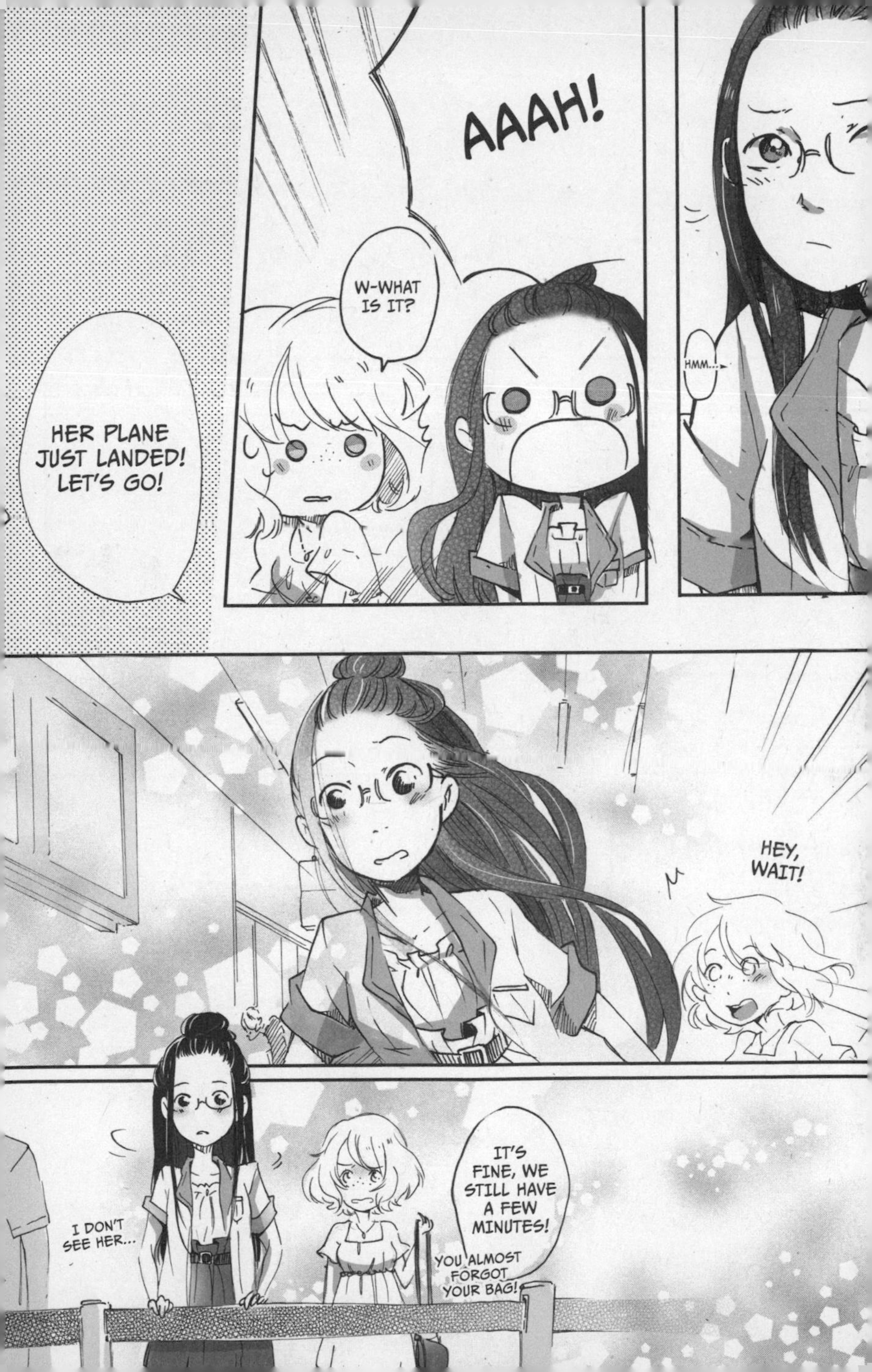
HMM...
AAAH!
W-WHAT IS IT?
HER PLANE JUST LANDED! LET'S GO!
HEY, WAIT!
IT'S FINE, WE STILL HAVE A FEW MINUTES!
YOU ALMOST FORGOT YOUR BAG!
I DON'T SEE HER...

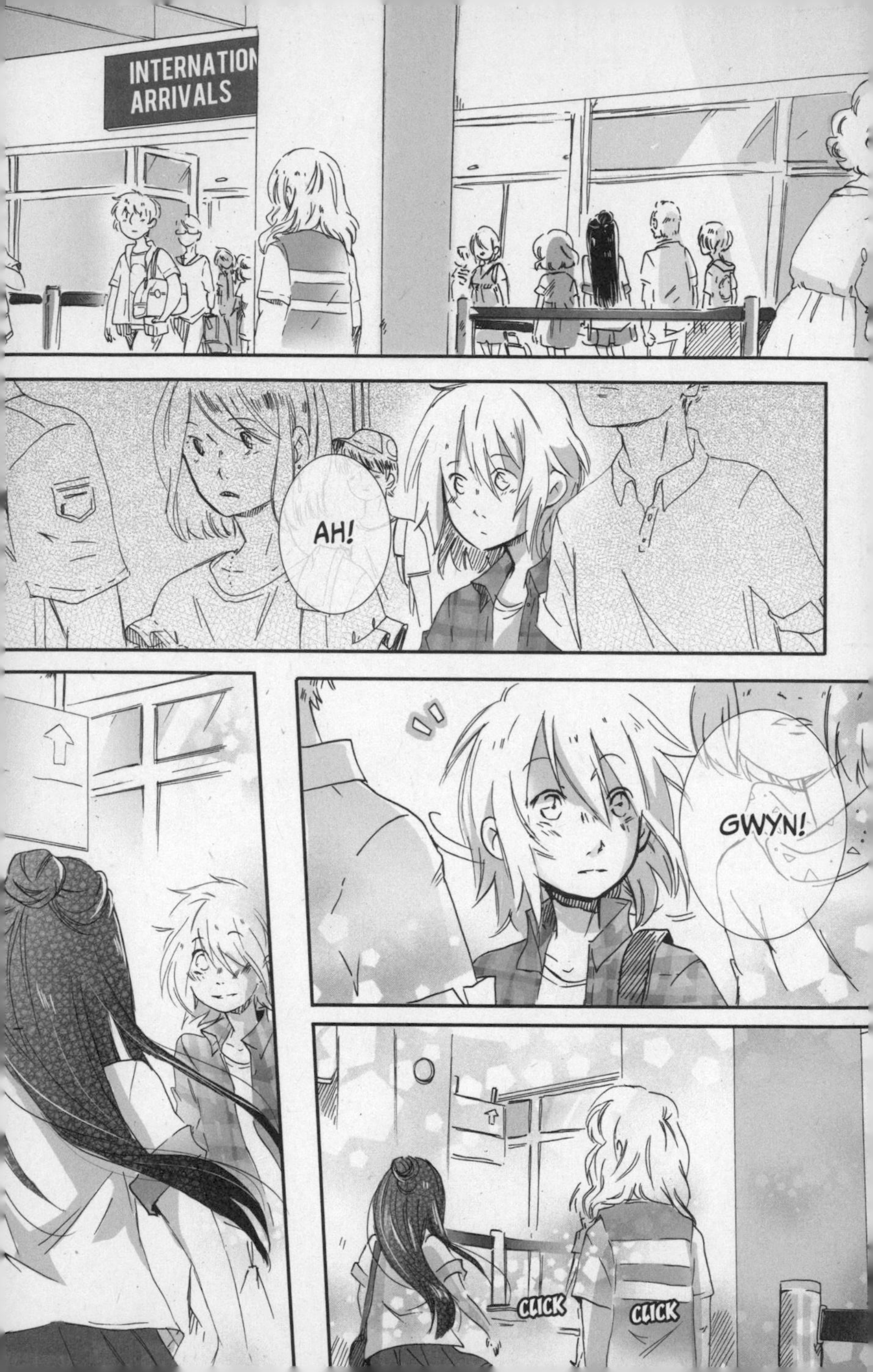
INTERNATION
ARRIVALS
AH!
GWYN!
CLICK
CLICK

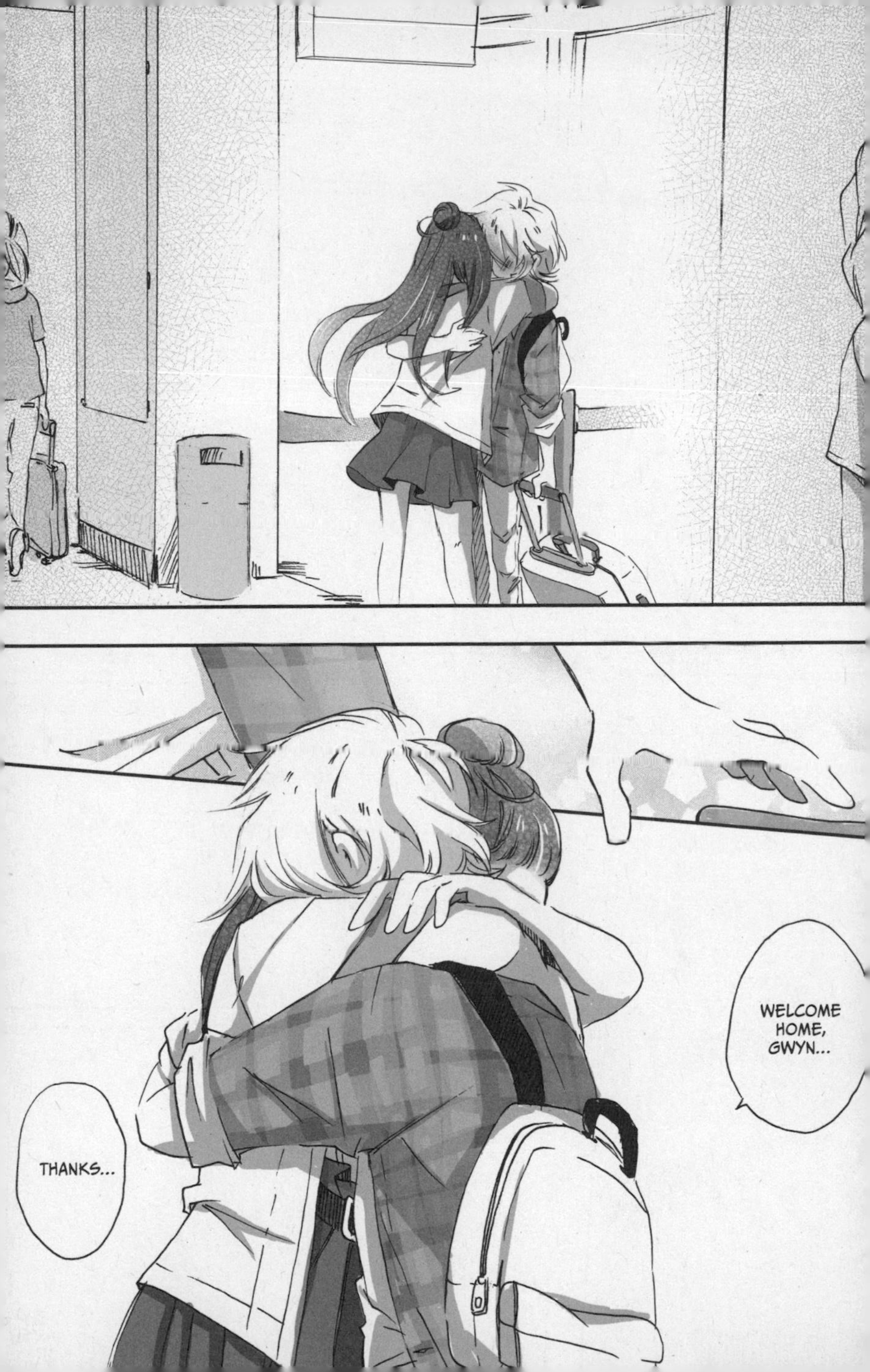
WELCOME HOME, GWYN...
THANKS...

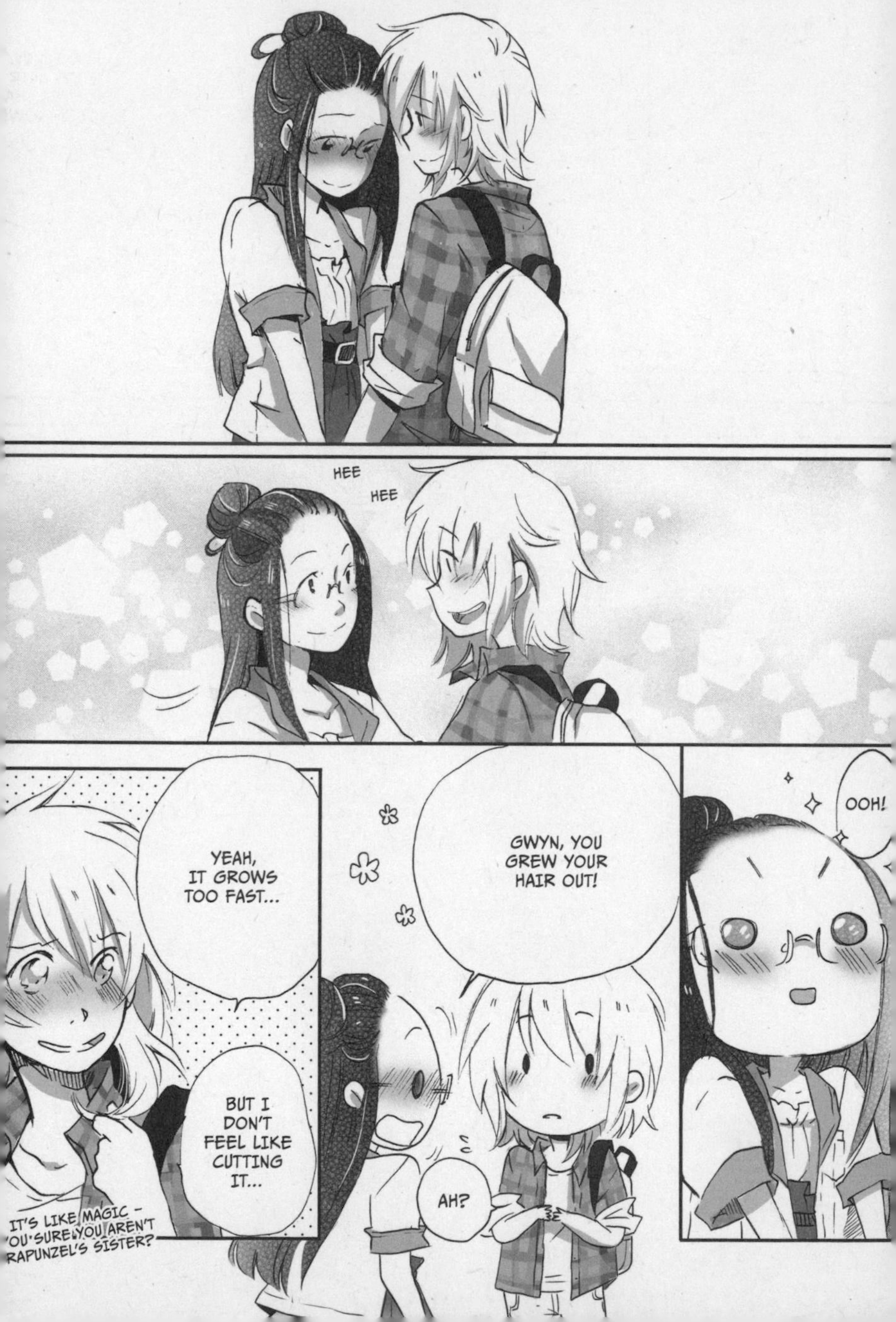
HEE
HEE
OOH!
GWYN, YOU GREW YOUR HAIR OUT!
AH?
YEAH, IT GROWS TOO FAST...
BUT I DON'T FEEL LIKE CUTTING IT...
IT'S LIKE MAGIC - OU SURE YOU AREN'T RAPUNZEL'S SISTER?

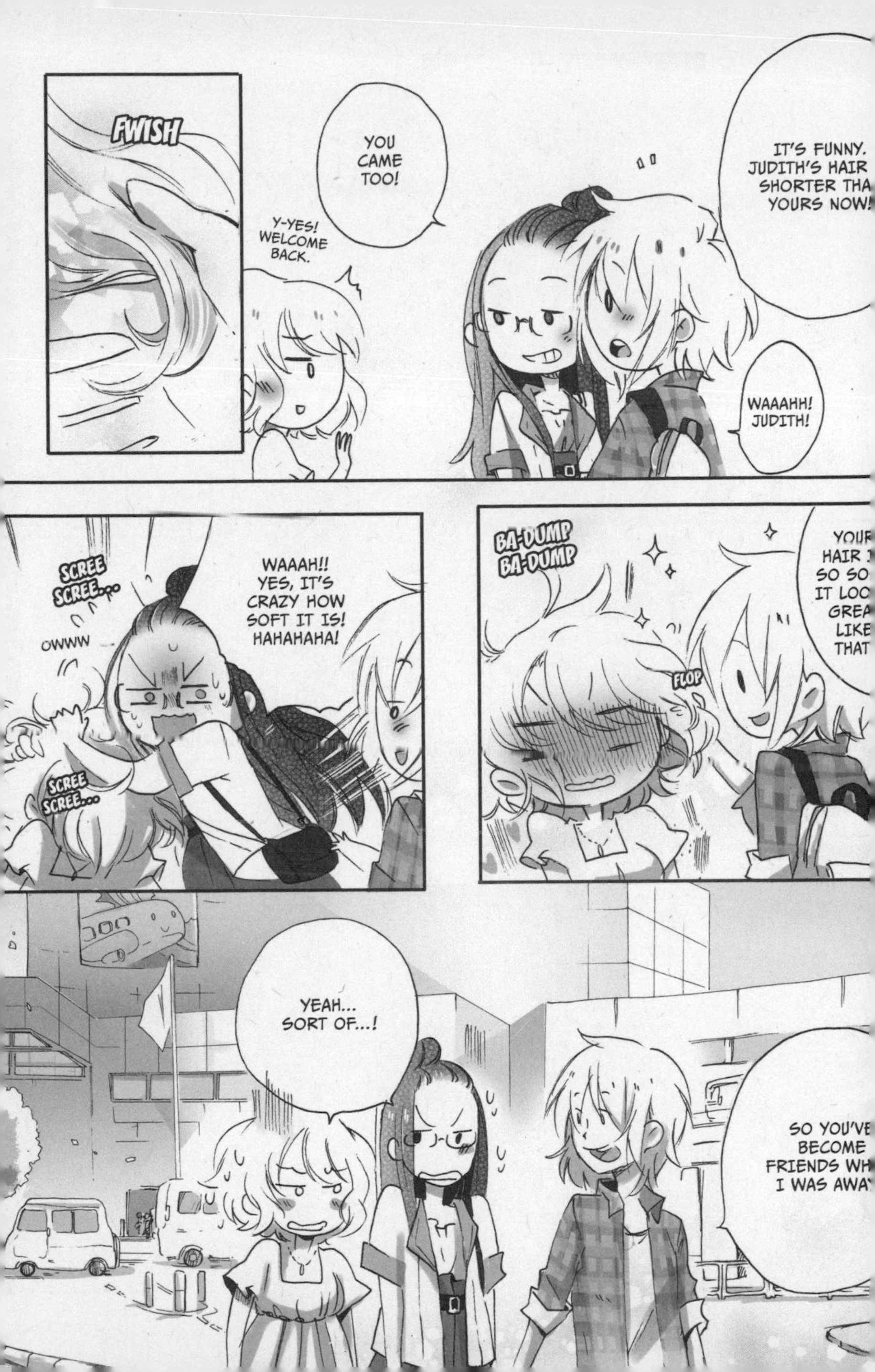
IT'S FUNNY. JUDITH'S HAIR SHORTER THA YOURS NOW!
WAAAHH! JUDITH!
YOU CAME TOO!
Y-YES! WELCOME BACK.
FWISH
YOUR HAIR I SO SO IT LOO GREA LIKE THAT
BA-DUMP BA-DUMP
FLOP
WAAAH!! YES, IT'S CRAZY HOW SOFT IT IS! HAHAHAHA!
SCREE SCREE...
OWWW
SCREE SCREE...
SO YOU'VE BECOME FRIENDS WH I WAS AWA
YEAH... SORT OF...!

Chapter 13
New Beginning

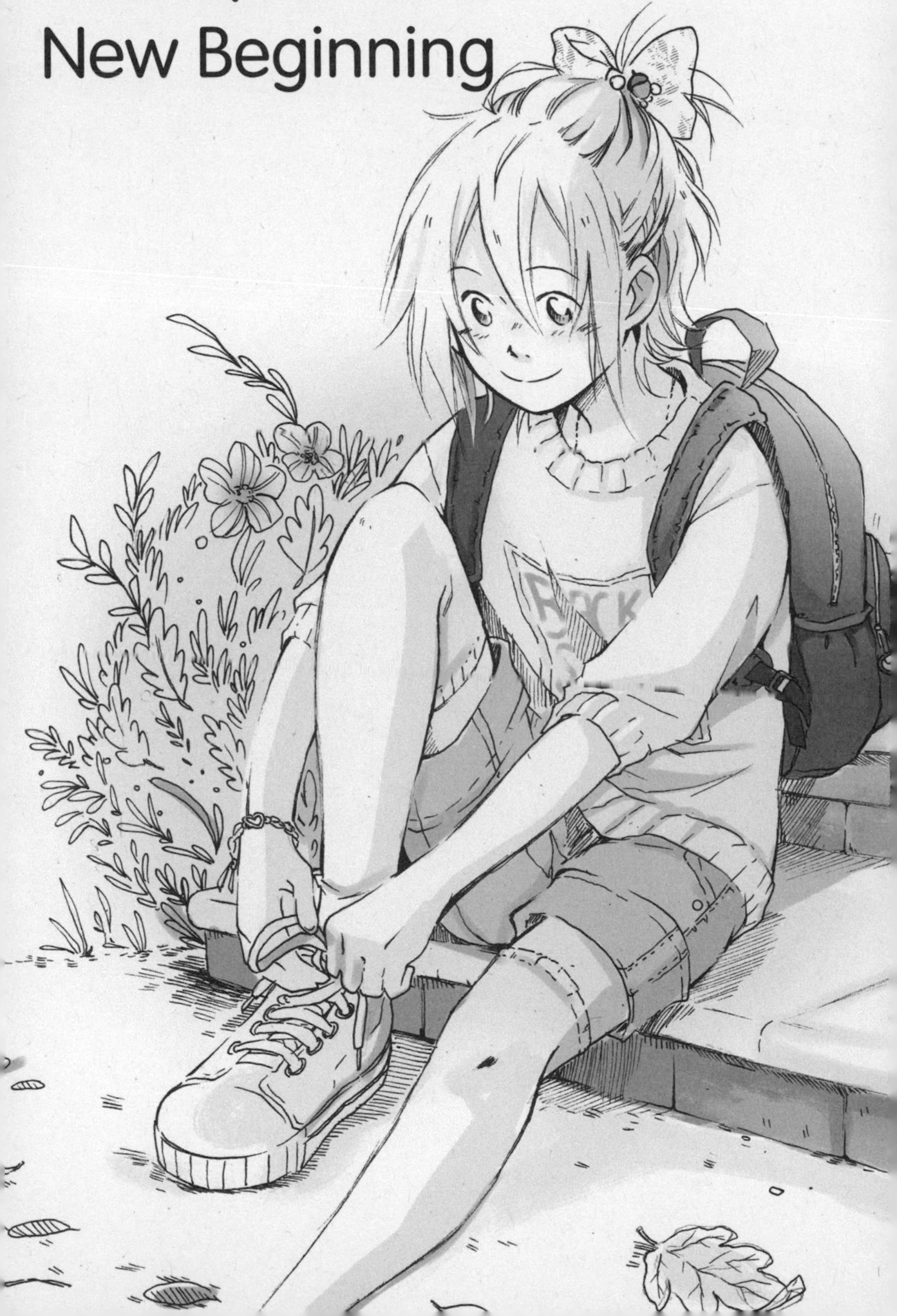

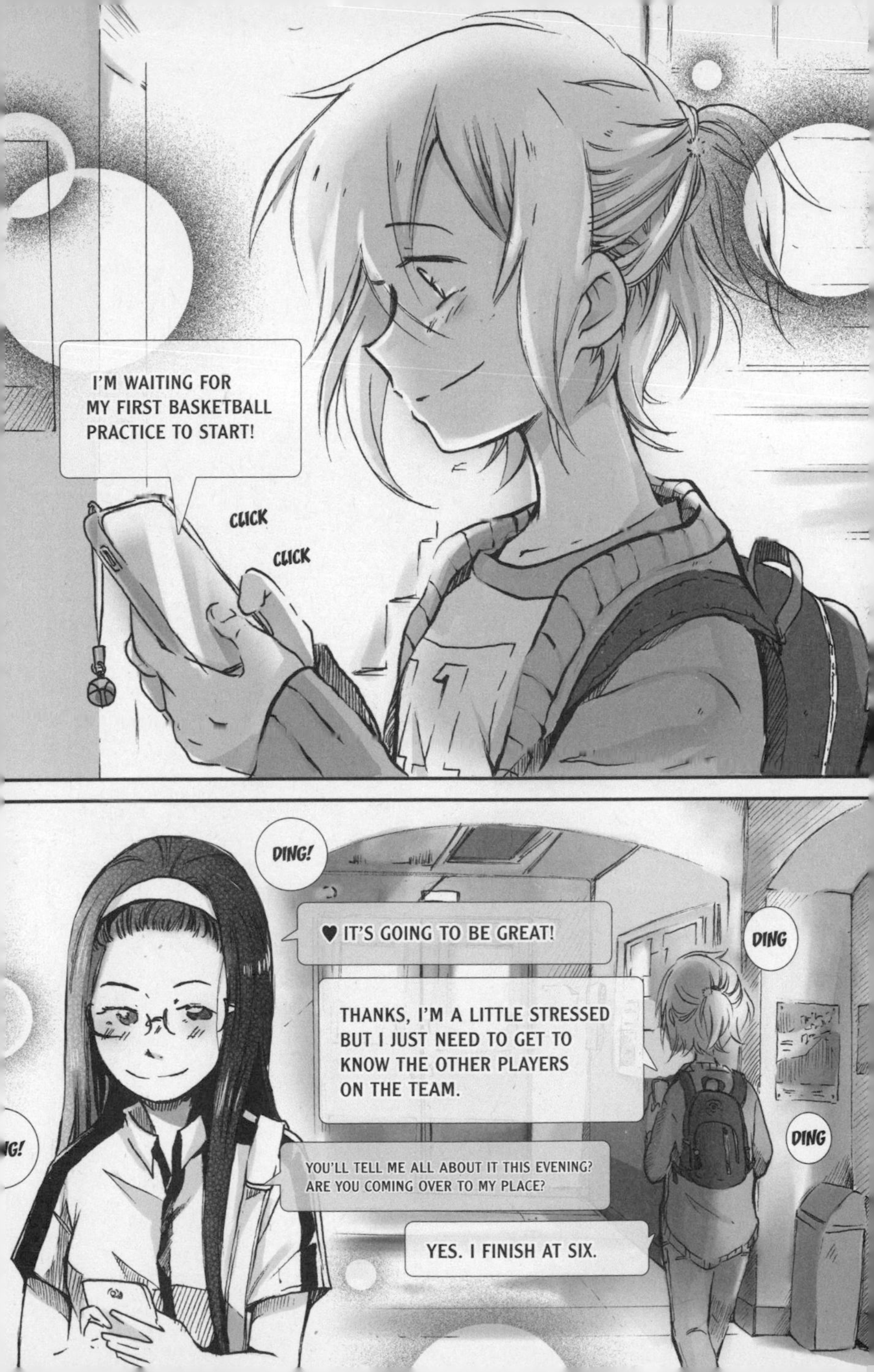
I'M WAITING FOR MY FIRST BASKETBALL PRACTICE TO START!
CLICK
CLICK
DING!
♥ IT'S GOING TO BE GREAT!
DING
THANKS, I'M A LITTLE STRESSED BUT I JUST NEED TO GET TO KNOW THE OTHER PLAYERS ON THE TEAM.
DING
YOU'LL TELL ME ALL ABOUT IT THIS EVENING? ARE YOU COMING OVER TO MY PLACE?
YES. I FINISH AT SIX.

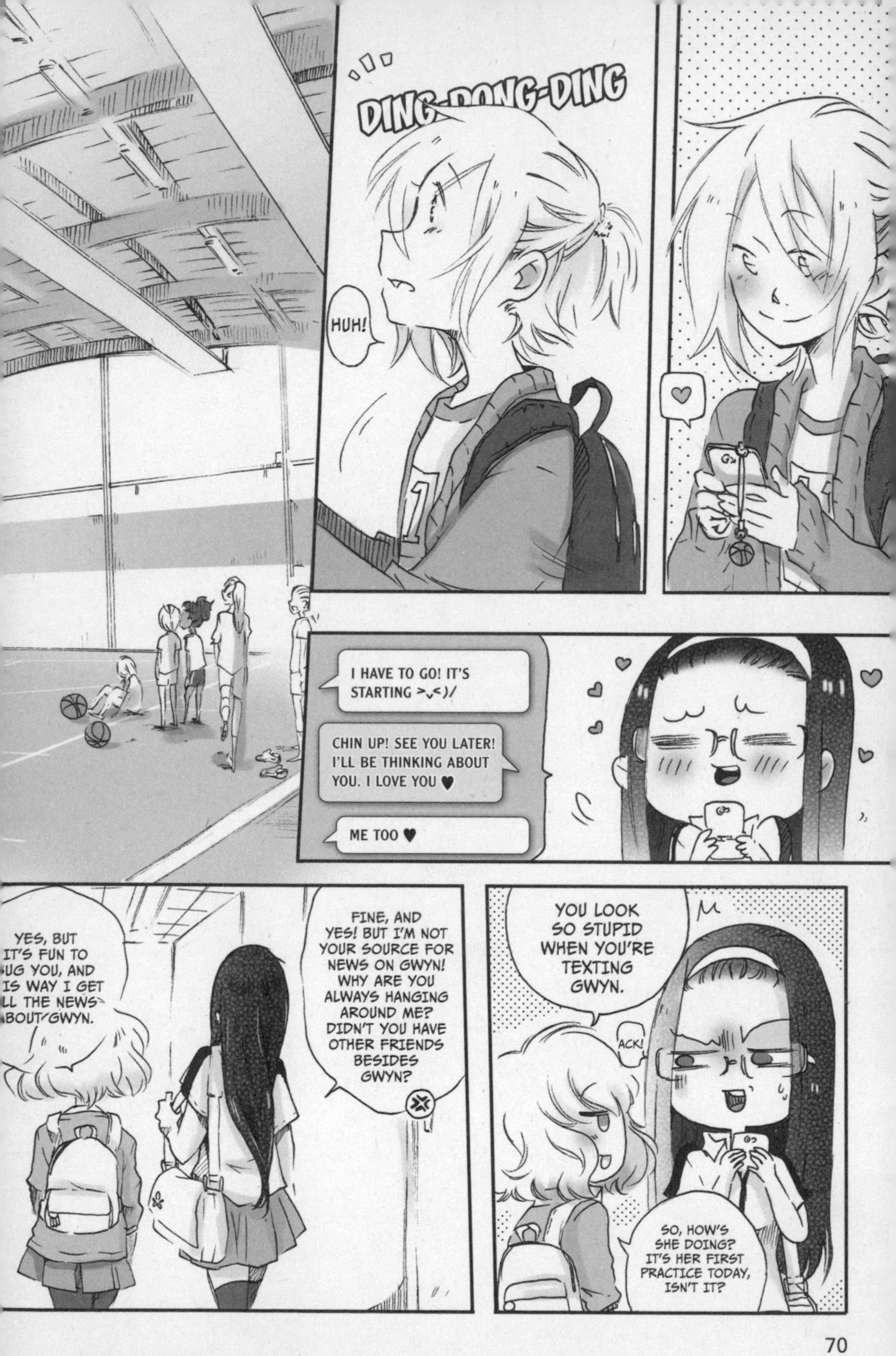
DING-DONG-DING
HUH!
I HAVE TO GO! IT'S STARTING >ᴗ<)/
CHIN UP! SEE YOU LATER! I'LL BE THINKING ABOUT YOU. I LOVE YOU ♥
ME TOO ♥
YOU LOOK SO STUPID WHEN YOU'RE TEXTING GWYN.
ACK!
SO, HOW'S SHE DOING? IT'S HER FIRST PRACTICE TODAY, ISN'T IT?
FINE, AND YES! BUT I'M NOT YOUR SOURCE FOR NEWS ON GWYN! WHY ARE YOU ALWAYS HANGING AROUND ME? DIDN'T YOU HAVE OTHER FRIENDS BESIDES GWYN?
YES, BUT IT'S FUN TO UG YOU, AND IS WAY I GET LL THE NEWS BOUT GWYN.

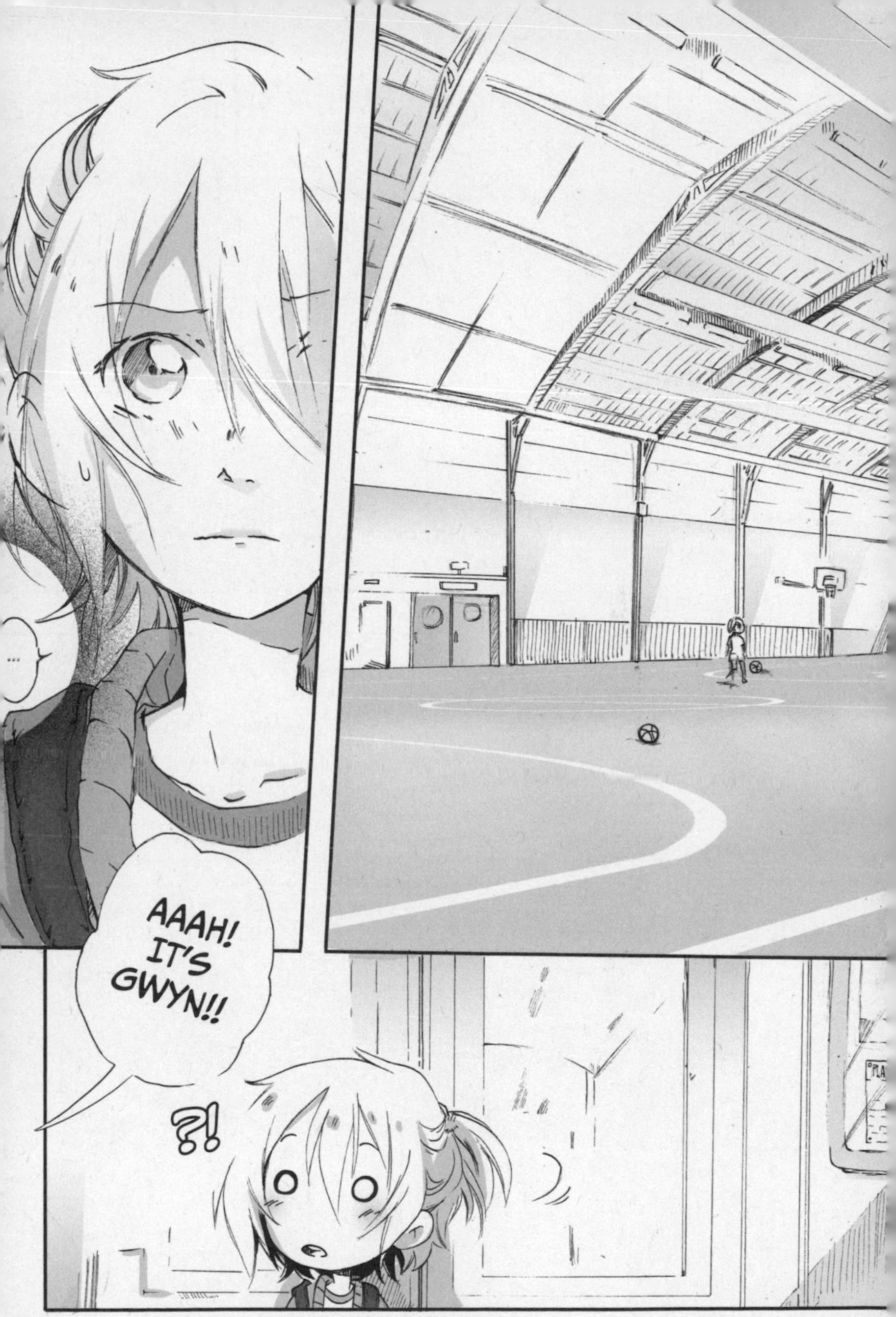
...
AAAH! IT'S GWYN!!
?!

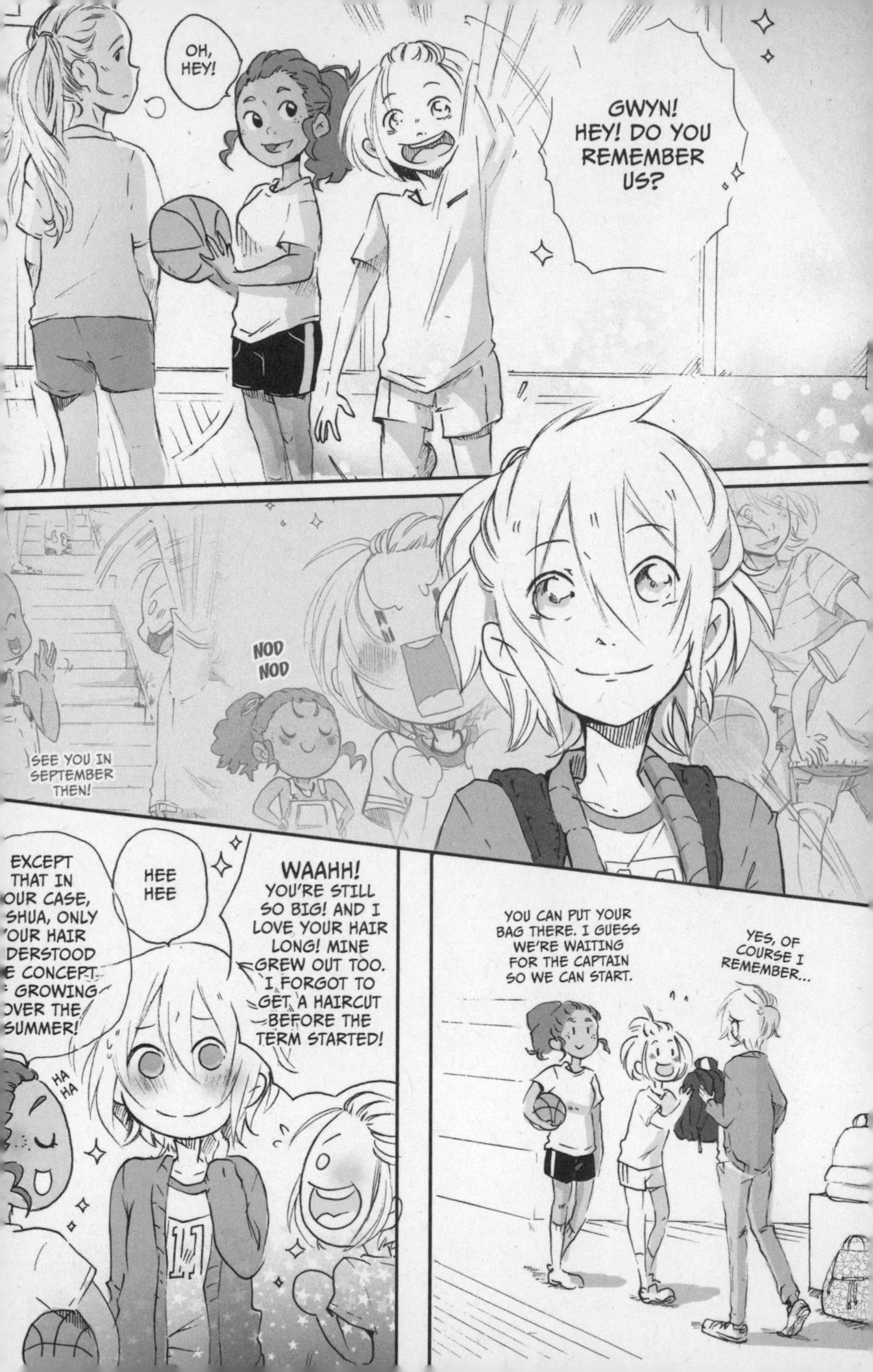

OH, HEY!
GWYN! HEY! DO YOU REMEMBER US?
NOD NOD
SEE YOU IN SEPTEMBER THEN!
WAAHH! YOU'RE STILL SO BIG! AND I LOVE YOUR HAIR LONG! MINE GREW OUT TOO. I FORGOT TO GET A HAIRCUT BEFORE THE TERM STARTED!
HEE HEE
HA HA
YES, OF COURSE I REMEMBER...
YOU CAN PUT YOUR BAG THERE. I GUESS WE'RE WAITING FOR THE CAPTAIN SO WE CAN START.

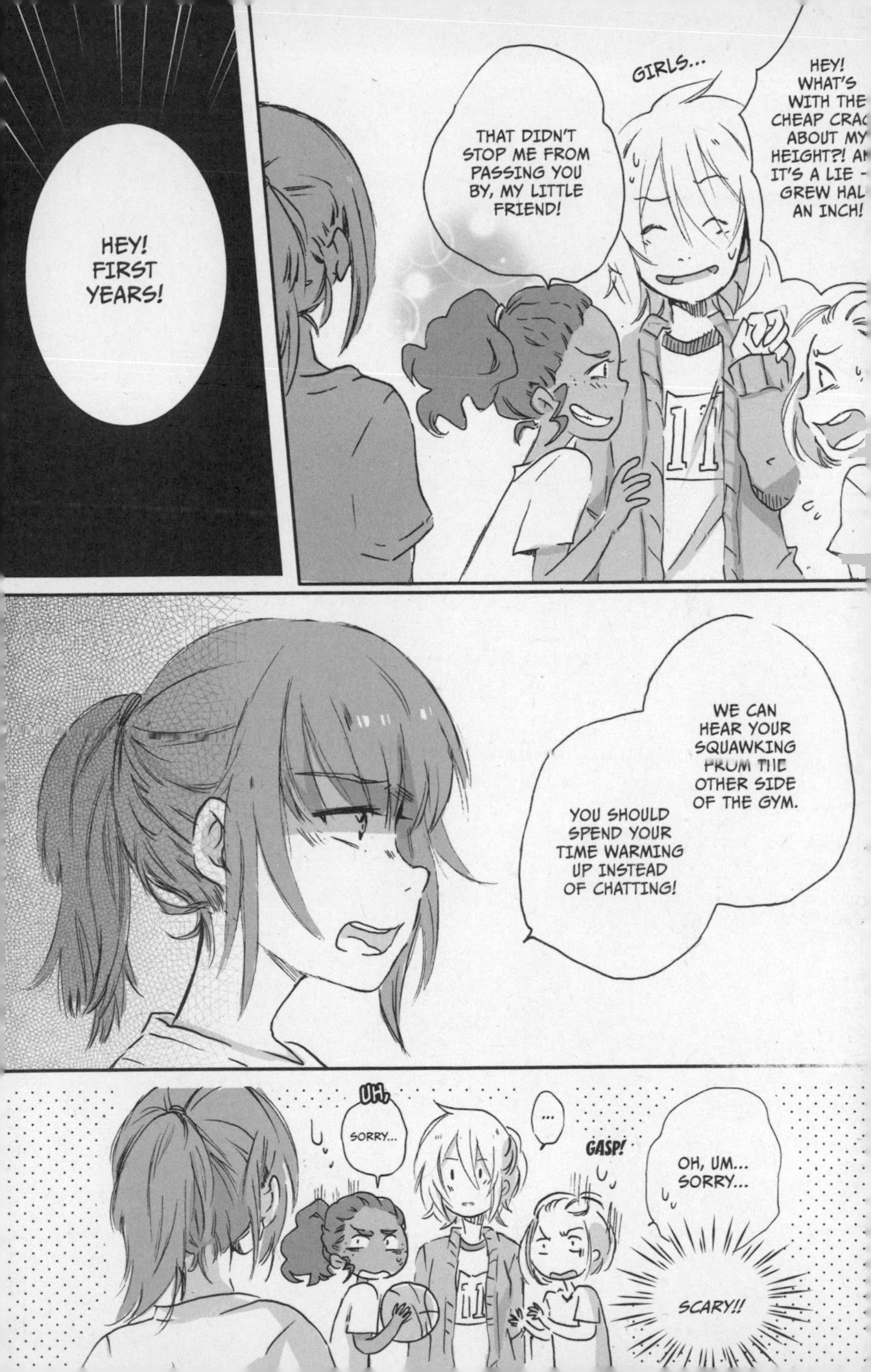
HEY! WHAT'S WITH THE CHEAP CRAC ABOUT MY HEIGHT?! AN IT'S A LIE - GREW HAL AN INCH!
GIRLS...
THAT DIDN'T STOP ME FROM PASSING YOU BY, MY LITTLE FRIEND!
HEY! FIRST YEARS!
WE CAN HEAR YOUR SQUAWKING FROM THE OTHER SIDE OF THE GYM.
YOU SHOULD SPEND YOUR TIME WARMING UP INSTEAD OF CHATTING!
OH, UM... SORRY...
SCARY!!
GASP!
...
UH,
SORRY...

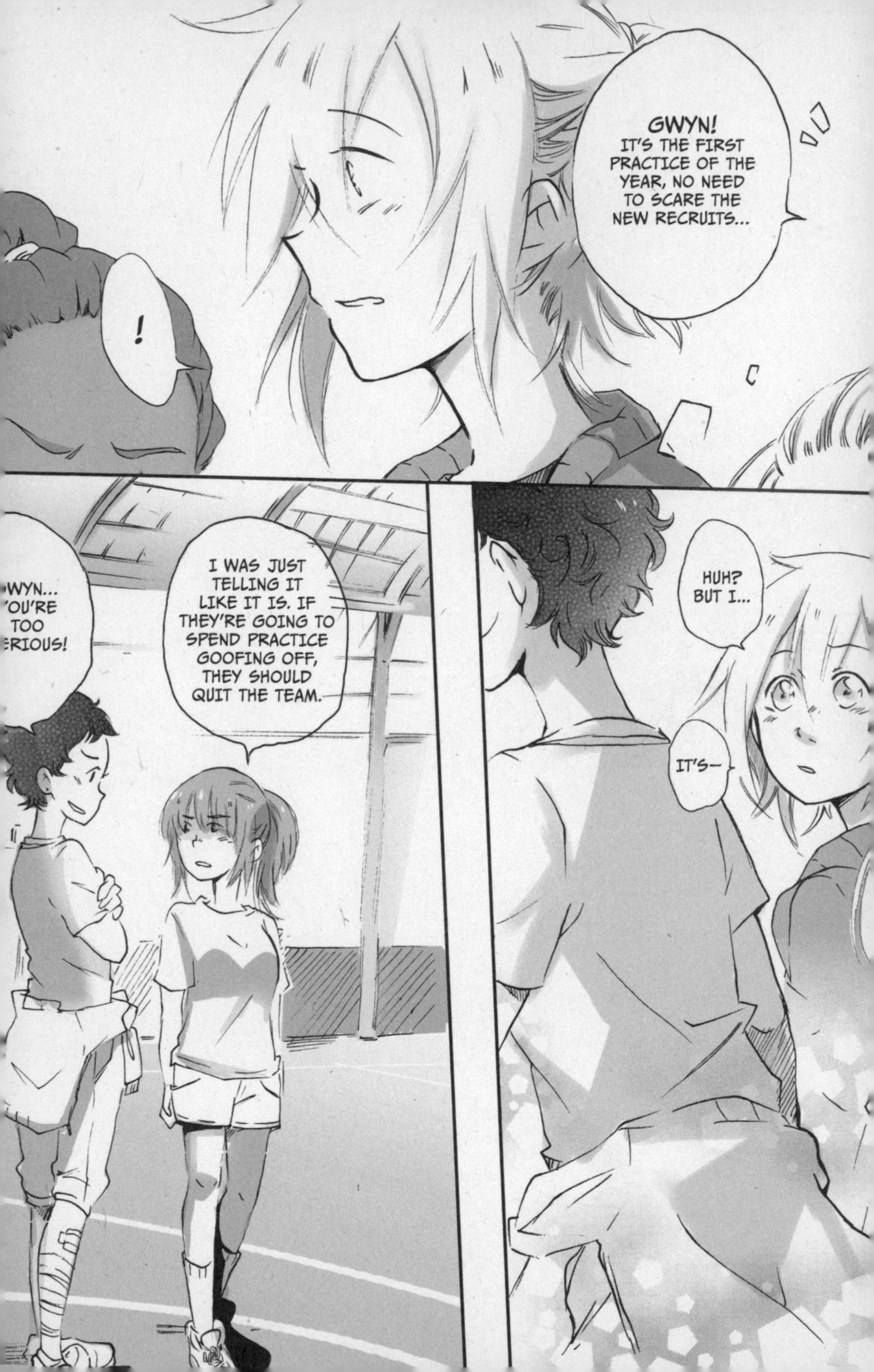
GWYN! IT'S THE FIRST PRACTICE OF THE YEAR, NO NEED TO SCARE THE NEW RECRUITS...
!
HUH? BUT I...
IT'S—
I WAS JUST TELLING IT LIKE IT IS. IF THEY'RE GOING TO SPEND PRACTICE GOOFING OFF, THEY SHOULD QUIT THE TEAM.
WYN... OU'RE TOO ERIOUS!

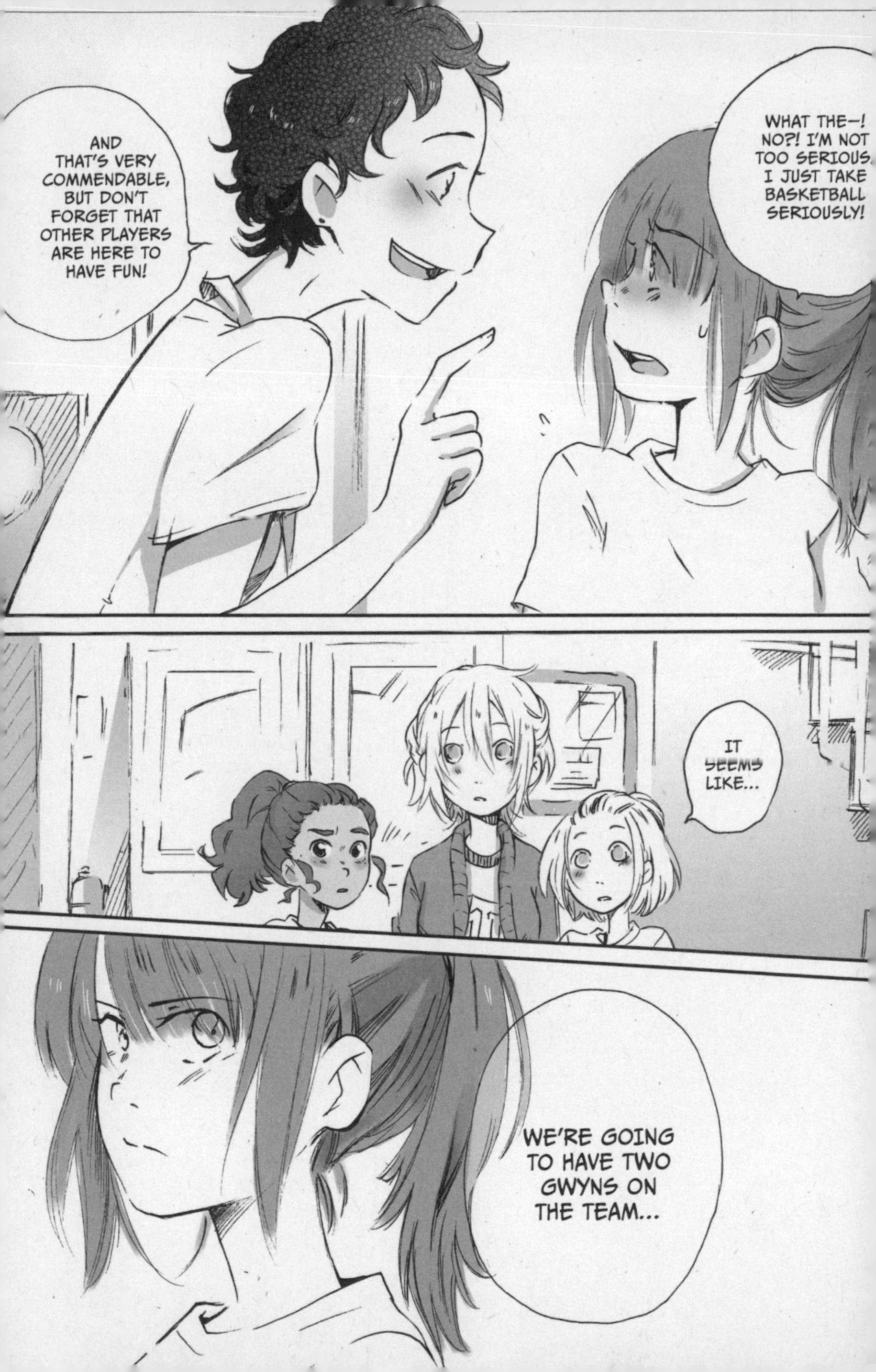
WHAT THE—! NO?! I'M NOT TOO SERIOUS. I JUST TAKE BASKETBALL SERIOUSLY!
AND THAT'S VERY COMMENDABLE, BUT DON'T FORGET THAT OTHER PLAYERS ARE HERE TO HAVE FUN!
IT SEEMS LIKE...
WE'RE GOING TO HAVE TWO GWYNS ON THE TEAM...

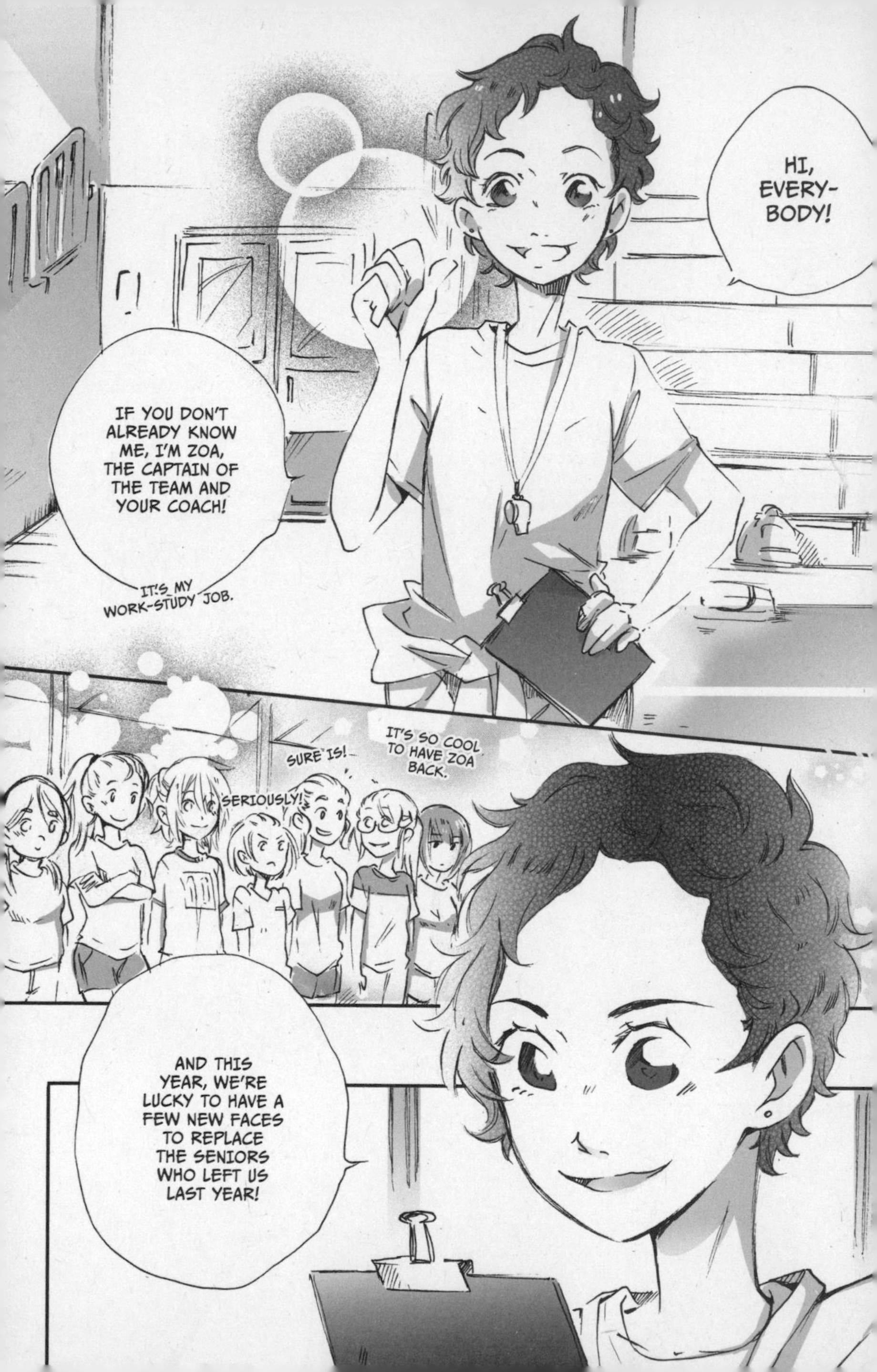
HI, EVERY-BODY!
IF YOU DON'T ALREADY KNOW ME, I'M ZOA, THE CAPTAIN OF THE TEAM AND YOUR COACH!
IT'S MY WORK-STUDY JOB.
IT'S SO COOL TO HAVE ZOA BACK.
SURE IS!
SERIOUSLY!
AND THIS YEAR, WE'RE LUCKY TO HAVE A FEW NEW FACES TO REPLACE THE SENIORS WHO LEFT US LAST YEAR!

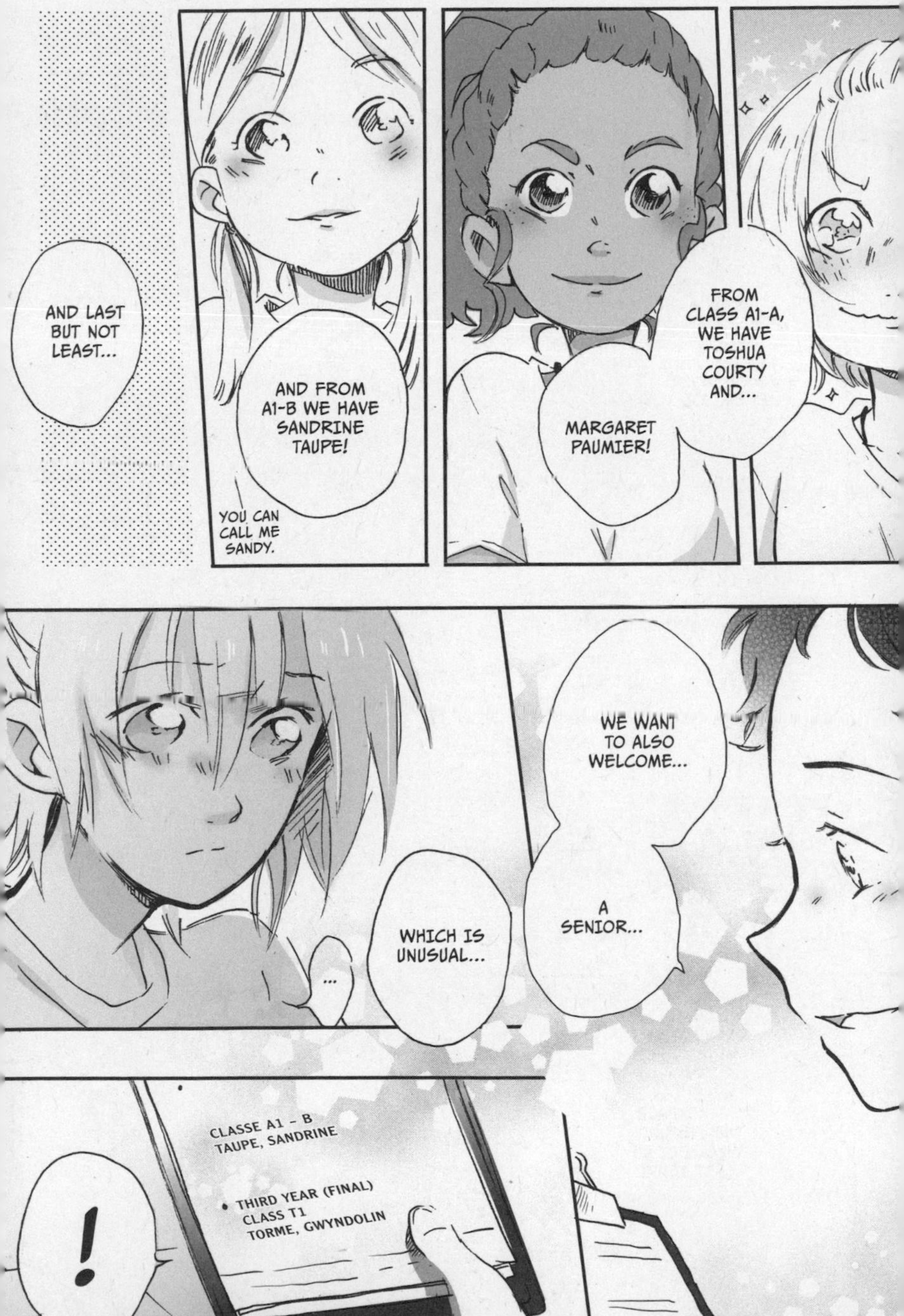
FROM CLASS A1-A, WE HAVE TOSHUA COURTY AND...
MARGARET PAUMIER!
AND FROM A1-B WE HAVE SANDRINE TAUPE!
YOU CAN CALL ME SANDY.
AND LAST BUT NOT LEAST...
WE WANT TO ALSO WELCOME...
A SENIOR...
WHICH IS UNUSUAL...
...
CLASSE A1 - B
TAUPE, SANDRINE
THIRD YEAR (FINAL)
CLASS T1
TORME, GWYNDOLIN
!

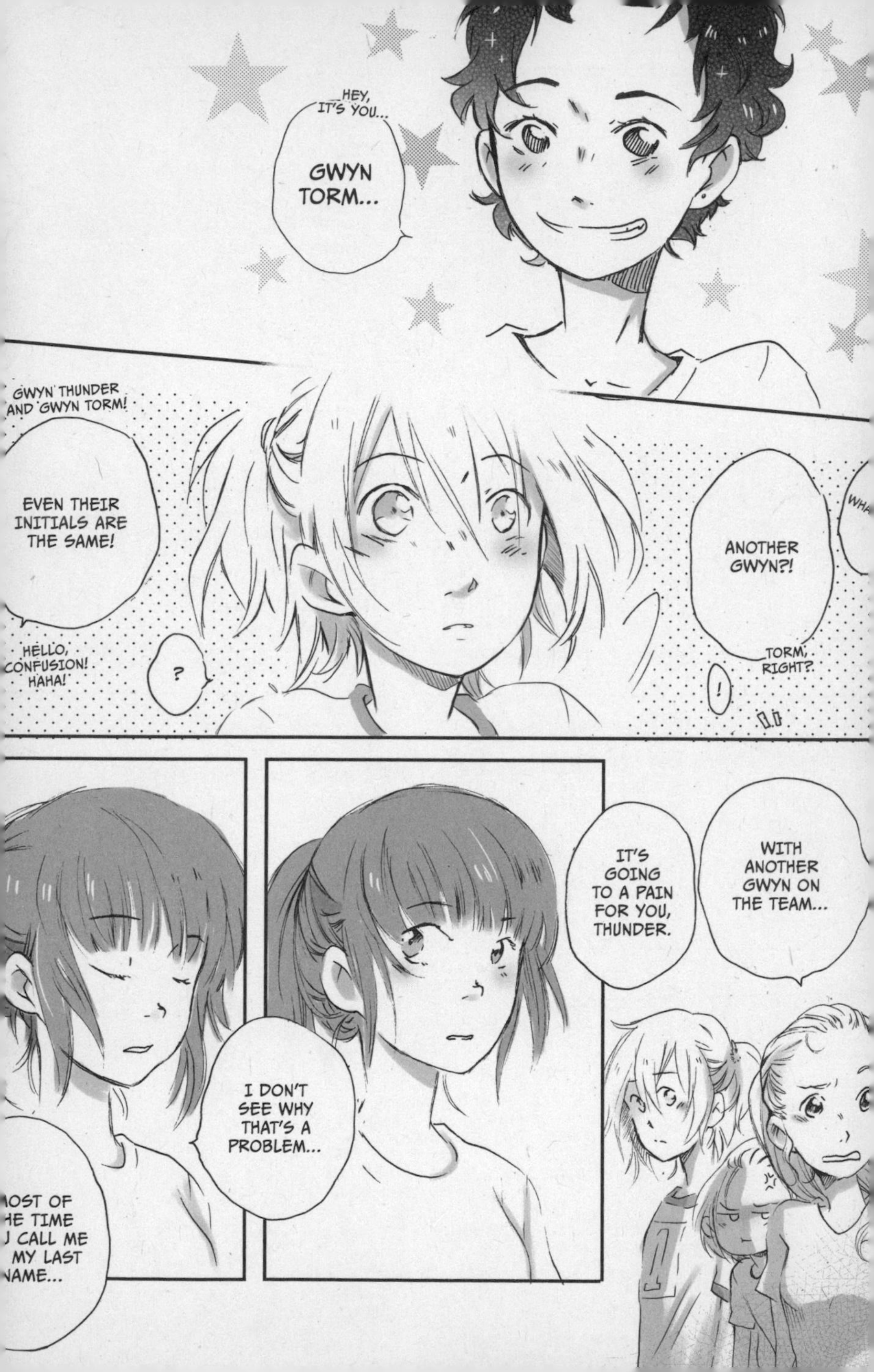
HEY, IT'S YOU...
GWYN TORM...
WHA
ANOTHER GWYN?!
TORM, RIGHT?.
!
?
GWYN THUNDER AND GWYN TORM!
EVEN THEIR INITIALS ARE THE SAME!
HELLO, CONFUSION! HAHA!
WITH ANOTHER GWYN ON THE TEAM...
IT'S GOING TO A PAIN FOR YOU, THUNDER.
I DON'T SEE WHY THAT'S A PROBLEM...
OST OF HE TIME CALL ME MY LAST NAME...

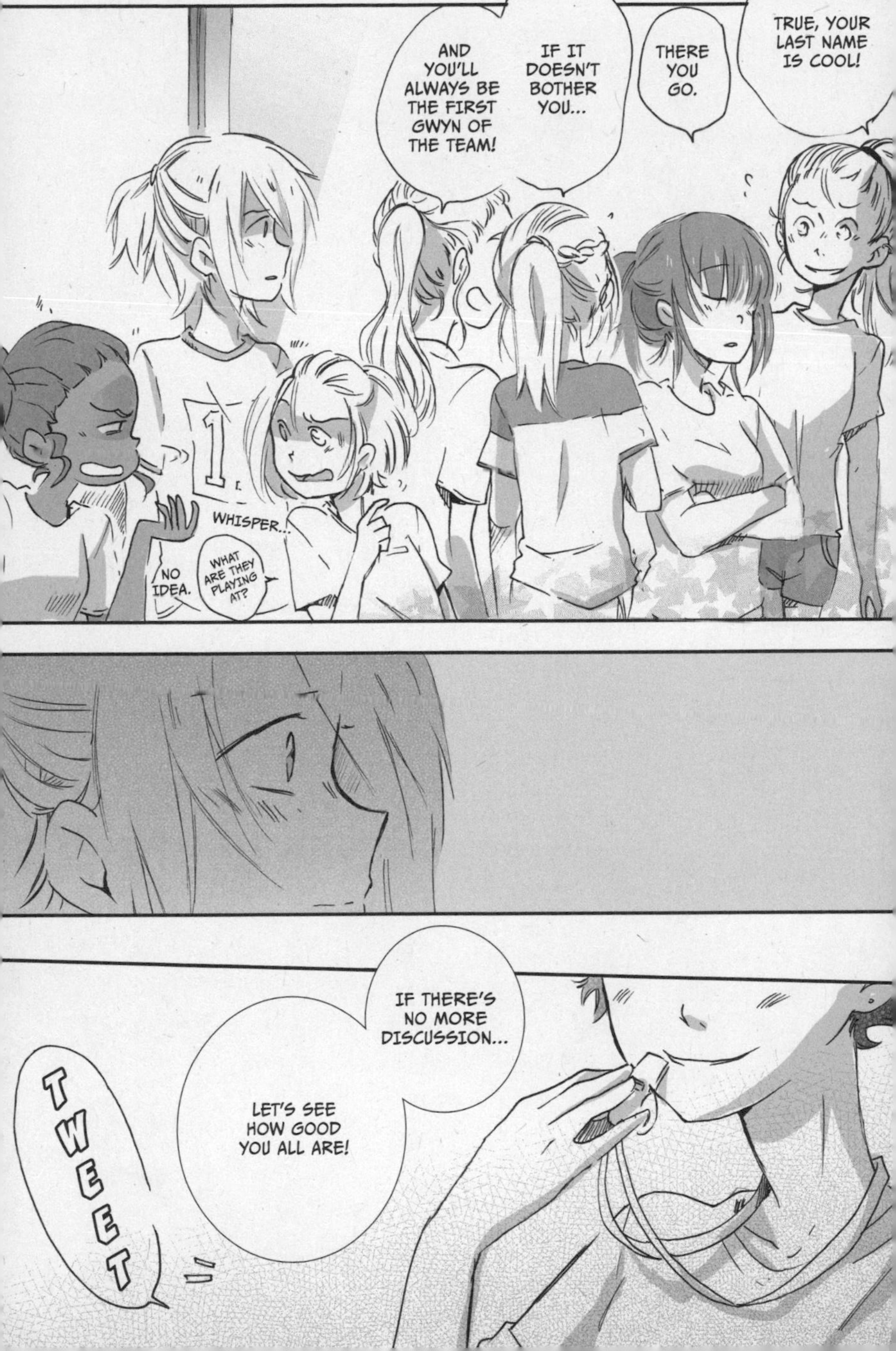
TRUE, YOUR LAST NAME IS COOL!
THERE YOU GO.
IF IT DOESN'T BOTHER YOU...
AND YOU'LL ALWAYS BE THE FIRST GWYN OF THE TEAM!
WHISPER...
WHAT ARE THEY PLAYING AT?
NO IDEA.
IF THERE'S NO MORE DISCUSSION...
LET'S SEE HOW GOOD YOU ALL ARE!
TWEET

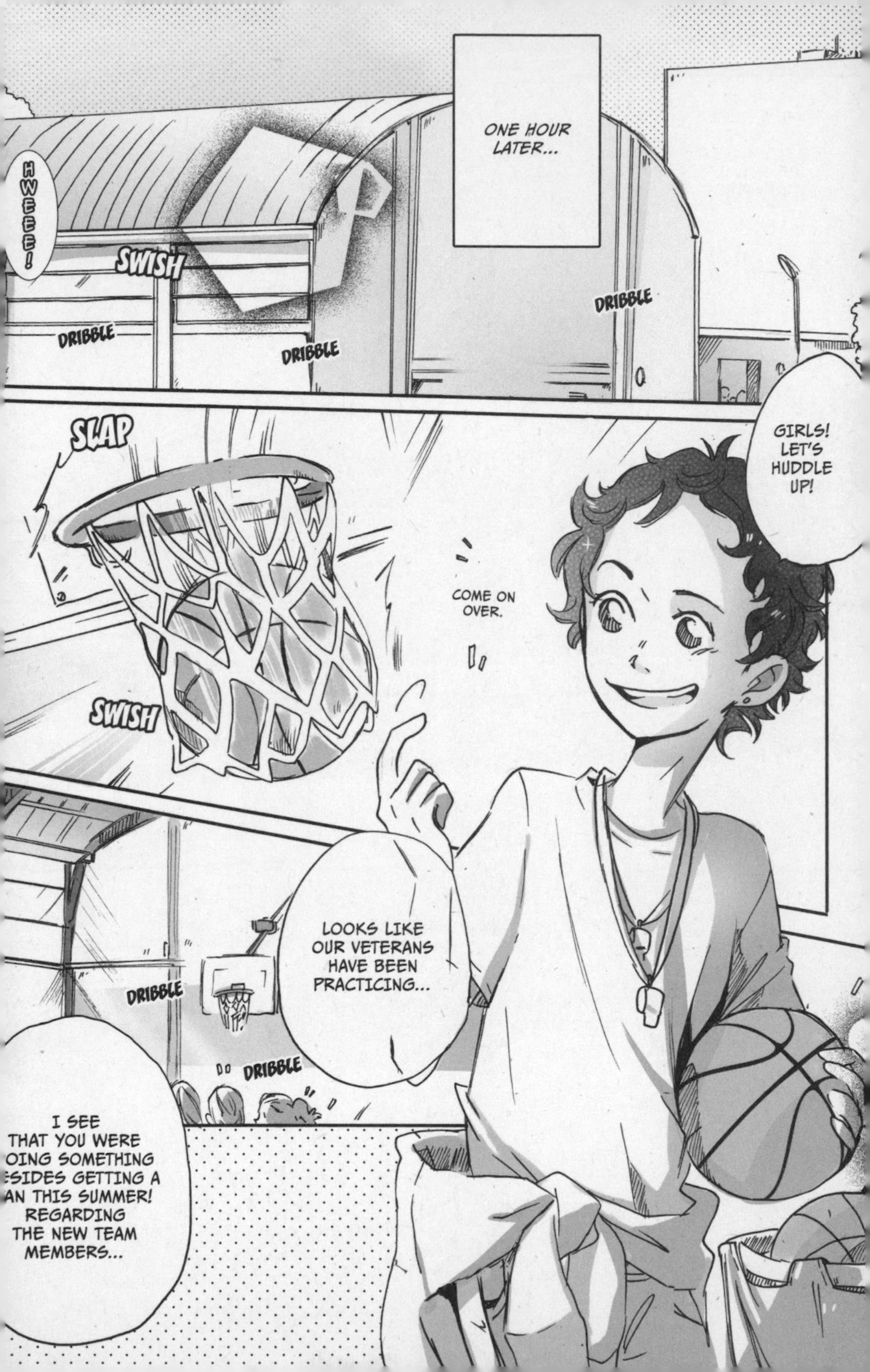
ONE HOUR LATER...
DRIBBLE
HWEEE!
SWISH
DRIBBLE
DRIBBLE
GIRLS! LET'S HUDDLE UP!
COME ON OVER.
LOOKS LIKE OUR VETERANS HAVE BEEN PRACTICING...
SLAP
SWISH
DRIBBLE
DRIBBLE
I SEE THAT YOU WERE OING SOMETHING ESIDES GETTING A AN THIS SUMMER! REGARDING THE NEW TEAM MEMBERS...

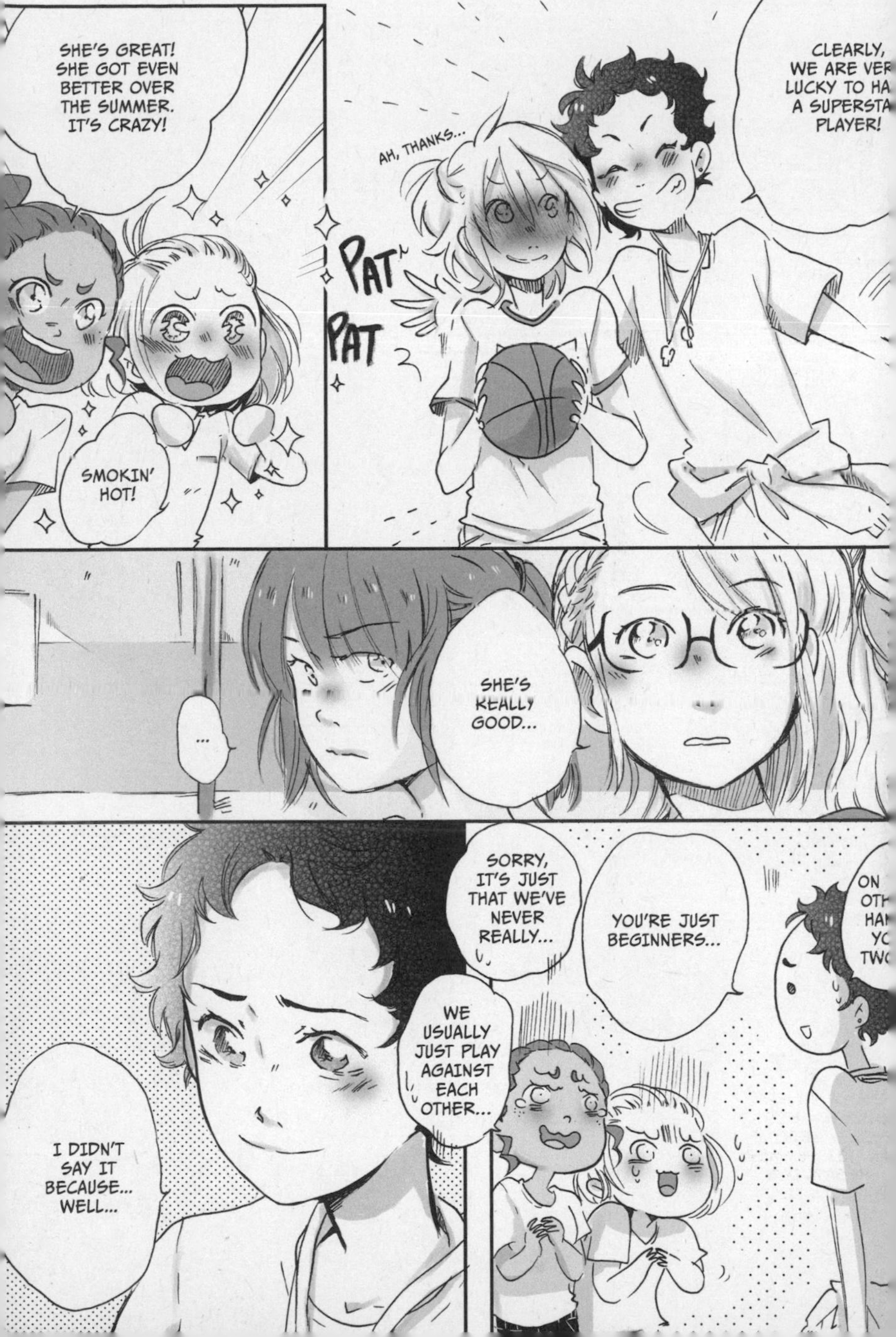
CLEARLY, WE ARE VER LUCKY TO HA A SUPERSTA PLAYER!
AH, THANKS...
PAT PAT
SHE'S GREAT! SHE GOT EVEN BETTER OVER THE SUMMER. IT'S CRAZY!
SMOKIN' HOT!
SHE'S REALLY GOOD...
...
ON OTH HA YO TWO
YOU'RE JUST BEGINNERS...
SORRY, IT'S JUST THAT WE'VE NEVER REALLY...
WE USUALLY JUST PLAY AGAINST EACH OTHER...
I DIDN'T SAY IT BECAUSE... WELL...

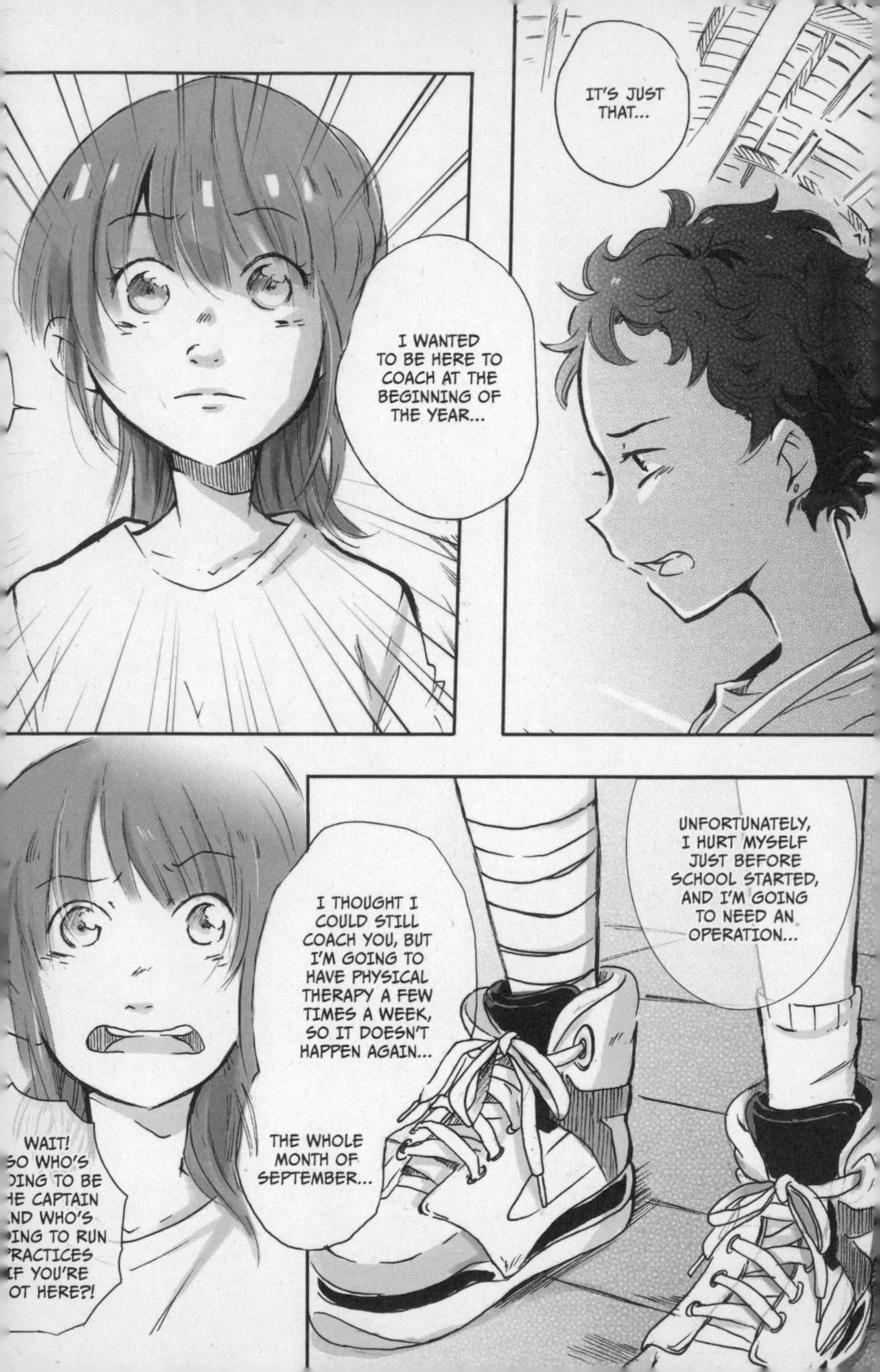
IT'S JUST THAT...
I WANTED TO BE HERE TO COACH AT THE BEGINNING OF THE YEAR...
UNFORTUNATELY, I HURT MYSELF JUST BEFORE SCHOOL STARTED, AND I'M GOING TO NEED AN OPERATION...
I THOUGHT I COULD STILL COACH YOU, BUT I'M GOING TO HAVE PHYSICAL THERAPY A FEW TIMES A WEEK, SO IT DOESN'T HAPPEN AGAIN...
THE WHOLE MONTH OF SEPTEMBER...
WAIT! SO WHO'S OING TO BE HE CAPTAIN ND WHO'S OING TO RUN RACTICES IF YOU'RE OT HERE?!

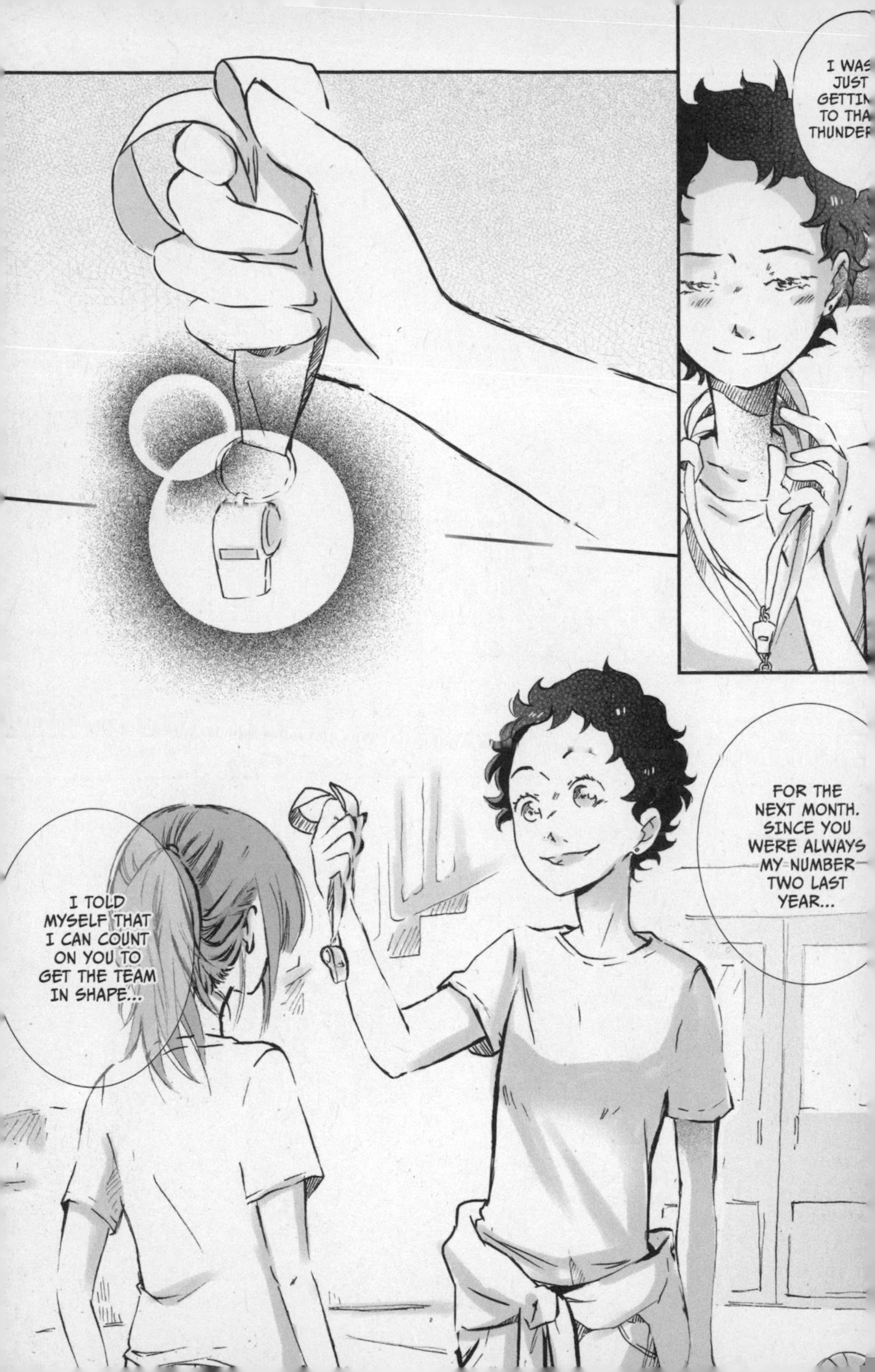
I WAS JUST GETTIN TO THA THUNDER
FOR THE NEXT MONTH. SINCE YOU WERE ALWAYS MY NUMBER TWO LAST YEAR...
I TOLD MYSELF THAT I CAN COUNT ON YOU TO GET THE TEAM IN SHAPE...

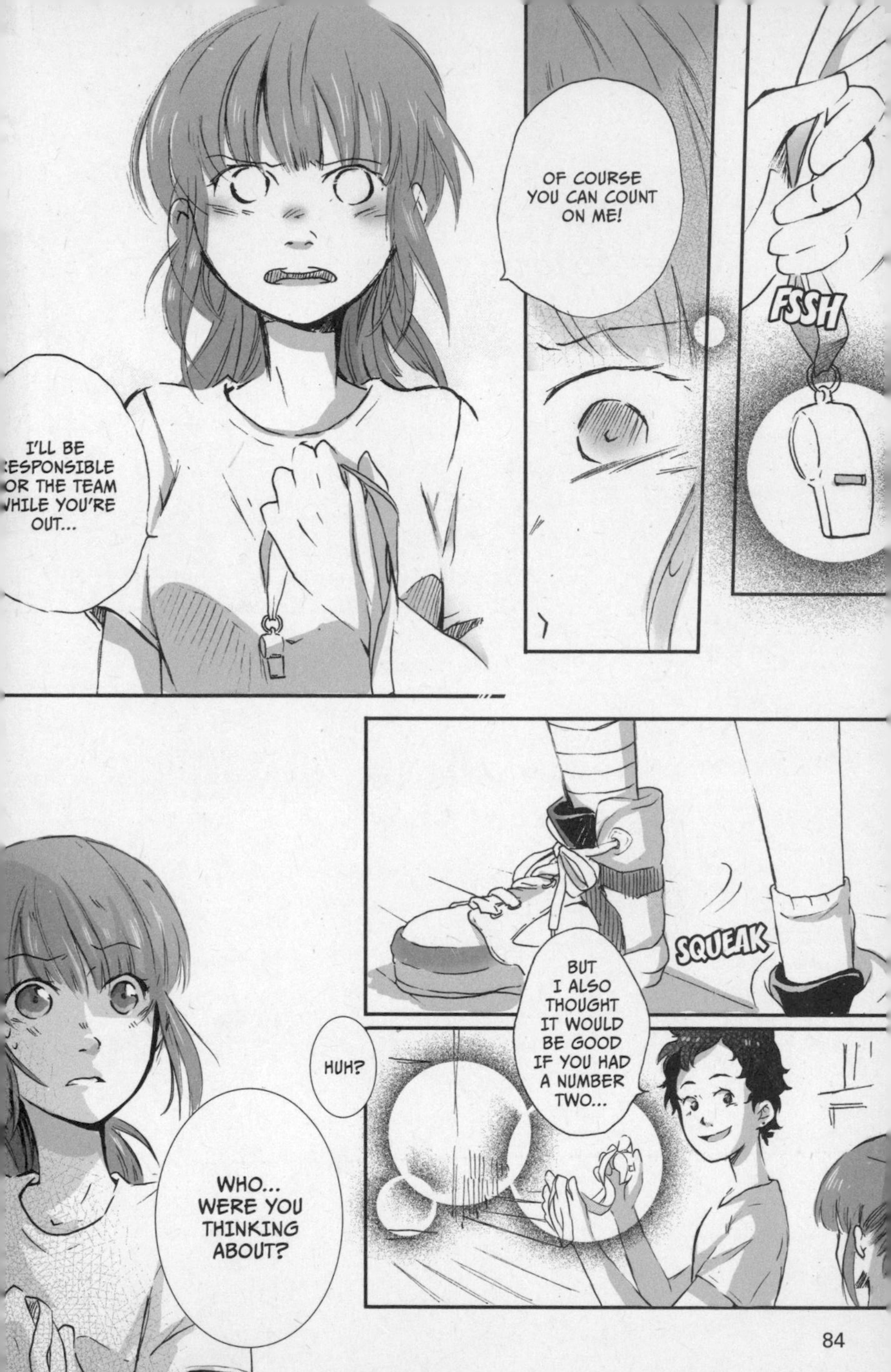
FSSH
OF COURSE YOU CAN COUNT ON ME!
I'LL BE ESPONSIBLE OR THE TEAM HILE YOU'RE OUT...
SQUEAK
BUT I ALSO THOUGHT IT WOULD BE GOOD IF YOU HAD A NUMBER TWO...
HUH?
WHO... WERE YOU THINKING ABOUT?

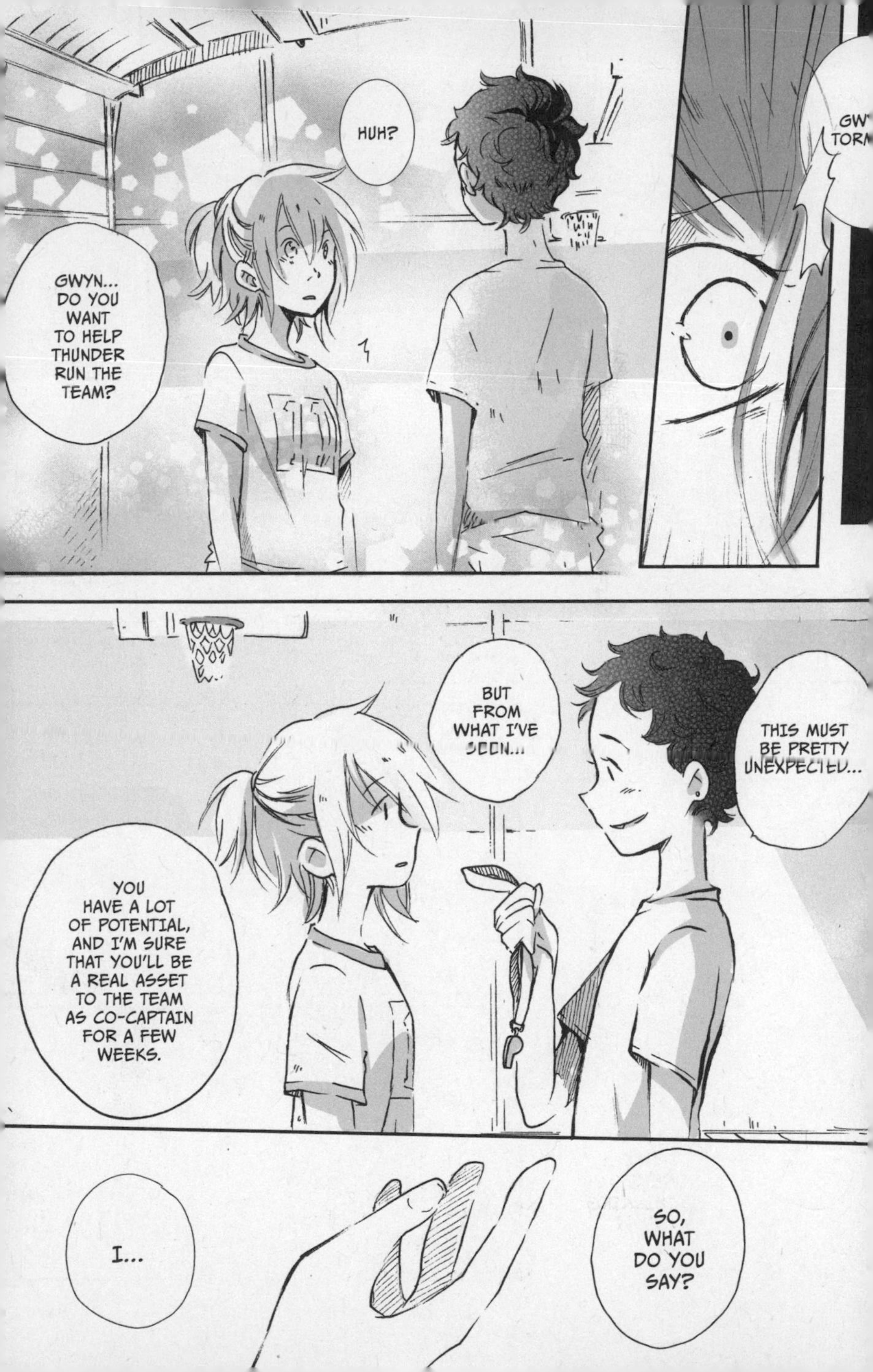
HUH?
GWYN... DO YOU WANT TO HELP THUNDER RUN THE TEAM?
THIS MUST BE PRETTY UNEXPECTED...
BUT FROM WHAT I'VE SEEN...
YOU HAVE A LOT OF POTENTIAL, AND I'M SURE THAT YOU'LL BE A REAL ASSET TO THE TEAM AS CO-CAPTAIN FOR A FEW WEEKS.
SO, WHAT DO YOU SAY?
I...

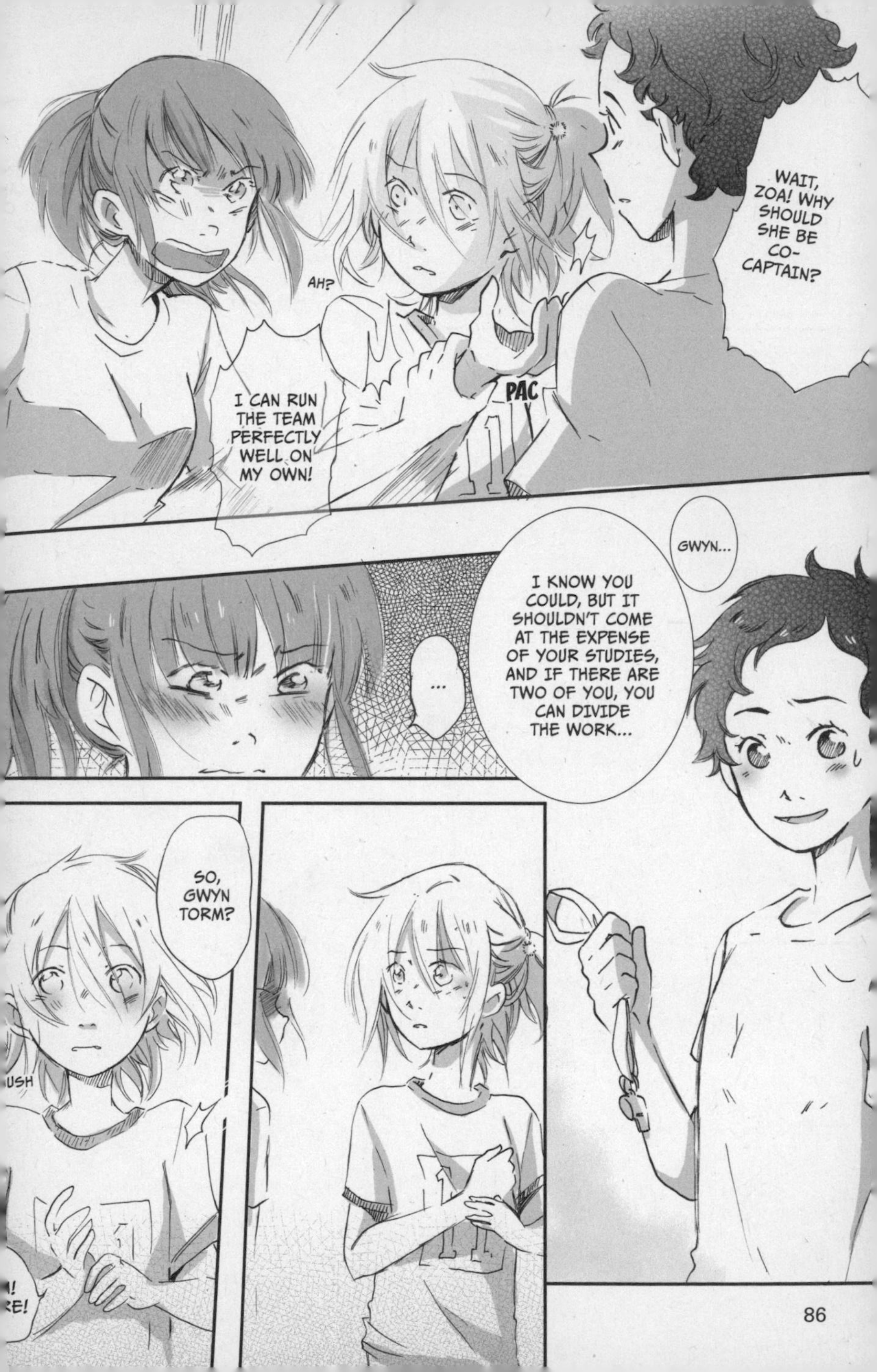
WAIT, ZOA! WHY SHOULD SHE BE CO-CAPTAIN?
AH?
I CAN RUN THE TEAM PERFECTLY WELL ON MY OWN!
GWYN...
I KNOW YOU COULD, BUT IT SHOULDN'T COME AT THE EXPENSE OF YOUR STUDIES, AND IF THERE ARE TWO OF YOU, YOU CAN DIVIDE THE WORK...
...
SO, GWYN TORM?

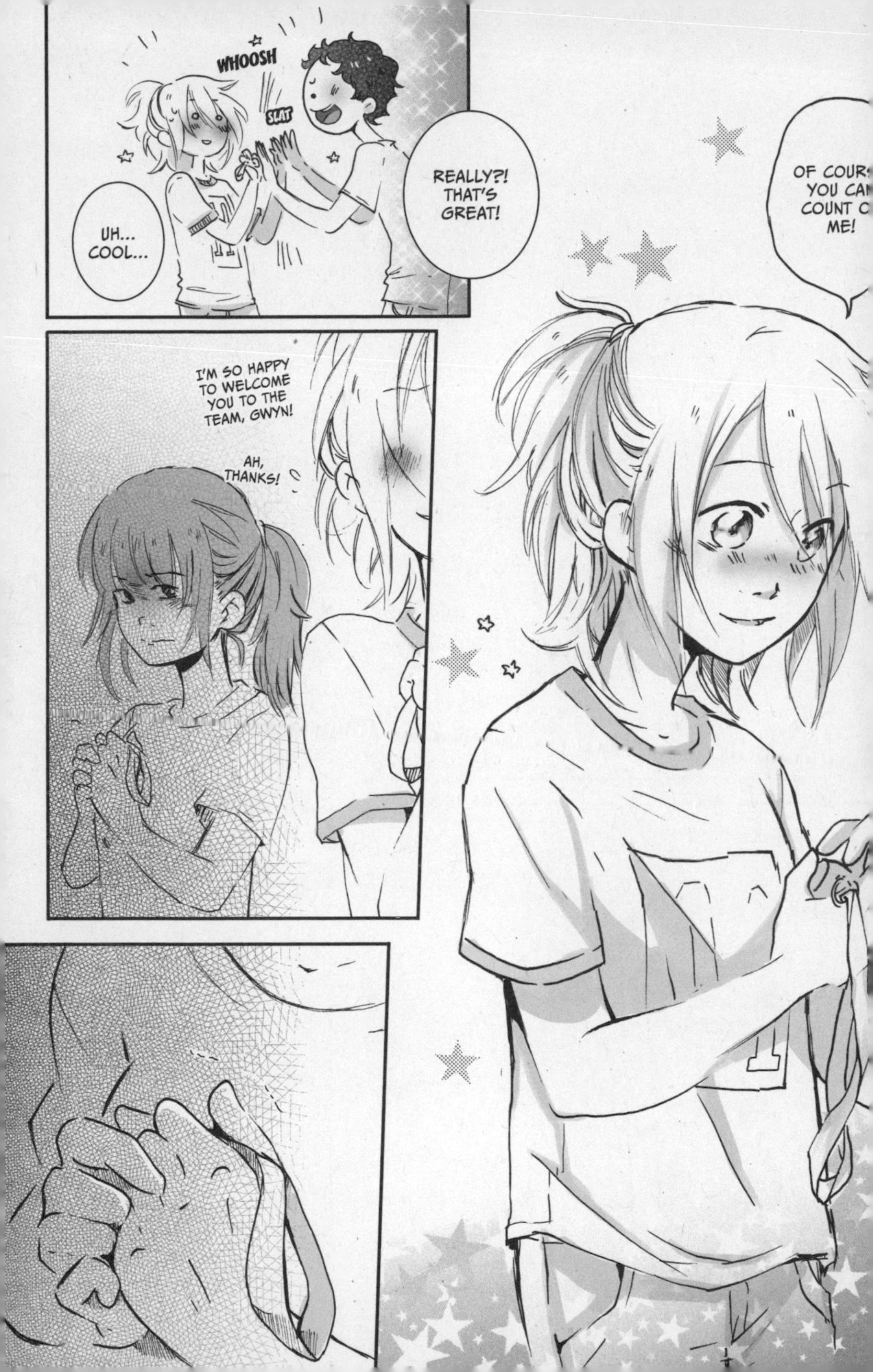
OF COUR YOU CA COUNT C ME!
REALLY?! THAT'S GREAT!
WHOOSH
SLAP
UH... COOL...
I'M SO HAPPY TO WELCOME YOU TO THE TEAM, GWYN!
AH, THANKS!

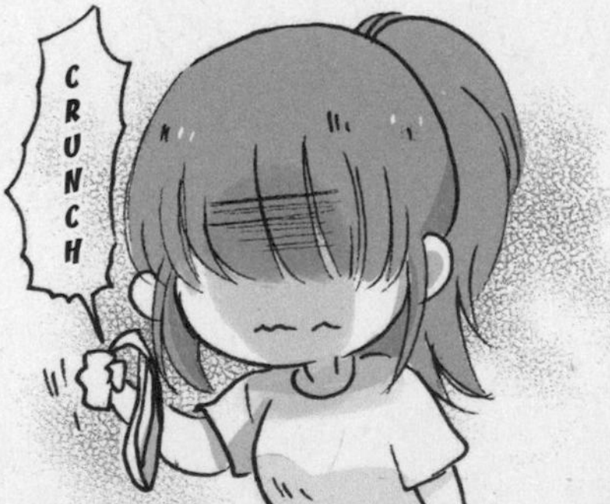
CRUNCH

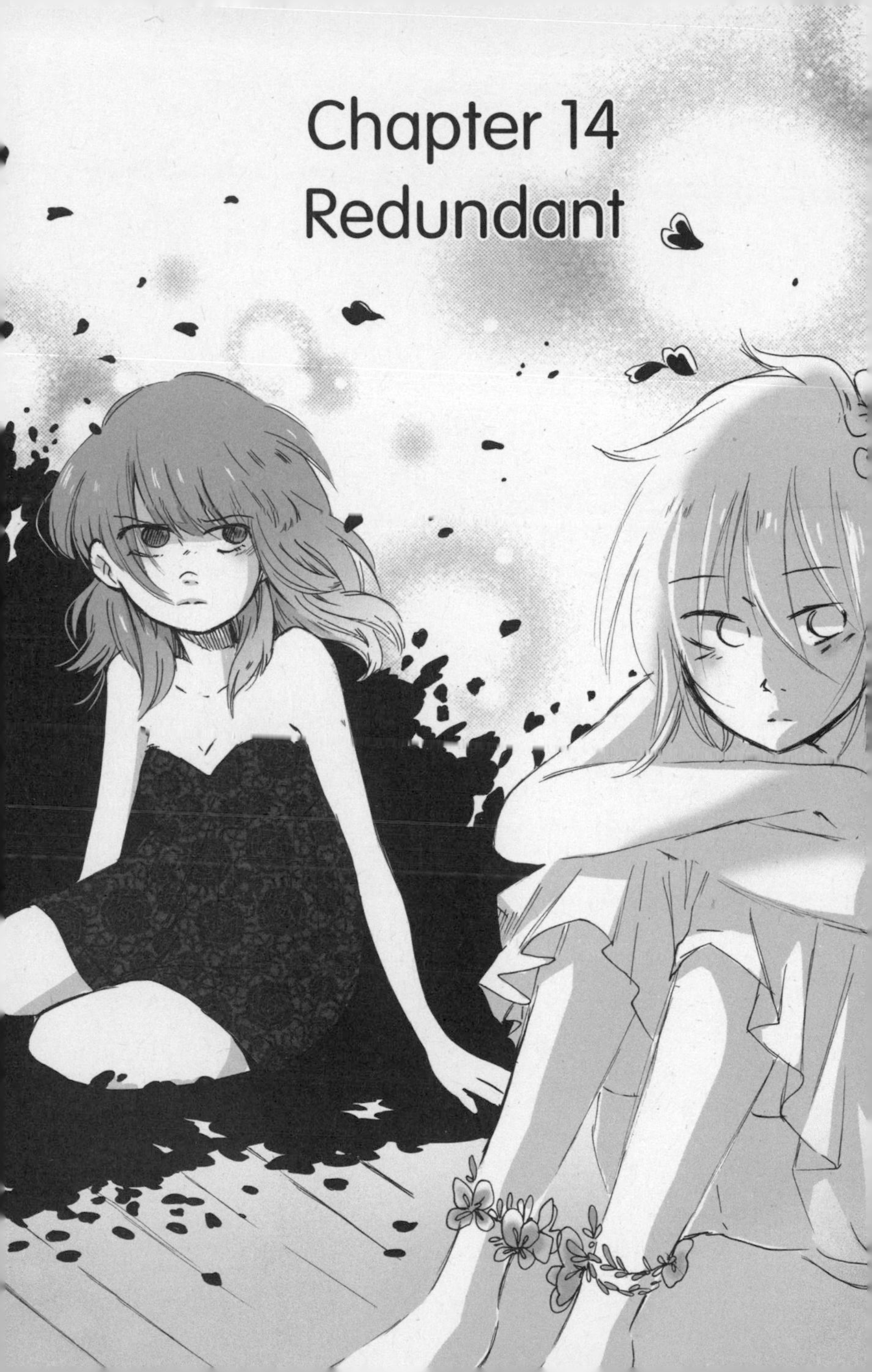
Chapter 14
Redundant

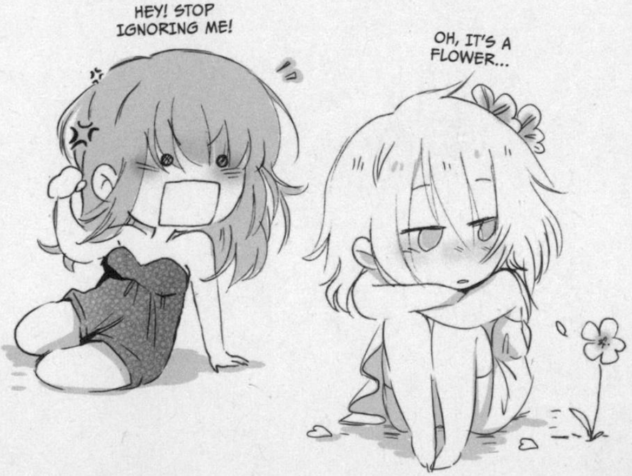
OH, IT'S A FLOWER...
HEY! STOP IGNORING ME!

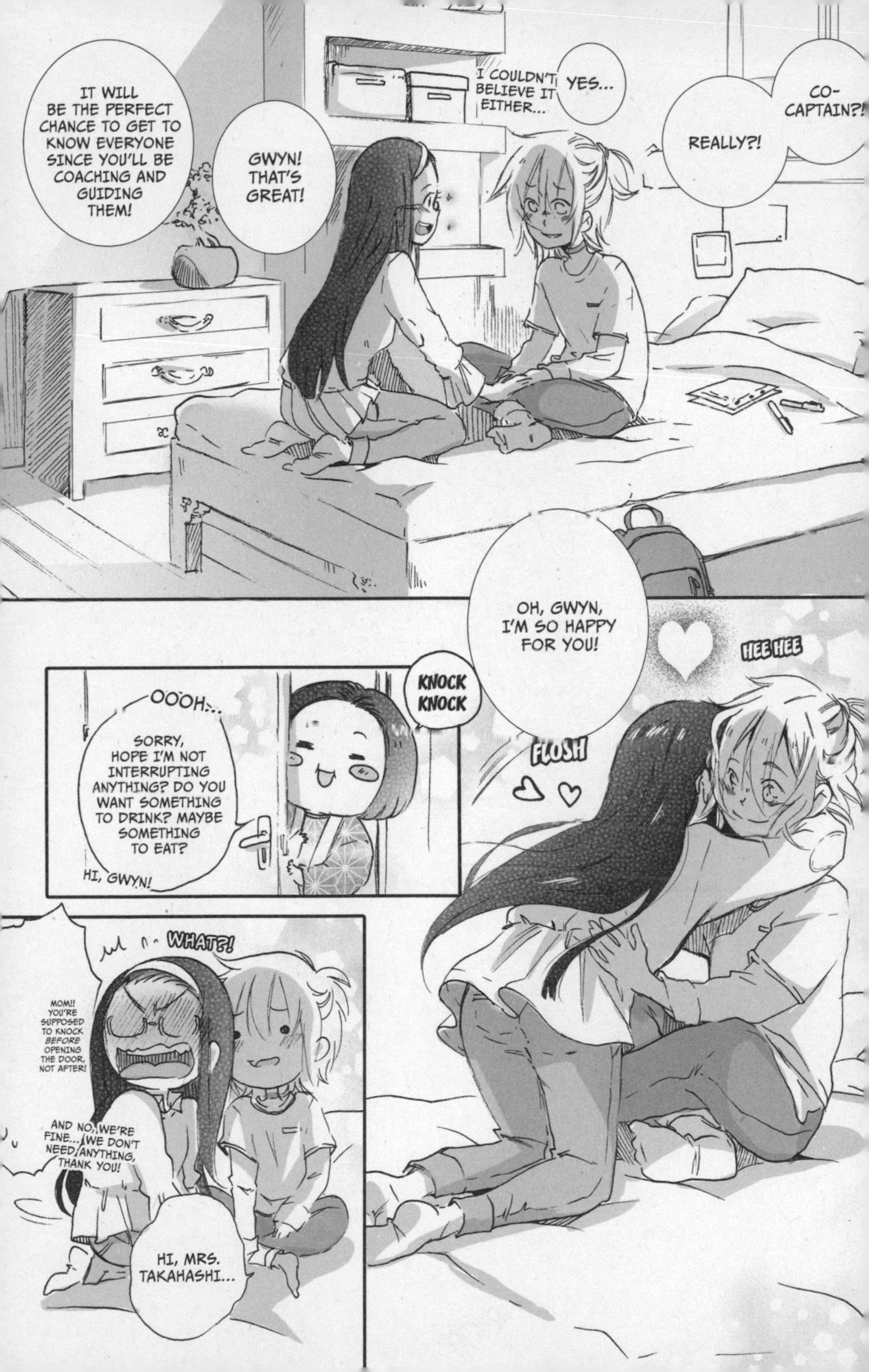
CO-CAPTAIN?!
REALLY?!
YES...
I COULDN'T BELIEVE IT EITHER...
GWYN! THAT'S GREAT!
IT WILL BE THE PERFECT CHANCE TO GET TO KNOW EVERYONE SINCE YOU'LL BE COACHING AND GUIDING THEM!
OH, GWYN, I'M SO HAPPY FOR YOU!
HEE HEE
FLOSH
KNOCK KNOCK
OOOH...
SORRY, HOPE I'M NOT INTERRUPTING ANYTHING? DO YOU WANT SOMETHING TO DRINK? MAYBE SOMETHING TO EAT?
HI, GWYN!
WHAT?!
MOM!! YOU'RE SUPPOSED TO KNOCK *BEFORE* OPENING THE DOOR, NOT AFTER!
AND NO, WE'RE FINE... WE DON'T NEED ANYTHING, THANK YOU!
HI, MRS. TAKAHASHI...

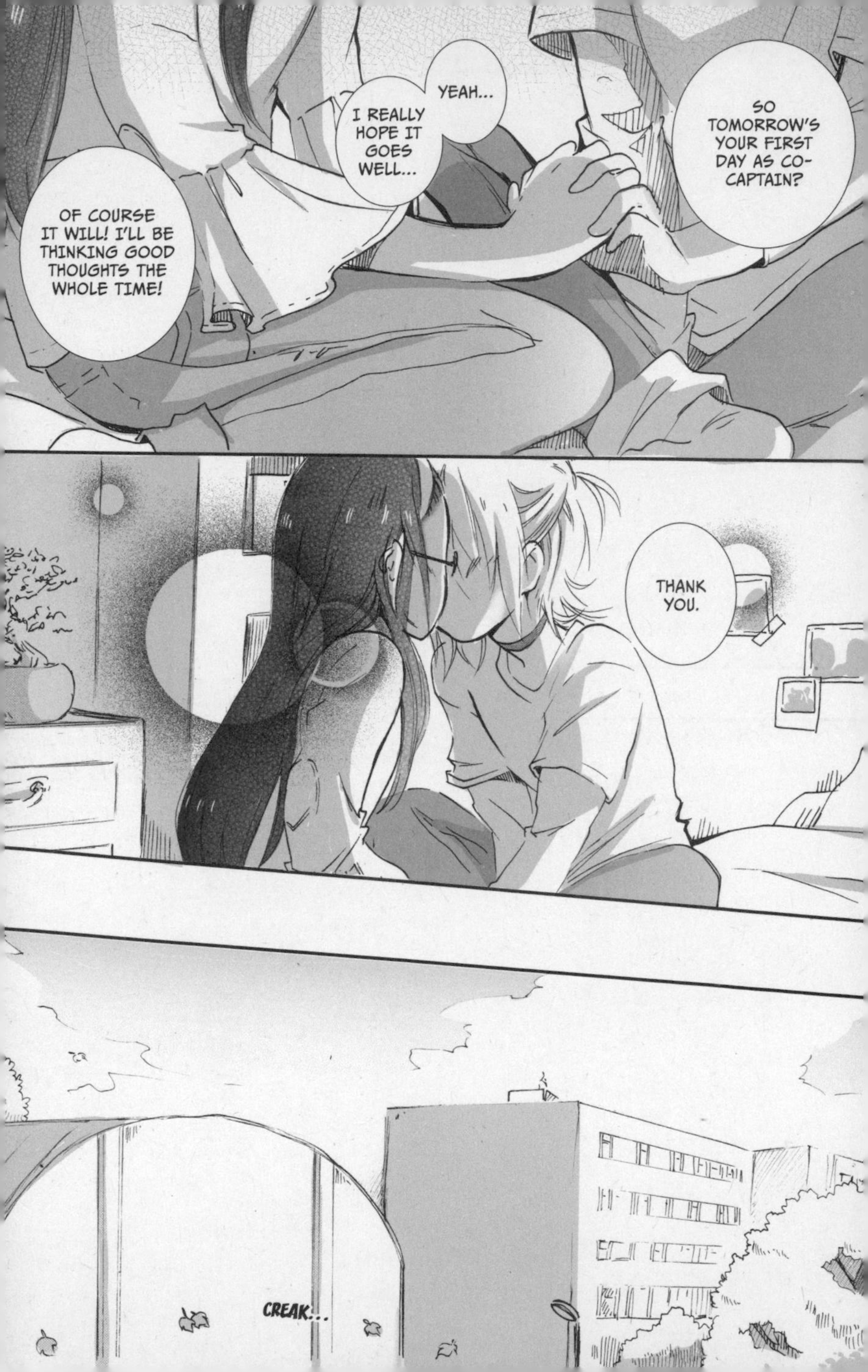
SO TOMORROW'S YOUR FIRST DAY AS CO-CAPTAIN?
YEAH...
I REALLY HOPE IT GOES WELL...
OF COURSE IT WILL! I'LL BE THINKING GOOD THOUGHTS THE WHOLE TIME!
THANK YOU.
CREAK...

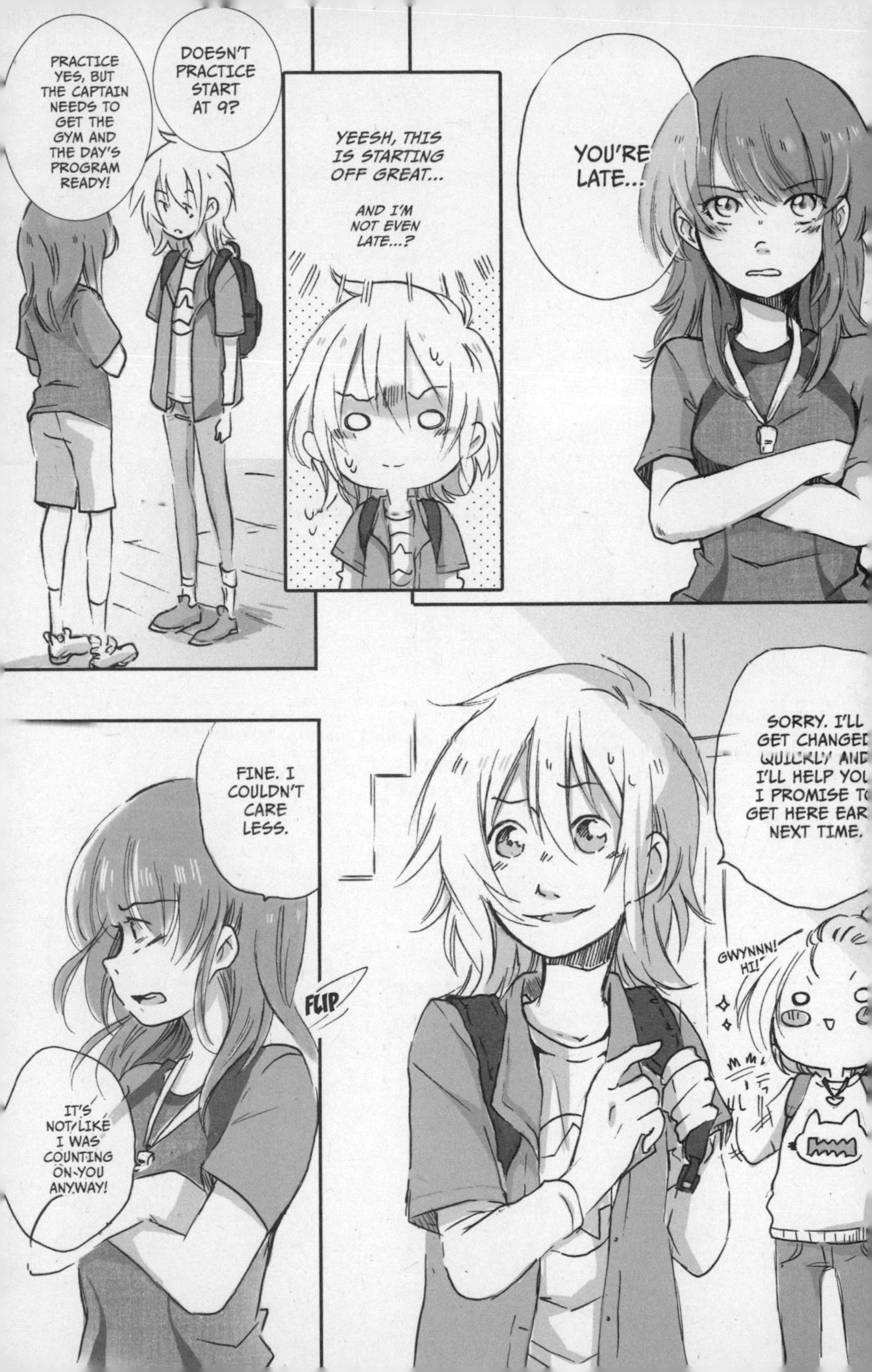
YOU'RE LATE...
YEESH, THIS IS STARTING OFF GREAT...
AND I'M NOT EVEN LATE...?
DOESN'T PRACTICE START AT 9?
PRACTICE YES, BUT THE CAPTAIN NEEDS TO GET THE GYM AND THE DAY'S PROGRAM READY!
SORRY. I'LL GET CHANGED QUICKLY AND I'LL HELP YOU I PROMISE TO GET HERE EAR NEXT TIME.
GWYNNN! HI!
FINE. I COULDN'T CARE LESS.
FLIP
IT'S NOT LIKE I WAS COUNTING ON YOU ANYWAY!

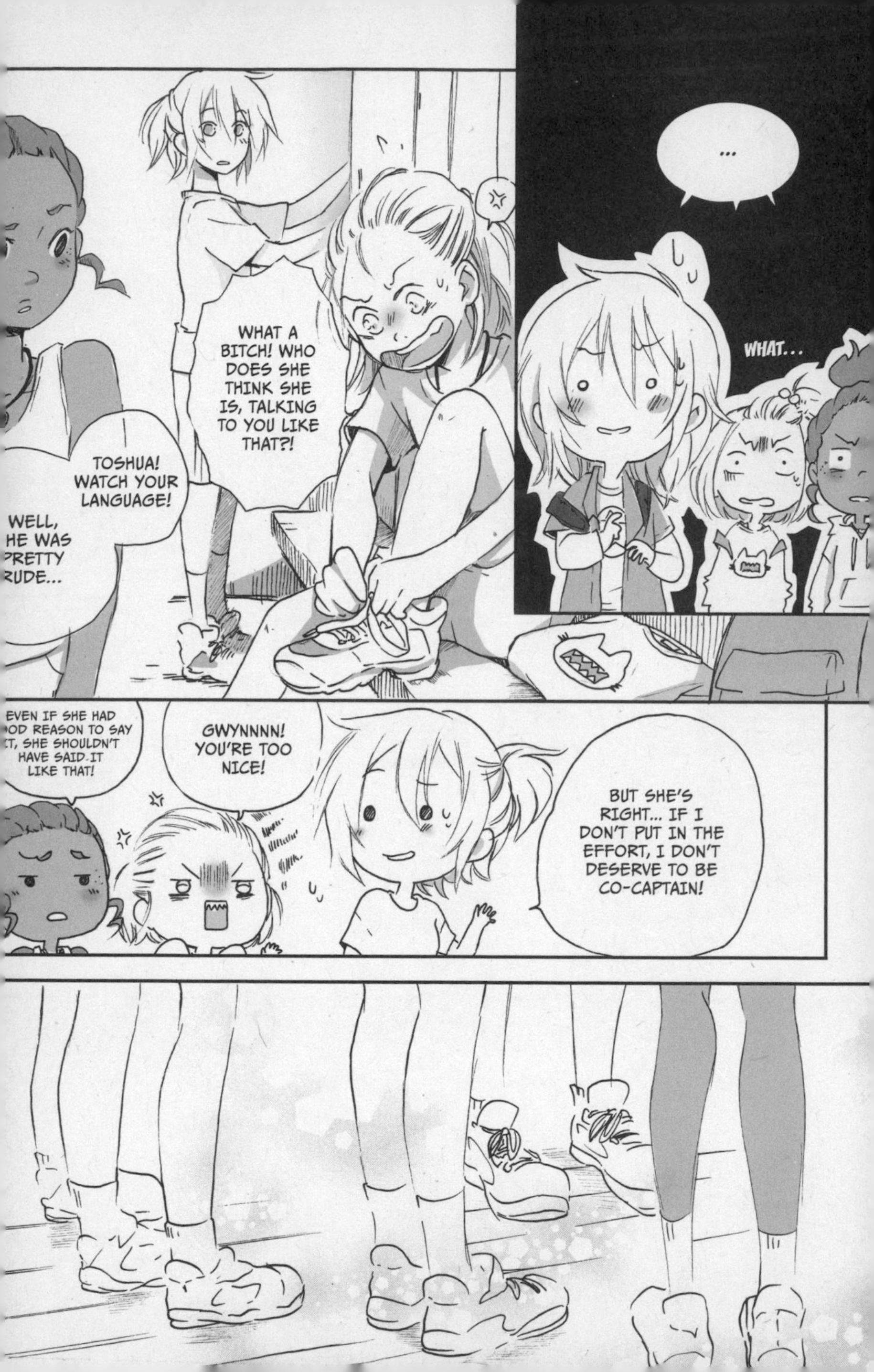
...
WHAT...
WHAT A BITCH! WHO DOES SHE THINK SHE IS, TALKING TO YOU LIKE THAT?!
TOSHUA! WATCH YOUR LANGUAGE!
WELL, HE WAS PRETTY RUDE...
BUT SHE'S RIGHT... IF I DON'T PUT IN THE EFFORT, I DON'T DESERVE TO BE CO-CAPTAIN!
GWYNNNN! YOU'RE TOO NICE!
EVEN IF SHE HAD OOD REASON TO SAY T, SHE SHOULDN'T HAVE SAID IT LIKE THAT!

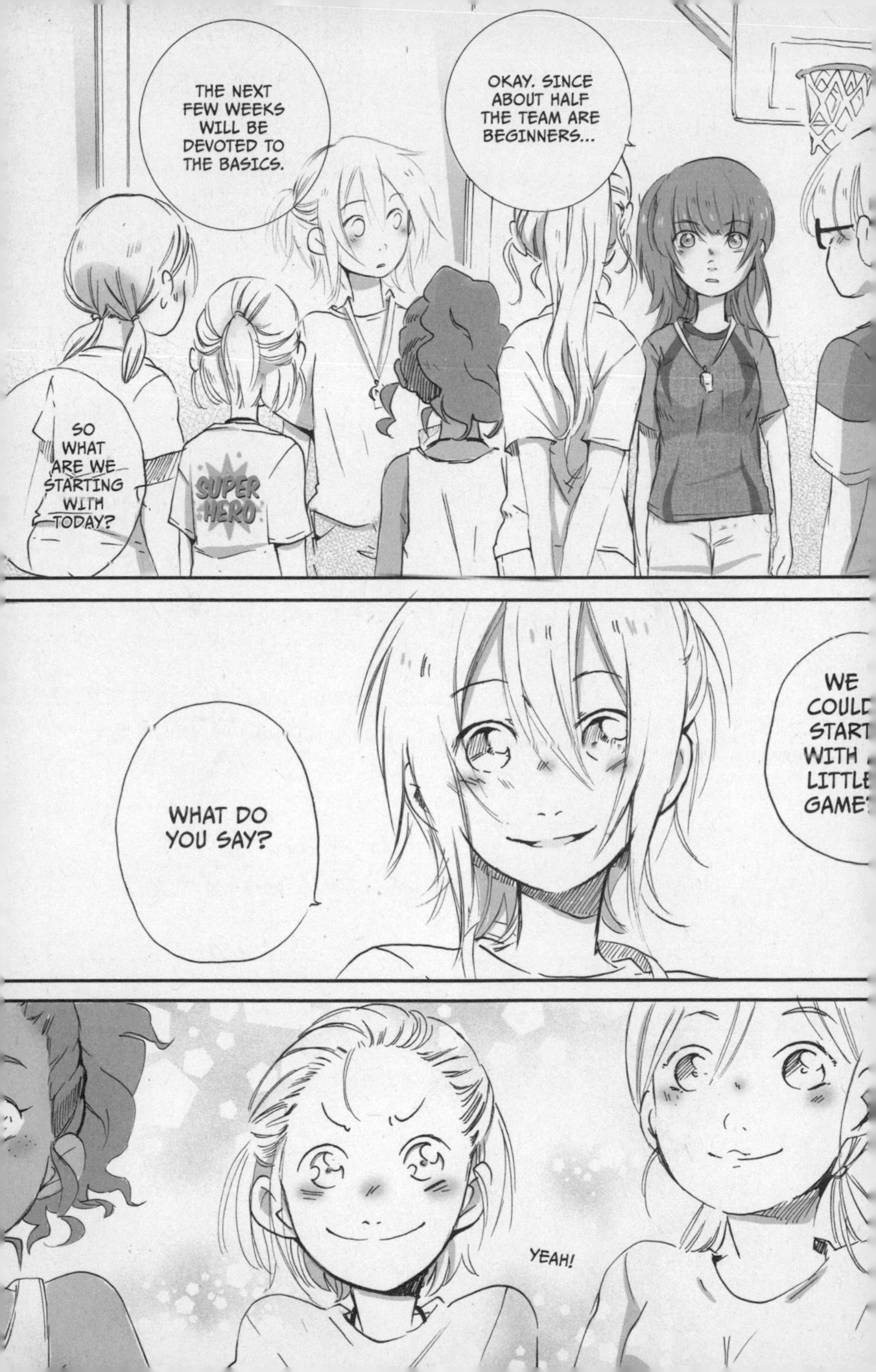
OKAY. SINCE ABOUT HALF THE TEAM ARE BEGINNERS...
THE NEXT FEW WEEKS WILL BE DEVOTED TO THE BASICS.
SUPER HERO
SO WHAT ARE WE STARTING WITH TODAY?
WE COULD START WITH LITTLE GAME
WHAT DO YOU SAY?
YEAH!

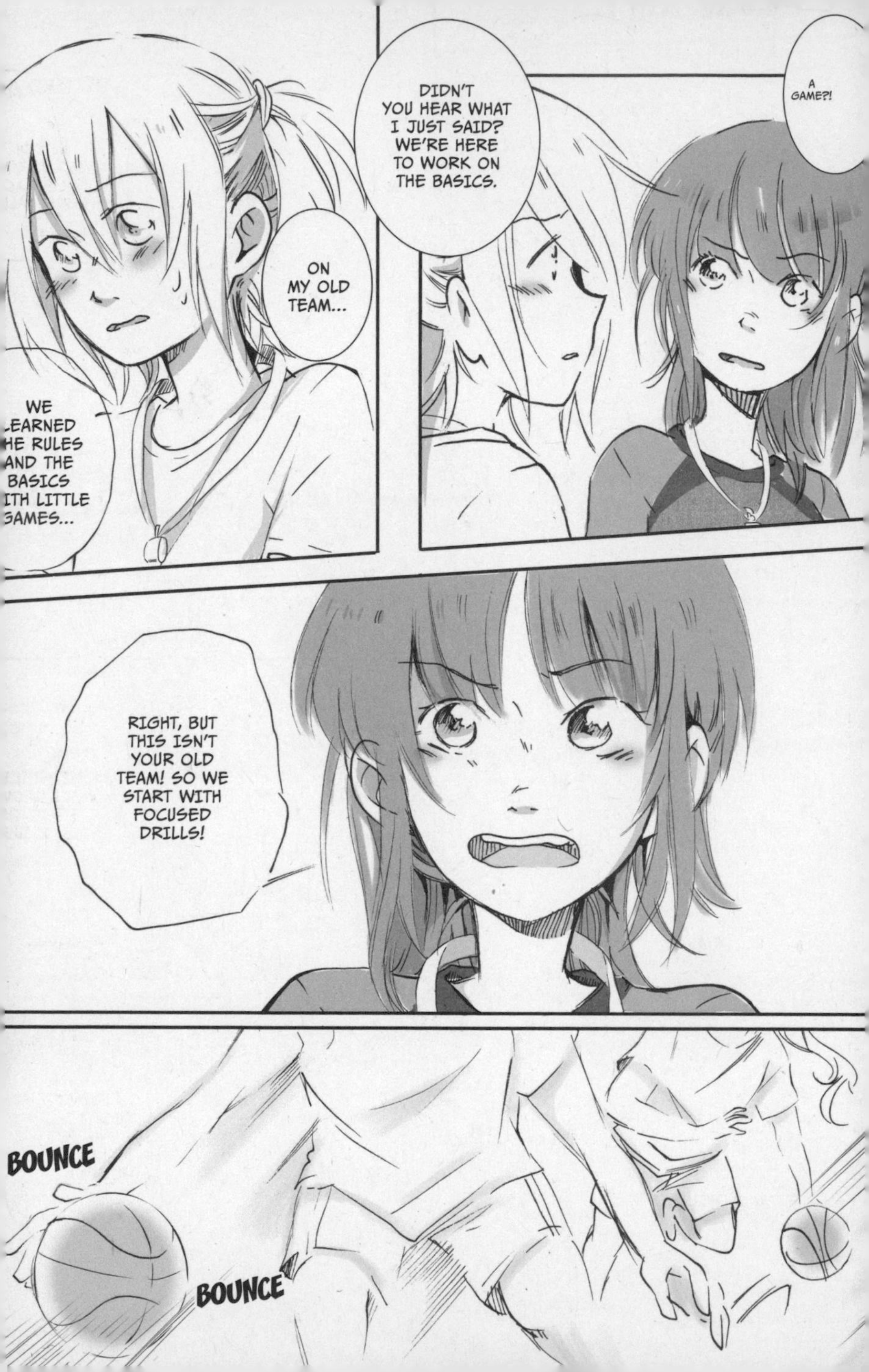
ON MY OLD TEAM...
WE LEARNED HE RULES AND THE BASICS ITH LITTLE GAMES...
A GAME?!
DIDN'T YOU HEAR WHAT I JUST SAID? WE'RE HERE TO WORK ON THE BASICS.
RIGHT, BUT THIS ISN'T YOUR OLD TEAM! SO WE START WITH FOCUSED DRILLS!
BOUNCE
BOUNCE

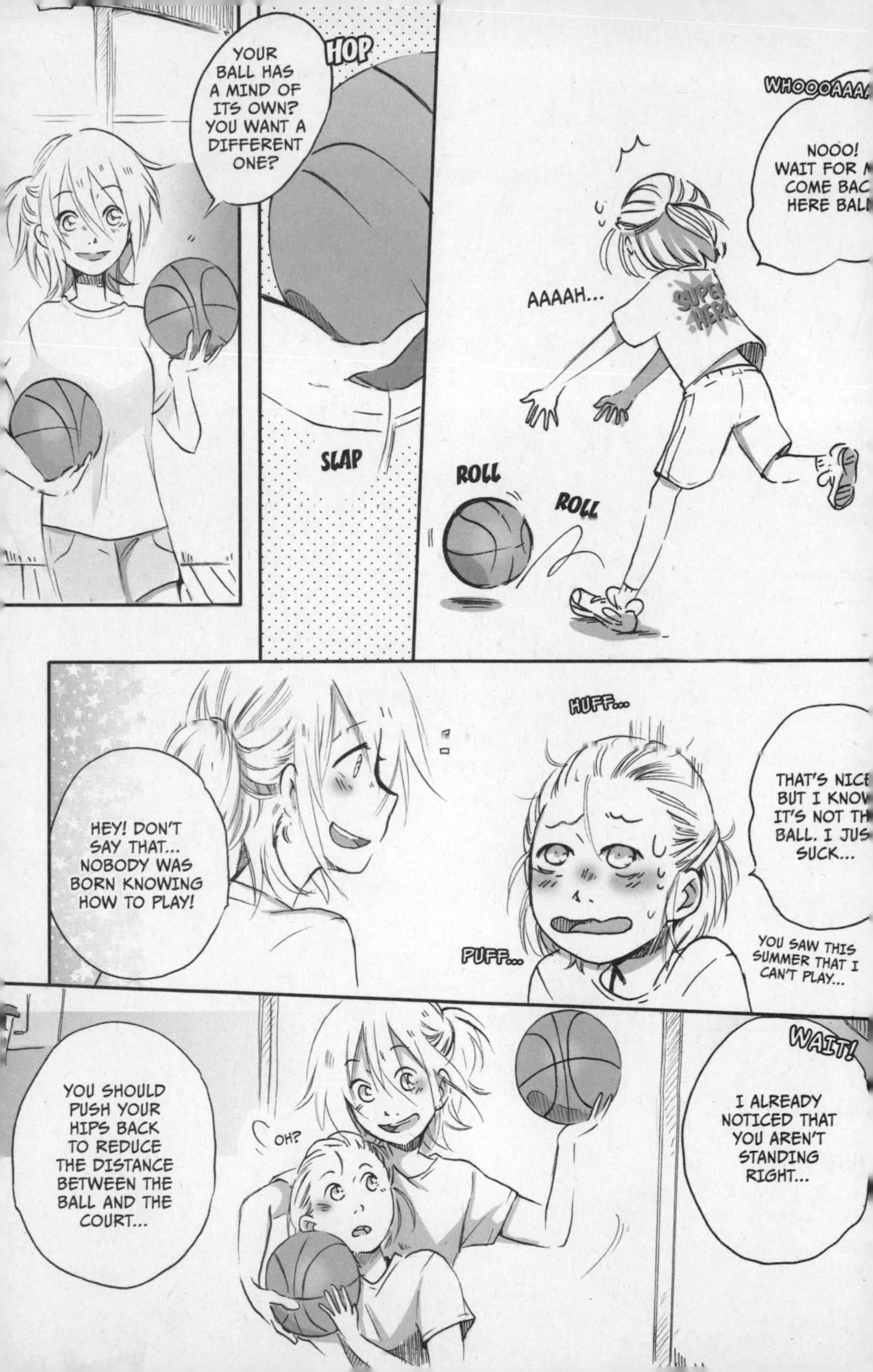
WHOOOAAAA
NOOO! WAIT FOR M COME BAC HERE BALL
AAAAH...
ROLL
ROLL
HOP
SLAP
YOUR BALL HAS A MIND OF ITS OWN? YOU WANT A DIFFERENT ONE?
HUFF...
THAT'S NICE BUT I KNOW IT'S NOT TH BALL. I JUS SUCK...
YOU SAW THIS SUMMER THAT I CAN'T PLAY...
PUFF...
HEY! DON'T SAY THAT... NOBODY WAS BORN KNOWING HOW TO PLAY!
WAIT!
I ALREADY NOTICED THAT YOU AREN'T STANDING RIGHT...
OH?
YOU SHOULD PUSH YOUR HIPS BACK TO REDUCE THE DISTANCE BETWEEN THE BALL AND THE COURT...

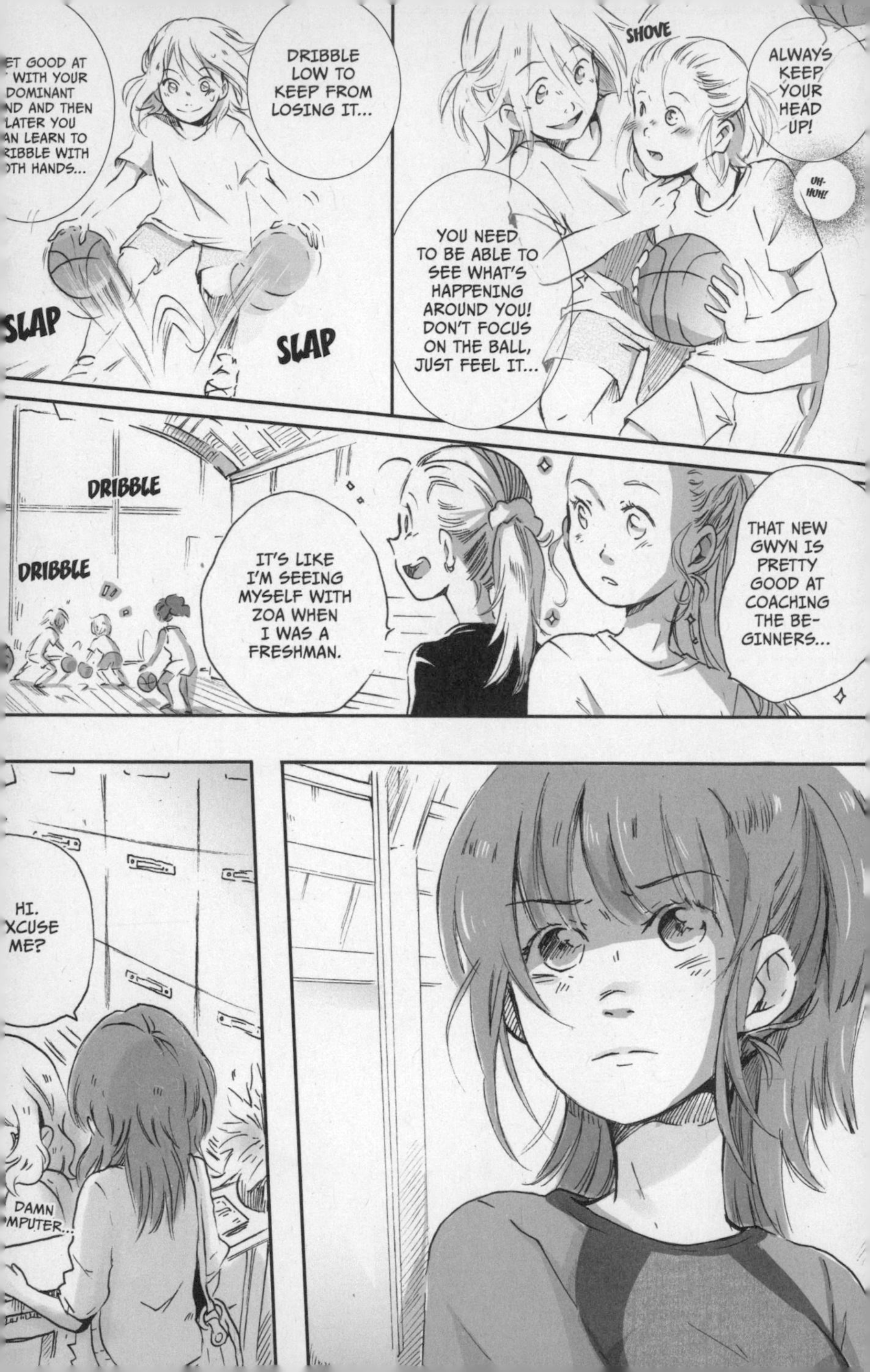
SHOVE
ALWAYS KEEP YOUR HEAD UP!
UH-HUH!
YOU NEED TO BE ABLE TO SEE WHAT'S HAPPENING AROUND YOU! DON'T FOCUS ON THE BALL, JUST FEEL IT...
DRIBBLE LOW TO KEEP FROM LOSING IT...
ET GOOD AT WITH YOUR DOMINANT ND AND THEN LATER YOU AN LEARN TO RIBBLE WITH OTH HANDS...
SLAP
SLAP
THAT NEW GWYN IS PRETTY GOOD AT COACHING THE BE-GINNERS...
IT'S LIKE I'M SEEING MYSELF WITH ZOA WHEN I WAS A FRESHMAN.
DRIBBLE
DRIBBLE
HI. XCUSE ME?
DAMN MPUTER...

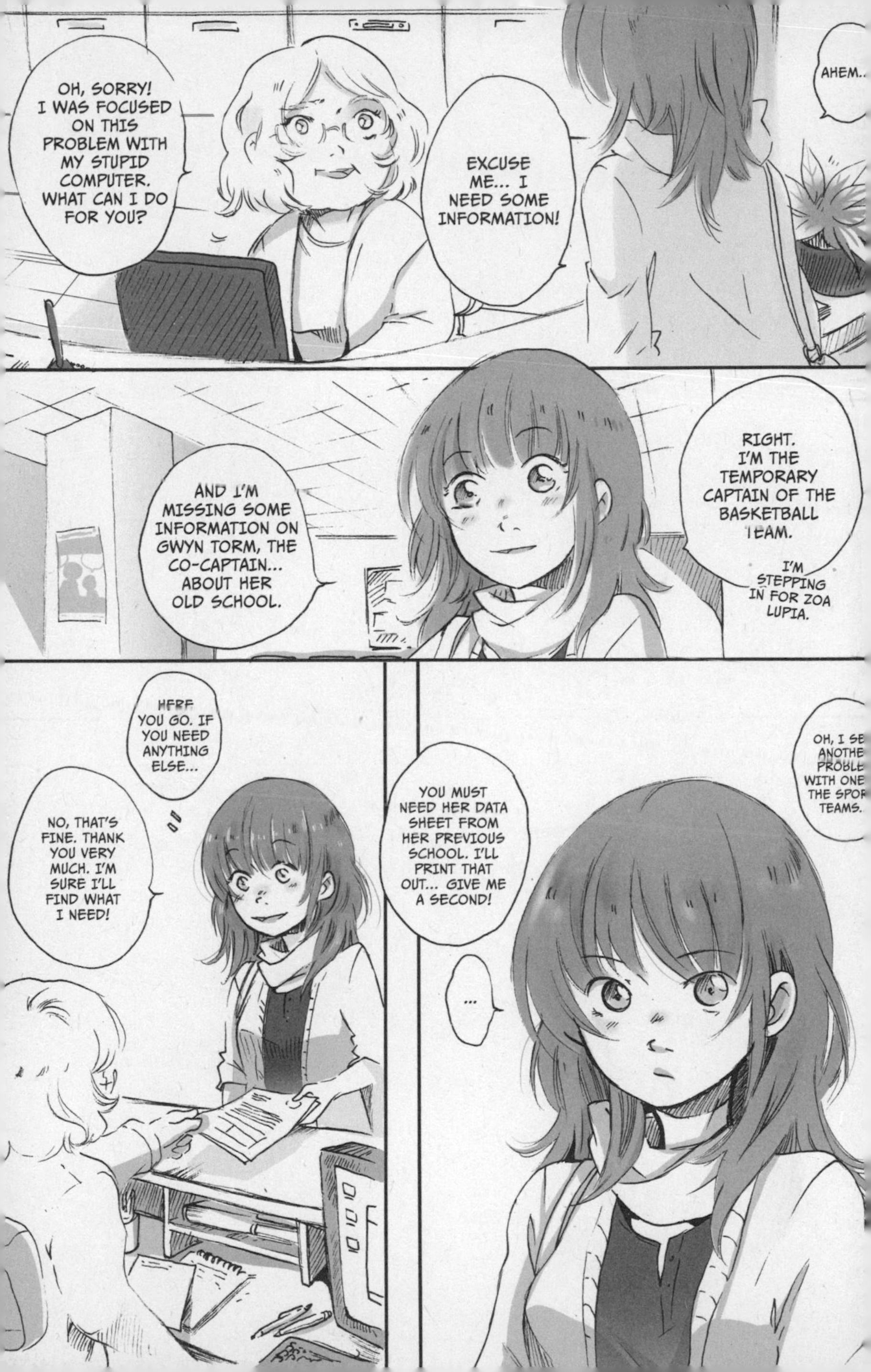
AHEM...
EXCUSE ME... I NEED SOME INFORMATION!
OH, SORRY! I WAS FOCUSED ON THIS PROBLEM WITH MY STUPID COMPUTER. WHAT CAN I DO FOR YOU?
RIGHT. I'M THE TEMPORARY CAPTAIN OF THE BASKETBALL TEAM.
I'M STEPPING IN FOR ZOA LUPIA.
AND I'M MISSING SOME INFORMATION ON GWYN TORM, THE CO-CAPTAIN... ABOUT HER OLD SCHOOL.
OH, I SE ANOTHE PROBLE WITH ONE THE SPOR TEAMS.
YOU MUST NEED HER DATA SHEET FROM HER PREVIOUS SCHOOL. I'LL PRINT THAT OUT... GIVE ME A SECOND!
...
HERE YOU GO. IF YOU NEED ANYTHING ELSE...
NO, THAT'S FINE. THANK YOU VERY MUCH. I'M SURE I'LL FIND WHAT I NEED!

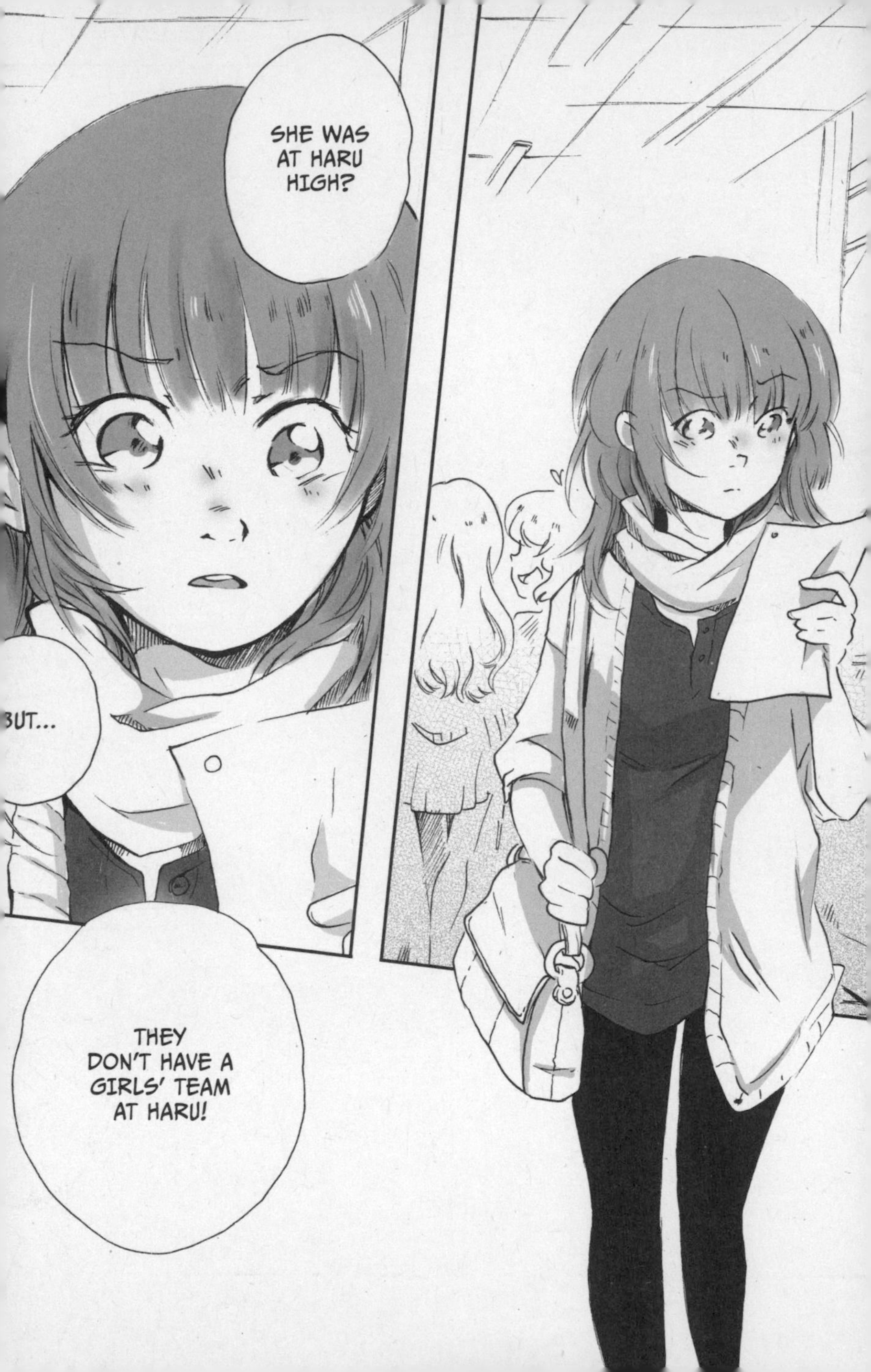
SHE WAS AT HARU HIGH?
BUT...
THEY DON'T HAVE A GIRLS' TEAM AT HARU!

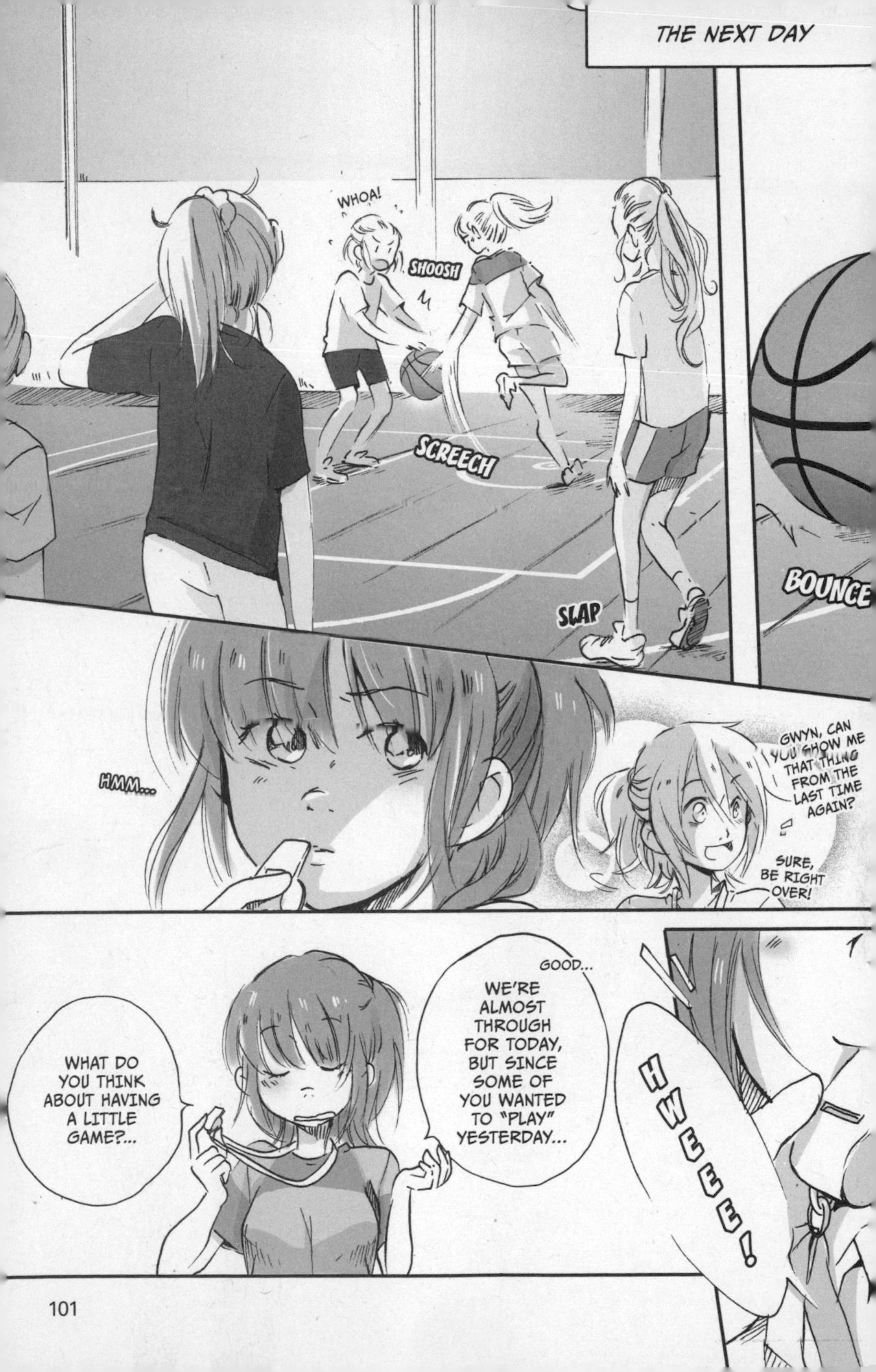
THE NEXT DAY
BOUNCE
WHOA!
SHOOSH
SCREECH
SLAP
GWYN, CAN YOU SHOW ME THAT THING FROM THE LAST TIME AGAIN?
SURE, BE RIGHT OVER!
HMM...
HWEEE!
GOOD...
WE'RE ALMOST THROUGH FOR TODAY, BUT SINCE SOME OF YOU WANTED TO "PLAY" YESTERDAY...
WHAT DO YOU THINK ABOUT HAVING A LITTLE GAME?...

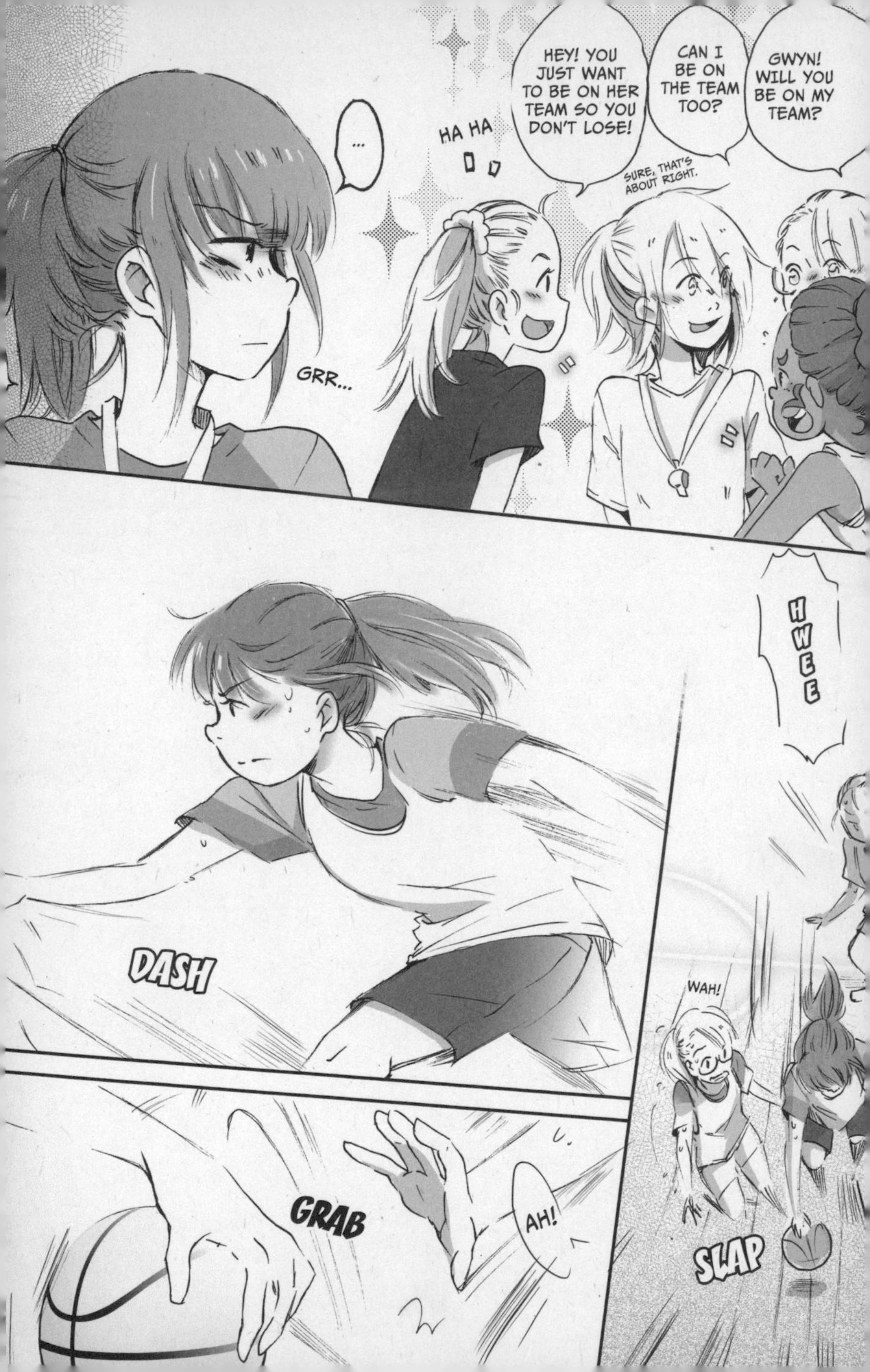
GWYN! WILL YOU BE ON MY TEAM?
CAN I BE ON THE TEAM TOO?
HEY! YOU JUST WANT TO BE ON HER TEAM SO YOU DON'T LOSE!
SURE, THAT'S ABOUT RIGHT.
HA HA
...
GRR...
HWEEE
WAH!
SLAP
DASH
AH!
GRAB

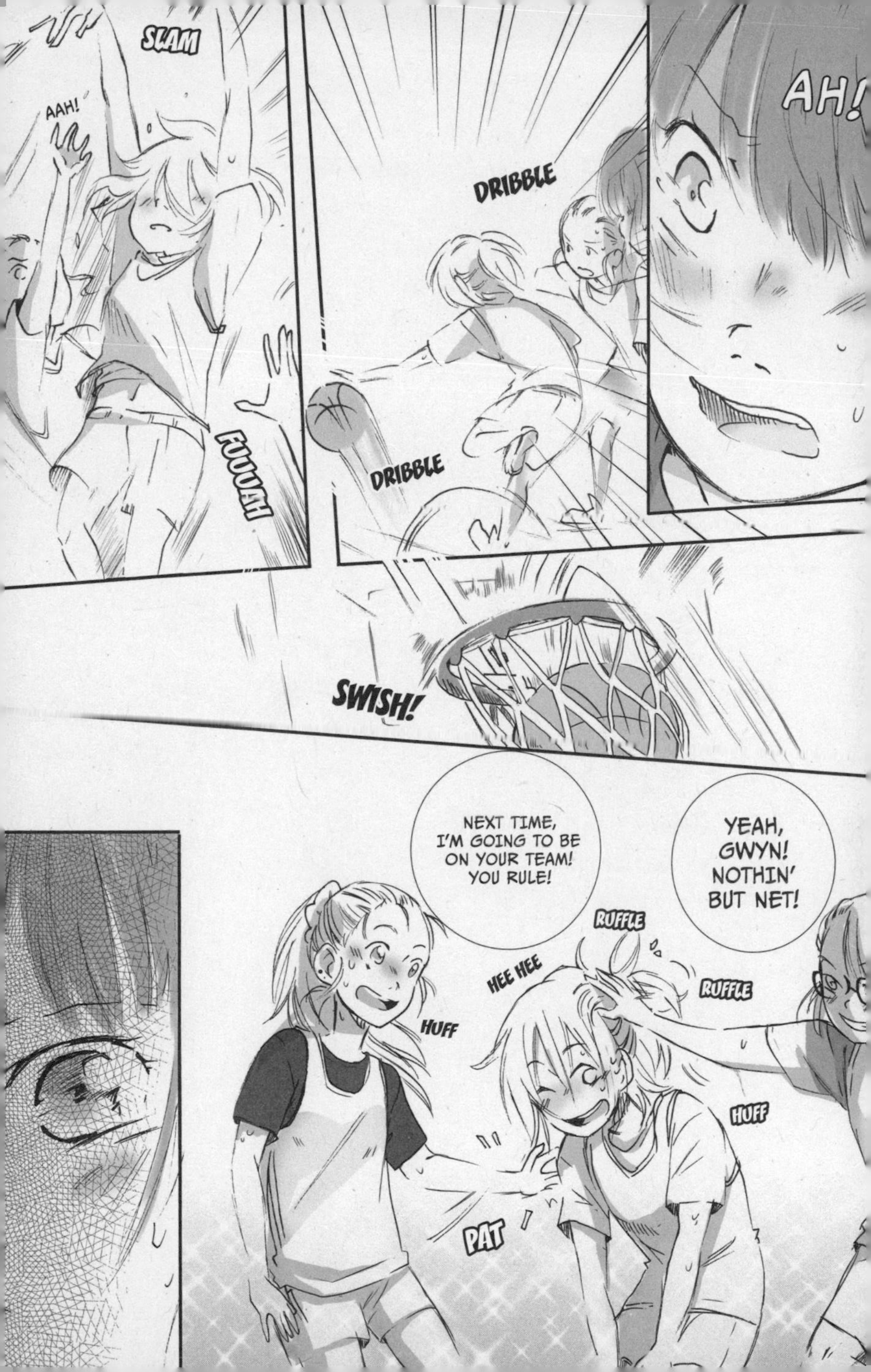
AH!
DRIBBLE
DRIBBLE
SLAM
AAH!
FUUUAH
SWISH!
YEAH, GWYN! NOTHIN' BUT NET!
NEXT TIME, I'M GOING TO BE ON YOUR TEAM! YOU RULE!
RUFFLE
RUFFLE
HEE HEE
HUFF
HUFF
PAT

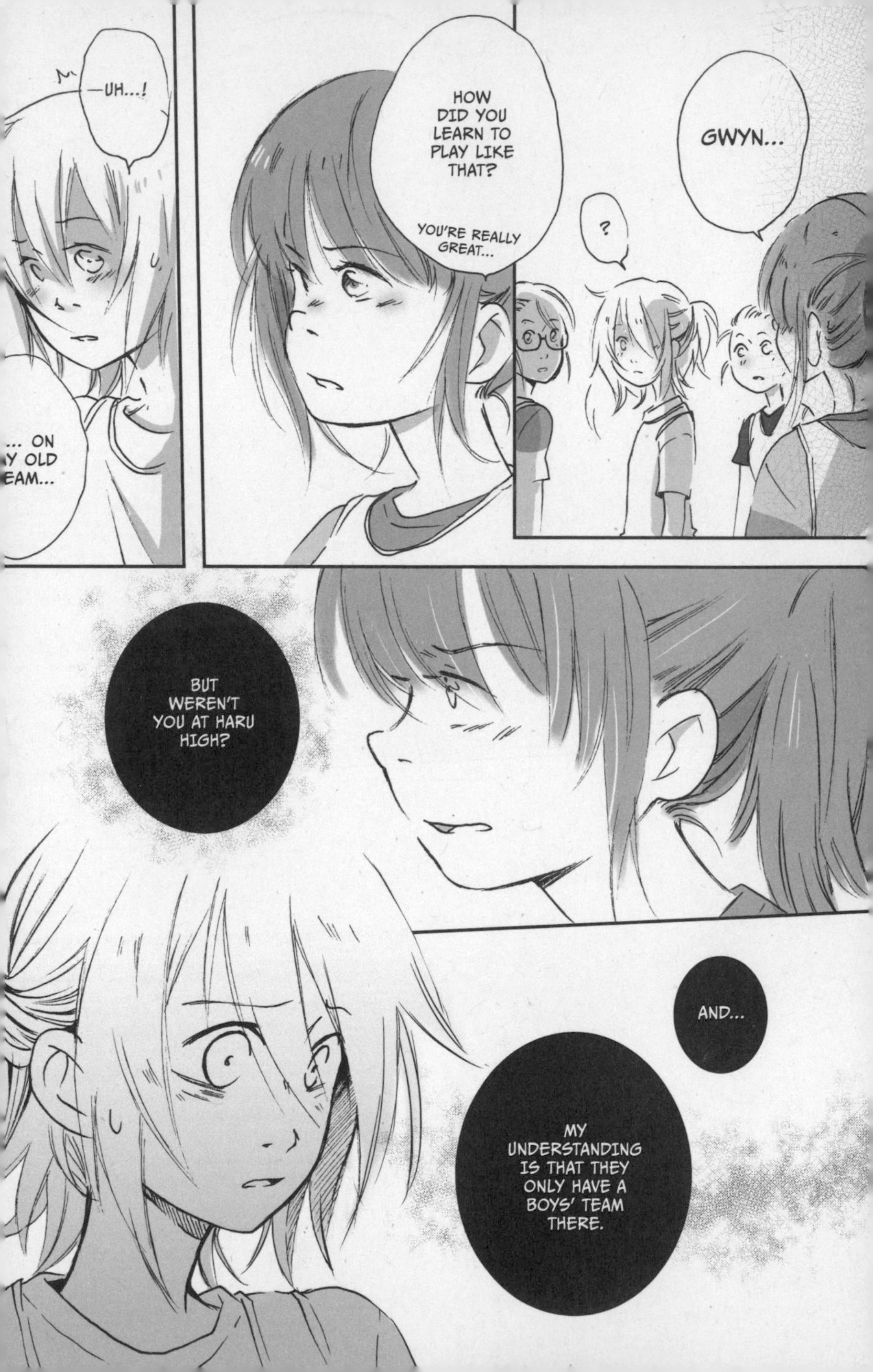
GWYN...
?
HOW DID YOU LEARN TO PLAY LIKE THAT?
YOU'RE REALLY GREAT...
—UH...!
... ON Y OLD EAM...
BUT WEREN'T YOU AT HARU HIGH?
AND...
MY UNDERSTANDING IS THAT THEY ONLY HAVE A BOYS' TEAM THERE.

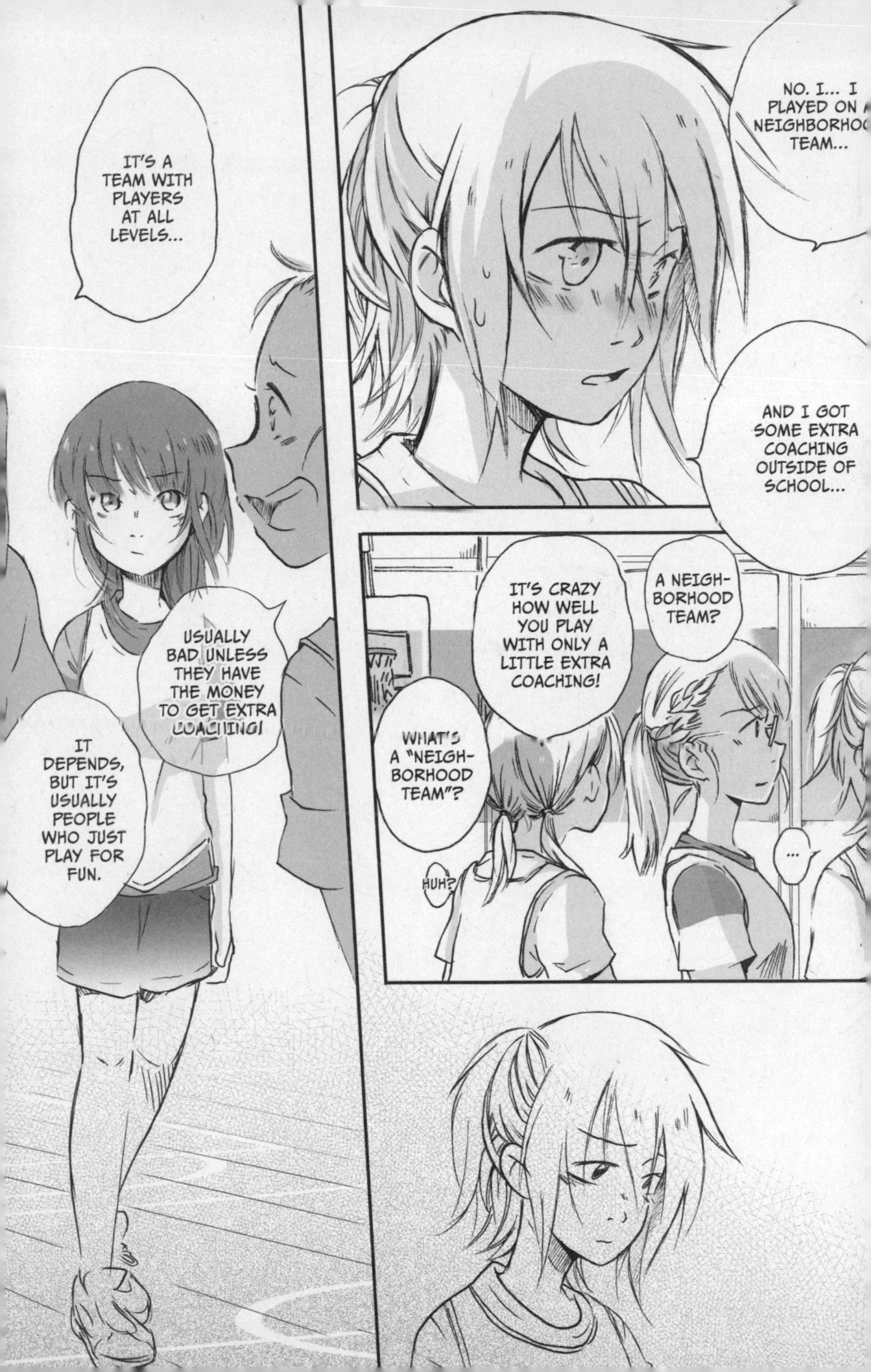
NO. I... I PLAYED ON NEIGHBORHO TEAM...
AND I GOT SOME EXTRA COACHING OUTSIDE OF SCHOOL...
A NEIGH-BORHOOD TEAM?
IT'S CRAZY HOW WELL YOU PLAY WITH ONLY A LITTLE EXTRA COACHING!
WHAT'S A "NEIGH-BORHOOD TEAM"?
...
HUH?
IT'S A TEAM WITH PLAYERS AT ALL LEVELS...
USUALLY BAD UNLESS THEY HAVE THE MONEY TO GET EXTRA COACHING!
IT DEPENDS, BUT IT'S USUALLY PEOPLE WHO JUST PLAY FOR FUN.

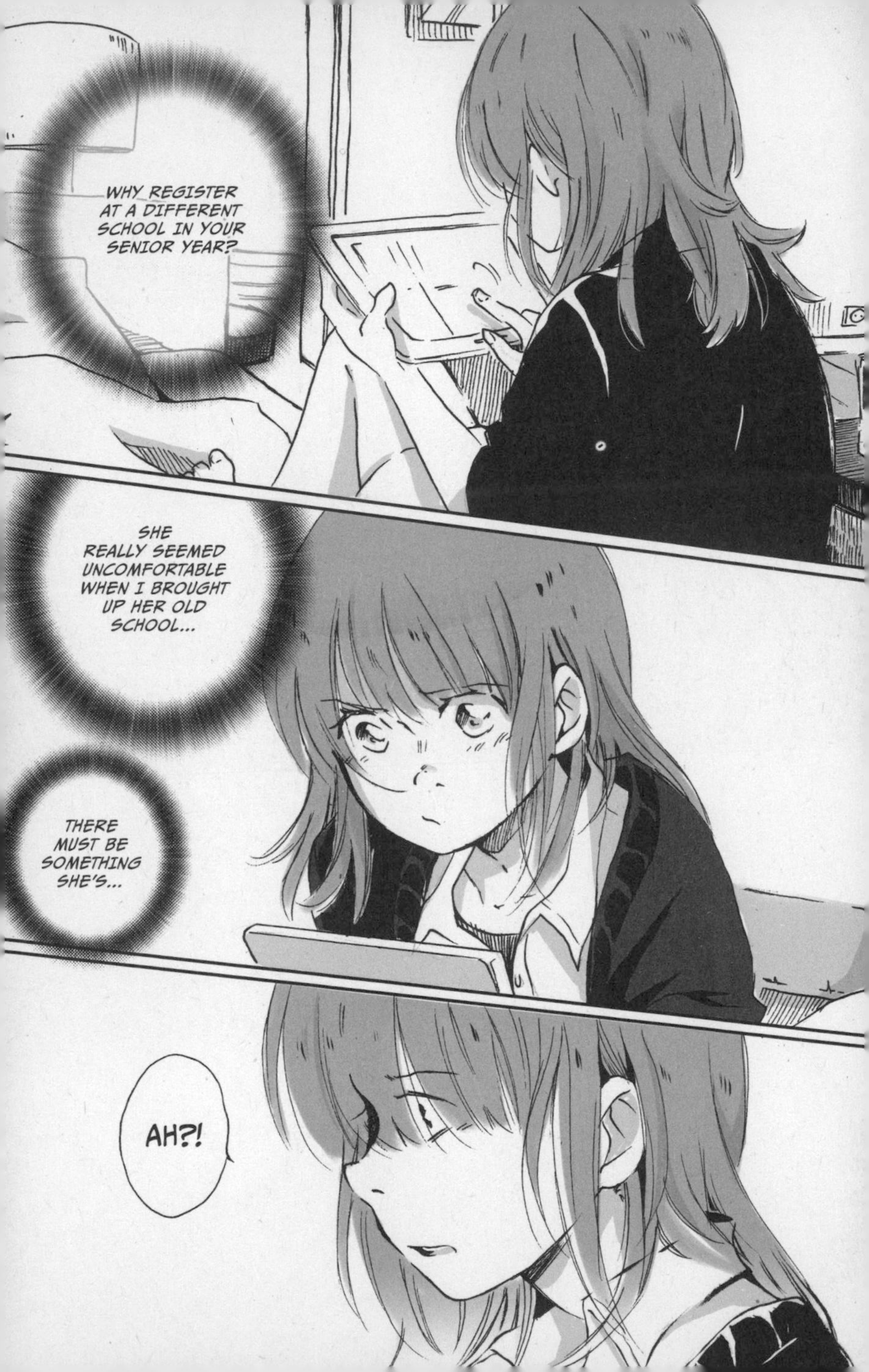
WHY REGISTER AT A DIFFERENT SCHOOL IN YOUR SENIOR YEAR?
SHE REALLY SEEMED UNCOMFORTABLE WHEN I BROUGHT UP HER OLD SCHOOL...
THERE MUST BE SOMETHING SHE'S...
AH?!

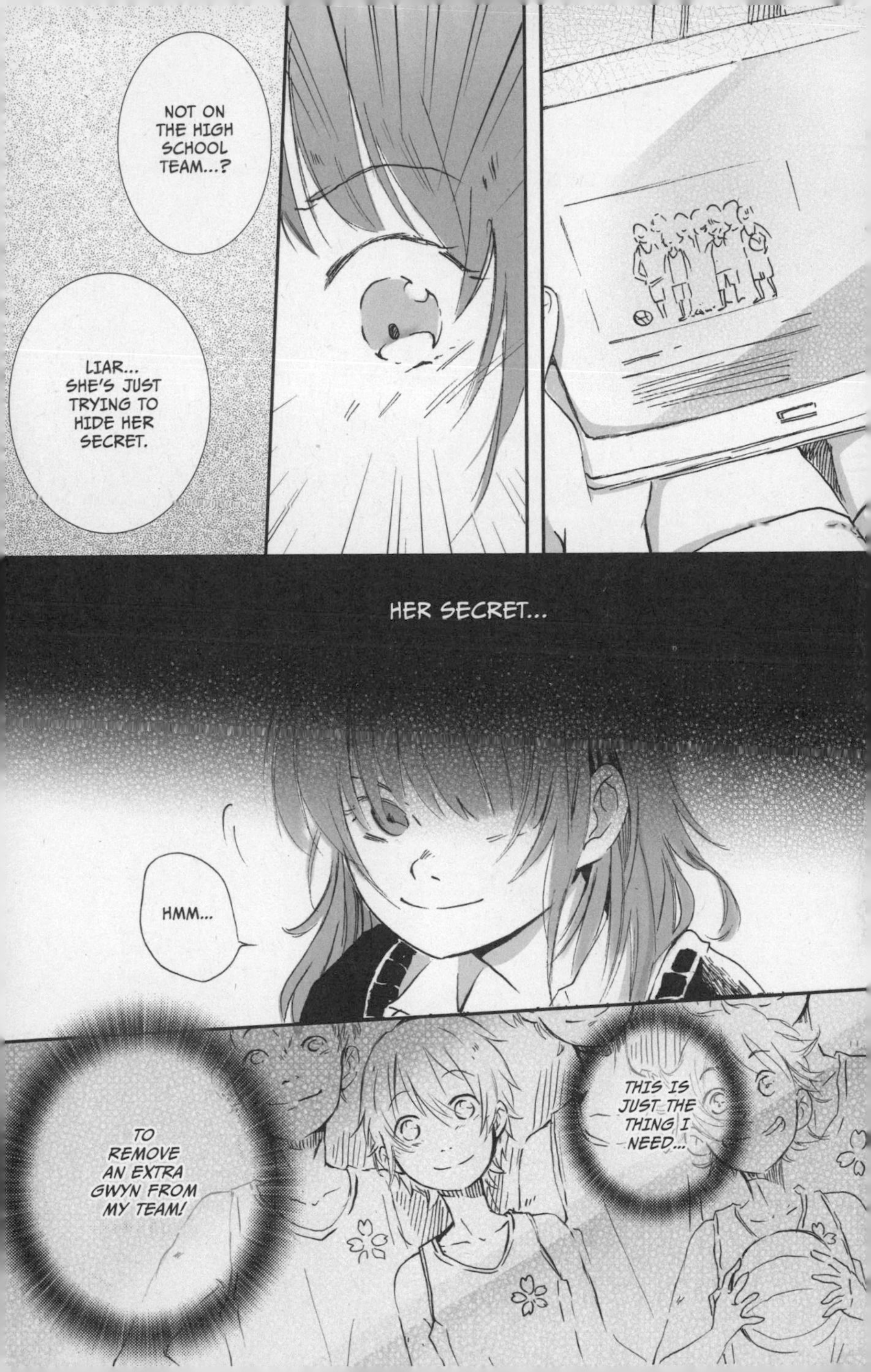
NOT ON THE HIGH SCHOOL TEAM...?
LIAR... SHE'S JUST TRYING TO HIDE HER SECRET.
HER SECRET...
HMM...
THIS IS JUST THE THING I NEED...
TO REMOVE AN EXTRA GWYN FROM MY TEAM!

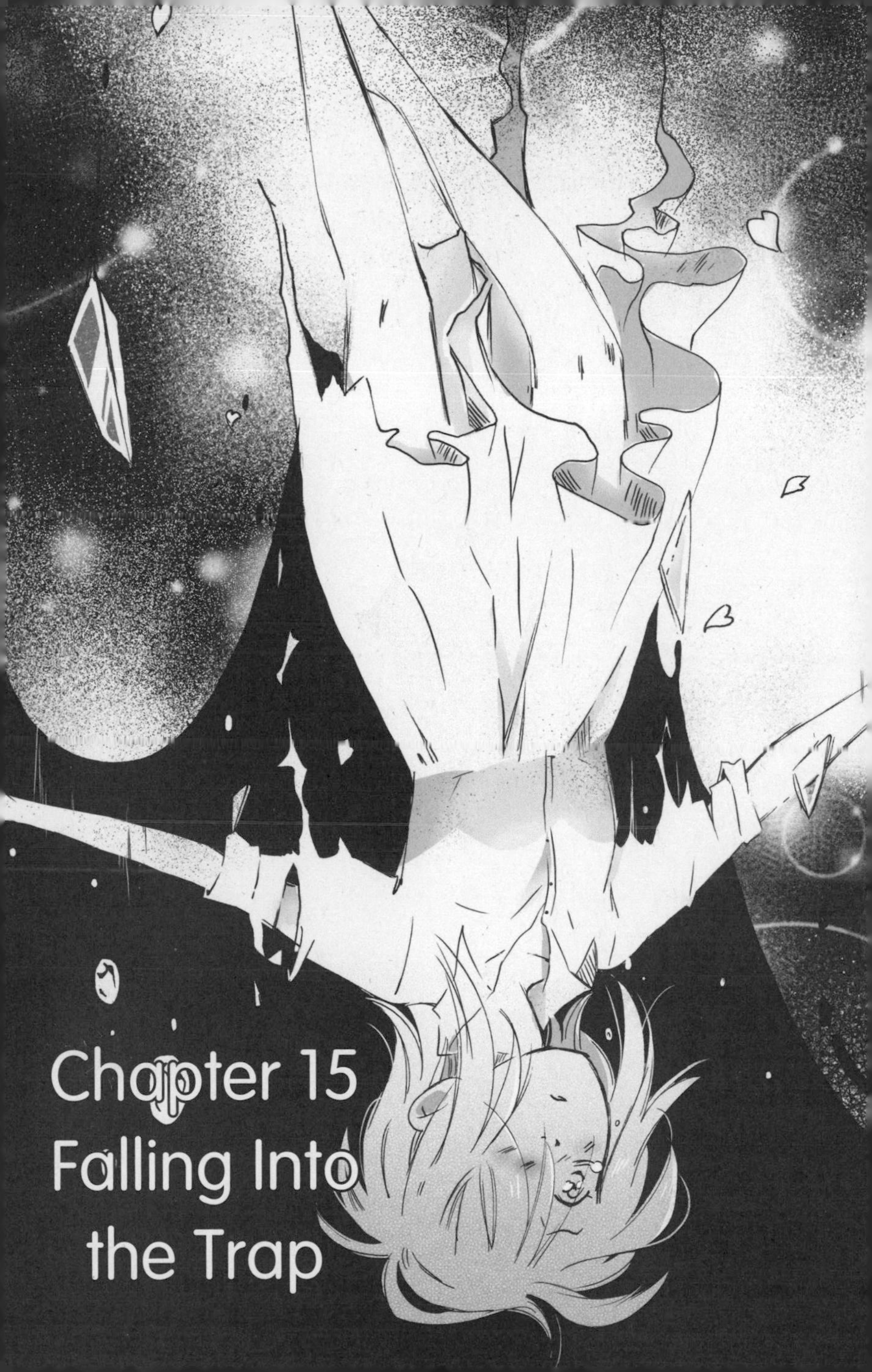
Chapter 15
Falling Into
the Trap

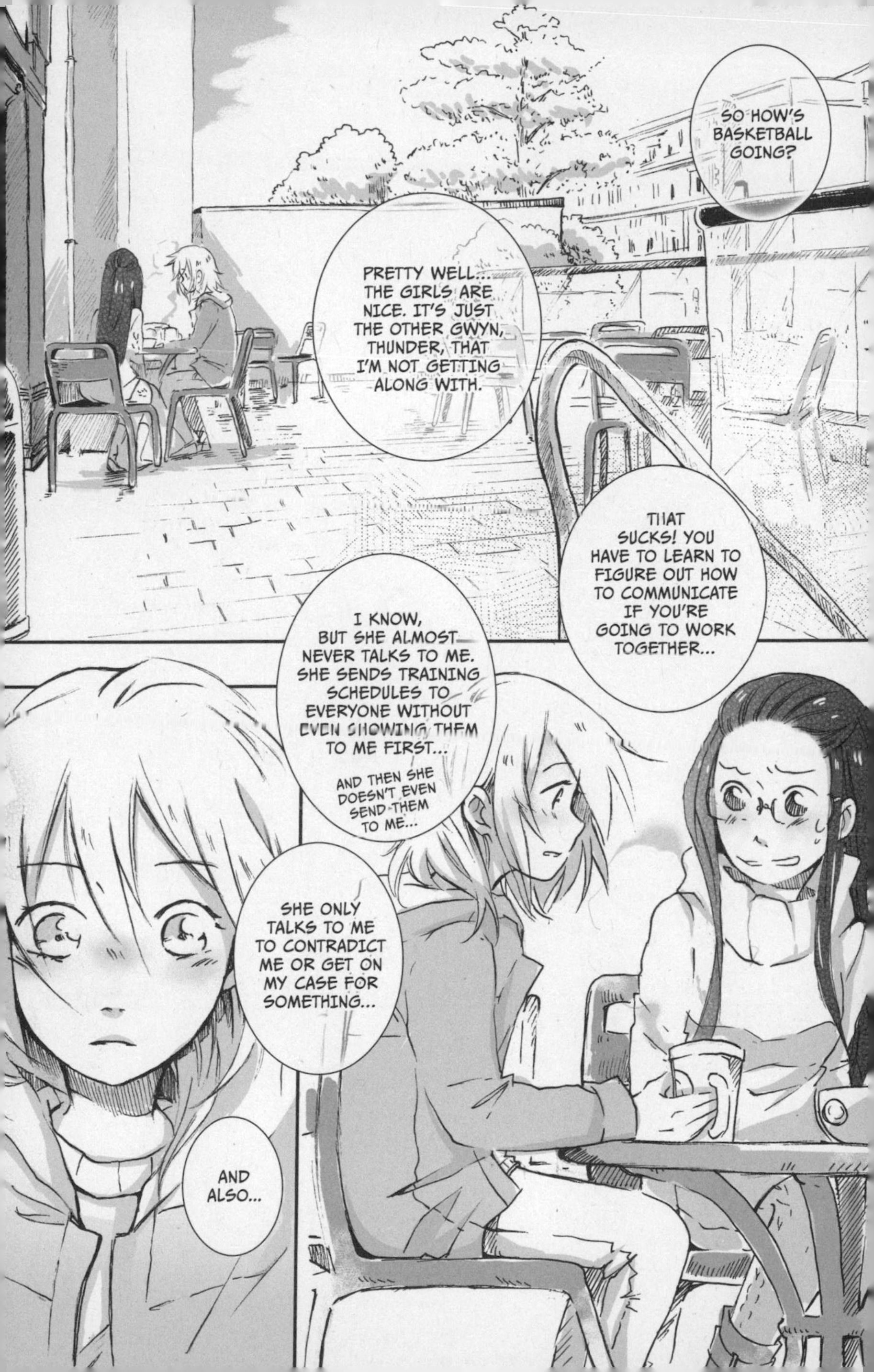
SO HOW'S BASKETBALL GOING?
PRETTY WELL... THE GIRLS ARE NICE. IT'S JUST THE OTHER GWYN, THUNDER, THAT I'M NOT GETTING ALONG WITH.
THAT SUCKS! YOU HAVE TO LEARN TO FIGURE OUT HOW TO COMMUNICATE IF YOU'RE GOING TO WORK TOGETHER...
I KNOW, BUT SHE ALMOST NEVER TALKS TO ME. SHE SENDS TRAINING SCHEDULES TO EVERYONE WITHOUT EVEN SHOWING THEM TO ME FIRST...
AND THEN SHE DOESN'T EVEN SEND THEM TO ME...
SHE ONLY TALKS TO ME TO CONTRADICT ME OR GET ON MY CASE FOR SOMETHING...
AND ALSO...

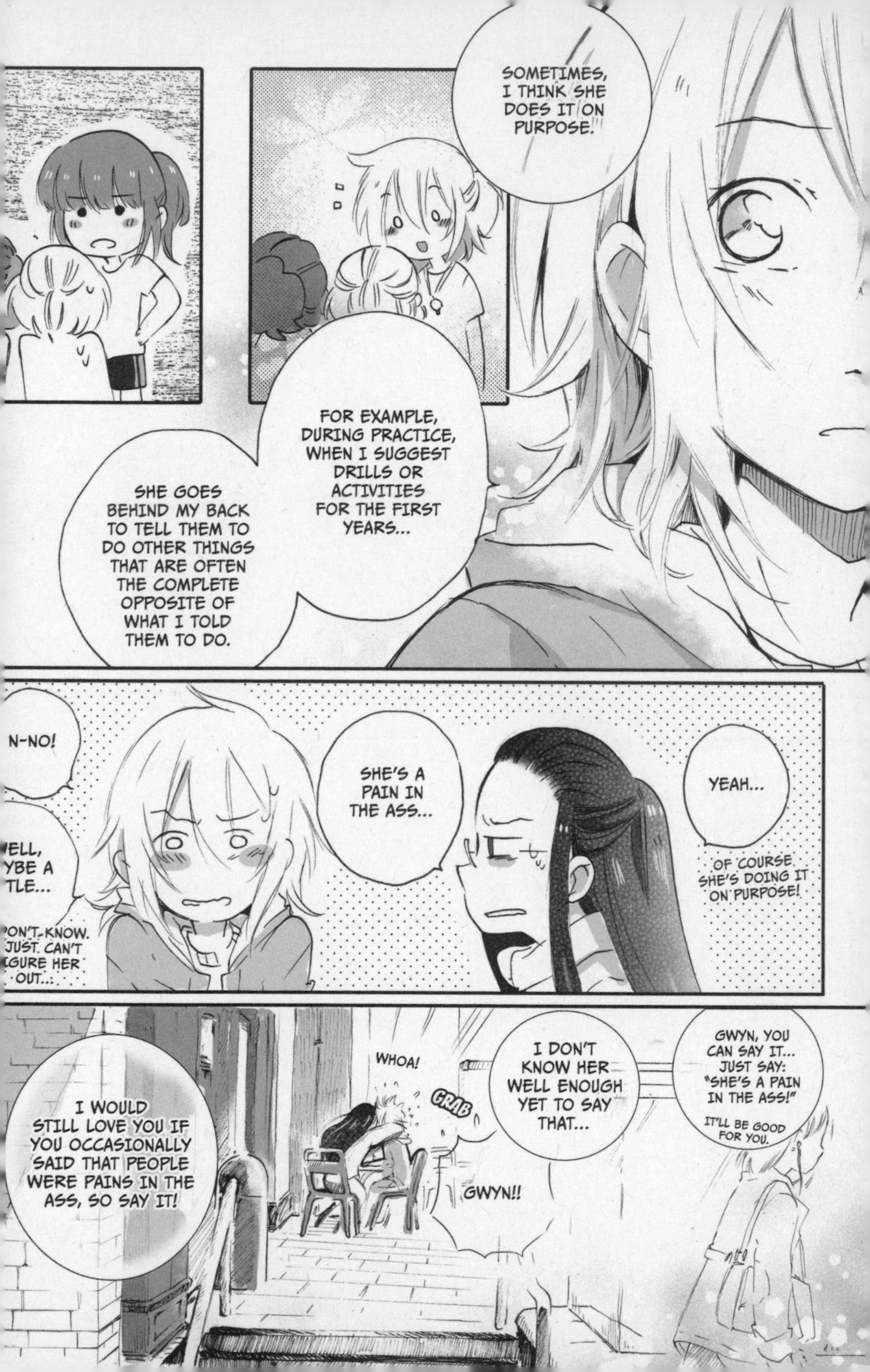
SOMETIMES, I THINK SHE DOES IT ON PURPOSE.
FOR EXAMPLE, DURING PRACTICE, WHEN I SUGGEST DRILLS OR ACTIVITIES FOR THE FIRST YEARS...
SHE GOES BEHIND MY BACK TO TELL THEM TO DO OTHER THINGS THAT ARE OFTEN THE COMPLETE OPPOSITE OF WHAT I TOLD THEM TO DO.
YEAH...
OF COURSE SHE'S DOING IT ON PURPOSE!
SHE'S A PAIN IN THE ASS...
N-NO!
ELL, YBE A TLE...
ON'T KNOW. JUST CAN'T IGURE HER OUT...
GWYN, YOU CAN SAY IT... JUST SAY: "SHE'S A PAIN IN THE ASS!"
IT'LL BE GOOD FOR YOU.
I DON'T KNOW HER WELL ENOUGH YET TO SAY THAT...
WHOA!
GRAB
GWYN!!
I WOULD STILL LOVE YOU IF YOU OCCASIONALLY SAID THAT PEOPLE WERE PAINS IN THE ASS, SO SAY IT!

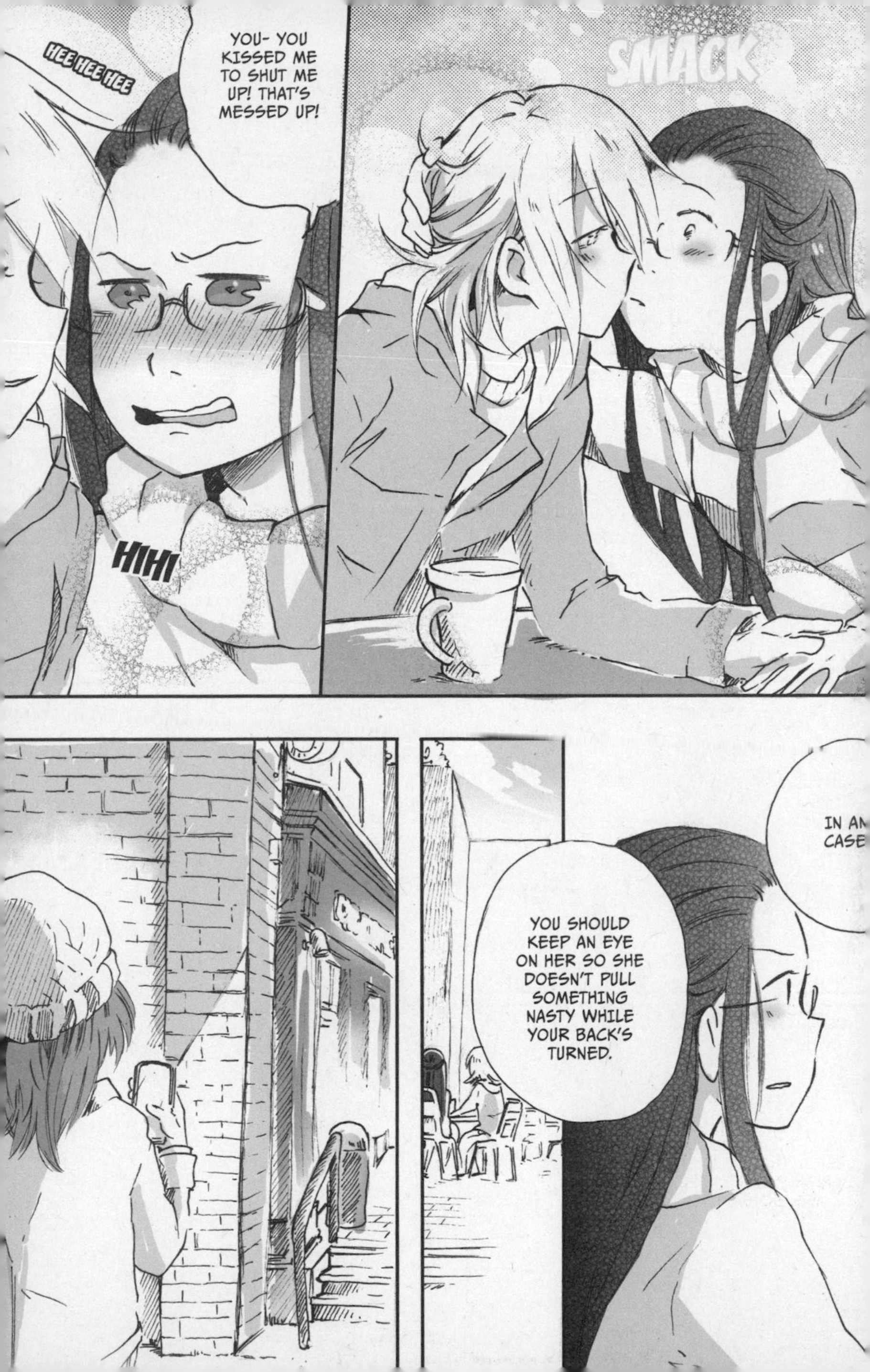
SMACK
YOU- YOU KISSED ME TO SHUT ME UP! THAT'S MESSED UP!
HEE HEE HEE
HIHI
IN AN CASE
YOU SHOULD KEEP AN EYE ON HER SO SHE DOESN'T PULL SOMETHING NASTY WHILE YOUR BACK'S TURNED.

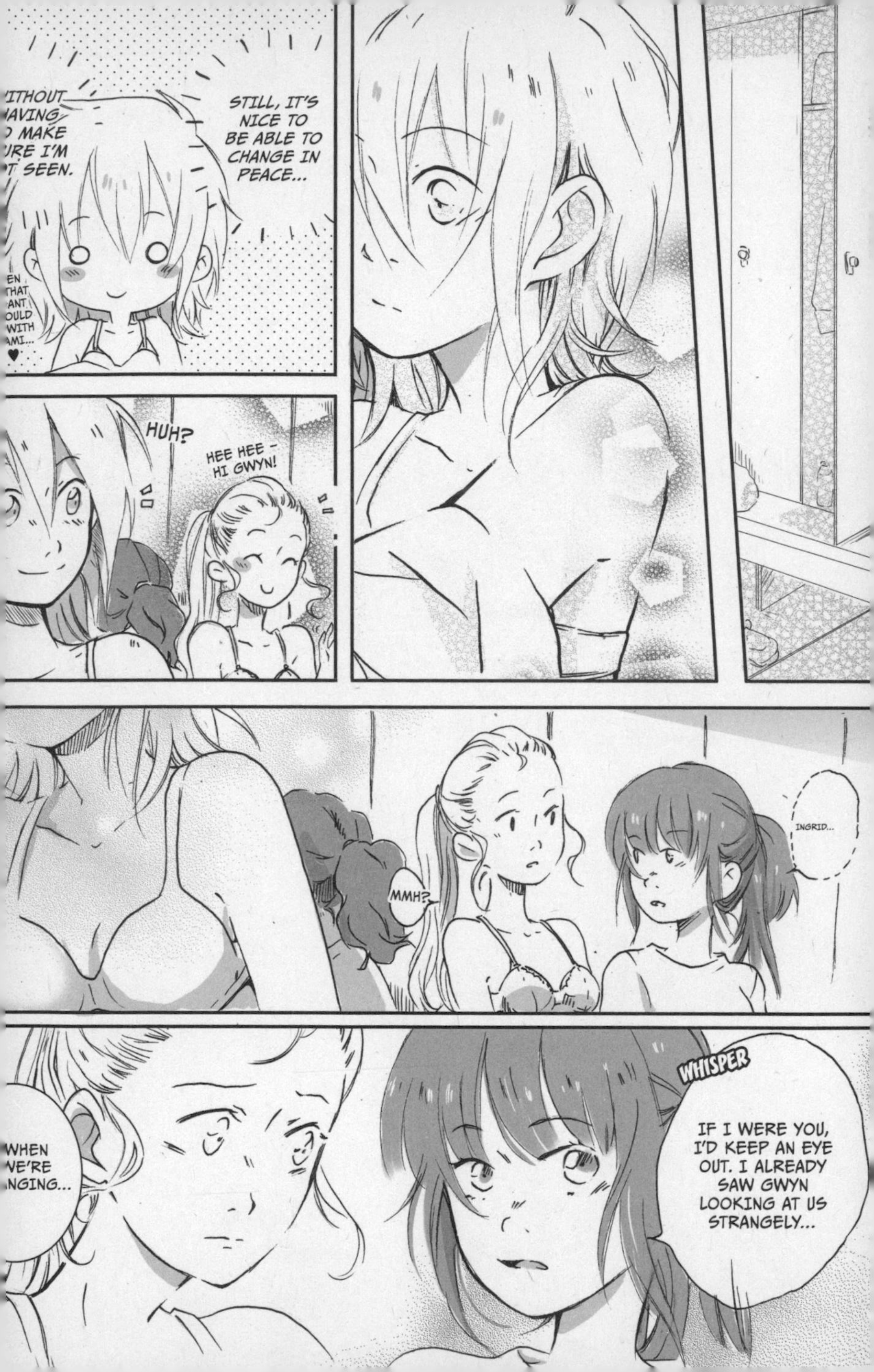
STILL, IT'S NICE TO BE ABLE TO CHANGE IN PEACE...
VITHOUT HAVING O MAKE URE I'M T SEEN.
EN THAT ANT OULD WITH AMI... ♥
HUH?
HEE HEE - HI GWYN!
INGRID...
MMH?
WHISPER
IF I WERE YOU, I'D KEEP AN EYE OUT. I ALREADY SAW GWYN LOOKING AT US STRANGELY...
WHEN VE'RE NGING...

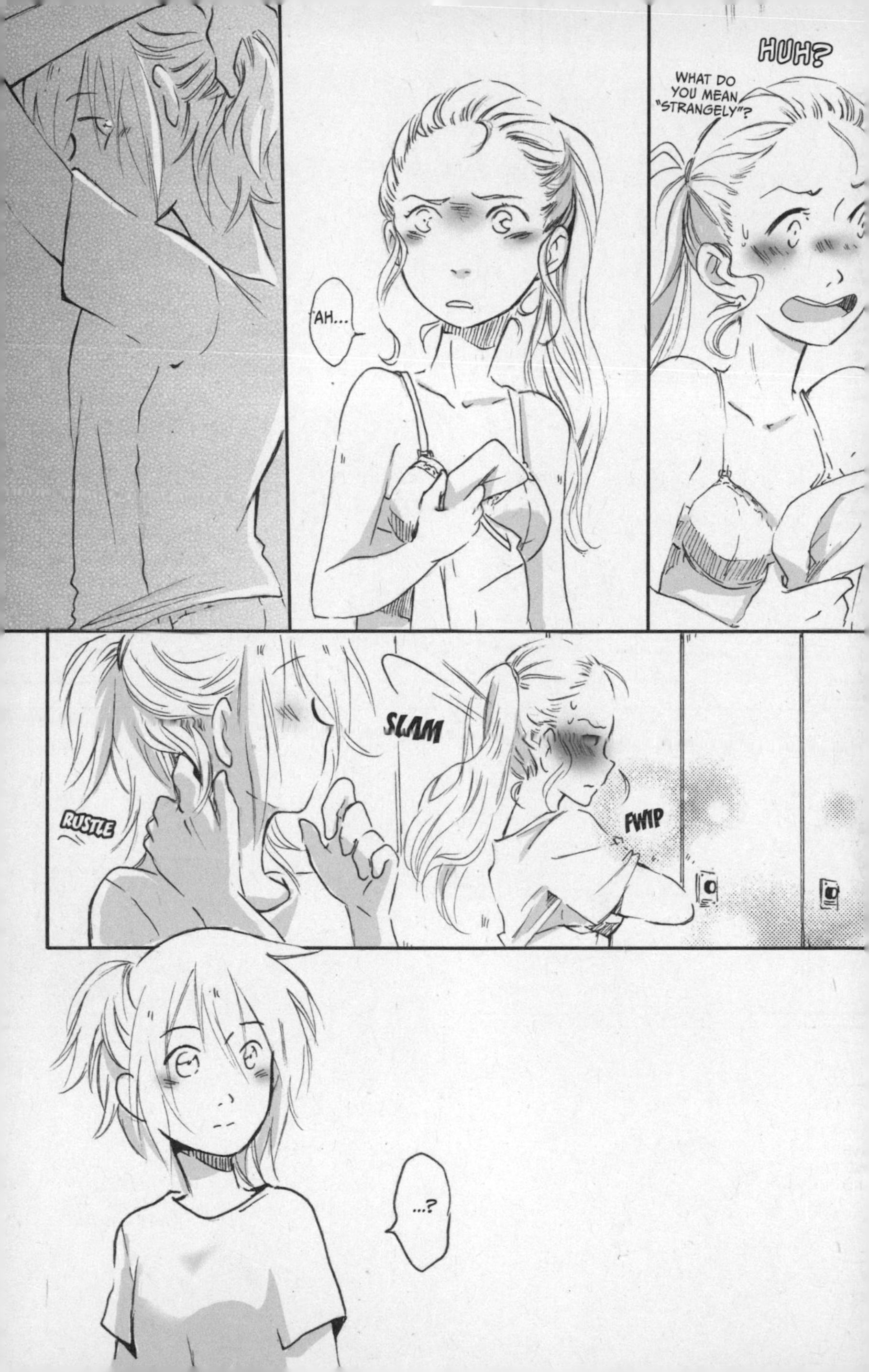
HUH?
WHAT DO YOU MEAN "STRANGELY"?
AH...
FWIP
SLAM
RUSTLE
...?

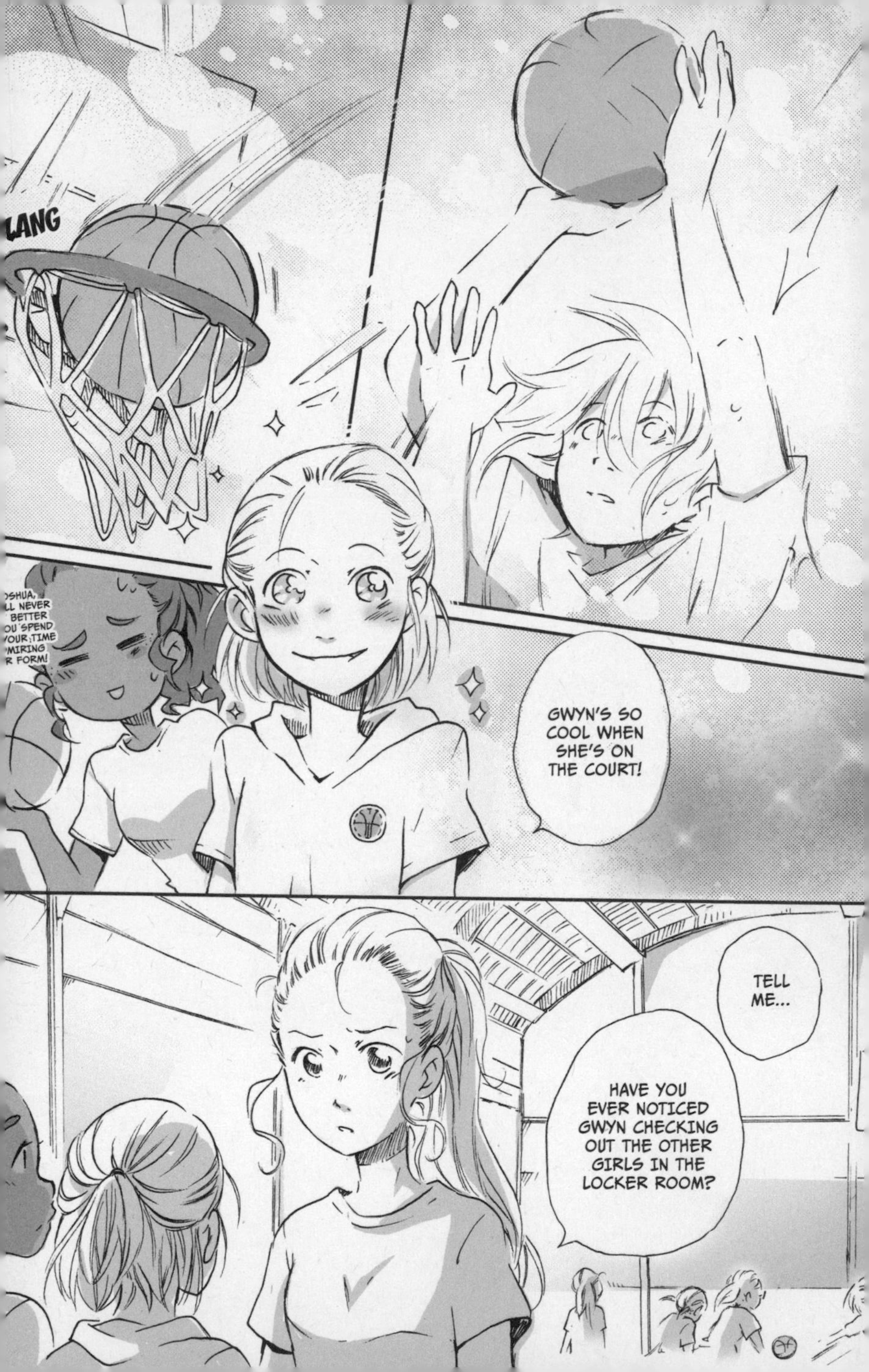
LANG
GWYN'S SO COOL WHEN SHE'S ON THE COURT!
TELL ME...
HAVE YOU EVER NOTICED GWYN CHECKING OUT THE OTHER GIRLS IN THE LOCKER ROOM?

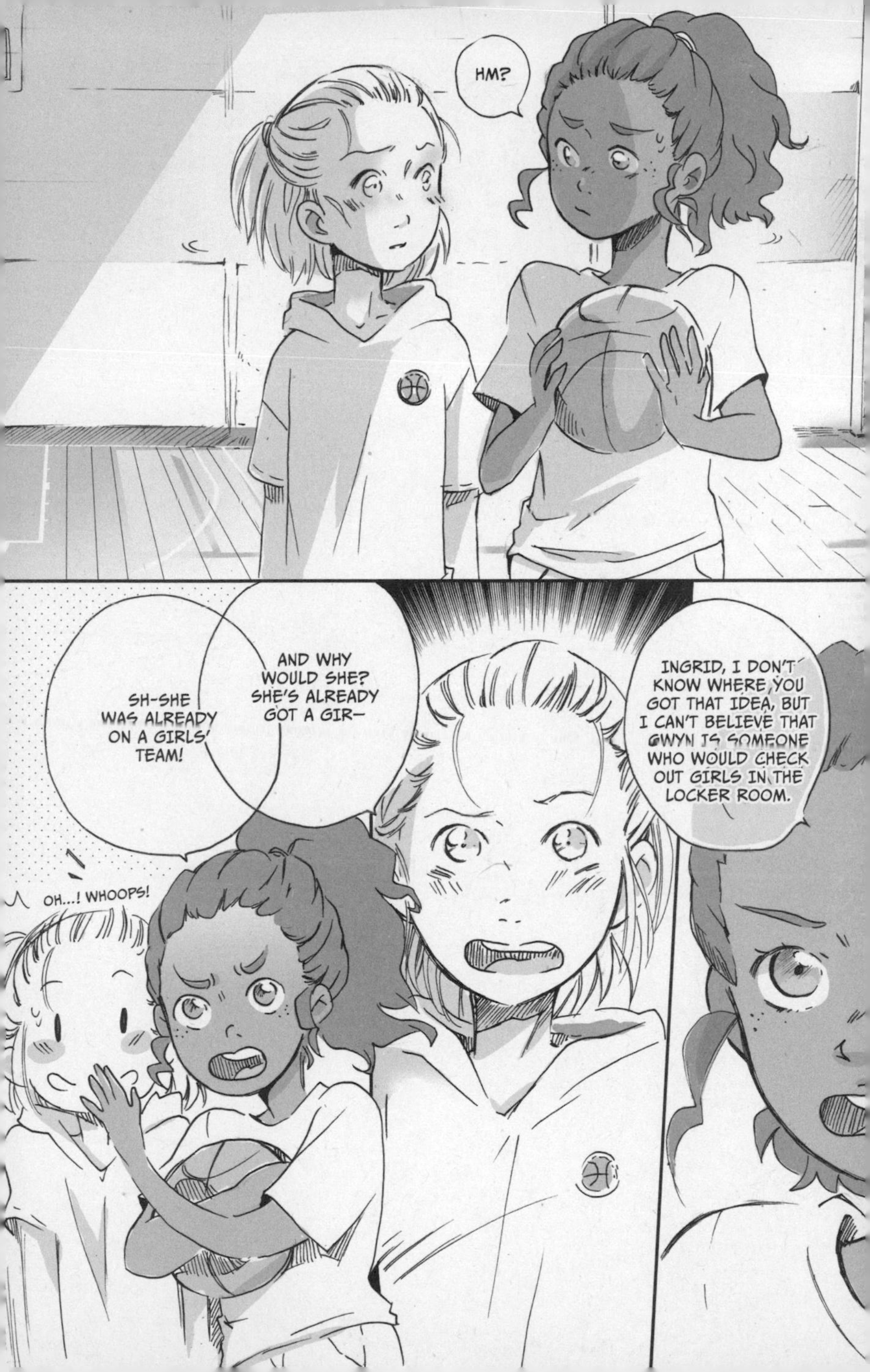
HM?
INGRID, I DON'T KNOW WHERE YOU GOT THAT IDEA, BUT I CAN'T BELIEVE THAT GWYN IS SOMEONE WHO WOULD CHECK OUT GIRLS IN THE LOCKER ROOM.
AND WHY WOULD SHE? SHE'S ALREADY GOT A GIR—
SH-SHE WAS ALREADY ON A GIRLS' TEAM!
OH...! WHOOPS!

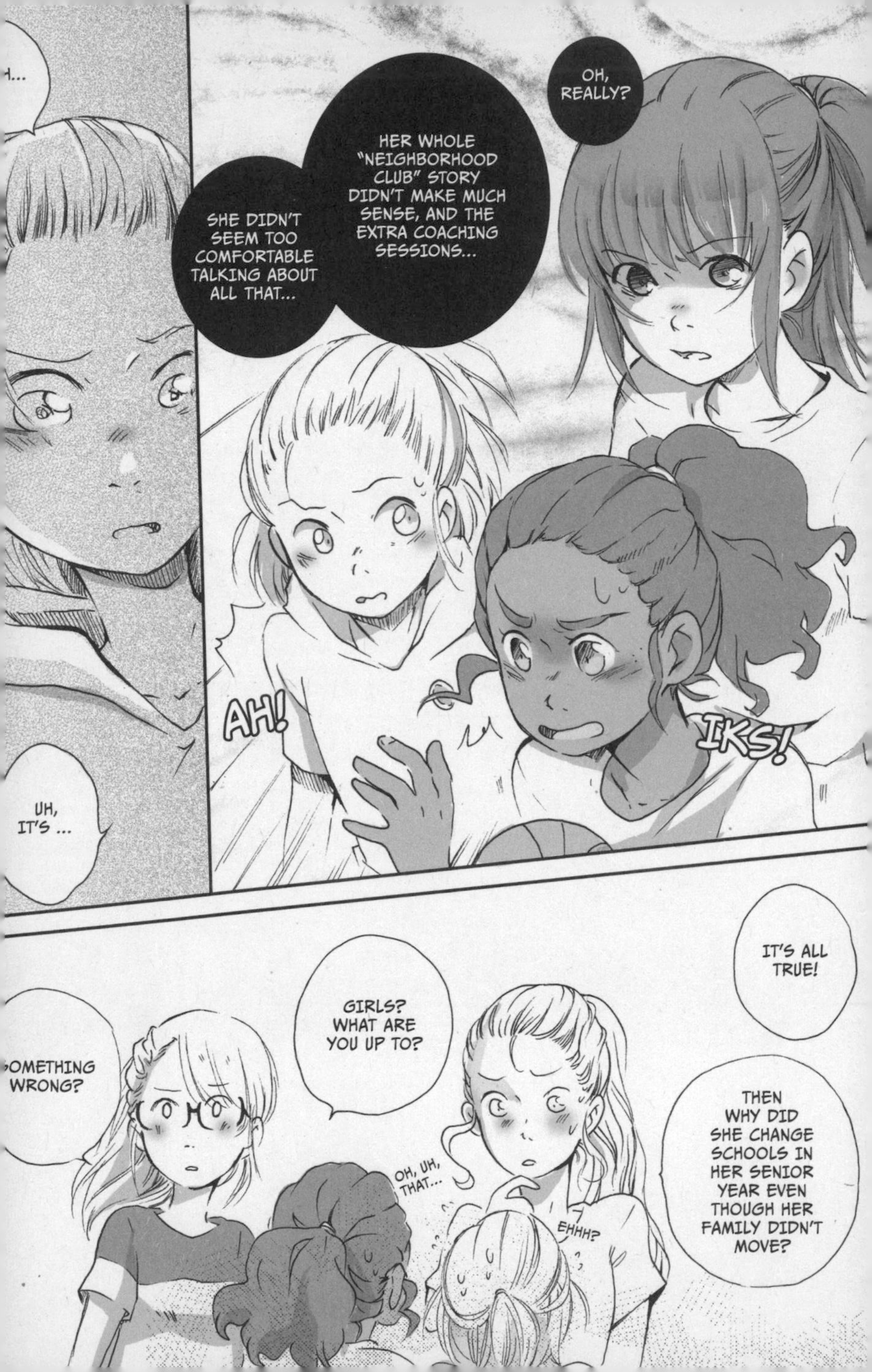
OH, REALLY?
HER WHOLE "NEIGHBORHOOD CLUB" STORY DIDN'T MAKE MUCH SENSE, AND THE EXTRA COACHING SESSIONS...
SHE DIDN'T SEEM TOO COMFORTABLE TALKING ABOUT ALL THAT...
IKS!
AH!
H...
UH, IT'S ...
IT'S ALL TRUE!
THEN WHY DID SHE CHANGE SCHOOLS IN HER SENIOR YEAR EVEN THOUGH HER FAMILY DIDN'T MOVE?
EHHH?
OH, UH, THAT...
GIRLS? WHAT ARE YOU UP TO?
OMETHING WRONG?

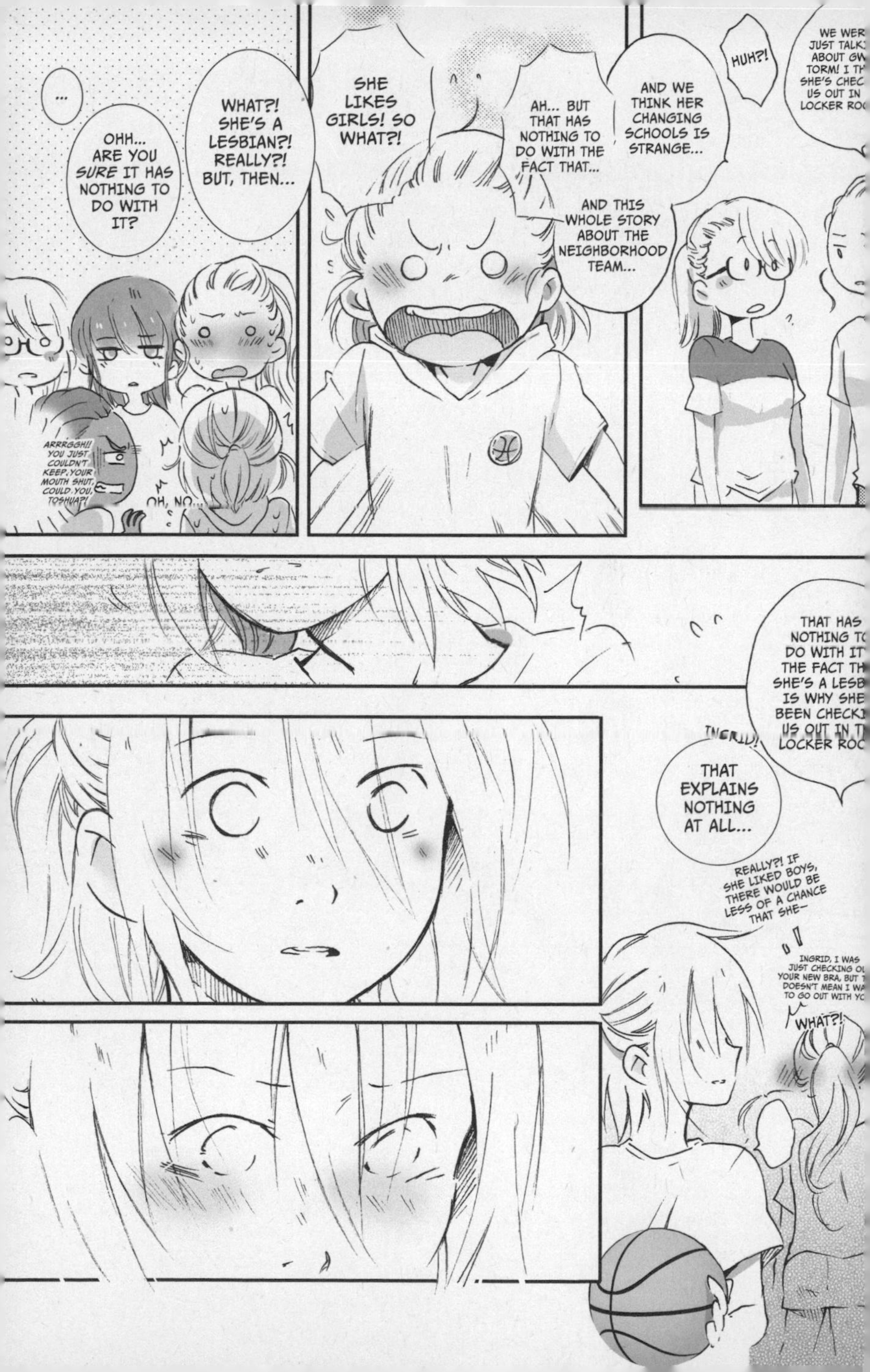
WE WER JUST TALK ABOUT GW TORM! I TH SHE'S CHEC US OUT IN LOCKER ROO
HUH?!
AND WE THINK HER CHANGING SCHOOLS IS STRANGE...
AH... BUT THAT HAS NOTHING TO DO WITH THE FACT THAT...
AND THIS WHOLE STORY ABOUT THE NEIGHBORHOOD TEAM...
SHE LIKES GIRLS! SO WHAT?!
WHAT?! SHE'S A LESBIAN?! REALLY?! BUT, THEN...
OHH... ARE YOU *SURE* IT HAS NOTHING TO DO WITH IT?
...
ARRRGGH!! YOU JUST COULDN'T KEEP YOUR MOUTH SHUT, COULD YOU, TOSHUA?!
OH, NO...
THAT HAS NOTHING TO DO WITH IT THE FACT TH SHE'S A LESB IS WHY SHE BEEN CHECKI US OUT IN T LOCKER ROO
INGRID!
THAT EXPLAINS NOTHING AT ALL...
REALLY?! IF SHE LIKED BOYS, THERE WOULD BE LESS OF A CHANCE THAT SHE—
INGRID, I WAS JUST CHECKING OU YOUR NEW BRA, BUT T DOESN'T MEAN I WA TO GO OUT WITH YO
WHAT?!

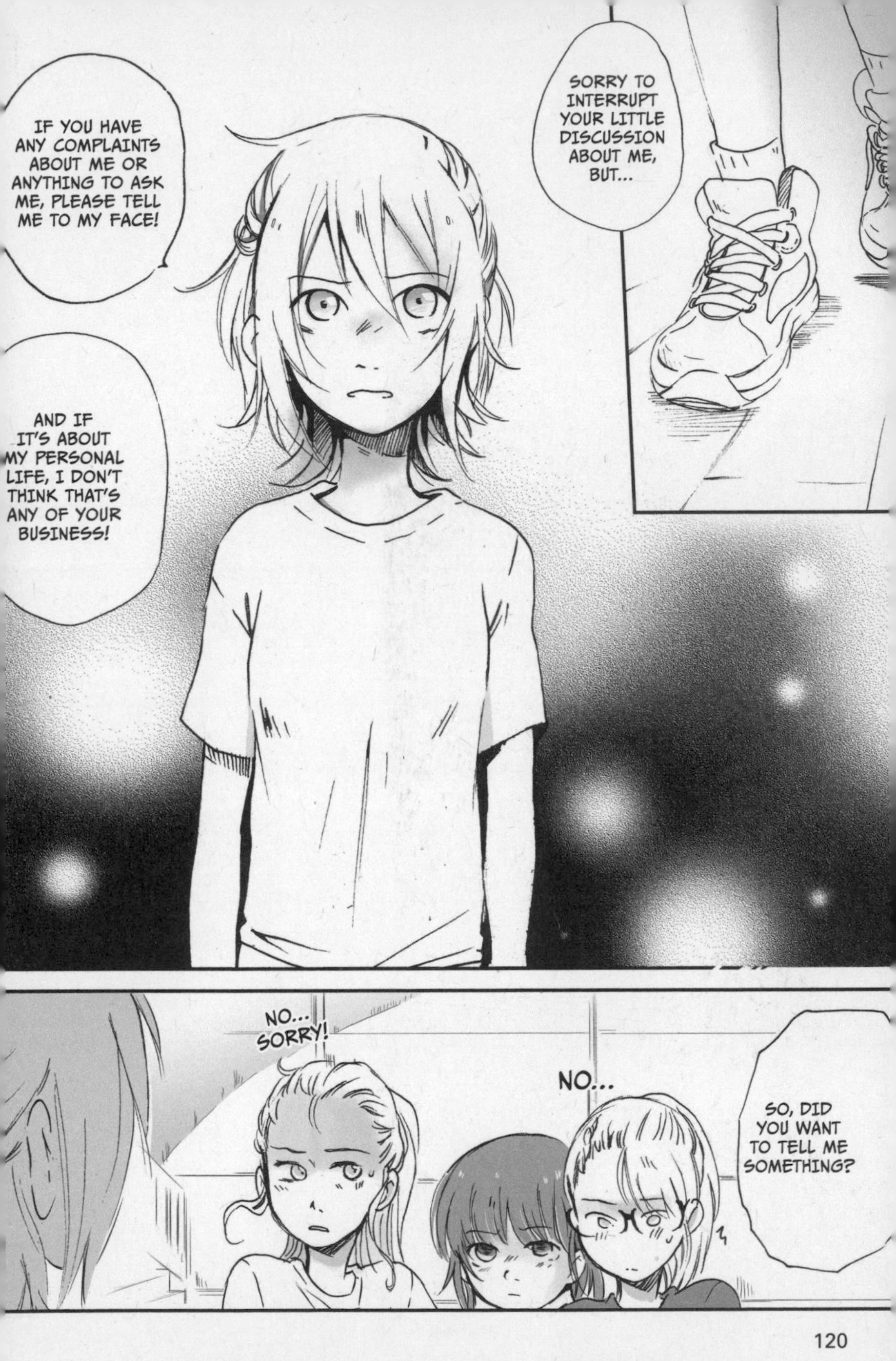
SORRY TO INTERRUPT YOUR LITTLE DISCUSSION ABOUT ME, BUT...
IF YOU HAVE ANY COMPLAINTS ABOUT ME OR ANYTHING TO ASK ME, PLEASE TELL ME TO MY FACE!
AND IF IT'S ABOUT MY PERSONAL LIFE, I DON'T THINK THAT'S ANY OF YOUR BUSINESS!
SO, DID YOU WANT TO TELL ME SOMETHING?
NO...
NO... SORRY!

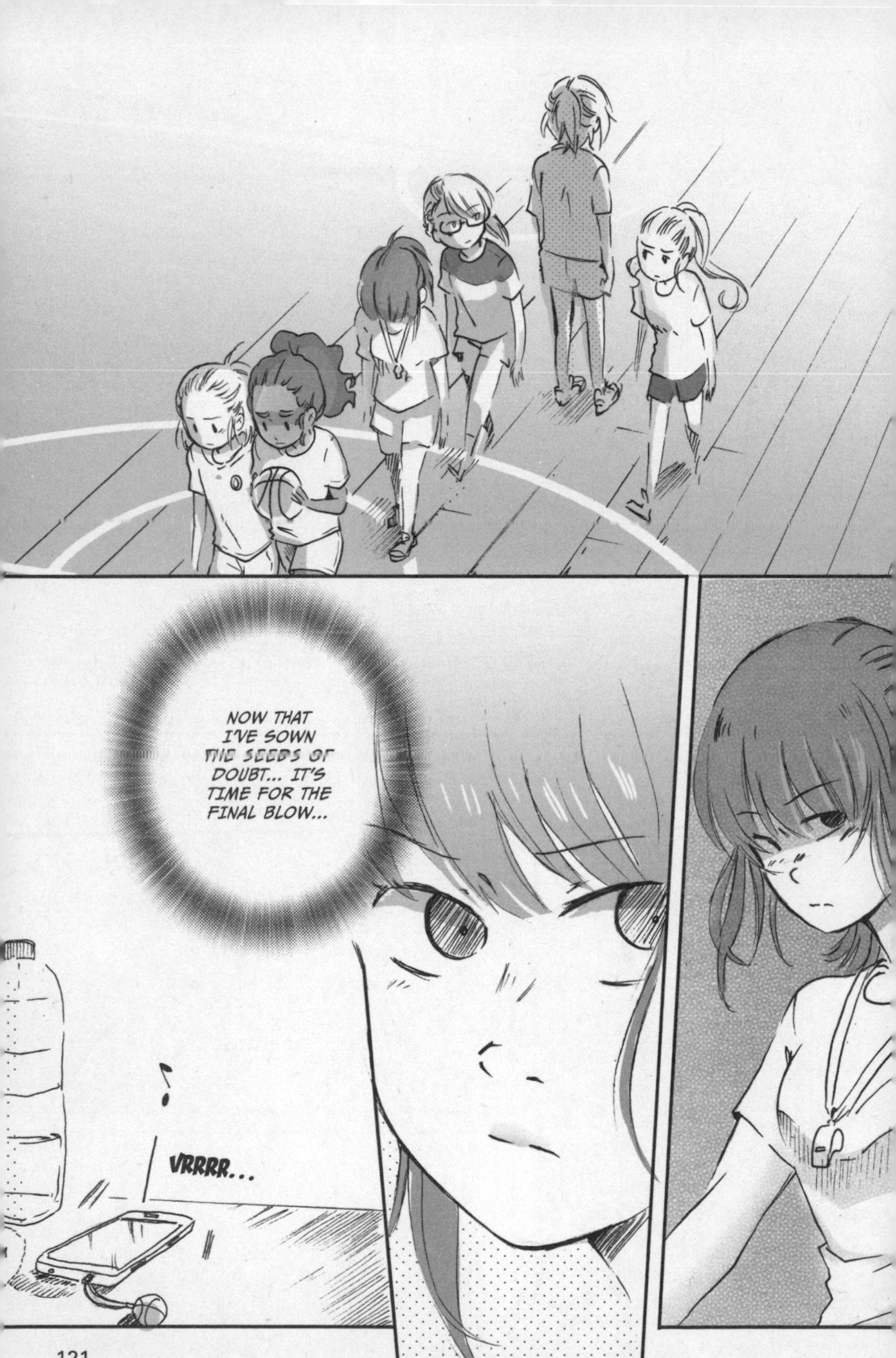
NOW THAT I'VE SOWN THE SEEDS OF DOUBT... IT'S TIME FOR THE FINAL BLOW...
VRRRR...

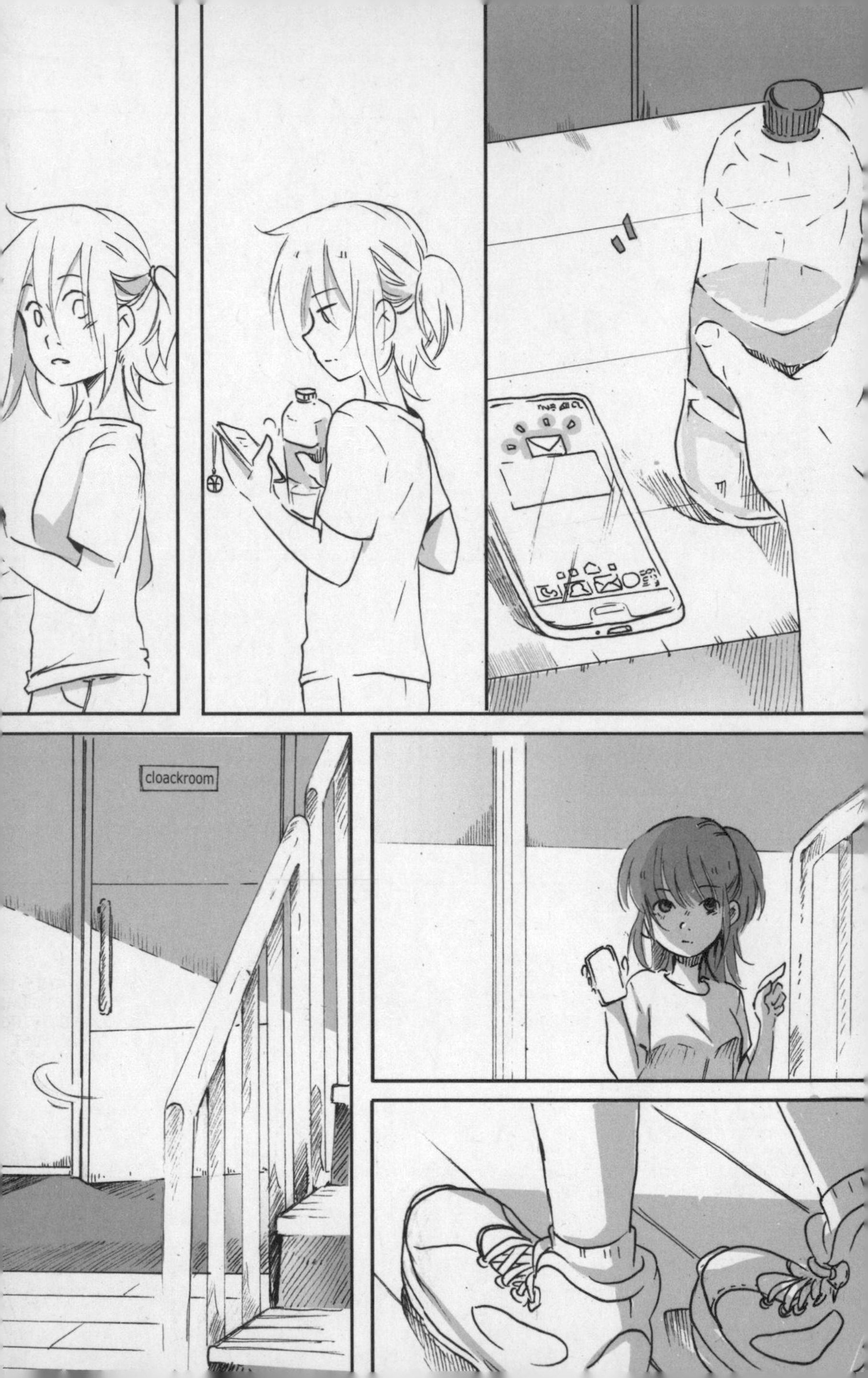
cloackroom

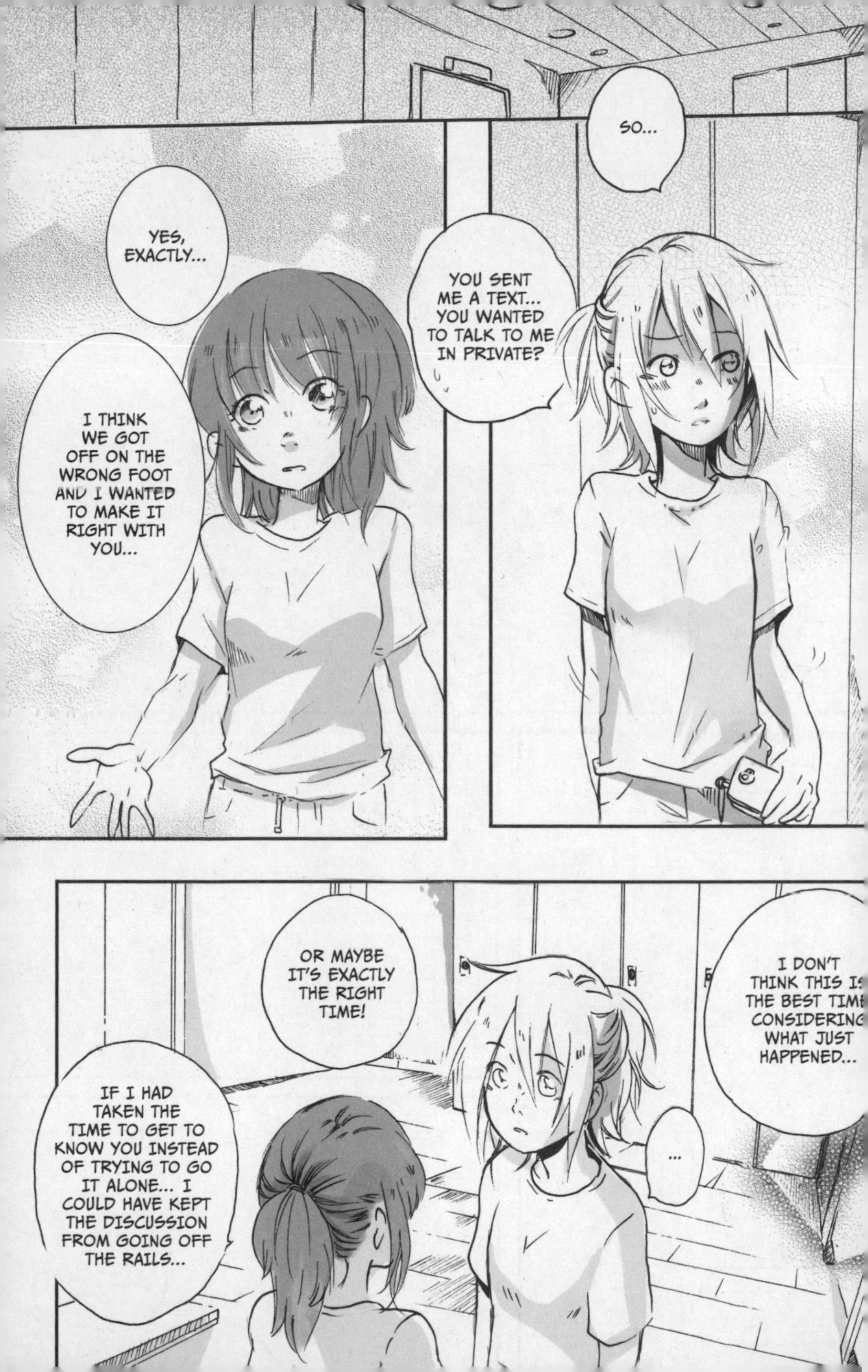
SO...
YOU SENT ME A TEXT... YOU WANTED TO TALK TO ME IN PRIVATE?
YES, EXACTLY...
I THINK WE GOT OFF ON THE WRONG FOOT AND I WANTED TO MAKE IT RIGHT WITH YOU...
I DON'T THINK THIS IS THE BEST TIME CONSIDERING WHAT JUST HAPPENED...
OR MAYBE IT'S EXACTLY THE RIGHT TIME!
...
IF I HAD TAKEN THE TIME TO GET TO KNOW YOU INSTEAD OF TRYING TO GO IT ALONE... I COULD HAVE KEPT THE DISCUSSION FROM GOING OFF THE RAILS...

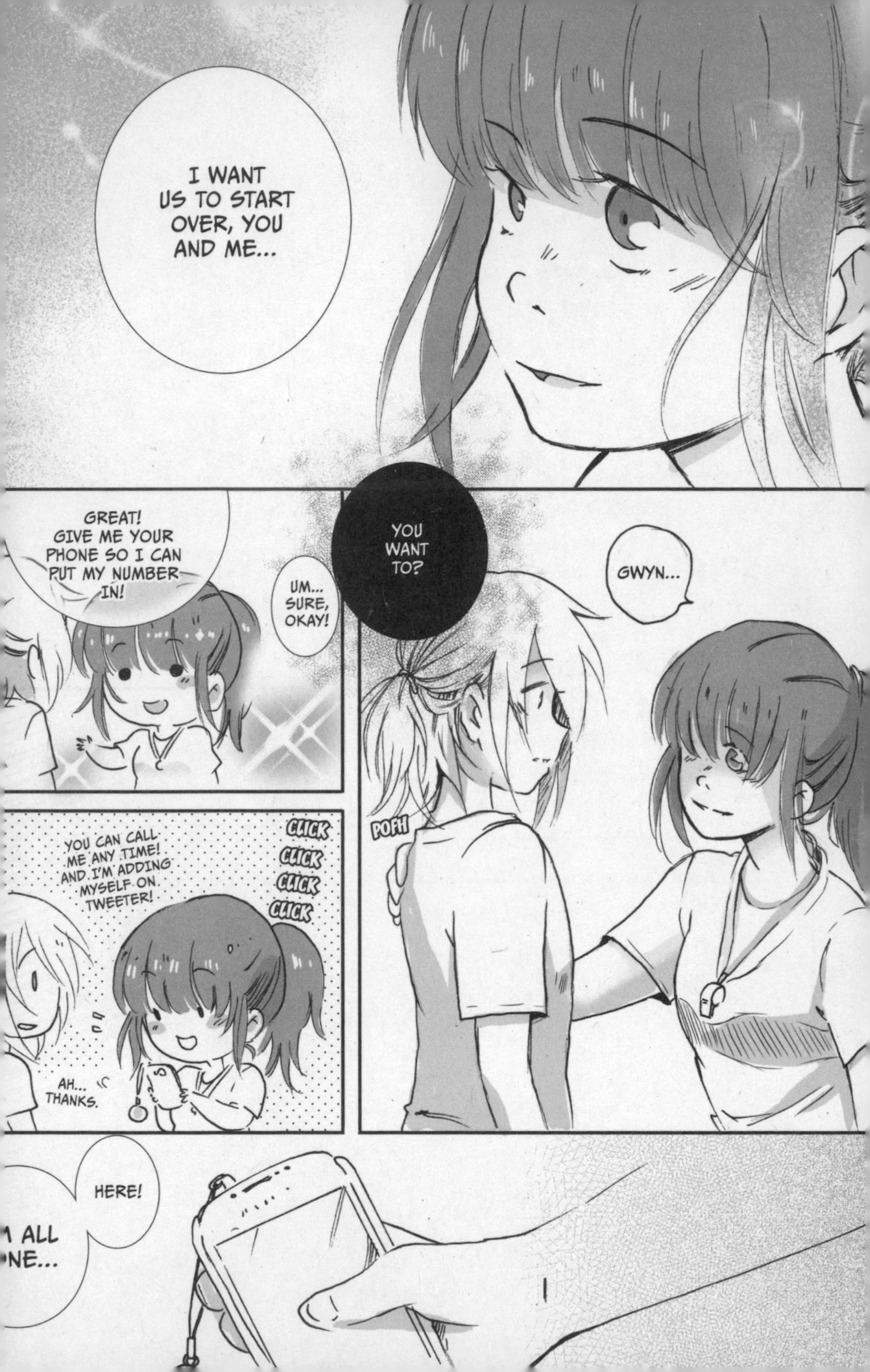
I WANT US TO START OVER, YOU AND ME...
GWYN...
YOU WANT TO?
POFH
UM... SURE, OKAY!
GREAT! GIVE ME YOUR PHONE SO I CAN PUT MY NUMBER IN!
CLICK
CLICK
CLICK
CLICK
YOU CAN CALL ME ANY TIME! AND I'M ADDING MYSELF ON TWEETER!
AH... THANKS.
HERE!
M ALL
NE...

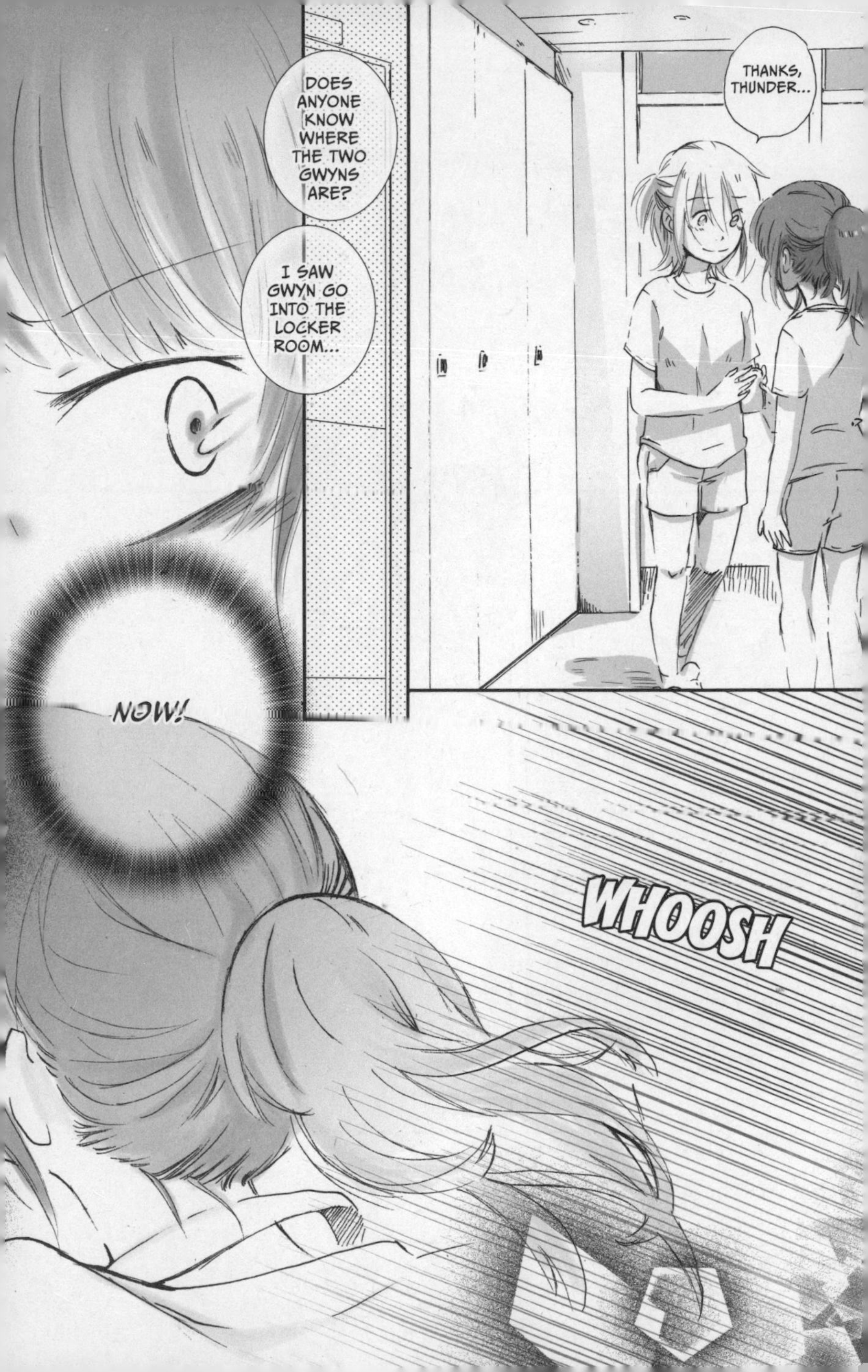
THANKS, THUNDER...
DOES ANYONE KNOW WHERE THE TWO GWYNS ARE?
I SAW GWYN GO INTO THE LOCKER ROOM...
NOW!
WHOOSH

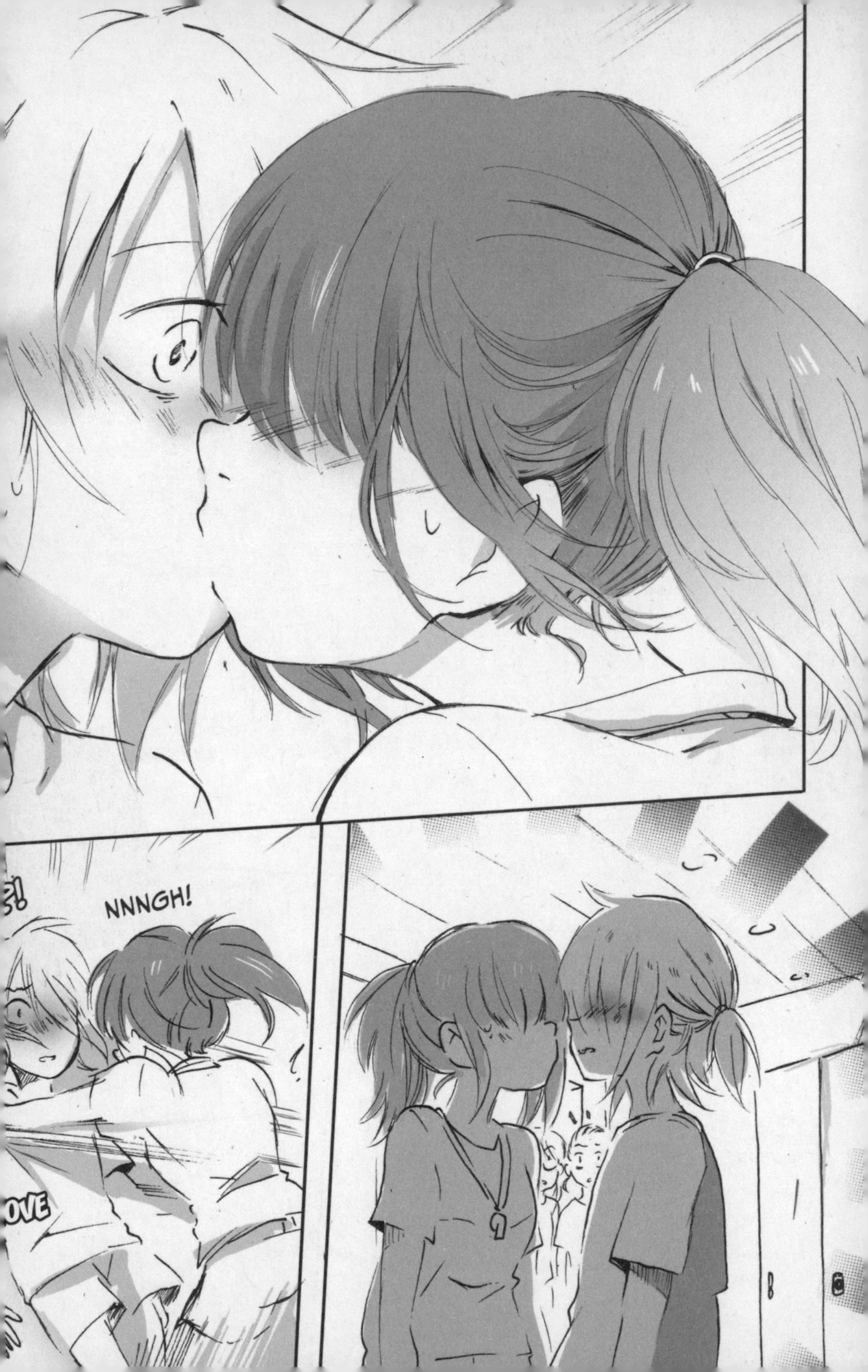
NNNGH!
OVE

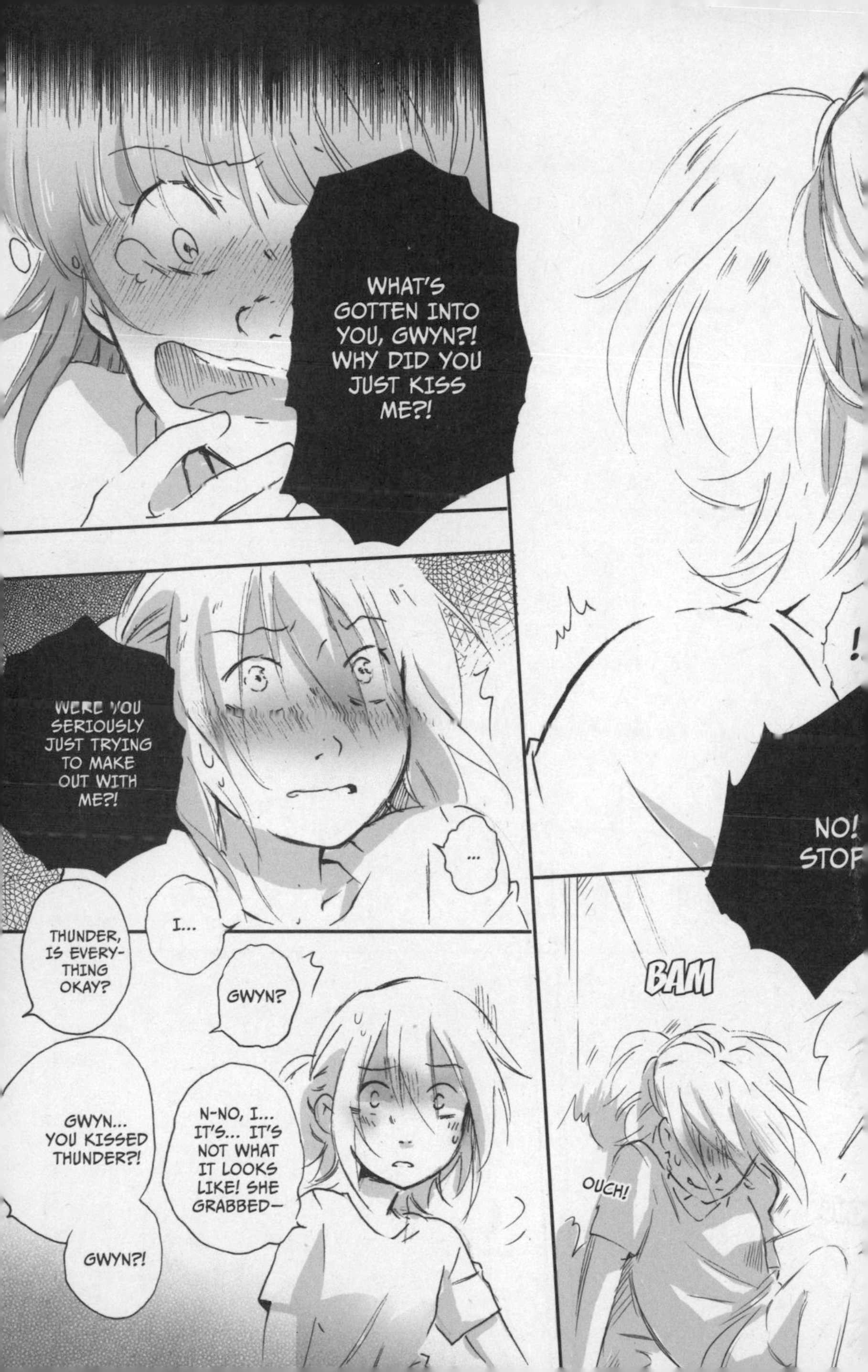
!
NO! STOP
BAM
OUCH!
WHAT'S GOTTEN INTO YOU, GWYN?! WHY DID YOU JUST KISS ME?!
WERE YOU SERIOUSLY JUST TRYING TO MAKE OUT WITH ME?!
...
I...
THUNDER, IS EVERY-THING OKAY?
GWYN?
GWYN... YOU KISSED THUNDER?!
GWYN?!
N-NO, I... IT'S... IT'S NOT WHAT IT LOOKS LIKE! SHE GRABBED—

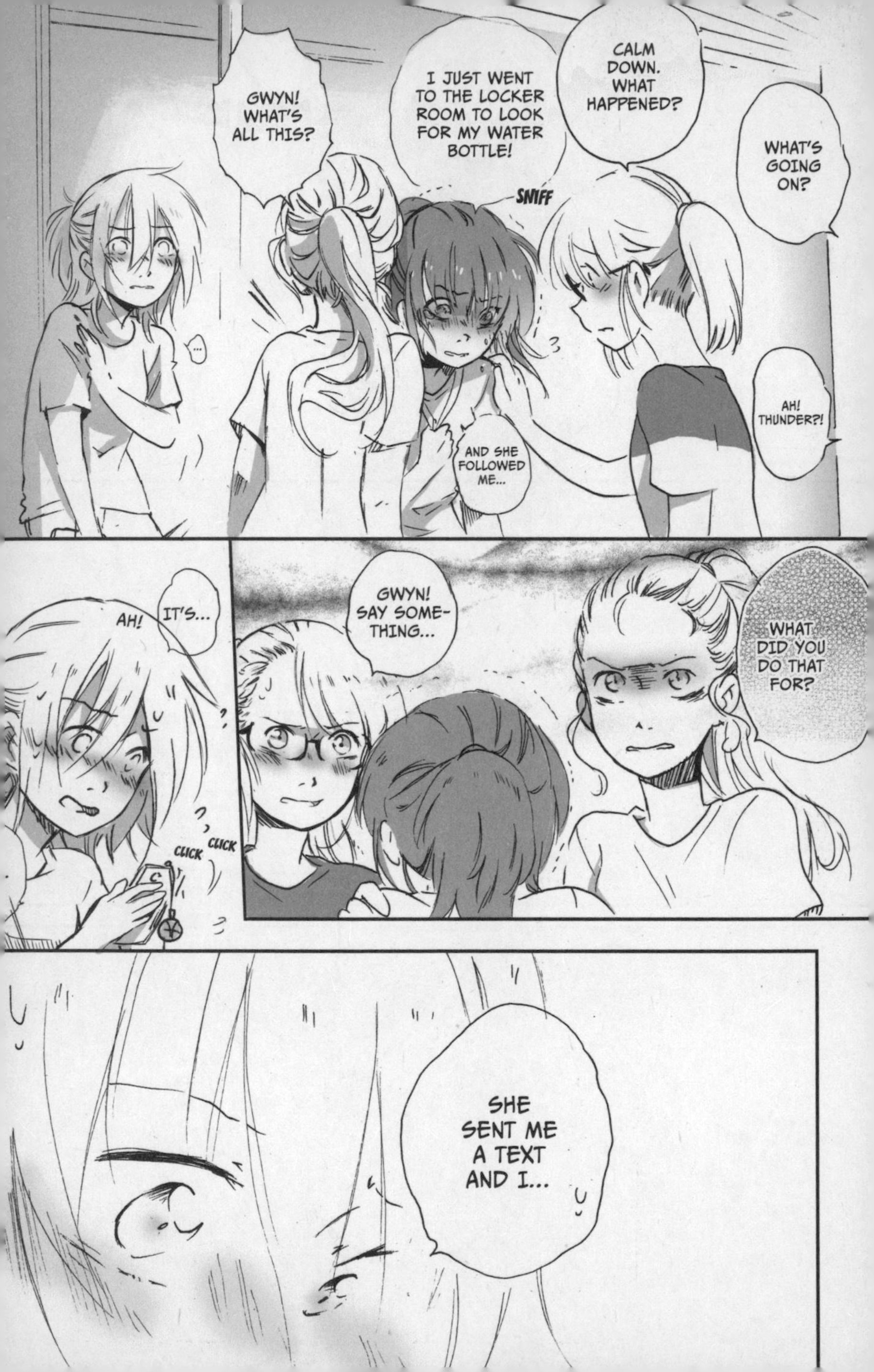

WHAT'S GOING ON?
CALM DOWN. WHAT HAPPENED?
I JUST WENT TO THE LOCKER ROOM TO LOOK FOR MY WATER BOTTLE!
SNIFF
GWYN! WHAT'S ALL THIS?
AH! THUNDER?!
AND SHE FOLLOWED ME...
...
WHAT DID YOU DO THAT FOR?
GWYN! SAY SOMETHING...
IT'S...
AH!
CLICK
CLICK
SHE SENT ME A TEXT AND I...

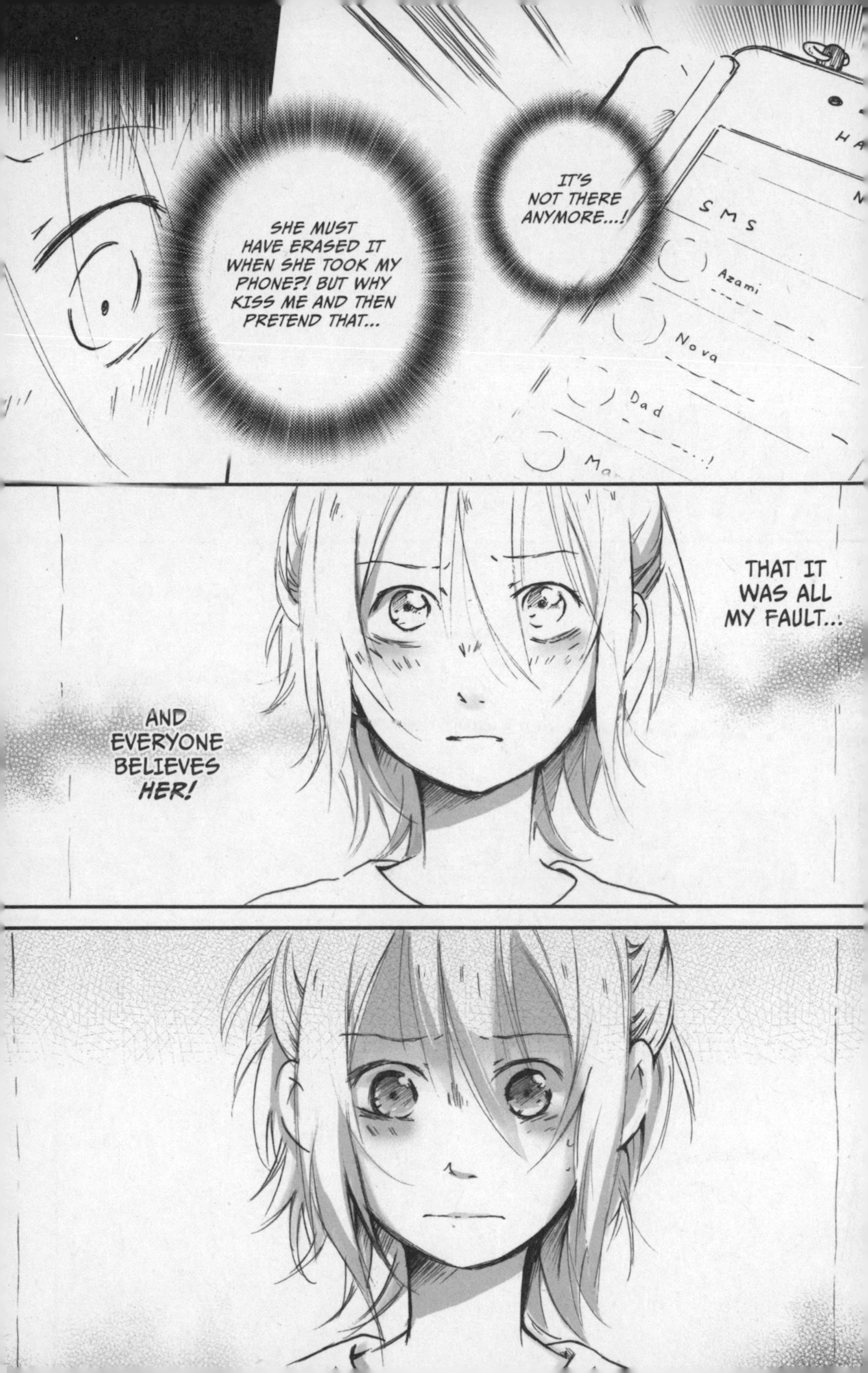
IT'S NOT THERE ANYMORE...!
SMS
Azami
Nova
Dad
SHE MUST HAVE ERASED IT WHEN SHE TOOK MY PHONE?! BUT WHY KISS ME AND THEN PRETEND THAT...
THAT IT WAS ALL MY FAULT...
AND EVERYONE BELIEVES HER!

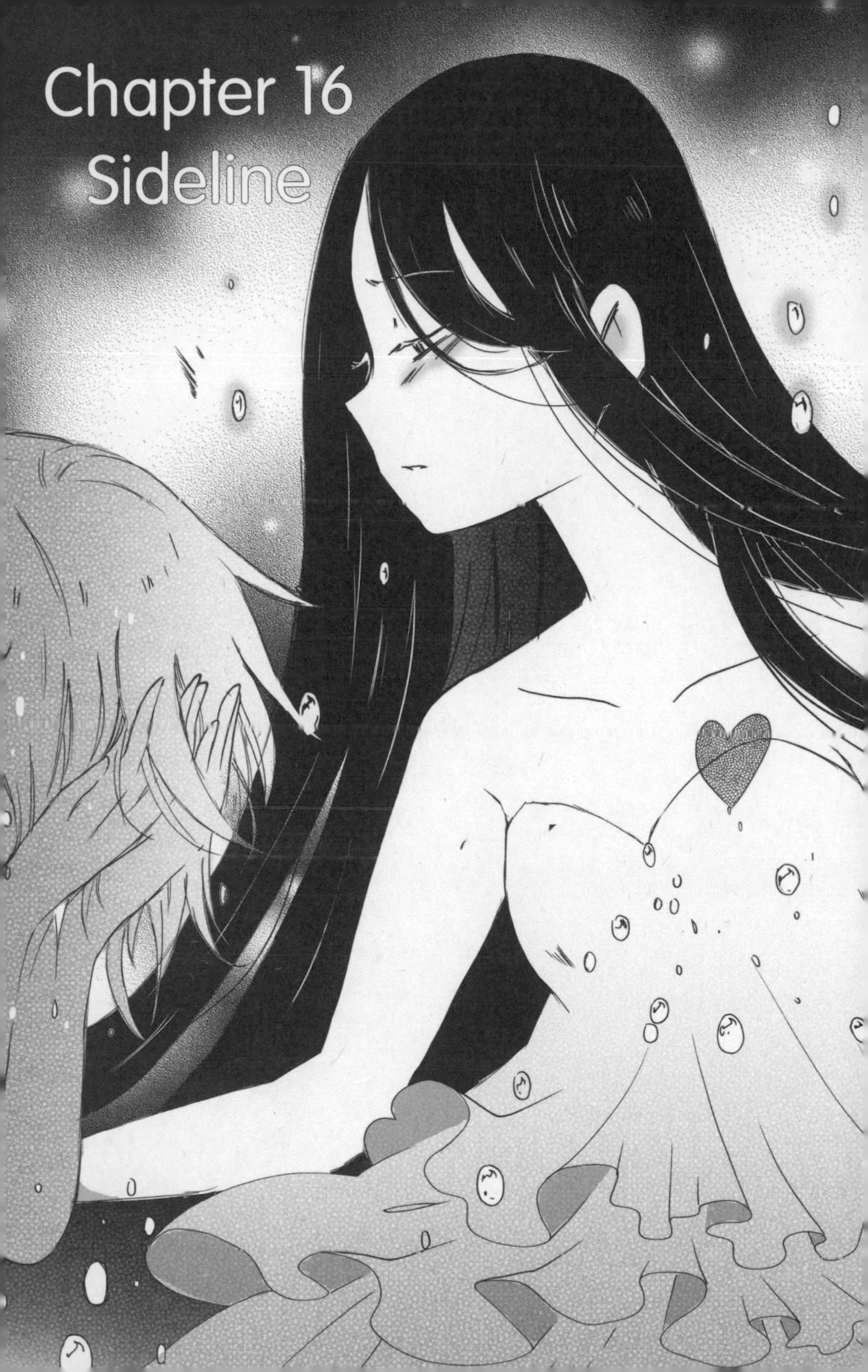
Chapter 16
Sideline

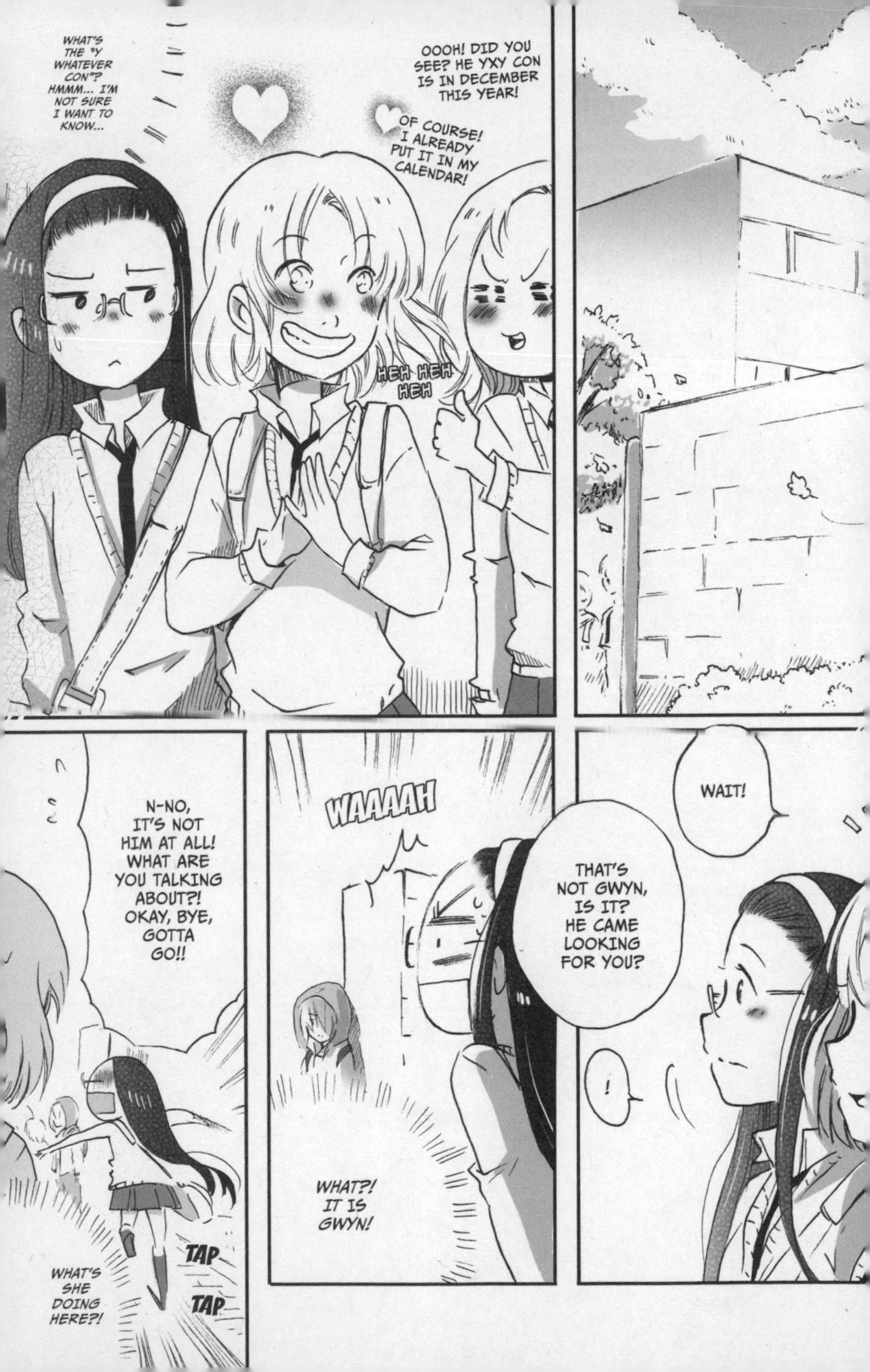
OOOH! DID YOU SEE? HE YXY CON IS IN DECEMBER THIS YEAR!
OF COURSE! I ALREADY PUT IT IN MY CALENDAR!
HEH HEH HEH
WHAT'S THE "Y WHATEVER CON"? HMMM... I'M NOT SURE I WANT TO KNOW...
WAIT!
THAT'S NOT GWYN, IS IT? HE CAME LOOKING FOR YOU?
!
WAAAAH
WHAT?! IT IS GWYN!
N-NO, IT'S NOT HIM AT ALL! WHAT ARE YOU TALKING ABOUT?! OKAY, BYE, GOTTA GO!!
TAP
TAP
WHAT'S SHE DOING HERE?!

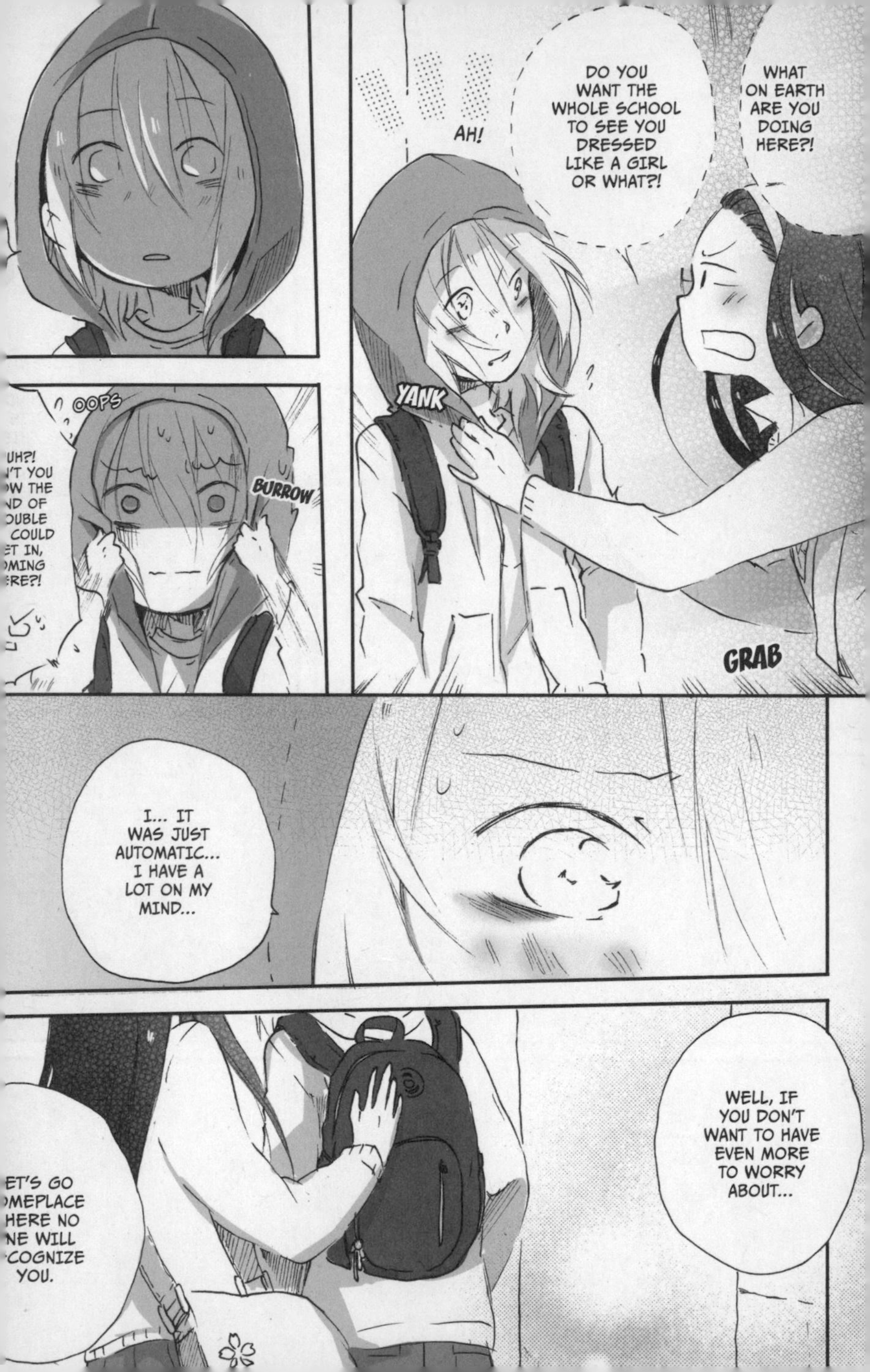
WHAT ON EARTH ARE YOU DOING HERE?!
DO YOU WANT THE WHOLE SCHOOL TO SEE YOU DRESSED LIKE A GIRL OR WHAT?!
AH!
YANK
GRAB
OOPS
UH?! 'T YOU W THE ND OF OUBLE COULD ET IN, OMING ERE?!
BURROW
I... IT WAS JUST AUTOMATIC... I HAVE A LOT ON MY MIND...
WELL, IF YOU DON'T WANT TO HAVE EVEN MORE TO WORRY ABOUT...
ET'S GO OMEPLACE HERE NO NE WILL COGNIZE YOU.

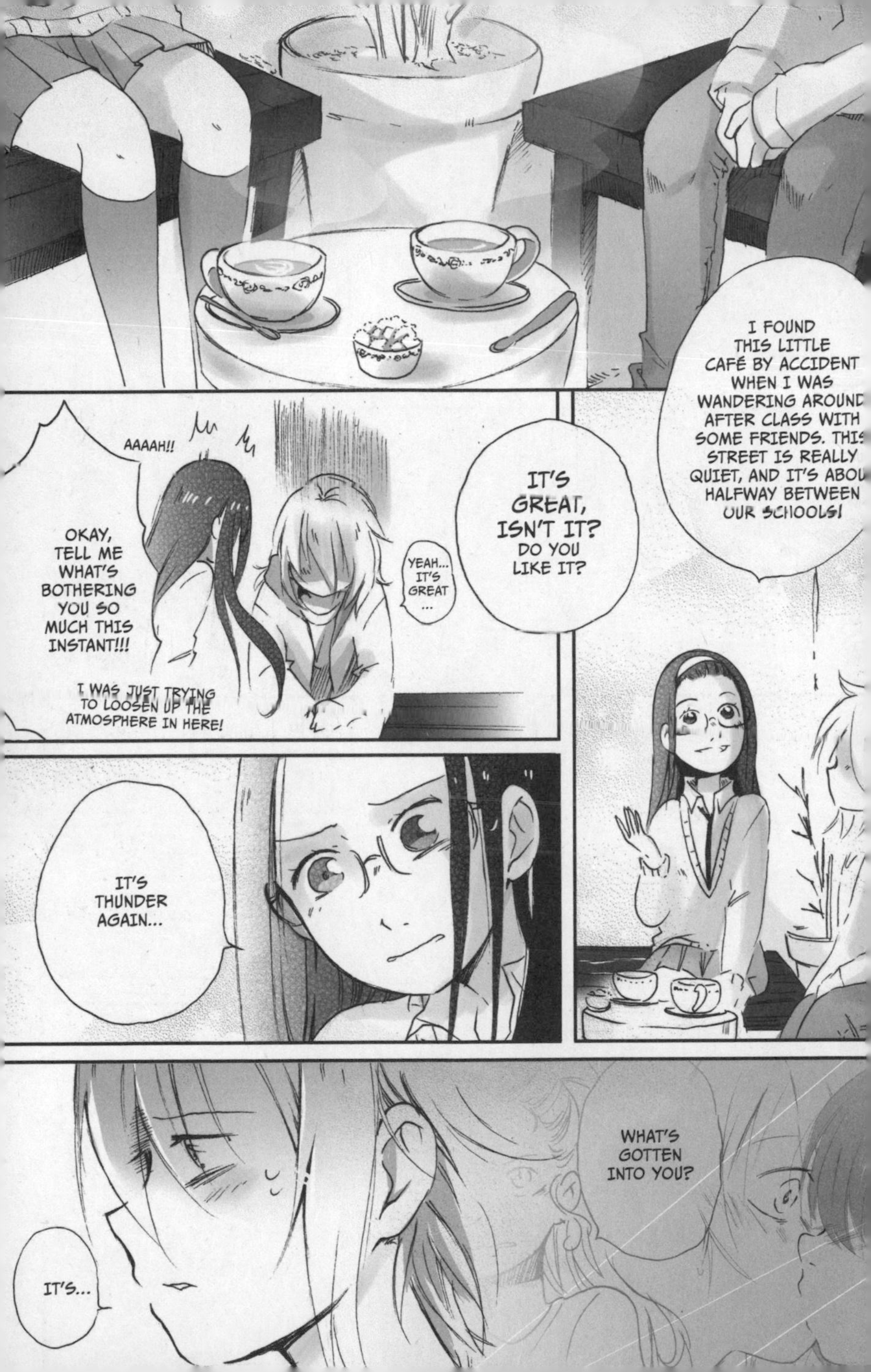
I FOUND THIS LITTLE CAFÉ BY ACCIDENT WHEN I WAS WANDERING AROUND AFTER CLASS WITH SOME FRIENDS. THIS STREET IS REALLY QUIET, AND IT'S ABOU HALFWAY BETWEEN OUR SCHOOLS!
IT'S GREAT, ISN'T IT? DO YOU LIKE IT?
YEAH... IT'S GREAT ...
AAAAH!!
OKAY, TELL ME WHAT'S BOTHERING YOU SO MUCH THIS INSTANT!!!
I WAS JUST TRYING TO LOOSEN UP THE ATMOSPHERE IN HERE!
IT'S THUNDER AGAIN...
WHAT'S GOTTEN INTO YOU?
IT'S...

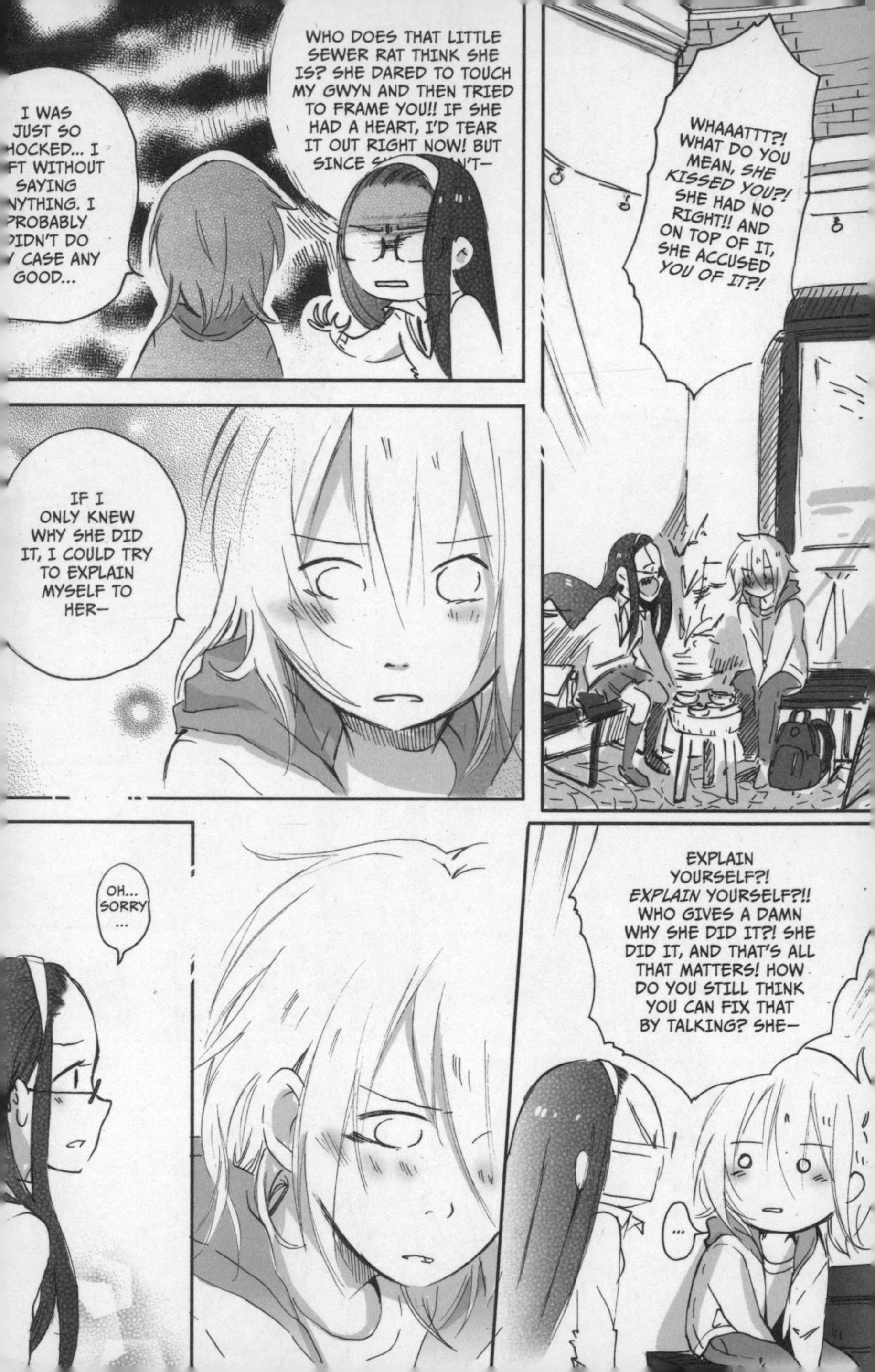
WHAAATTT?! WHAT DO YOU MEAN, SHE KISSED YOU?! SHE HAD NO RIGHT!! AND ON TOP OF IT, SHE ACCUSED YOU OF IT?!
WHO DOES THAT LITTLE SEWER RAT THINK SHE IS? SHE DARED TO TOUCH MY GWYN AND THEN TRIED TO FRAME YOU!! IF SHE HAD A HEART, I'D TEAR IT OUT RIGHT NOW! BUT SINCE SH N'T—
I WAS JUST SO HOCKED... I FT WITHOUT SAYING NYTHING. I PROBABLY IDN'T DO CASE ANY GOOD...
IF I ONLY KNEW WHY SHE DID IT, I COULD TRY TO EXPLAIN MYSELF TO HER—
EXPLAIN YOURSELF?! EXPLAIN YOURSELF?!! WHO GIVES A DAMN WHY SHE DID IT?! SHE DID IT, AND THAT'S ALL THAT MATTERS! HOW DO YOU STILL THINK YOU CAN FIX THAT BY TALKING? SHE—
...
OH... SORRY ...

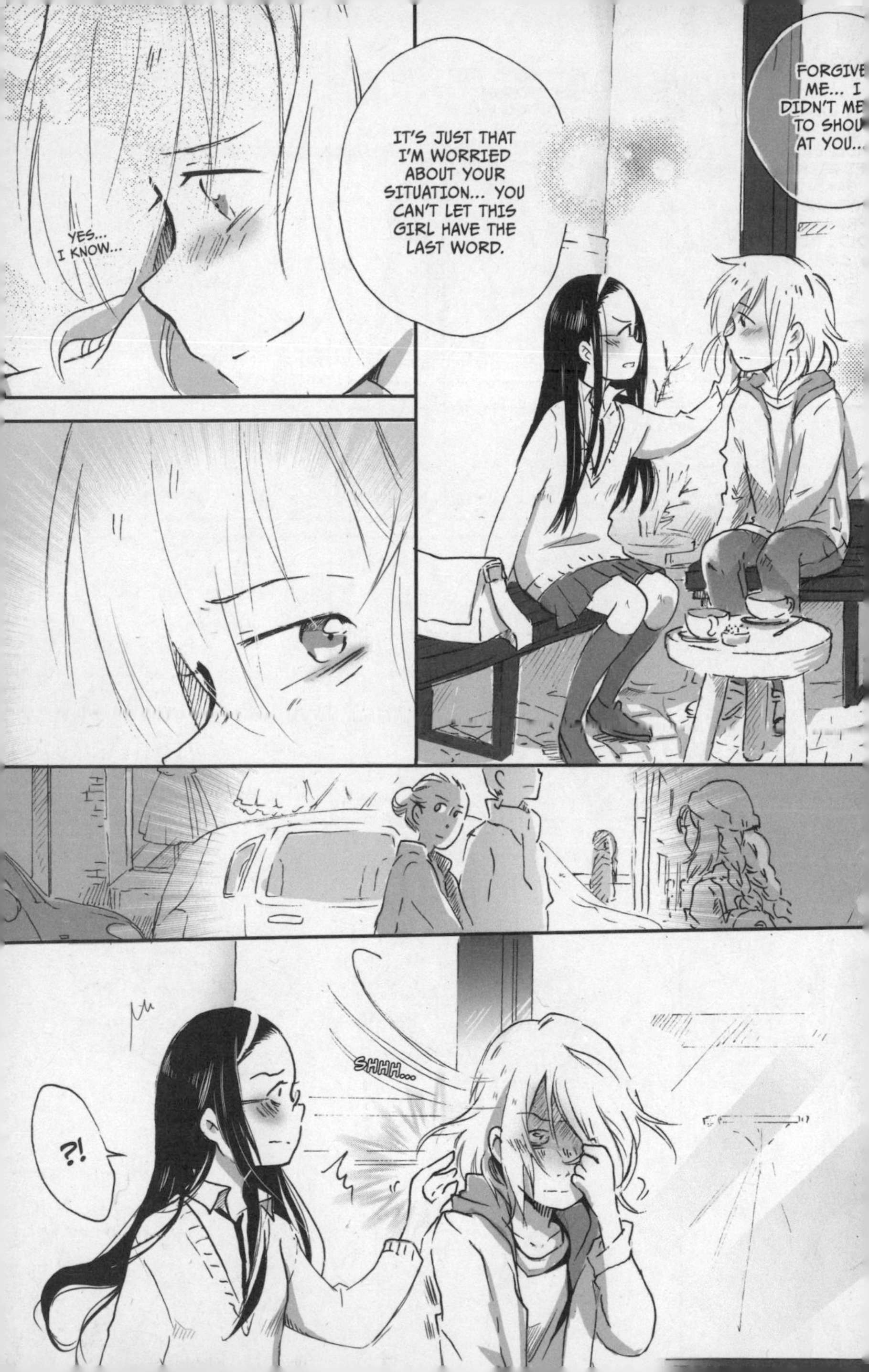

FORGIVE ME... I DIDN'T ME TO SHOU AT YOU...
IT'S JUST THAT I'M WORRIED ABOUT YOUR SITUATION... YOU CAN'T LET THIS GIRL HAVE THE LAST WORD.
YES... I KNOW...
SHHH...
?!

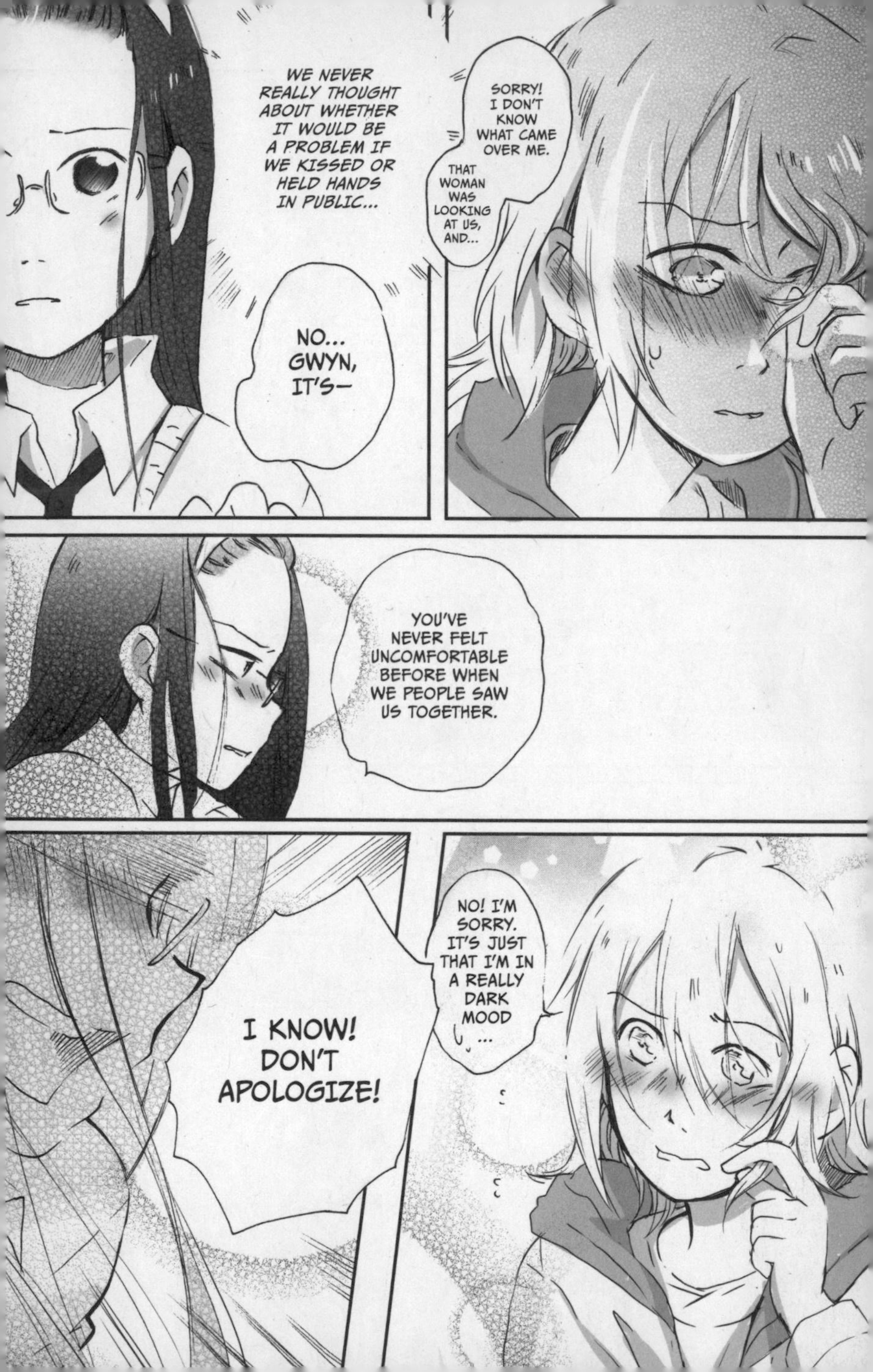
SORRY! I DON'T KNOW WHAT CAME OVER ME.
THAT WOMAN WAS LOOKING AT US, AND...
WE NEVER REALLY THOUGHT ABOUT WHETHER IT WOULD BE A PROBLEM IF WE KISSED OR HELD HANDS IN PUBLIC...
NO... GWYN, IT'S—
YOU'VE NEVER FELT UNCOMFORTABLE BEFORE WHEN WE PEOPLE SAW US TOGETHER.
NO! I'M SORRY. IT'S JUST THAT I'M IN A REALLY DARK MOOD...
I KNOW! DON'T APOLOGIZE!

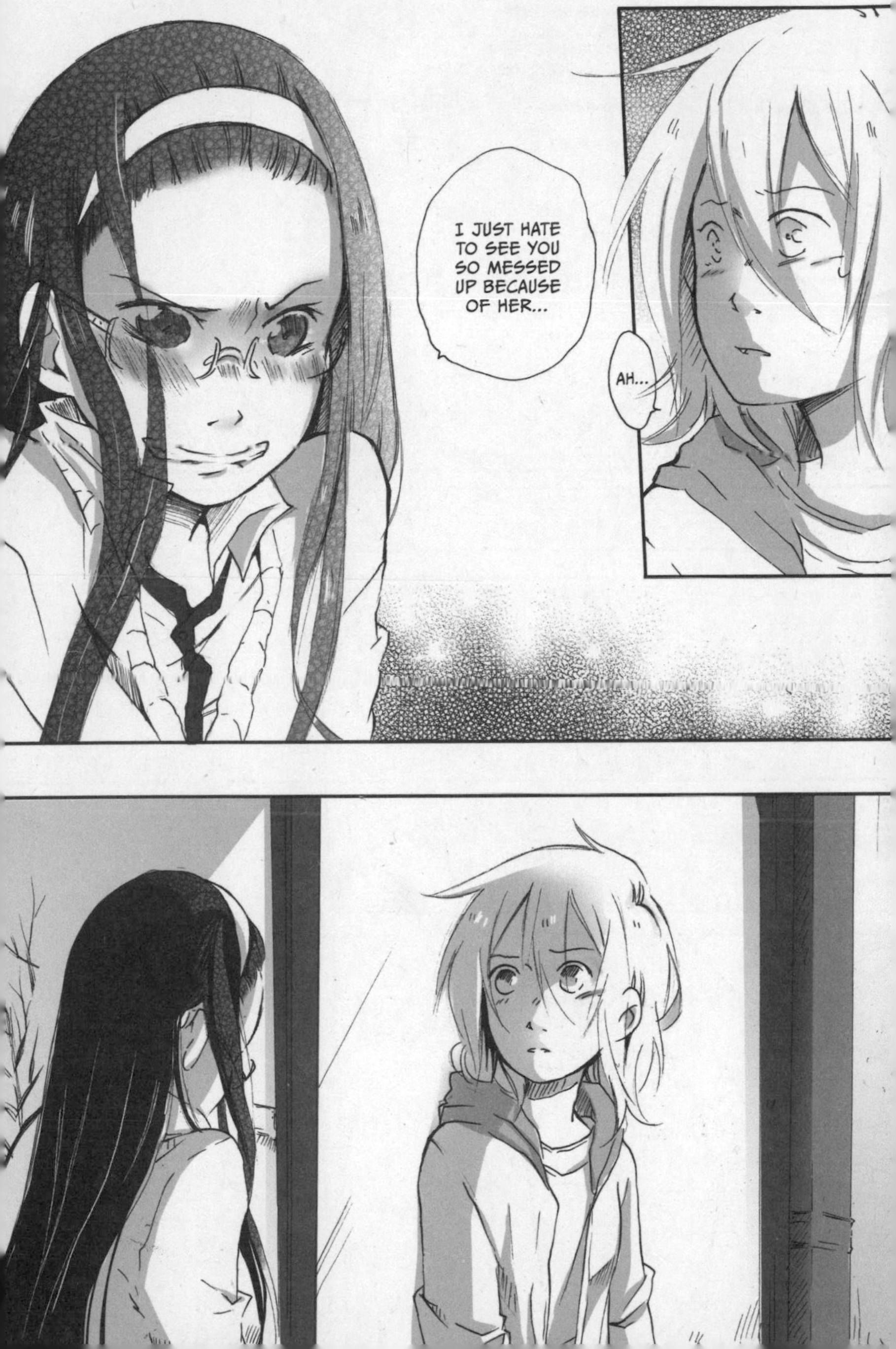
AH...
I JUST HATE TO SEE YOU SO MESSED UP BECAUSE OF HER...

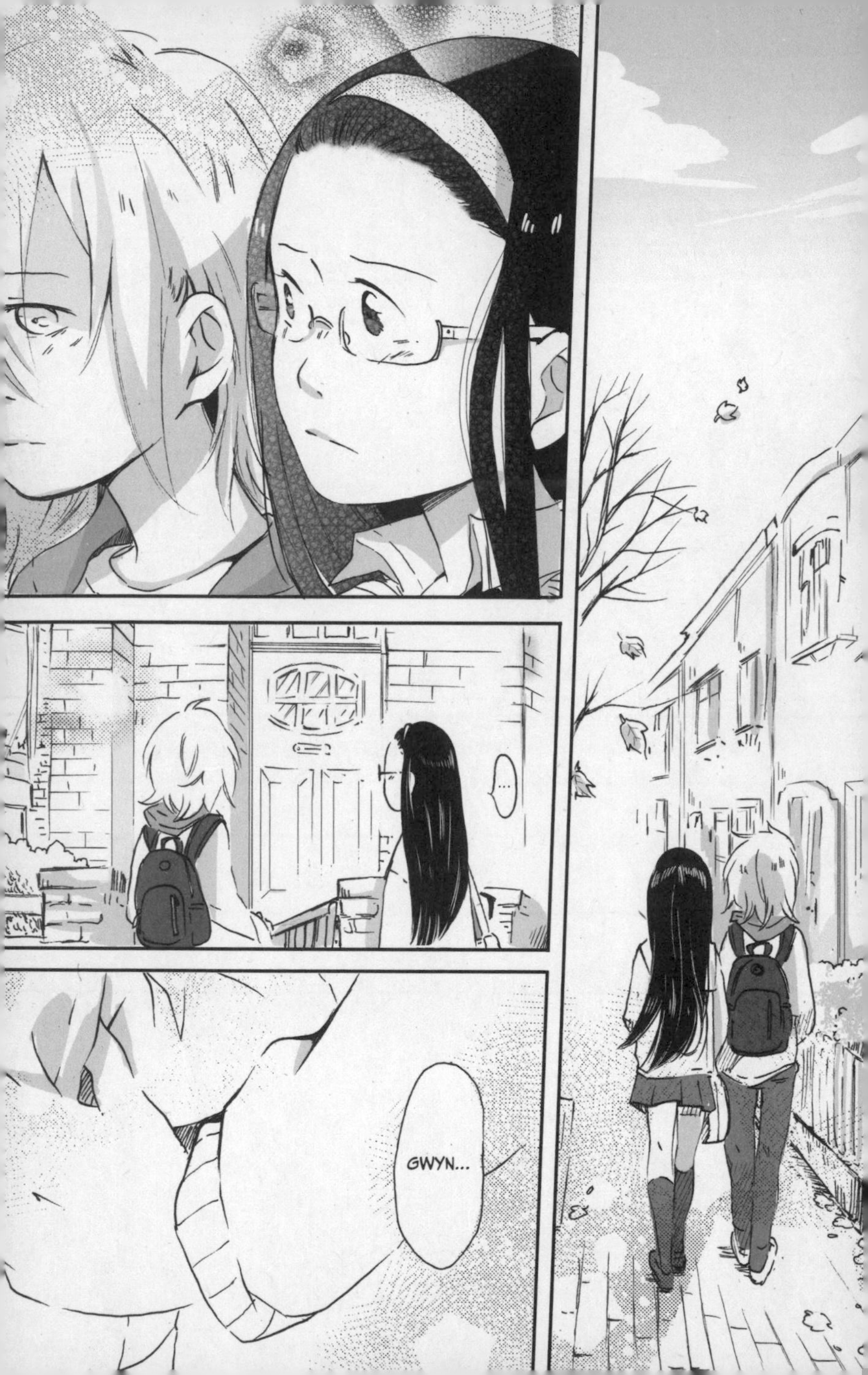
...
GWYN...

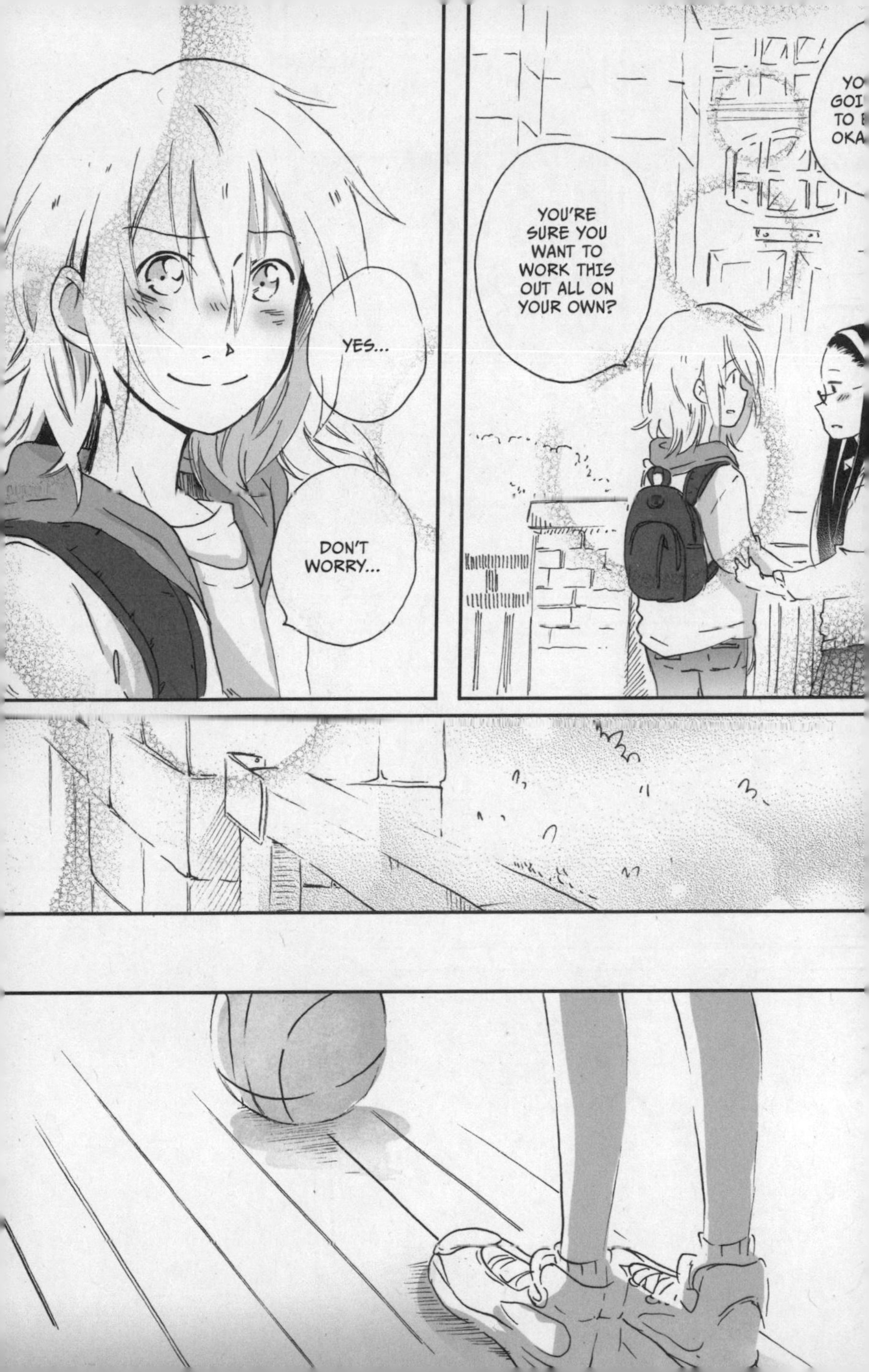
YOU'RE SURE YOU WANT TO WORK THIS OUT ALL ON YOUR OWN?
YES...
DON'T WORRY...

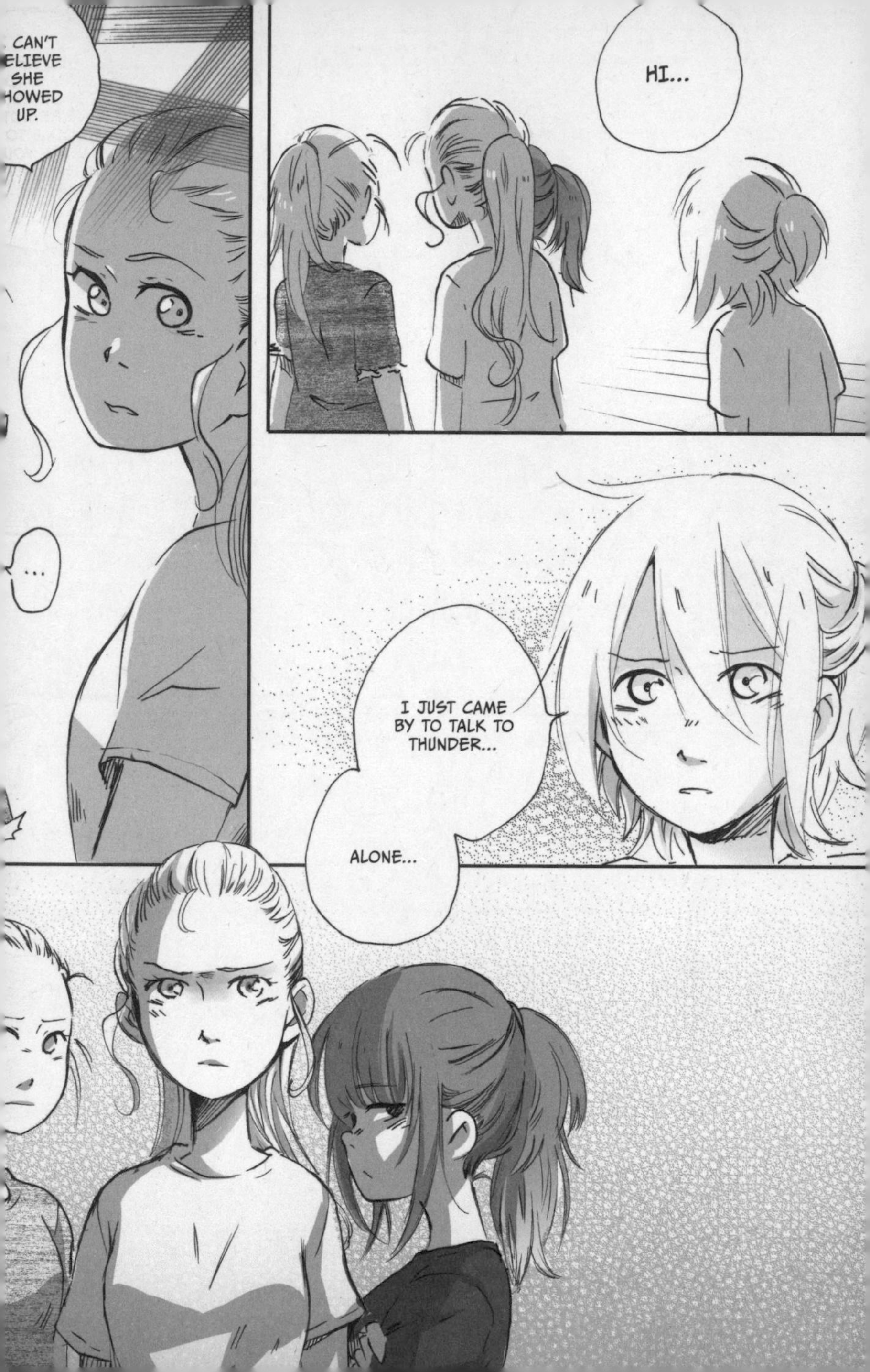
HI...
I JUST CAME BY TO TALK TO THUNDER...
ALONE...
CAN'T ELIEVE SHE HOWED UP.
...

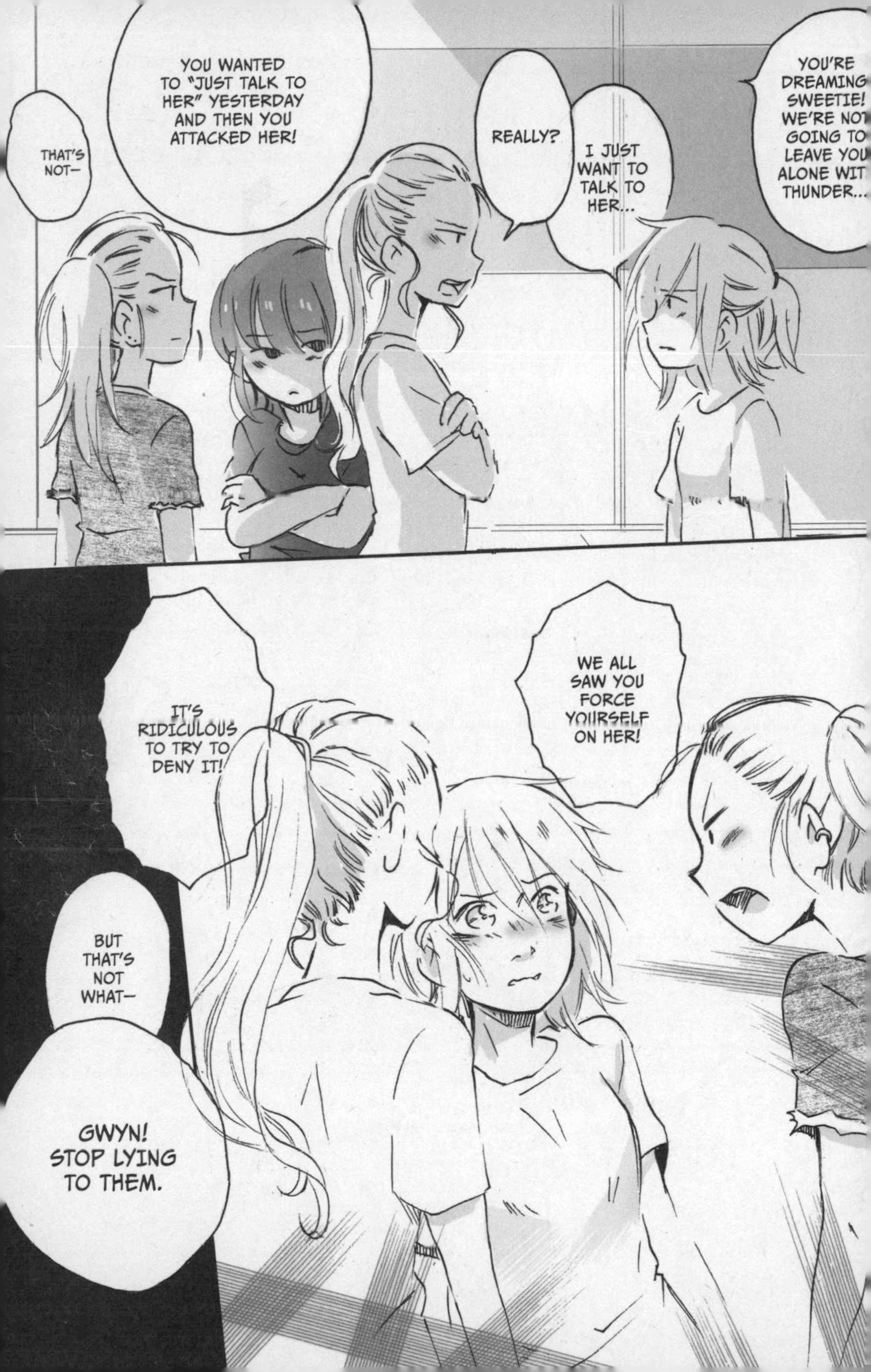
YOU'RE DREAMING SWEETIE! WE'RE NOT GOING TO LEAVE YOU ALONE WIT THUNDER...
I JUST WANT TO TALK TO HER...
REALLY?
YOU WANTED TO "JUST TALK TO HER" YESTERDAY AND THEN YOU ATTACKED HER!
THAT'S NOT—
WE ALL SAW YOU FORCE YOURSELF ON HER!
IT'S RIDICULOUS TO TRY TO DENY IT!
BUT THAT'S NOT WHAT—
GWYN! STOP LYING TO THEM.

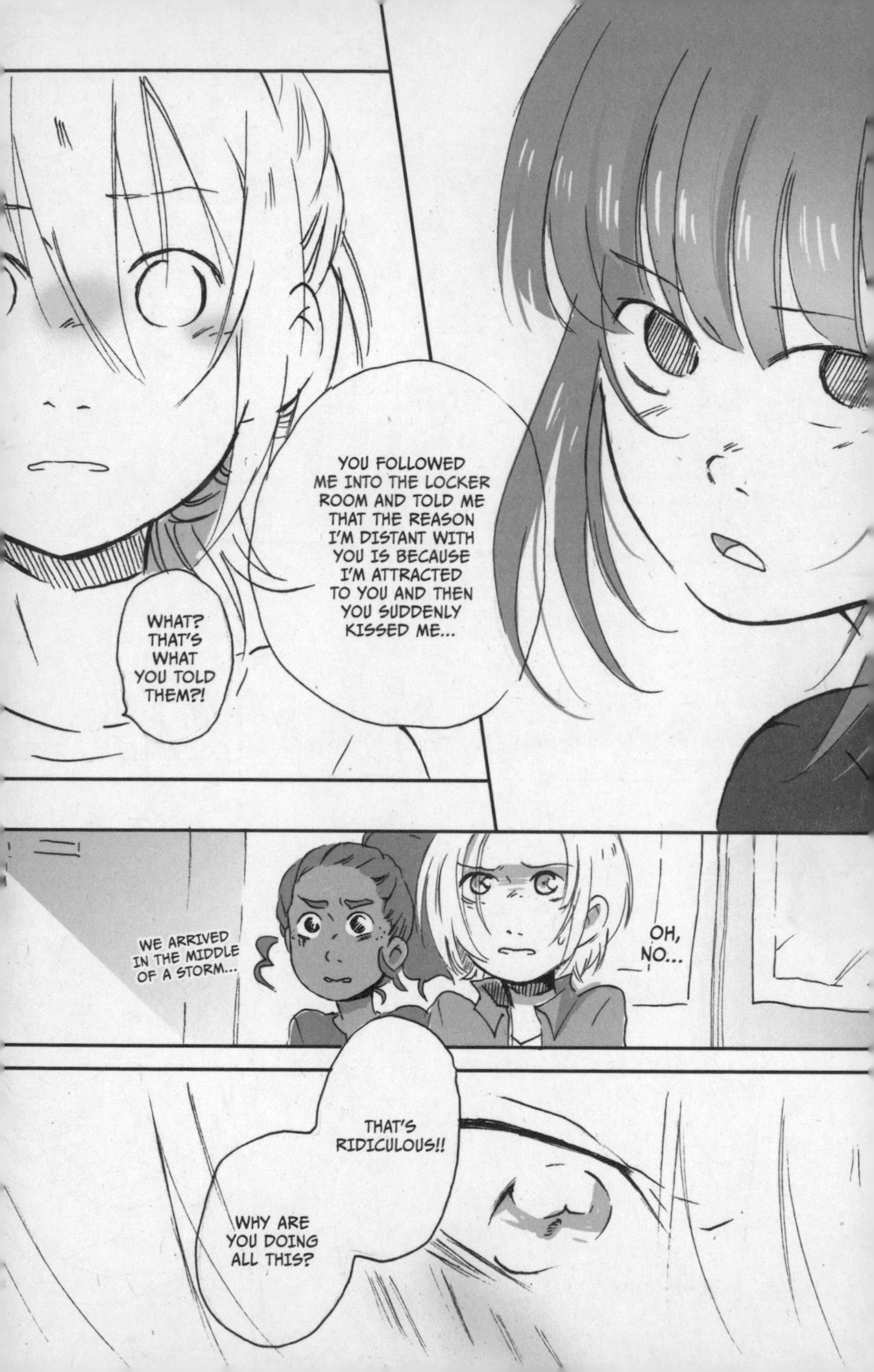
YOU FOLLOWED ME INTO THE LOCKER ROOM AND TOLD ME THAT THE REASON I'M DISTANT WITH YOU IS BECAUSE I'M ATTRACTED TO YOU AND THEN YOU SUDDENLY KISSED ME...
WHAT? THAT'S WHAT YOU TOLD THEM?!
OH, NO...
WE ARRIVED IN THE MIDDLE OF A STORM...
THAT'S RIDICULOUS!!
WHY ARE YOU DOING ALL THIS?

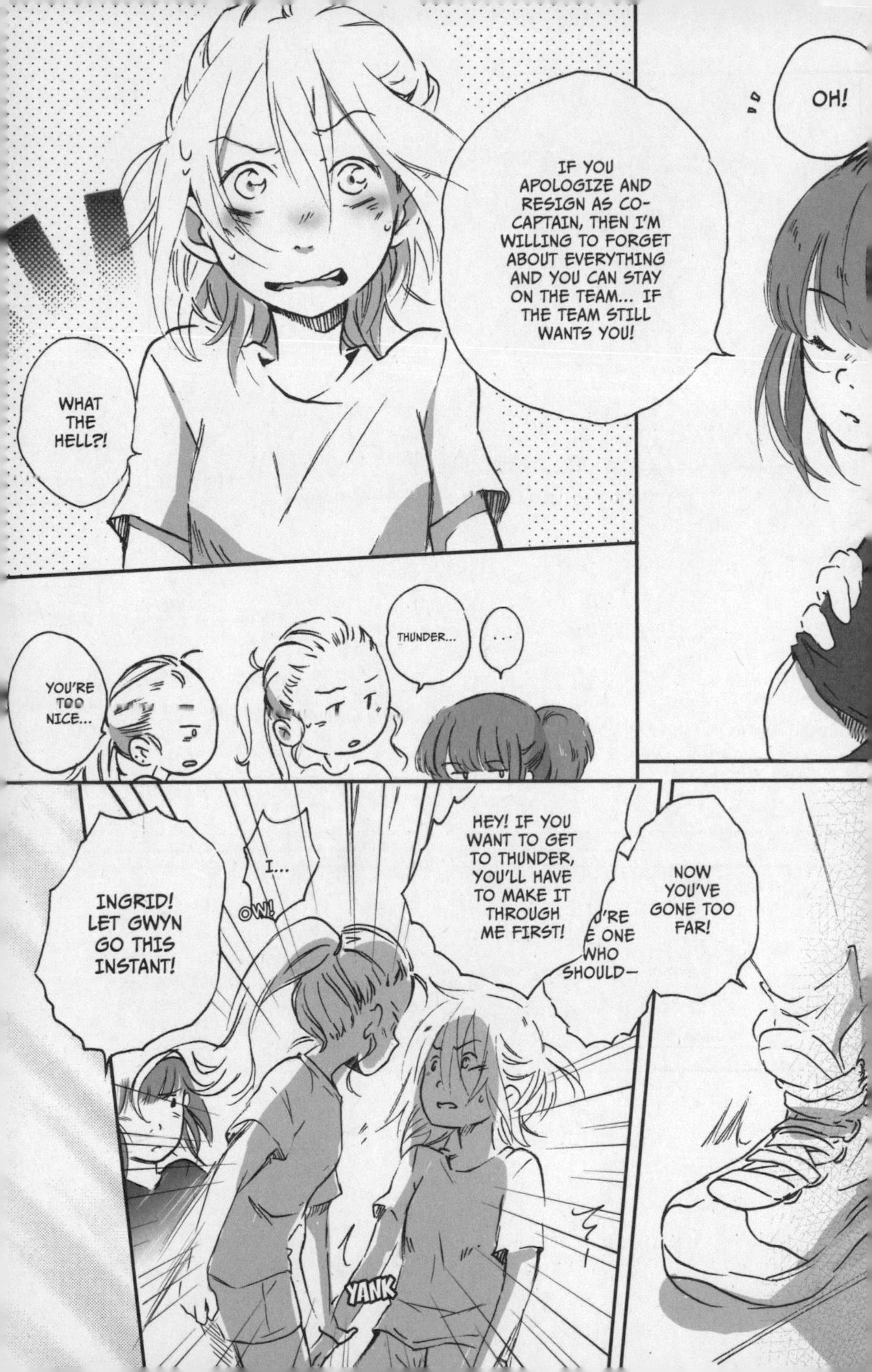
OH!
IF YOU APOLOGIZE AND RESIGN AS CO-CAPTAIN, THEN I'M WILLING TO FORGET ABOUT EVERYTHING AND YOU CAN STAY ON THE TEAM... IF THE TEAM STILL WANTS YOU!
WHAT THE HELL?!
THUNDER...
...
YOU'RE TOO NICE...
NOW YOU'VE GONE TOO FAR!
HEY! IF YOU WANT TO GET TO THUNDER, YOU'LL HAVE TO MAKE IT THROUGH ME FIRST!
U'RE E ONE WHO SHOULD—
I...
OW!
INGRID! LET GWYN GO THIS INSTANT!
YANK

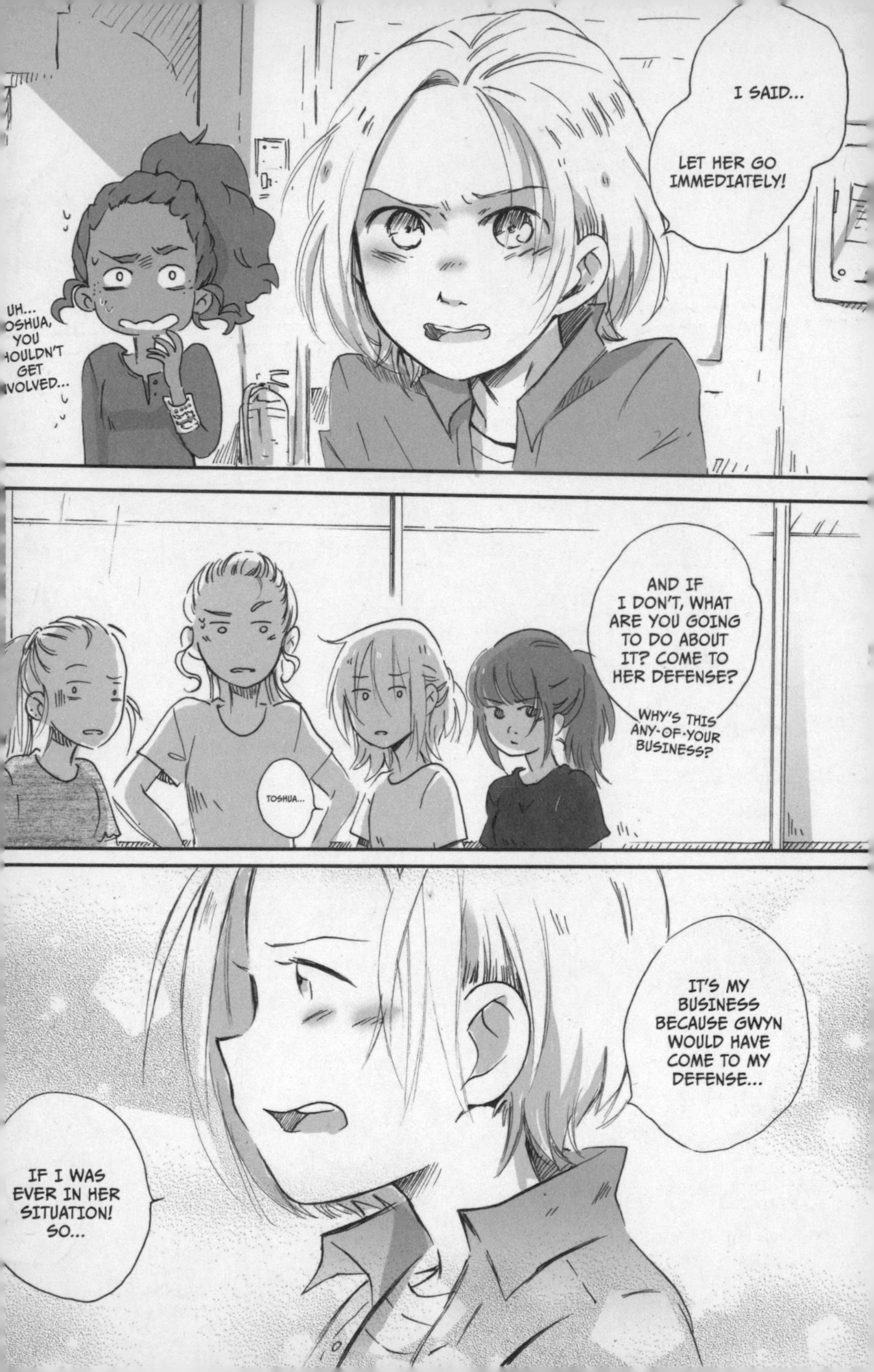
I SAID...
LET HER GO IMMEDIATELY!
UH... OSHUA, YOU HOULDN'T GET NVOLVED...
AND IF I DON'T, WHAT ARE YOU GOING TO DO ABOUT IT? COME TO HER DEFENSE?
WHY'S THIS ANY-OF-YOUR BUSINESS?
TOSHUA...
IT'S MY BUSINESS BECAUSE GWYN WOULD HAVE COME TO MY DEFENSE...
IF I WAS EVER IN HER SITUATION! SO...

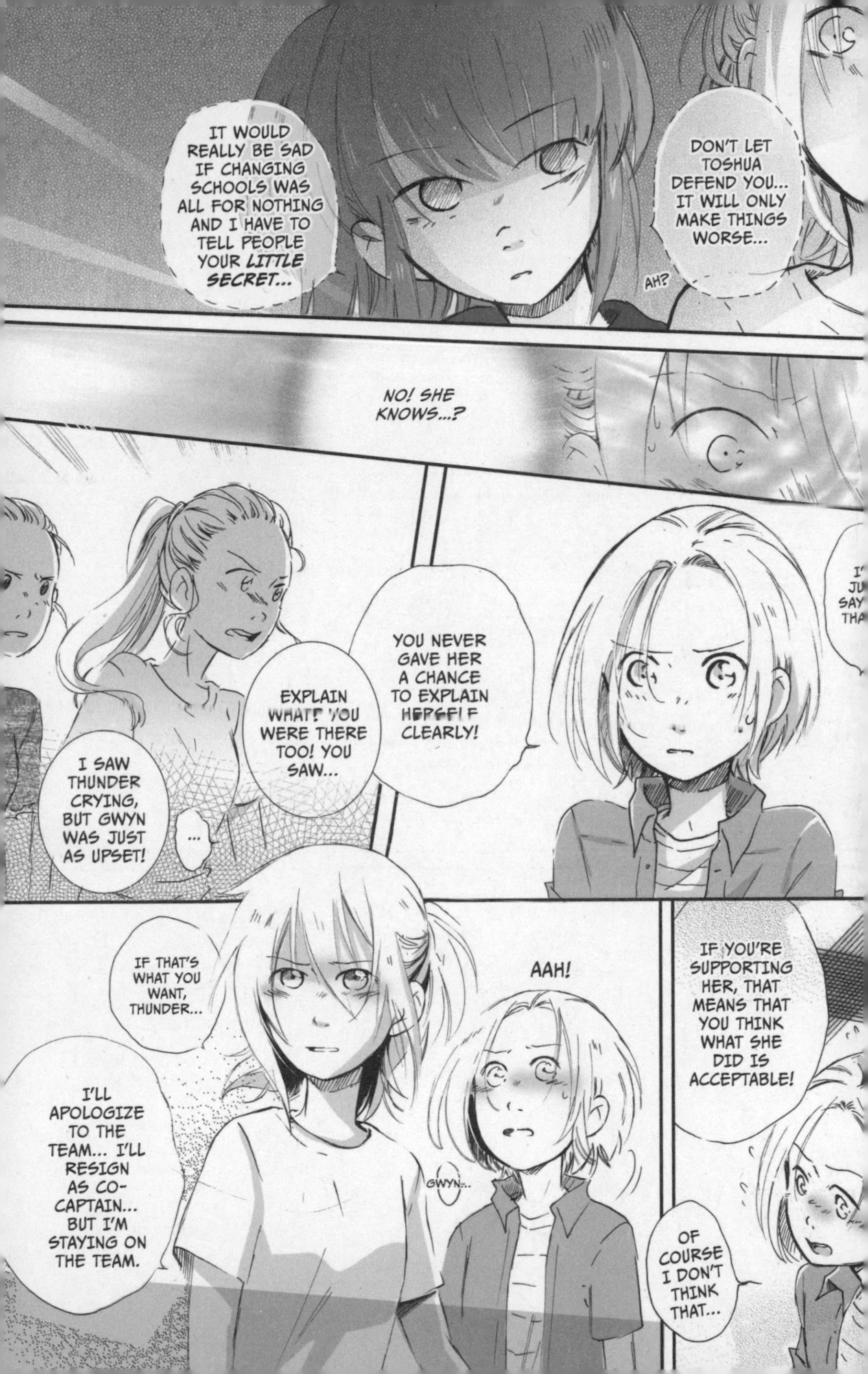
DON'T LET TOSHUA DEFEND YOU... IT WILL ONLY MAKE THINGS WORSE...
AH?
IT WOULD REALLY BE SAD IF CHANGING SCHOOLS WAS ALL FOR NOTHING AND I HAVE TO TELL PEOPLE YOUR *LITTLE SECRET*...
NO! SHE KNOWS...?
YOU NEVER GAVE HER A CHANCE TO EXPLAIN HERSELF CLEARLY!
EXPLAIN WHAT? YOU WERE THERE TOO! YOU SAW...
I SAW THUNDER CRYING, BUT GWYN WAS JUST AS UPSET!
...
IF YOU'RE SUPPORTING HER, THAT MEANS THAT YOU THINK WHAT SHE DID IS ACCEPTABLE!
OF COURSE I DON'T THINK THAT...
AAH!
IF THAT'S WHAT YOU WANT, THUNDER...
I'LL APOLOGIZE TO THE TEAM... I'LL RESIGN AS CO-CAPTAIN... BUT I'M STAYING ON THE TEAM.
GWYN...

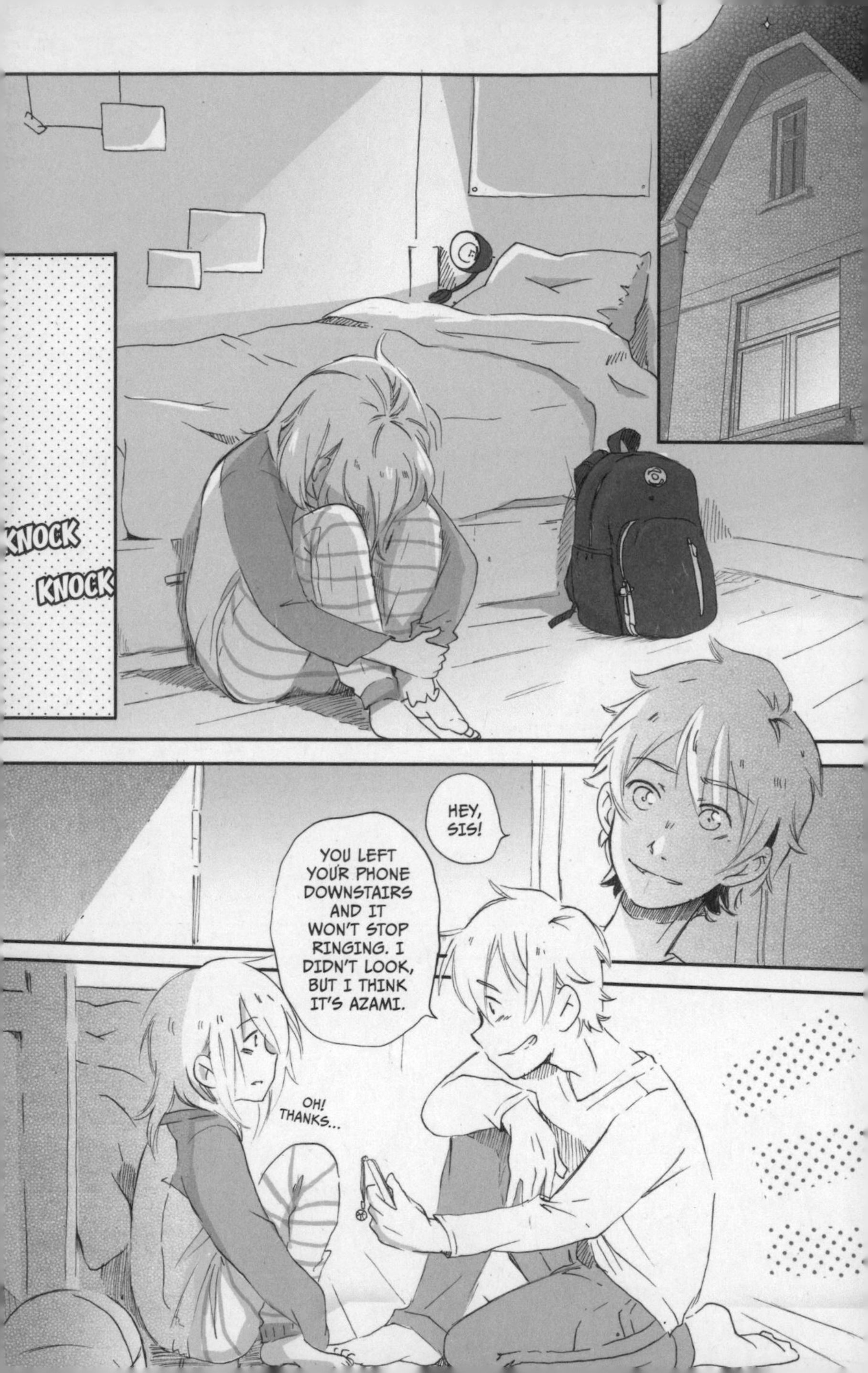
KNOCK
KNOCK
HEY, SIS!
YOU LEFT YOUR PHONE DOWNSTAIRS AND IT WON'T STOP RINGING. I DIDN'T LOOK, BUT I THINK IT'S AZAMI.
OH! THANKS...

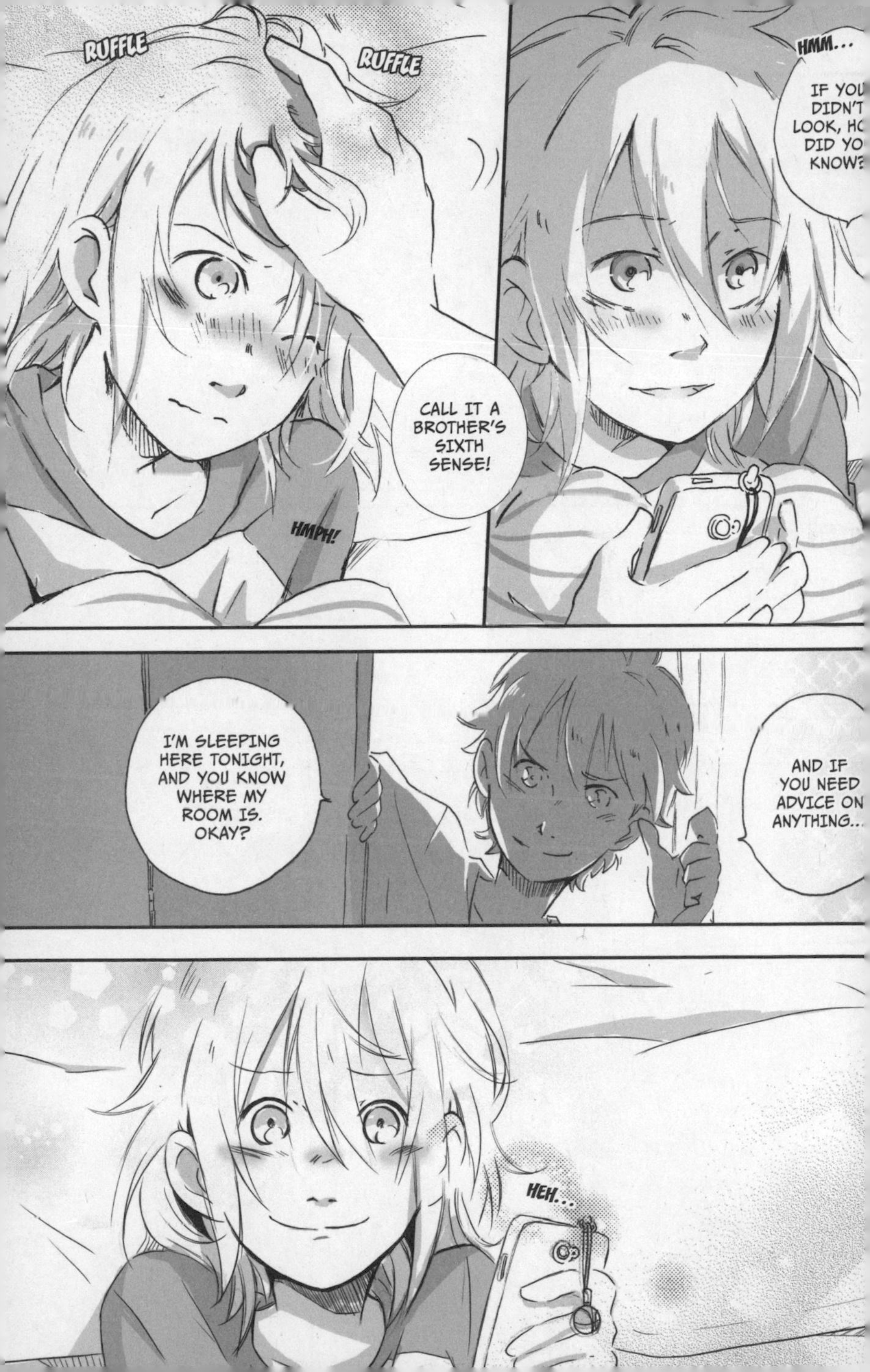
HMM...
IF YOU DIDN'T LOOK, HO DID YO KNOW?
RUFFLE
RUFFLE
CALL IT A BROTHER'S SIXTH SENSE!
HMPH!
AND IF YOU NEED ADVICE ON ANYTHING...
I'M SLEEPING HERE TONIGHT, AND YOU KNOW WHERE MY ROOM IS. OKAY?
HEH...

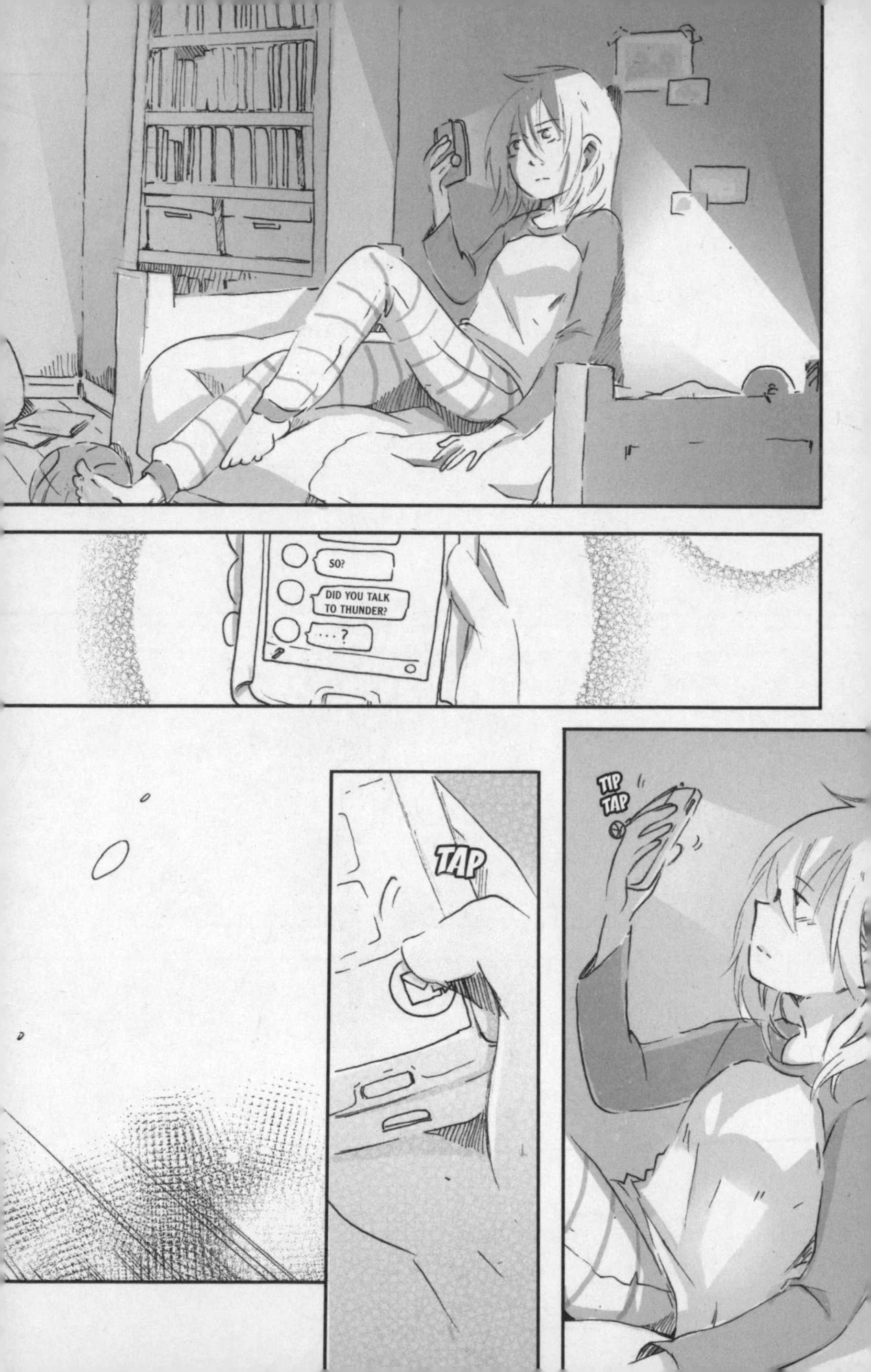
SO?
DID YOU TALK TO THUNDER?
...?
TIP TAP
TAP

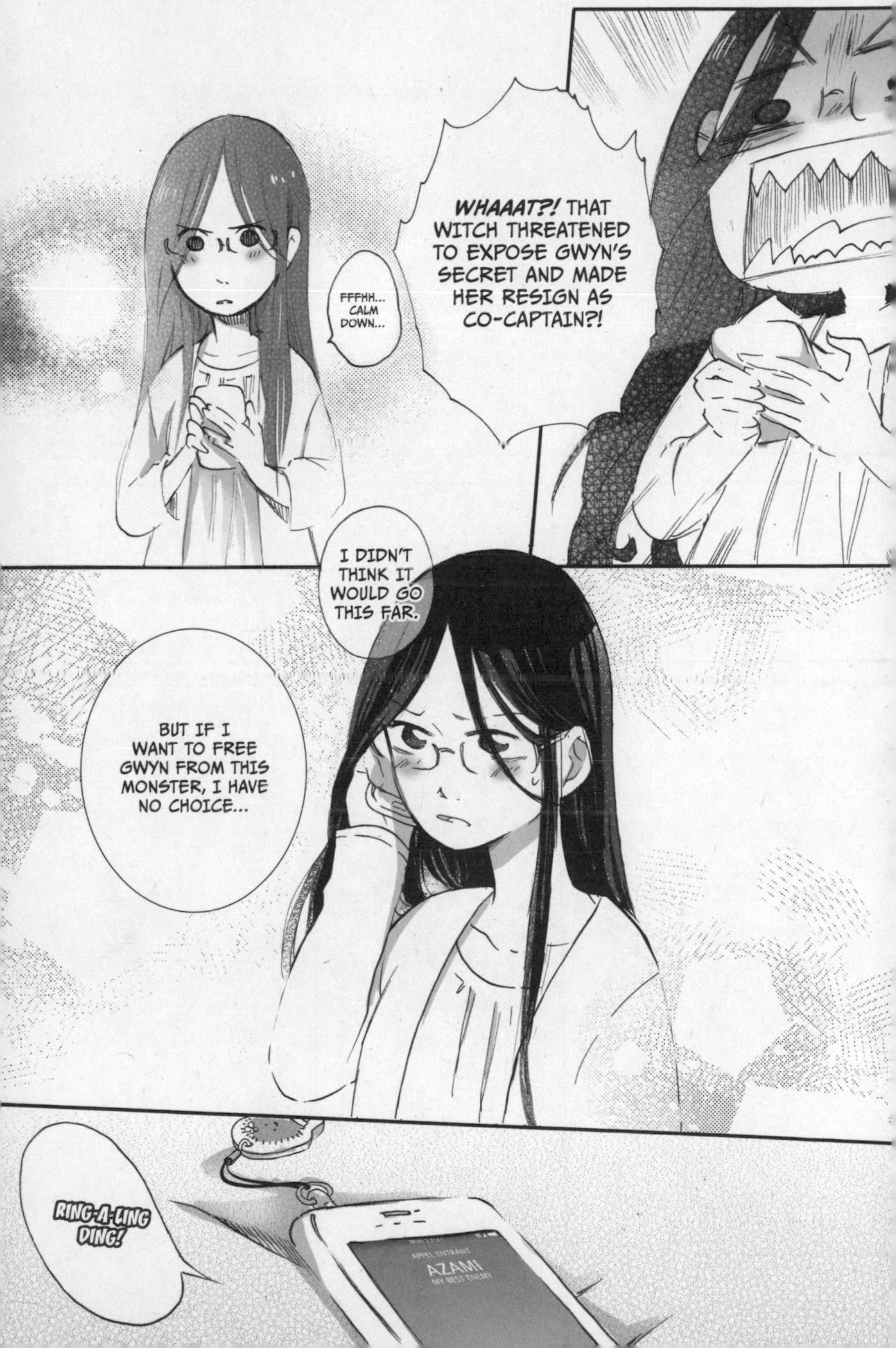
WHAAAT?! THAT WITCH THREATENED TO EXPOSE GWYN'S SECRET AND MADE HER RESIGN AS CO-CAPTAIN?!
FFFHH... CALM DOWN...
I DIDN'T THINK IT WOULD GO THIS FAR.
BUT IF I WANT TO FREE GWYN FROM THIS MONSTER, I HAVE NO CHOICE...
RING-A-LING DING!
APPEL ENTRANT
AZAMI
MY BEST ENEMY

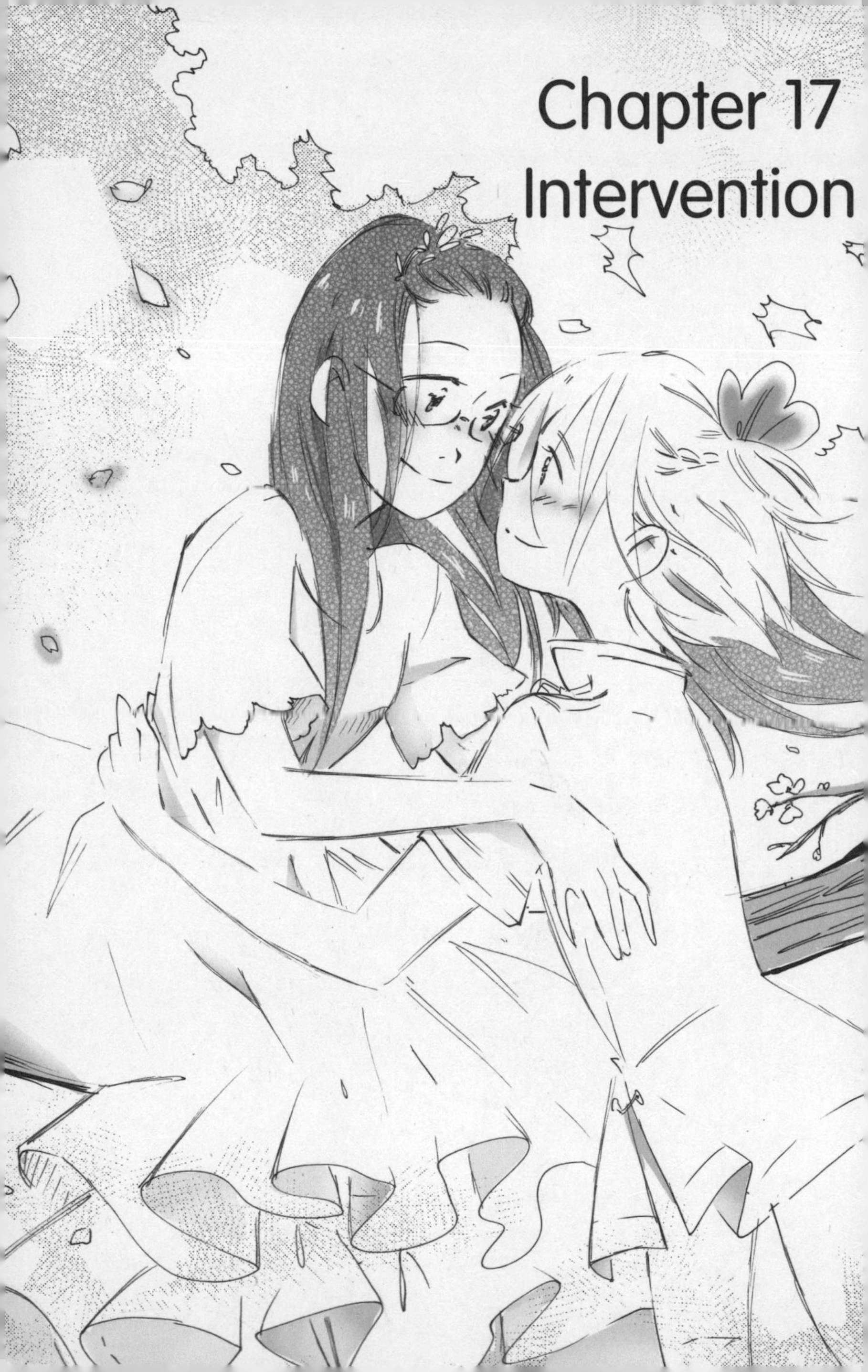
Chapter 17
Intervention

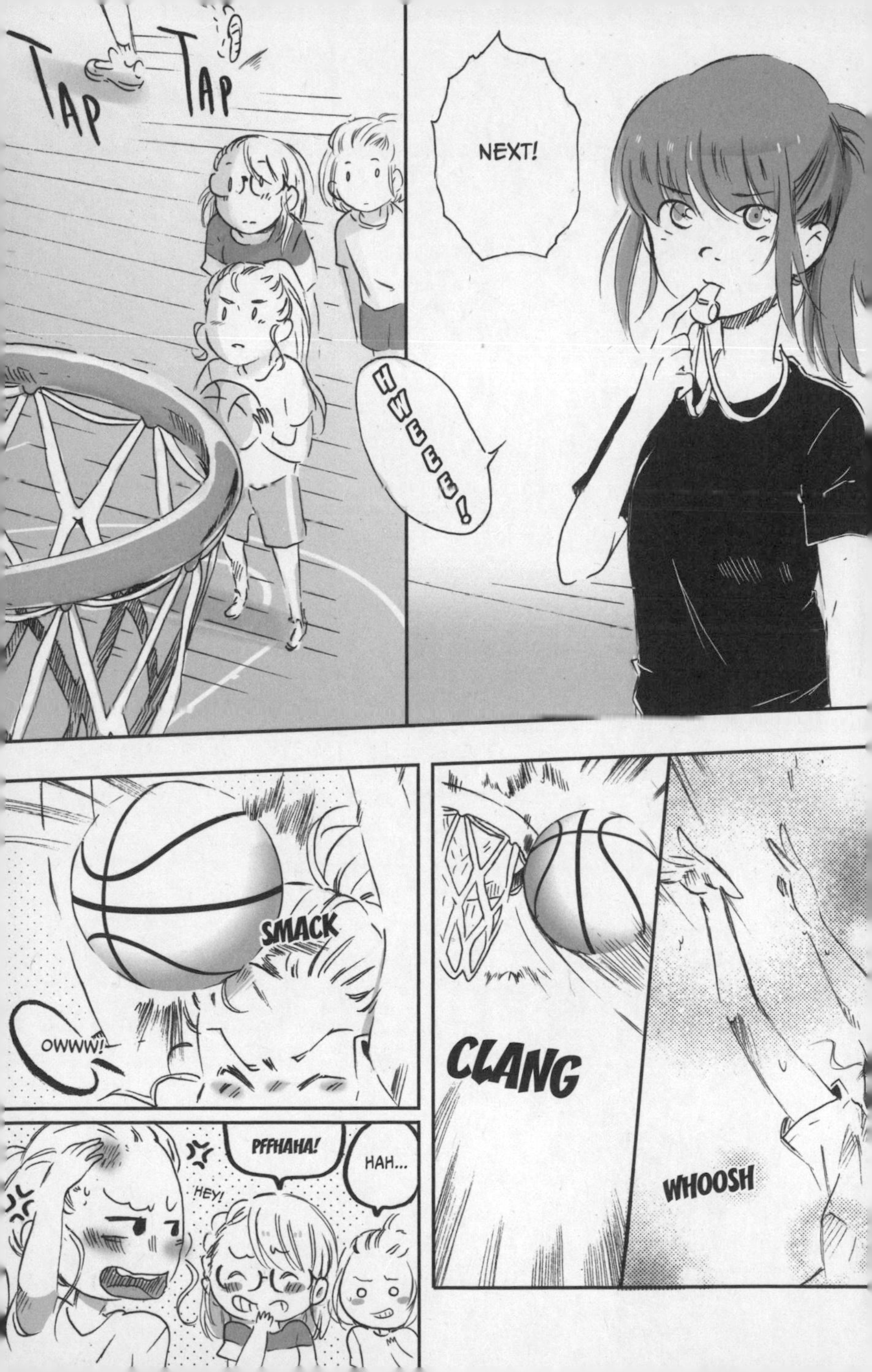
NEXT!
HWEEEE!
TAP TAP
WHOOSH
CLANG
SMACK
OWWW!
HAH...
PFFHAHA!
HEY!

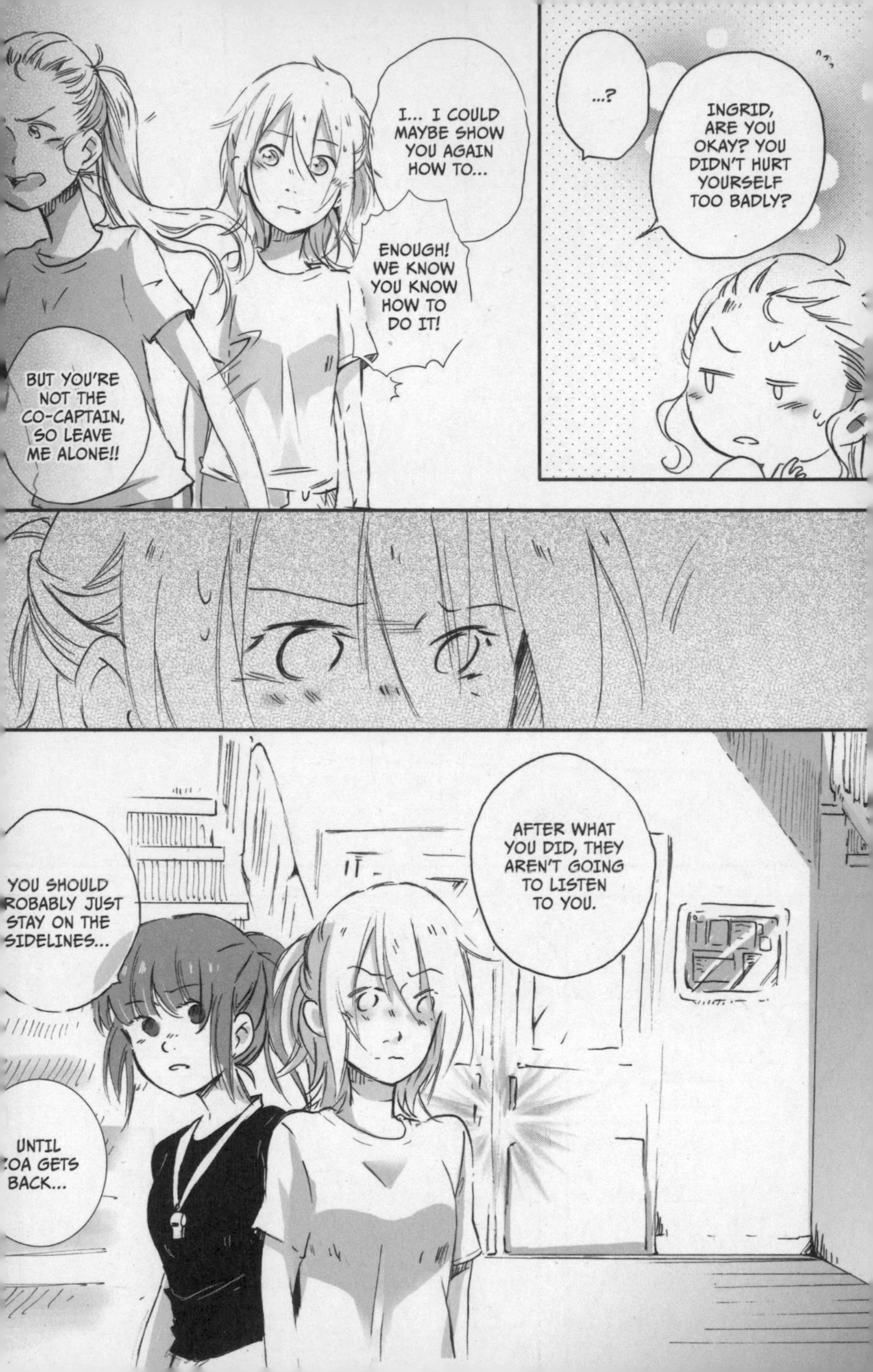
INGRID, ARE YOU OKAY? YOU DIDN'T HURT YOURSELF TOO BADLY?
...?
I... I COULD MAYBE SHOW YOU AGAIN HOW TO...
ENOUGH! WE KNOW YOU KNOW HOW TO DO IT!
BUT YOU'RE NOT THE CO-CAPTAIN, SO LEAVE ME ALONE!!
AFTER WHAT YOU DID, THEY AREN'T GOING TO LISTEN TO YOU.
YOU SHOULD ROBABLY JUST STAY ON THE IDELINES...
UNTIL OA GETS BACK...

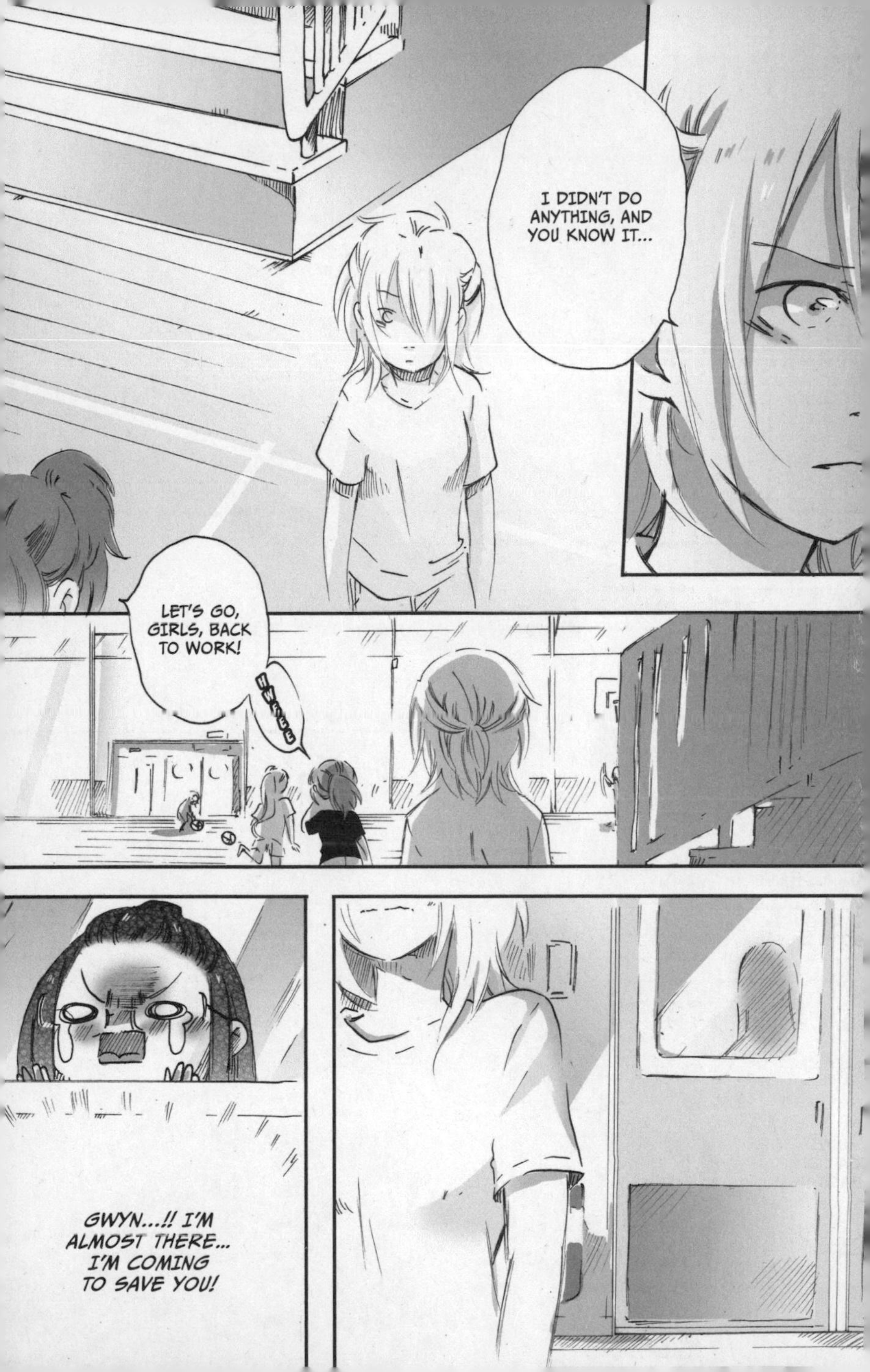
I DIDN'T DO ANYTHING, AND YOU KNOW IT...
LET'S GO, GIRLS, BACK TO WORK!
HWEEE
GWYN...!! I'M ALMOST THERE... I'M COMING TO SAVE YOU!

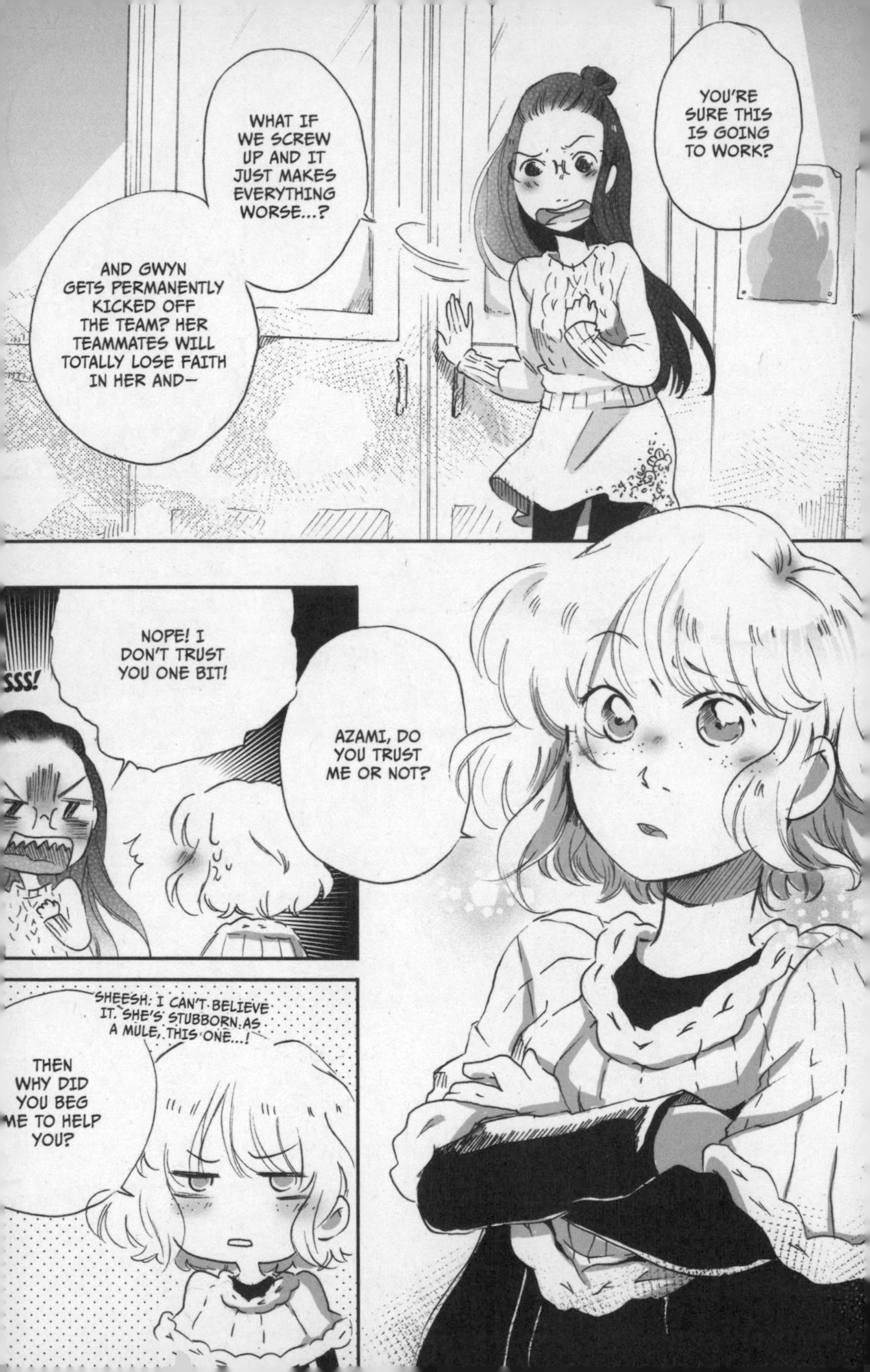
YOU'RE SURE THIS IS GOING TO WORK?
WHAT IF WE SCREW UP AND IT JUST MAKES EVERYTHING WORSE...?
AND GWYN GETS PERMANENTLY KICKED OFF THE TEAM? HER TEAMMATES WILL TOTALLY LOSE FAITH IN HER AND—
AZAMI, DO YOU TRUST ME OR NOT?
NOPE! I DON'T TRUST YOU ONE BIT!
SSS!
SHEESH. I CAN'T BELIEVE IT. SHE'S STUBBORN AS A MULE, THIS ONE...!
THEN WHY DID YOU BEG ME TO HELP YOU?

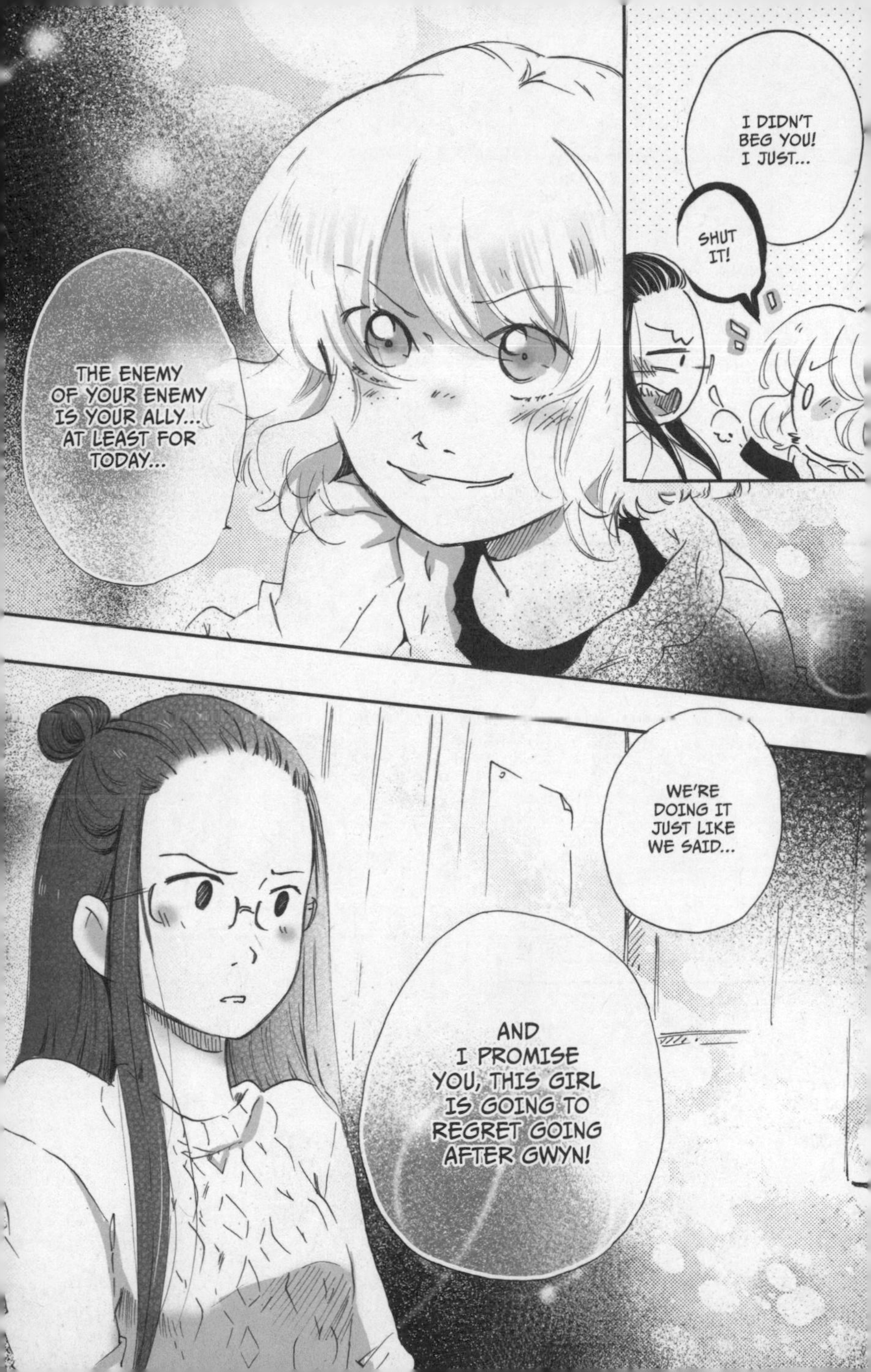
I DIDN'T BEG YOU! I JUST...
SHUT IT!
THE ENEMY OF YOUR ENEMY IS YOUR ALLY... AT LEAST FOR TODAY...
WE'RE DOING IT JUST LIKE WE SAID...
AND I PROMISE YOU, THIS GIRL IS GOING TO REGRET GOING AFTER GWYN!

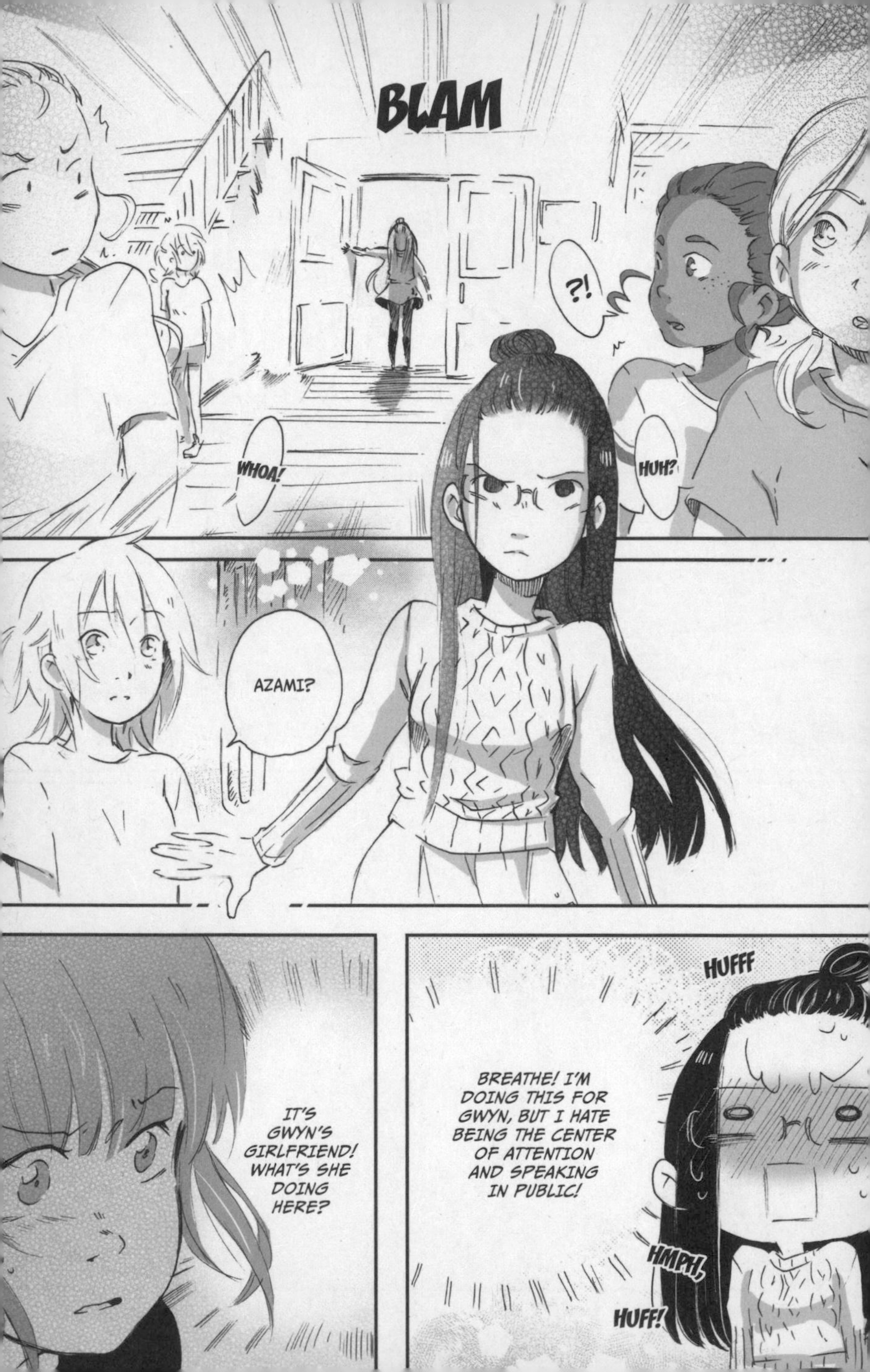
BLAM
?!
HUH?
WHOA!
AZAMI?
HUFFF
BREATHE! I'M DOING THIS FOR GWYN, BUT I HATE BEING THE CENTER OF ATTENTION AND SPEAKING IN PUBLIC!
HMPH,
HUFF!
IT'S GWYN'S GIRLFRIEND! WHAT'S SHE DOING HERE?

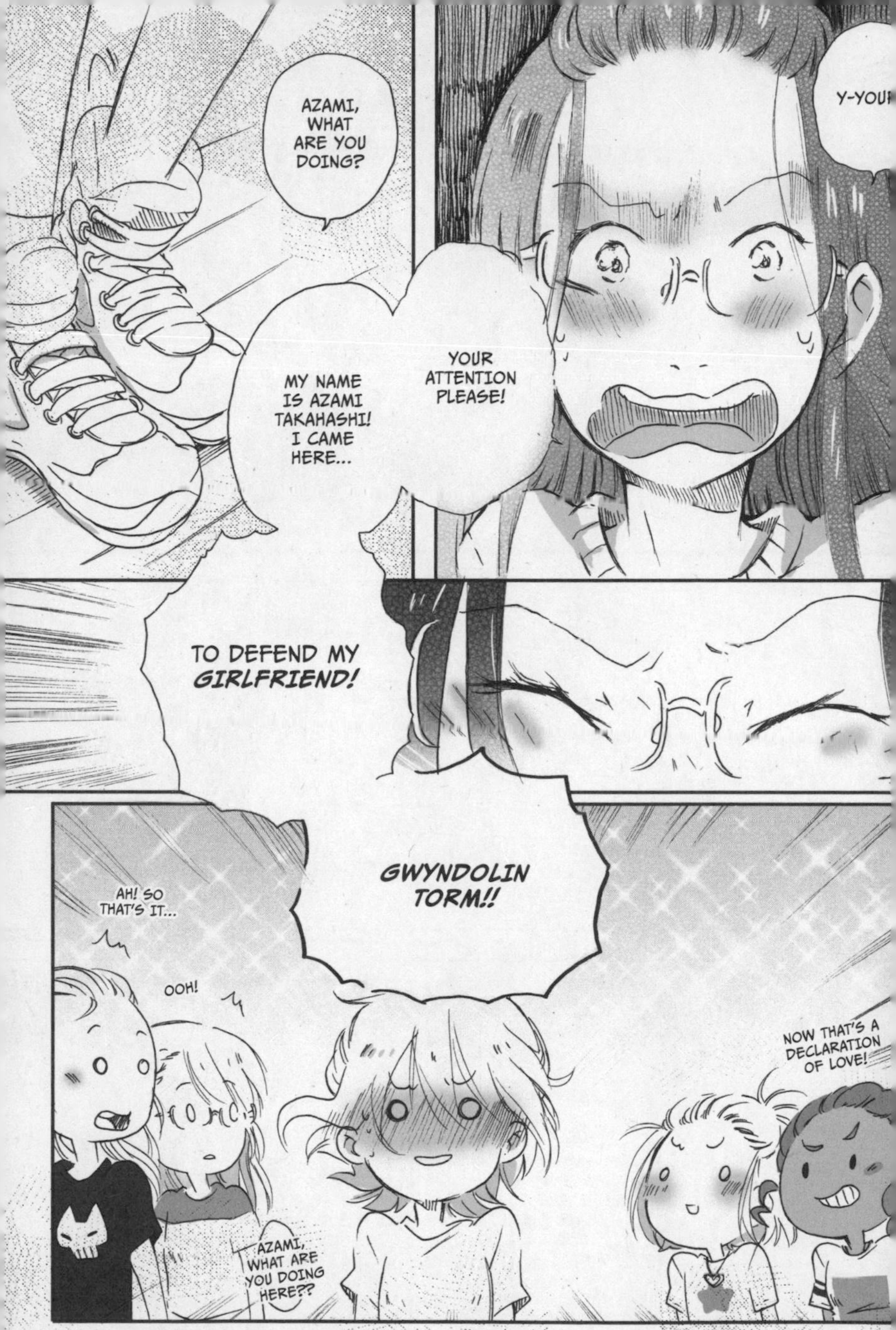
Y-YOU!
YOUR ATTENTION PLEASE!
MY NAME IS AZAMI TAKAHASHI! I CAME HERE...
AZAMI, WHAT ARE YOU DOING?
TO DEFEND MY *GIRLFRIEND!*
GWYNDOLIN TORM!!
NOW THAT'S A DECLARATION OF LOVE!
AH! SO THAT'S IT...
OOH!
AZAMI, WHAT ARE YOU DOING HERE??

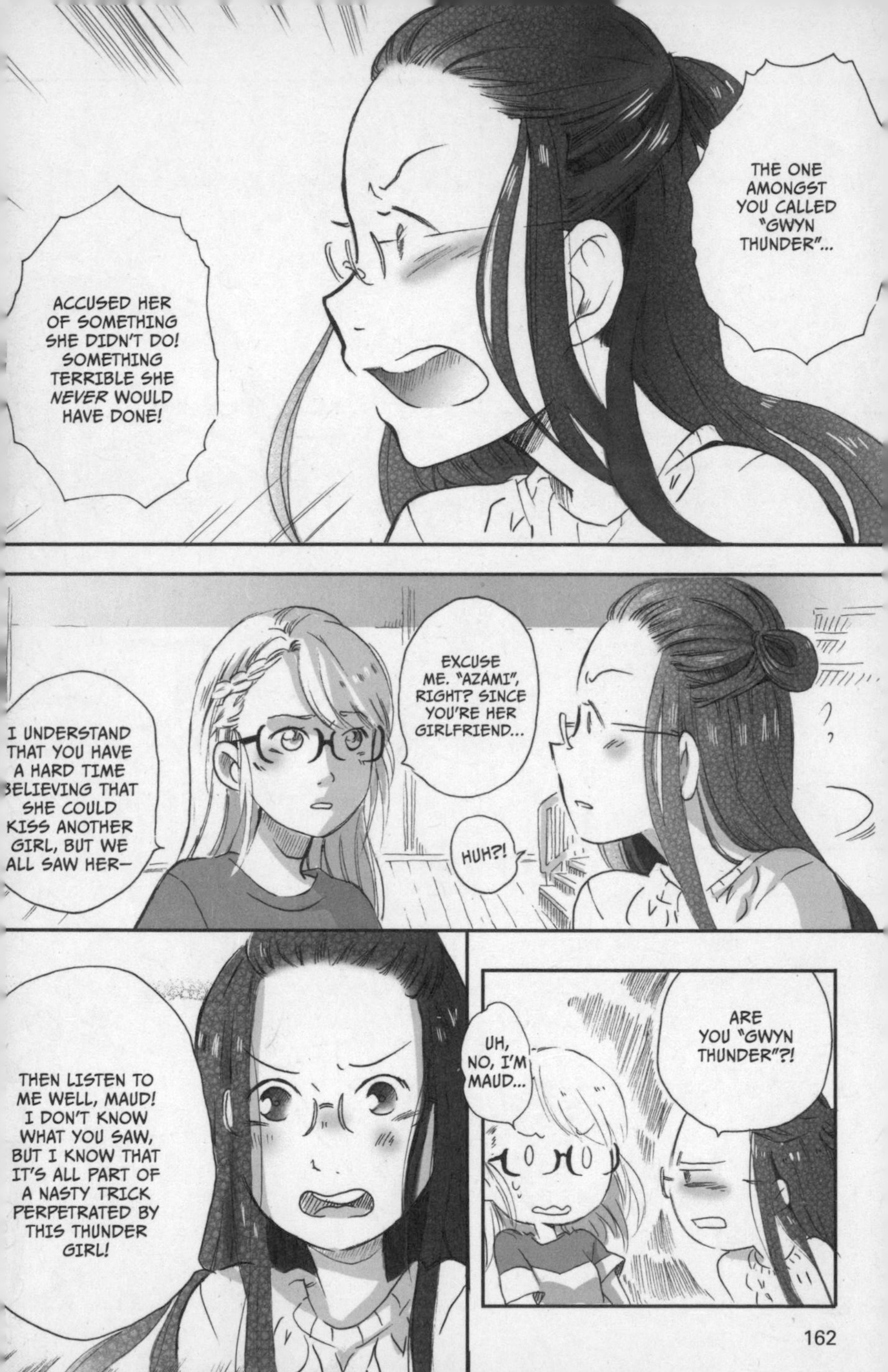
THE ONE AMONGST YOU CALLED "GWYN THUNDER"...
ACCUSED HER OF SOMETHING SHE DIDN'T DO! SOMETHING TERRIBLE SHE *NEVER* WOULD HAVE DONE!
EXCUSE ME. "AZAMI", RIGHT? SINCE YOU'RE HER GIRLFRIEND...
HUH?!
I UNDERSTAND THAT YOU HAVE A HARD TIME BELIEVING THAT SHE COULD KISS ANOTHER GIRL, BUT WE ALL SAW HER—
ARE YOU "GWYN THUNDER"?!
UH, NO, I'M MAUD...
THEN LISTEN TO ME WELL, MAUD! I DON'T KNOW WHAT YOU SAW, BUT I KNOW THAT IT'S ALL PART OF A NASTY TRICK PERPETRATED BY THIS THUNDER GIRL!

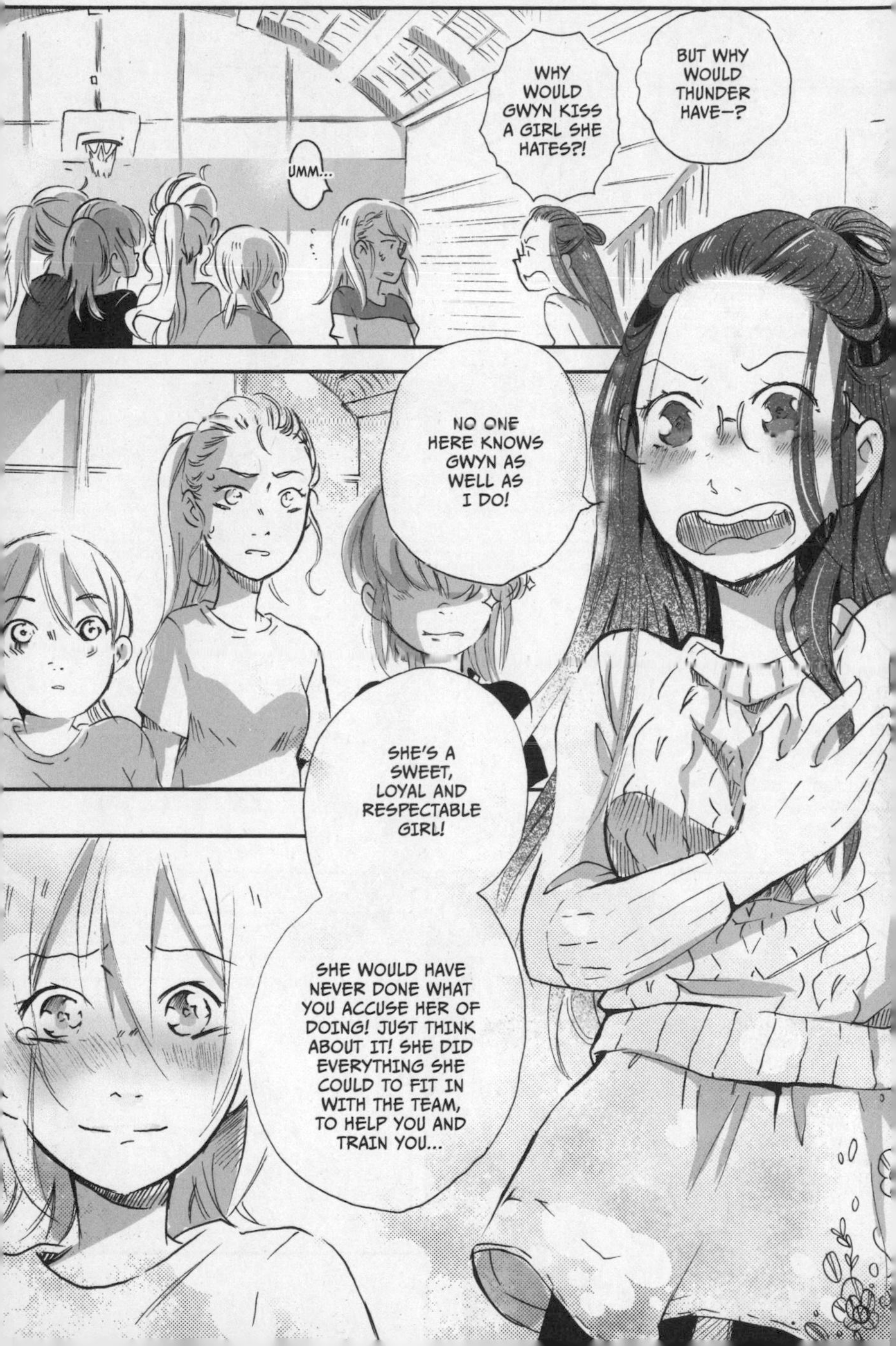
BUT WHY WOULD THUNDER HAVE—?
WHY WOULD GWYN KISS A GIRL SHE HATES?!
UMM...
NO ONE HERE KNOWS GWYN AS WELL AS I DO!
SHE'S A SWEET, LOYAL AND RESPECTABLE GIRL!
SHE WOULD HAVE NEVER DONE WHAT YOU ACCUSE HER OF DOING! JUST THINK ABOUT IT! SHE DID EVERYTHING SHE COULD TO FIT IN WITH THE TEAM, TO HELP YOU AND TRAIN YOU...

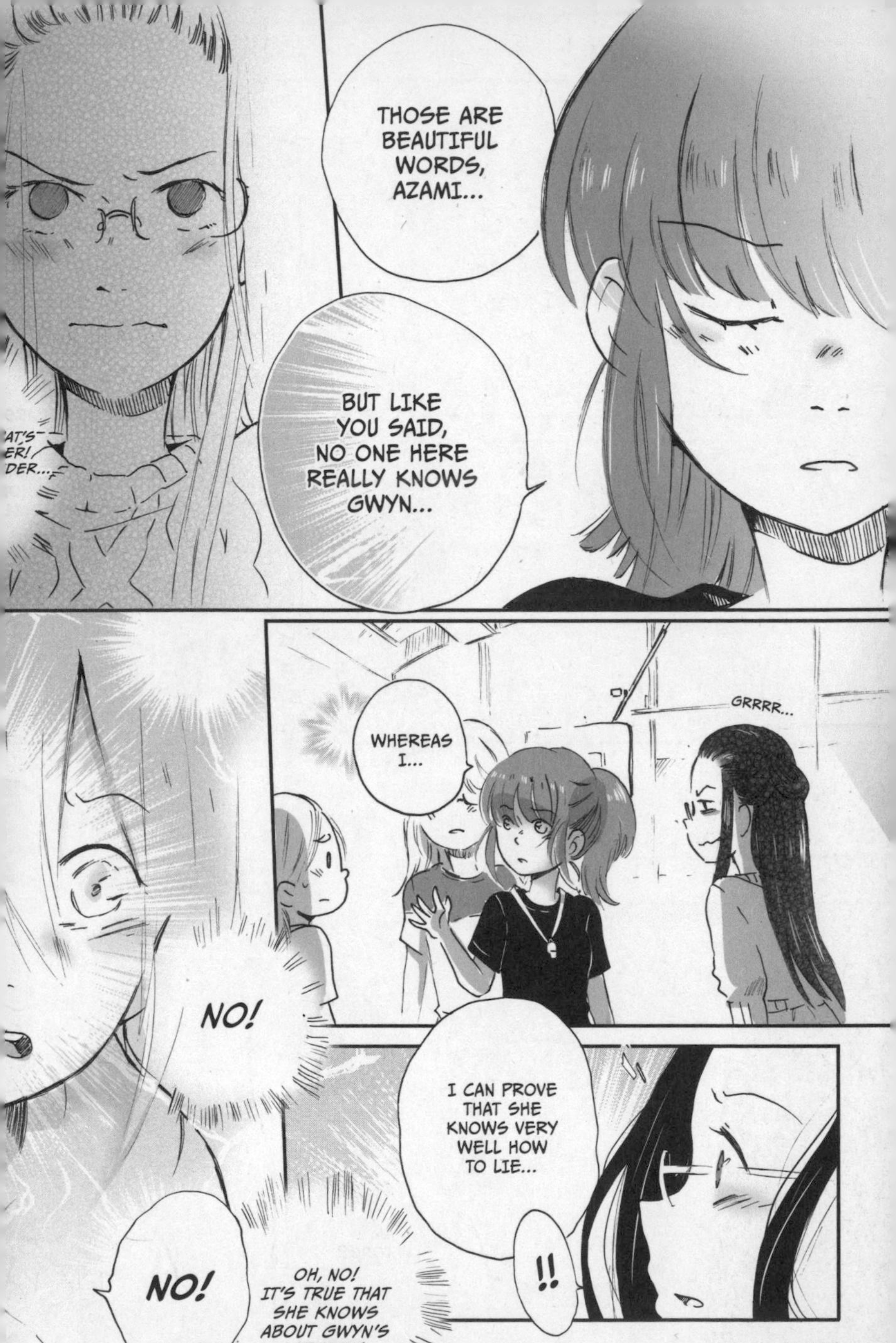
THOSE ARE BEAUTIFUL WORDS, AZAMI...
BUT LIKE YOU SAID, NO ONE HERE REALLY KNOWS GWYN...
GRRRR...
WHEREAS I...
I CAN PROVE THAT SHE KNOWS VERY WELL HOW TO LIE...
!!
NO!
NO!
OH, NO! IT'S TRUE THAT SHE KNOWS ABOUT GWYN'S SECRET!

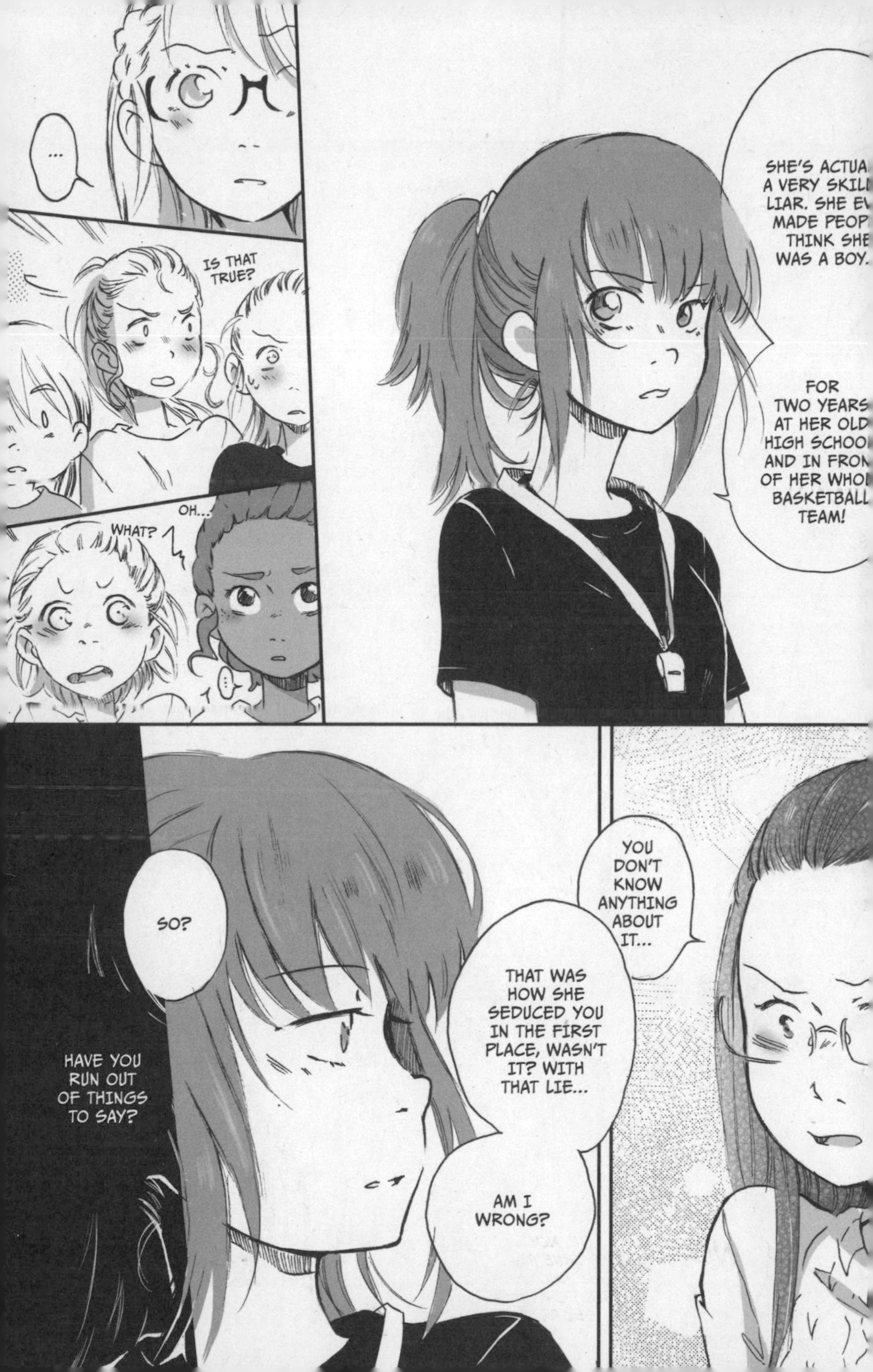
SHE'S ACTUA A VERY SKILL LIAR. SHE EV MADE PEOP THINK SHE WAS A BOY.
FOR TWO YEARS AT HER OLD HIGH SCHOO AND IN FRON OF HER WHO BASKETBALL TEAM!
...
IS THAT TRUE?
OH...
WHAT?
...
YOU DON'T KNOW ANYTHING ABOUT IT...
SO?
THAT WAS HOW SHE SEDUCED YOU IN THE FIRST PLACE, WASN'T IT? WITH THAT LIE...
HAVE YOU RUN OUT OF THINGS TO SAY?
AM I WRONG?

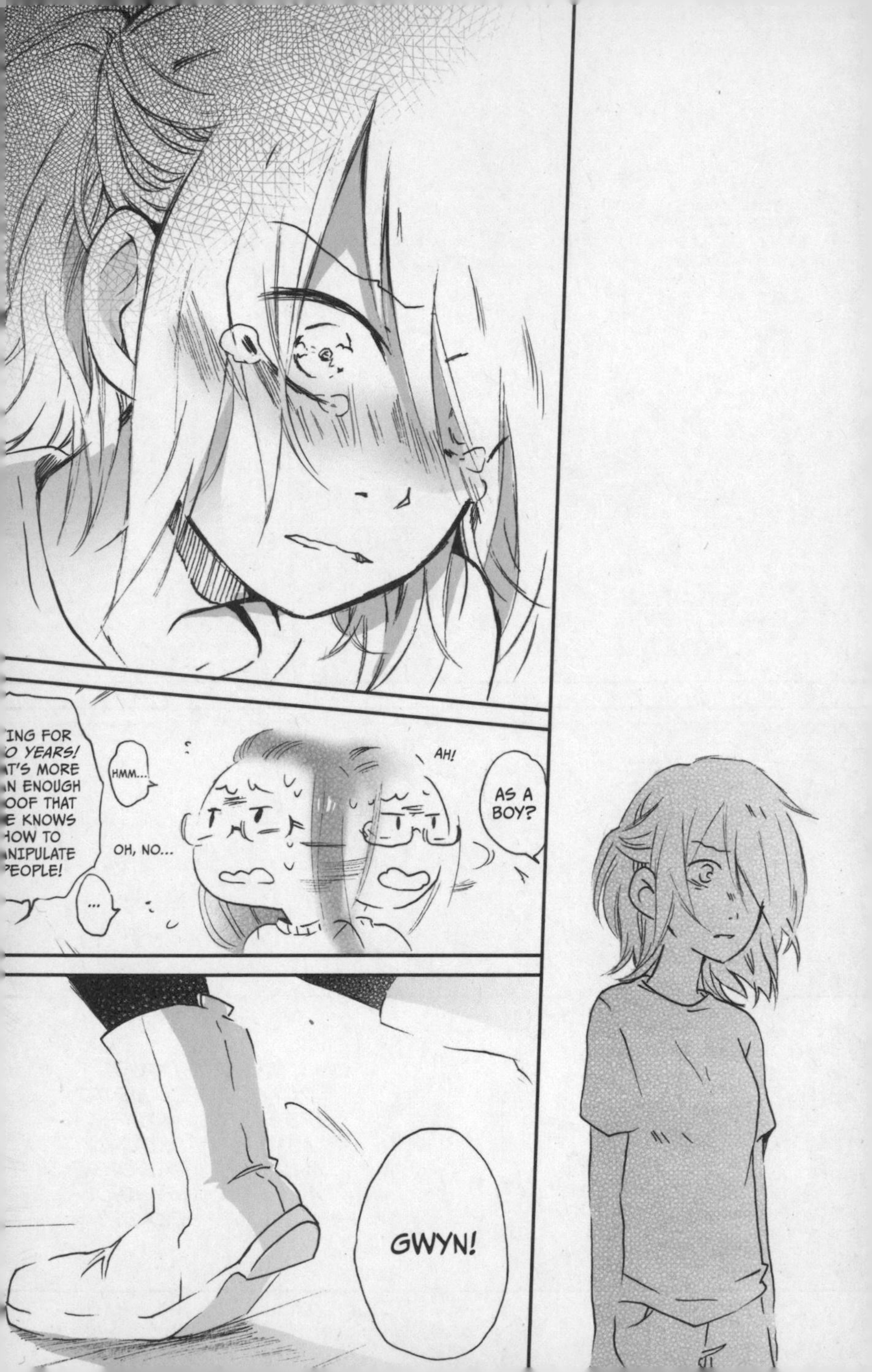
AS A BOY?
AH!
HMM...
ING FOR O YEARS! T'S MORE N ENOUGH OOF THAT E KNOWS HOW TO NIPULATE PEOPLE!
OH, NO...
...
GWYN!

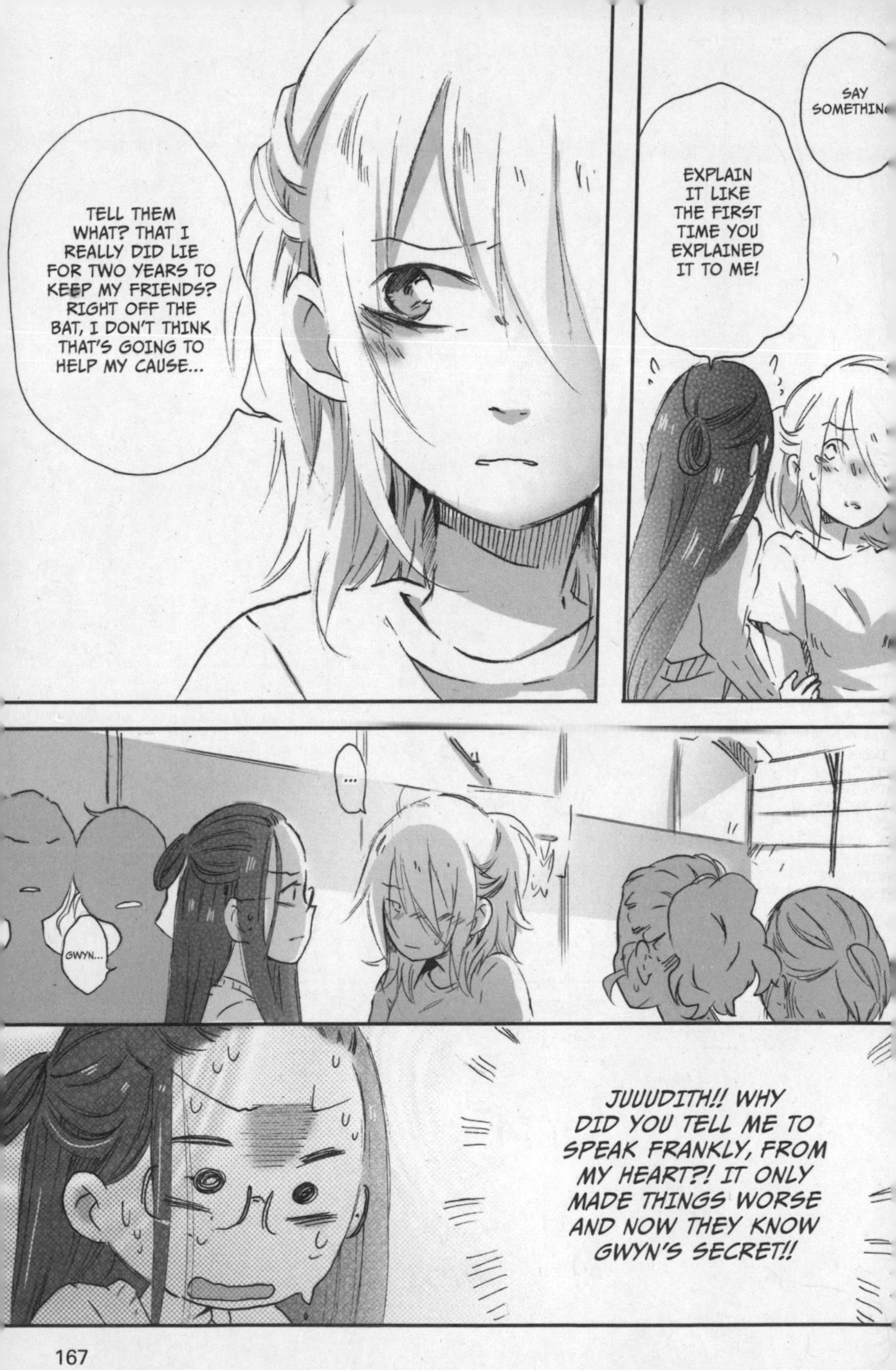
SAY SOMETHIN
EXPLAIN IT LIKE THE FIRST TIME YOU EXPLAINED IT TO ME!
TELL THEM WHAT? THAT I REALLY DID LIE FOR TWO YEARS TO KEEP MY FRIENDS? RIGHT OFF THE BAT, I DON'T THINK THAT'S GOING TO HELP MY CAUSE...
...
GWYN...
JUUUDITH!! WHY DID YOU TELL ME TO SPEAK FRANKLY, FROM MY HEART?! IT ONLY MADE THINGS WORSE AND NOW THEY KNOW GWYN'S SECRET!!

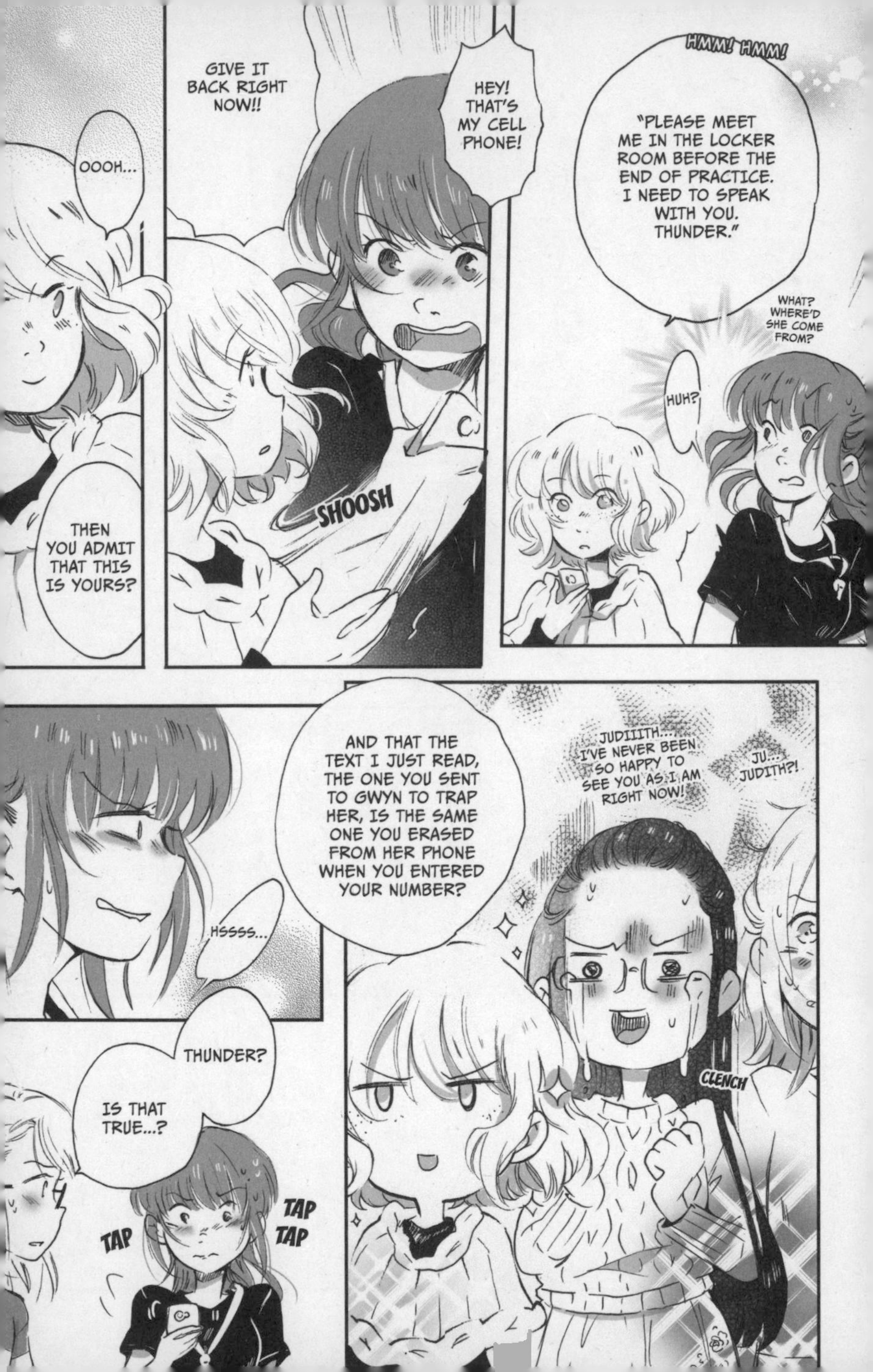
HMM! HMM!
"PLEASE MEET ME IN THE LOCKER ROOM BEFORE THE END OF PRACTICE. I NEED TO SPEAK WITH YOU. THUNDER."
WHAT? WHERE'D SHE COME FROM?
HUH?
HEY! THAT'S MY CELL PHONE!
GIVE IT BACK RIGHT NOW!!
SHOOSH
OOOH...
THEN YOU ADMIT THAT THIS IS YOURS?
AND THAT THE TEXT I JUST READ, THE ONE YOU SENT TO GWYN TO TRAP HER, IS THE SAME ONE YOU ERASED FROM HER PHONE WHEN YOU ENTERED YOUR NUMBER?
JU... JUDITH?!
JUDIIITH... I'VE NEVER BEEN SO HAPPY TO SEE YOU AS I AM RIGHT NOW!
CLENCH
HSSSS...
THUNDER?
IS THAT TRUE...?
TAP TAP
TAP

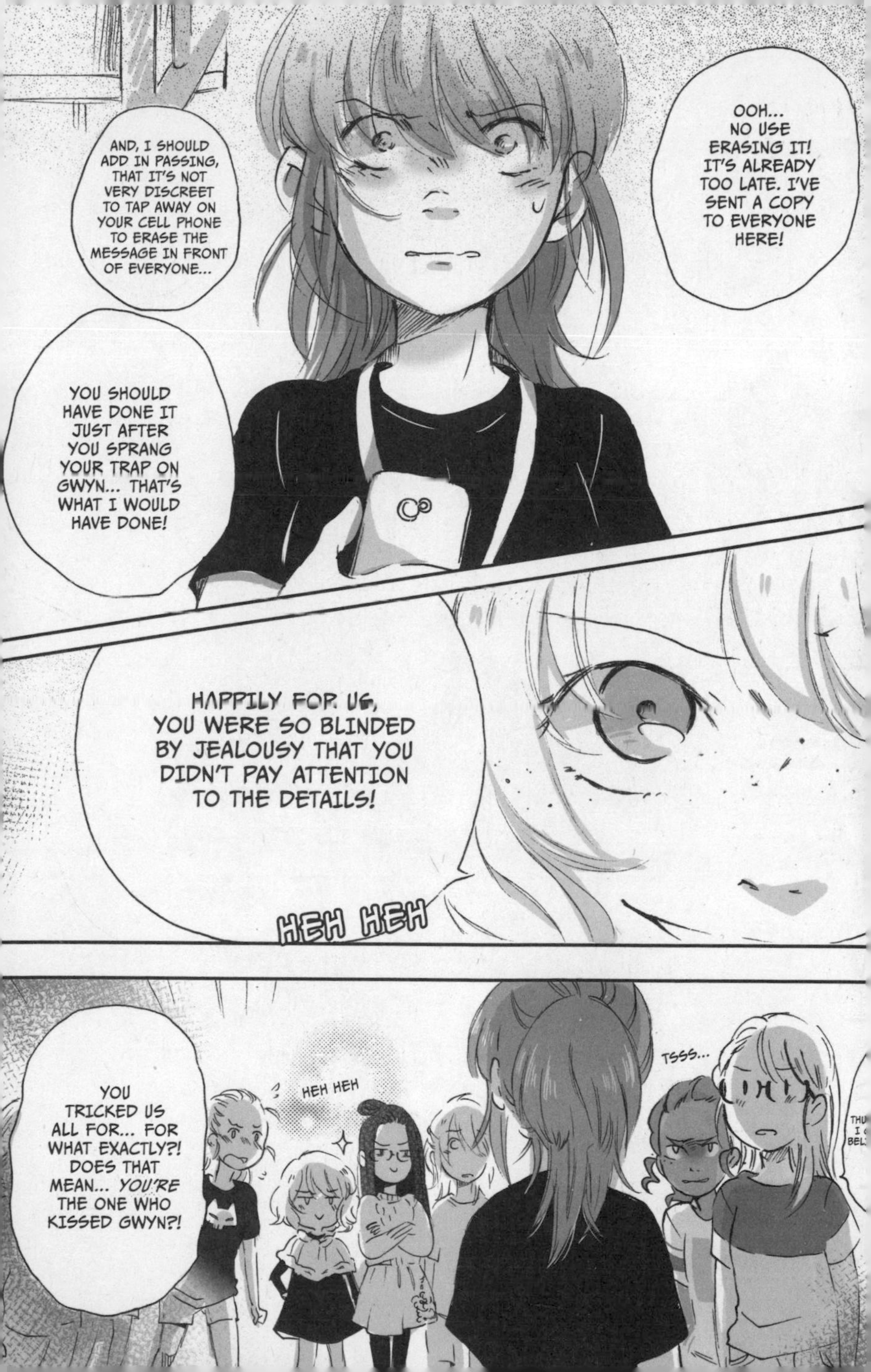
OOH... NO USE ERASING IT! IT'S ALREADY TOO LATE. I'VE SENT A COPY TO EVERYONE HERE!
AND, I SHOULD ADD IN PASSING, THAT IT'S NOT VERY DISCREET TO TAP AWAY ON YOUR CELL PHONE TO ERASE THE MESSAGE IN FRONT OF EVERYONE...
YOU SHOULD HAVE DONE IT JUST AFTER YOU SPRANG YOUR TRAP ON GWYN... THAT'S WHAT I WOULD HAVE DONE!
HAPPILY FOR US, YOU WERE SO BLINDED BY JEALOUSY THAT YOU DIDN'T PAY ATTENTION TO THE DETAILS!
HEH HEH
TSSS...
HEH HEH
YOU TRICKED US ALL FOR... FOR WHAT EXACTLY?! DOES THAT MEAN... *YOU'RE* THE ONE WHO KISSED GWYN?!

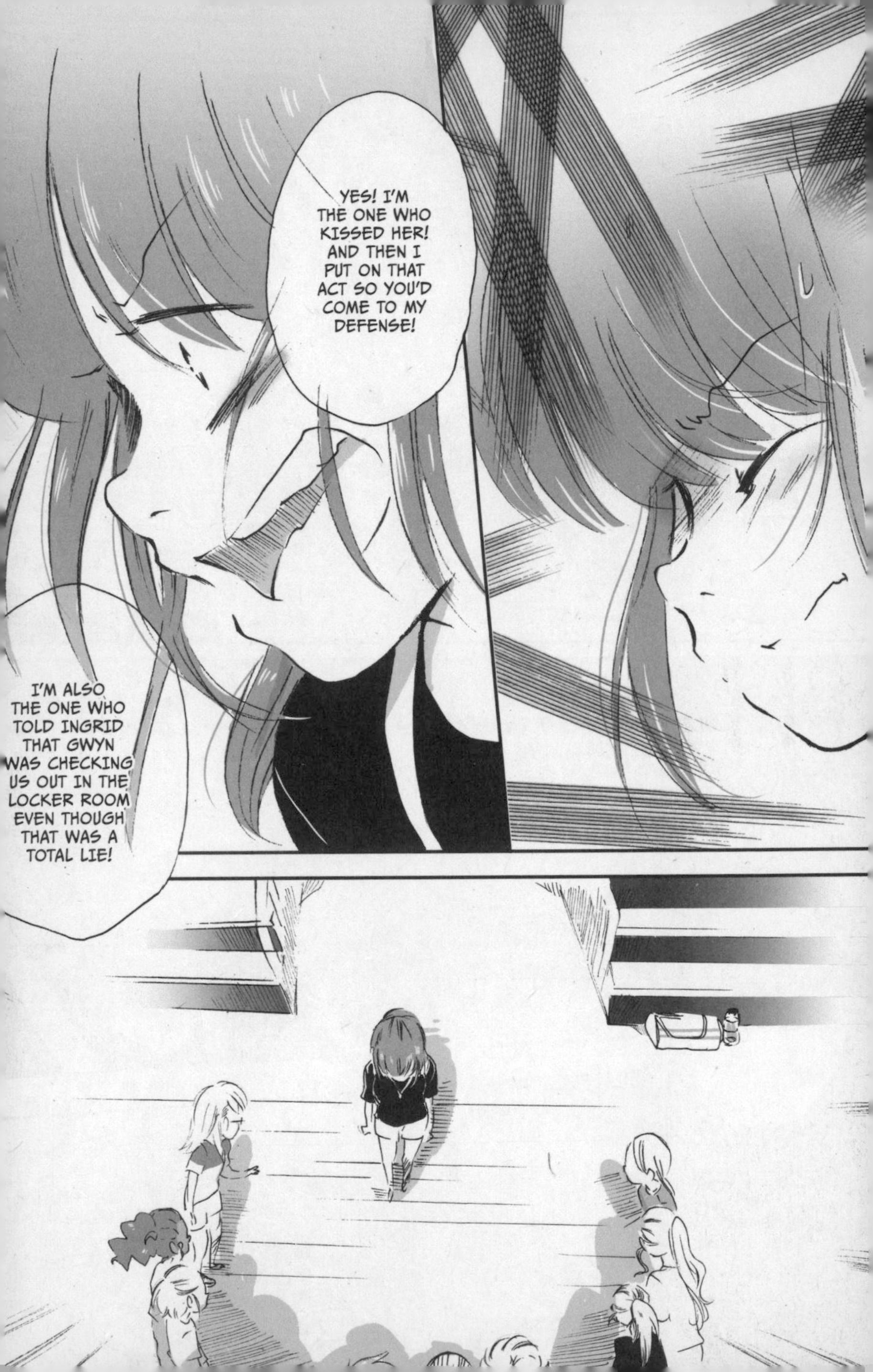
YES! I'M THE ONE WHO KISSED HER! AND THEN I PUT ON THAT ACT SO YOU'D COME TO MY DEFENSE!
I'M ALSO THE ONE WHO TOLD INGRID THAT GWYN WAS CHECKING US OUT IN THE LOCKER ROOM EVEN THOUGH THAT WAS A TOTAL LIE!

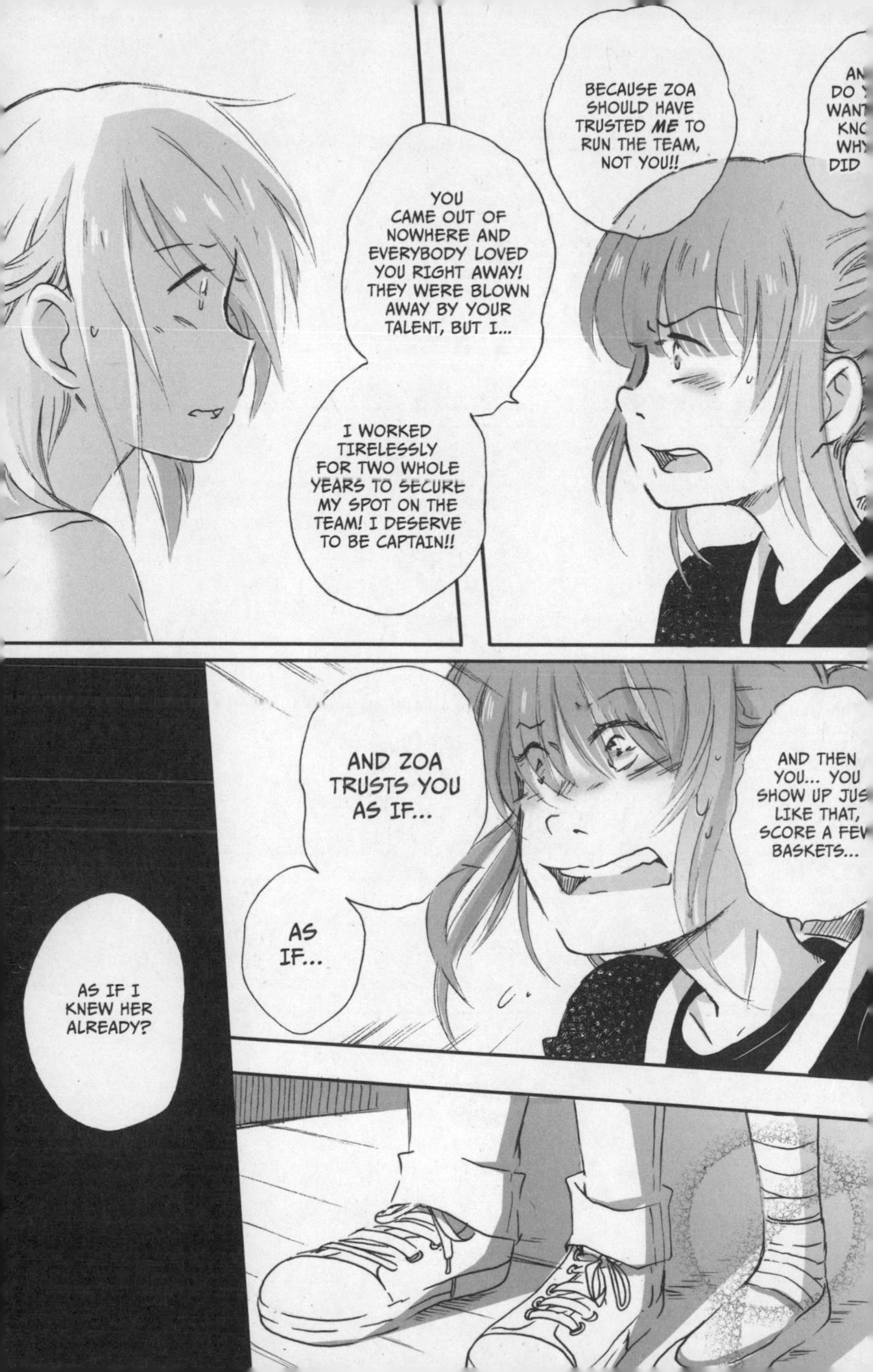
BECAUSE ZOA SHOULD HAVE TRUSTED *ME* TO RUN THE TEAM, NOT YOU!!
YOU CAME OUT OF NOWHERE AND EVERYBODY LOVED YOU RIGHT AWAY! THEY WERE BLOWN AWAY BY YOUR TALENT, BUT I...
I WORKED TIRELESSLY FOR TWO WHOLE YEARS TO SECURE MY SPOT ON THE TEAM! I DESERVE TO BE CAPTAIN!!
AND THEN YOU... YOU SHOW UP JUS LIKE THAT, SCORE A FEW BASKETS...
AND ZOA TRUSTS YOU AS IF...
AS IF...
AS IF I KNEW HER ALREADY?

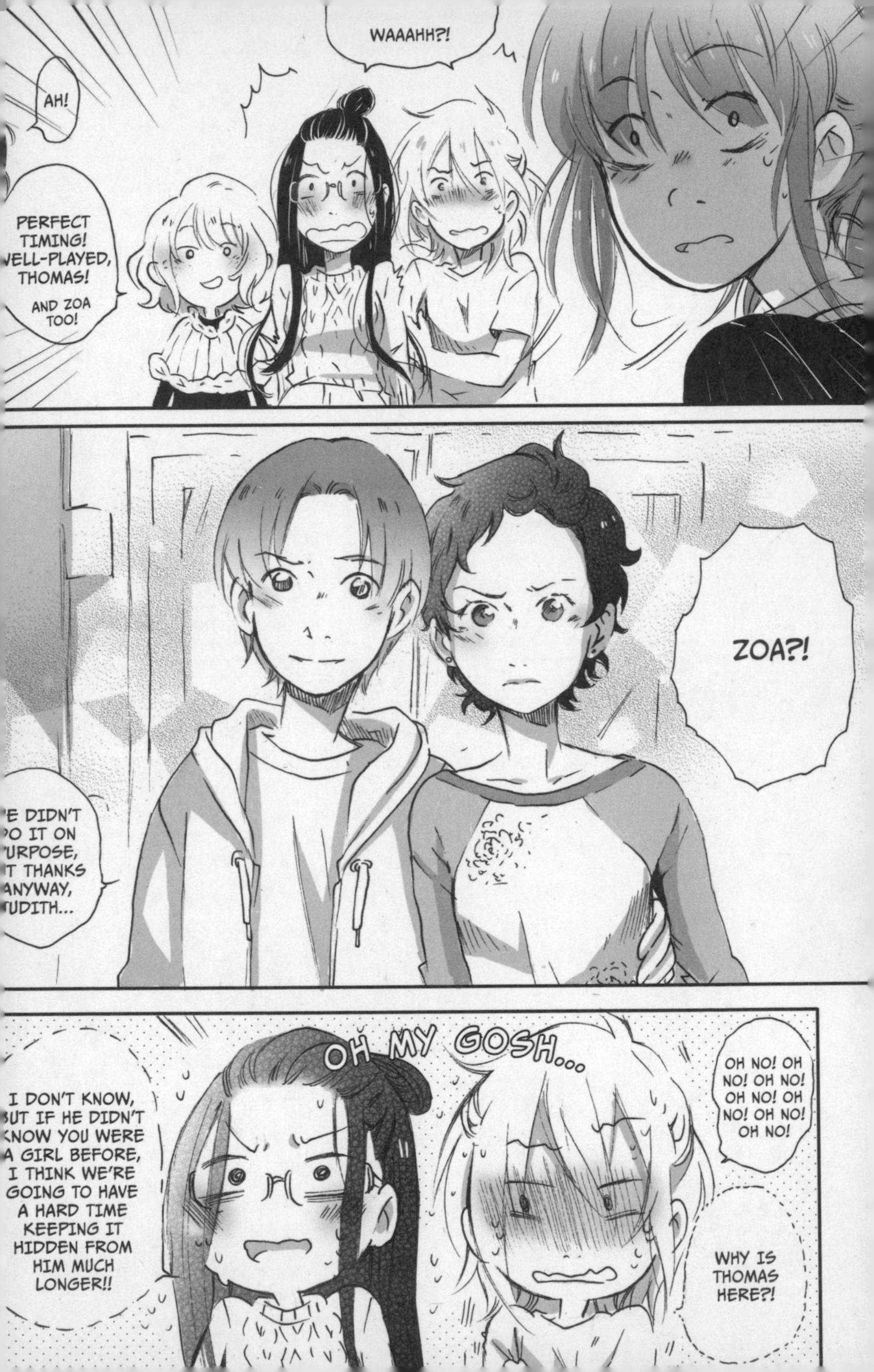
AH!
WAAAHH?!
PERFECT TIMING! ELL-PLAYED, THOMAS!
AND ZOA TOO!
ZOA?!
E DIDN'T O IT ON URPOSE, T THANKS NYWAY, UDITH...
OH MY GOSH...
I DON'T KNOW, UT IF HE DIDN'T NOW YOU WERE A GIRL BEFORE, I THINK WE'RE GOING TO HAVE A HARD TIME KEEPING IT HIDDEN FROM HIM MUCH LONGER!!
OH NO! OH NO! OH NO! OH NO! OH NO! OH NO! OH NO!
WHY IS THOMAS HERE?!

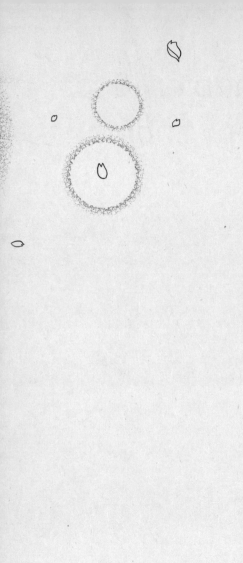

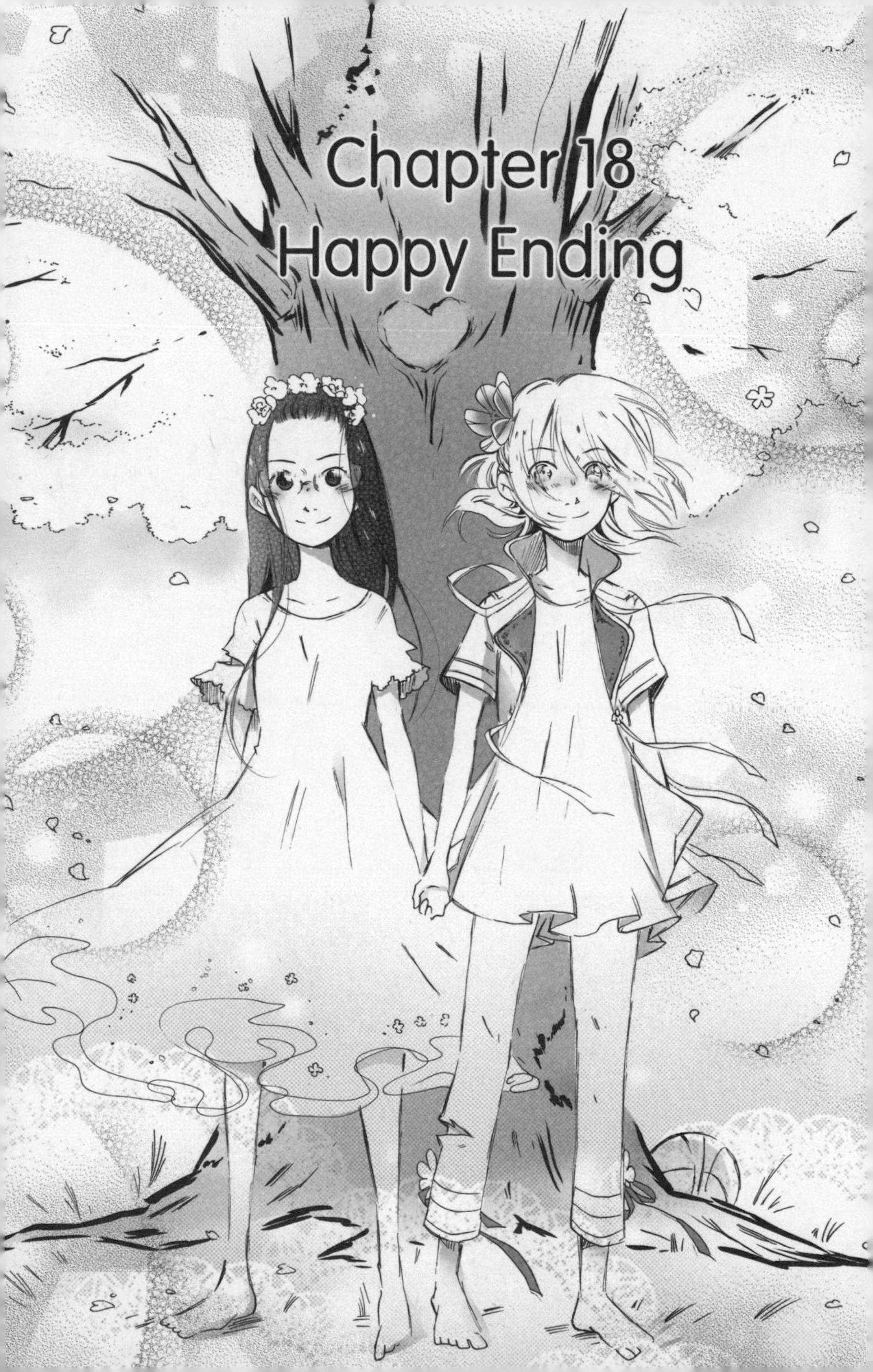
Chapter 18
Happy Ending

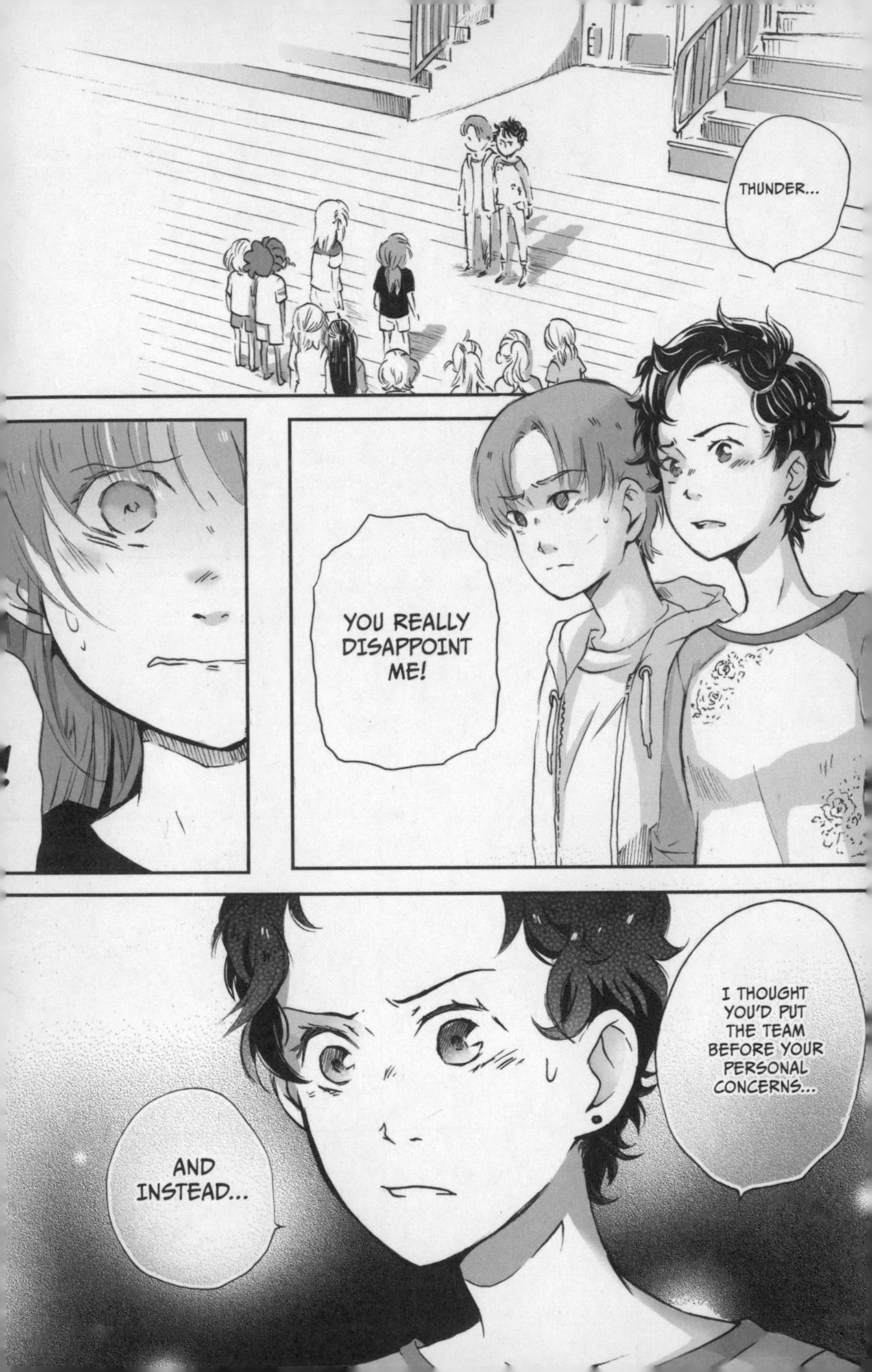
THUNDER...
YOU REALLY DISAPPOINT ME!
I THOUGHT YOU'D PUT THE TEAM BEFORE YOUR PERSONAL CONCERNS...
AND INSTEAD...

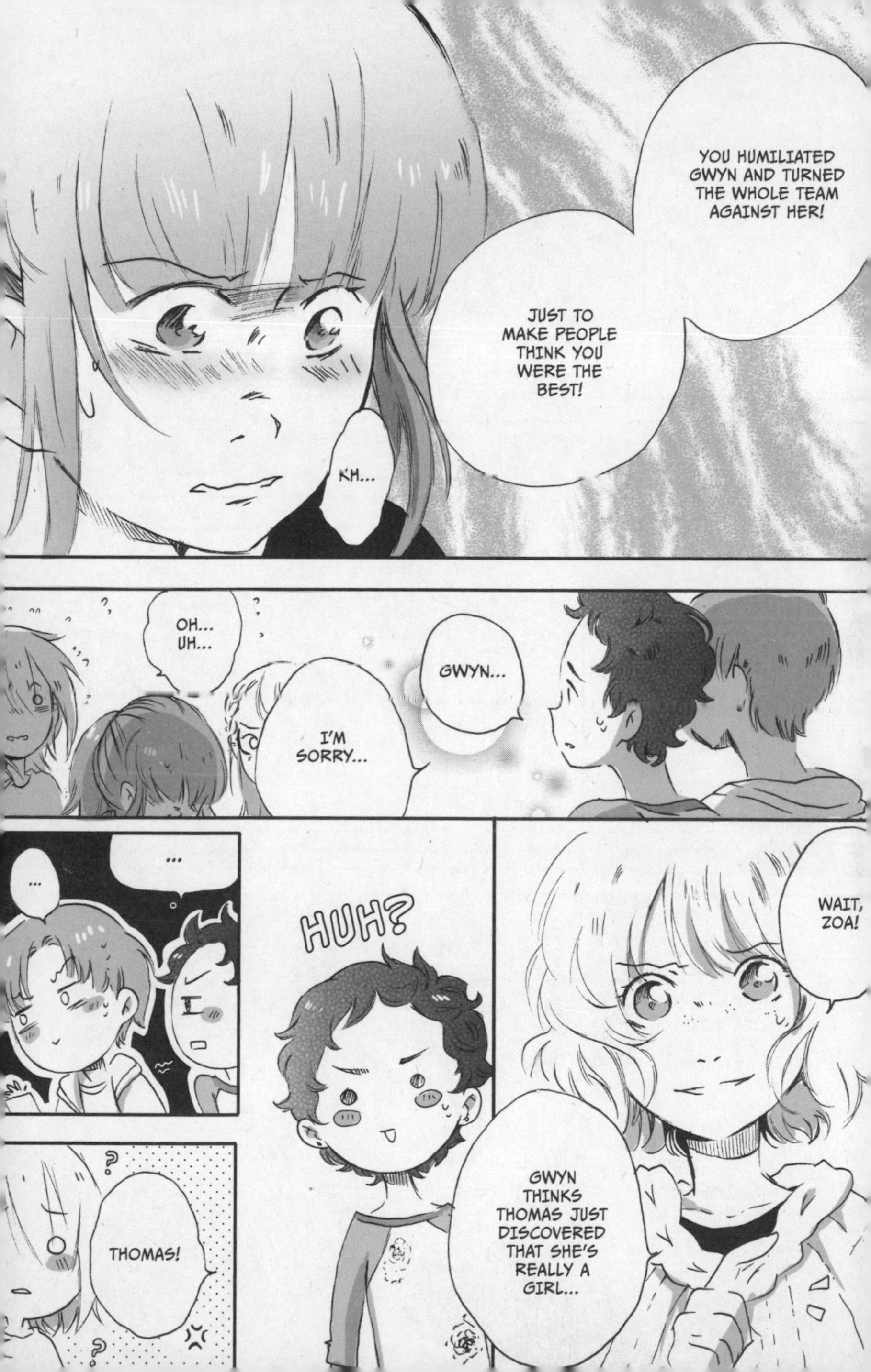
YOU HUMILIATED GWYN AND TURNED THE WHOLE TEAM AGAINST HER!
JUST TO MAKE PEOPLE THINK YOU WERE THE BEST!
KH...
GWYN...
I'M SORRY...
OH... UH...
WAIT, ZOA!
GWYN THINKS THOMAS JUST DISCOVERED THAT SHE'S REALLY A GIRL...
HUH?
...
...
THOMAS!

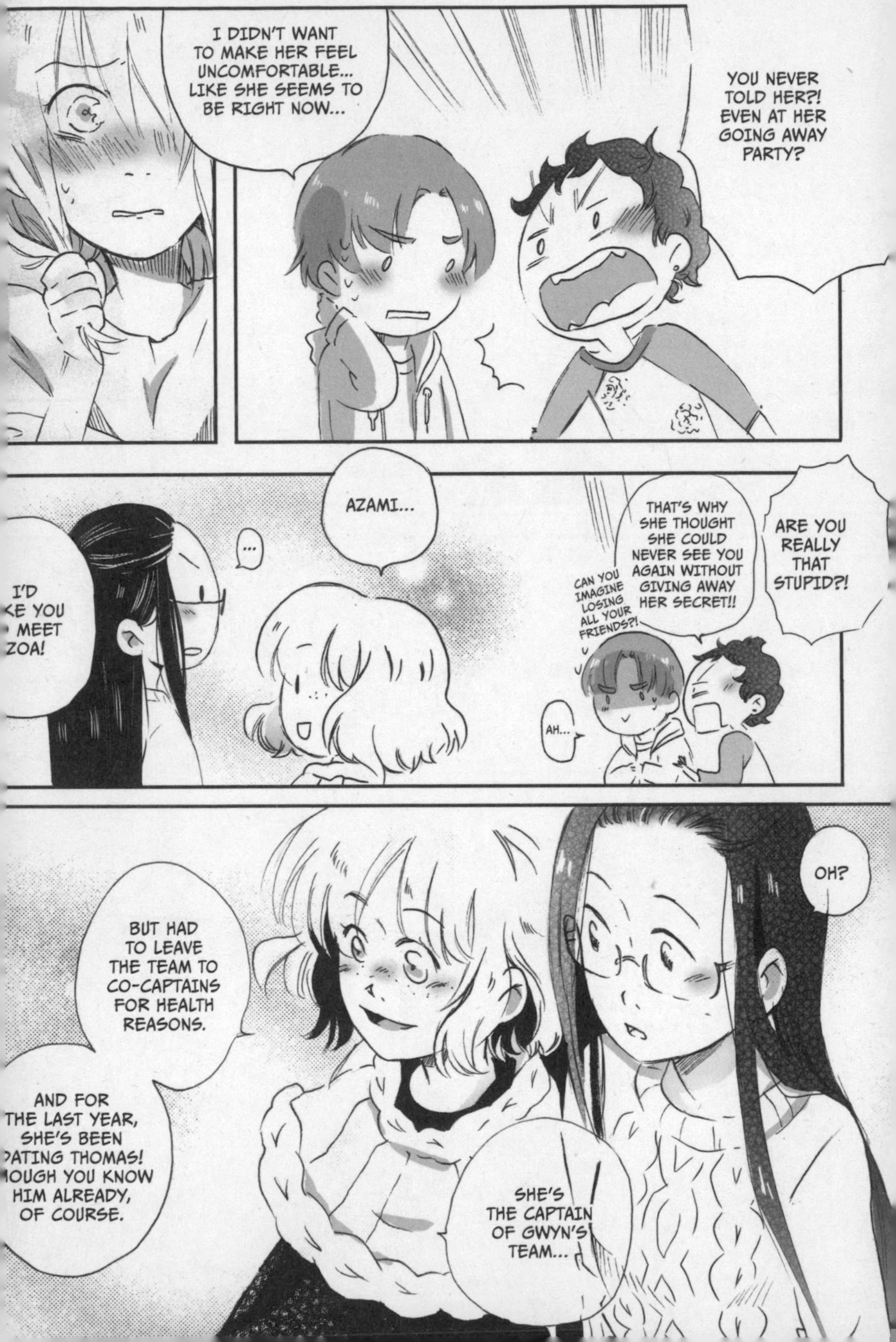
YOU NEVER TOLD HER?! EVEN AT HER GOING AWAY PARTY?
I DIDN'T WANT TO MAKE HER FEEL UNCOMFORTABLE... LIKE SHE SEEMS TO BE RIGHT NOW...
ARE YOU REALLY THAT STUPID?!
THAT'S WHY SHE THOUGHT SHE COULD NEVER SEE YOU AGAIN WITHOUT GIVING AWAY HER SECRET!!
CAN YOU IMAGINE LOSING ALL YOUR FRIENDS?!
AH...
AZAMI...
...
I'D
E YOU
MEET
ZOA!
OH?
SHE'S THE CAPTAIN OF GWYN'S TEAM...
BUT HAD TO LEAVE THE TEAM TO CO-CAPTAINS FOR HEALTH REASONS.
AND FOR THE LAST YEAR, SHE'S BEEN
ATING THOMAS!
HOUGH YOU KNOW
HIM ALREADY, OF COURSE.

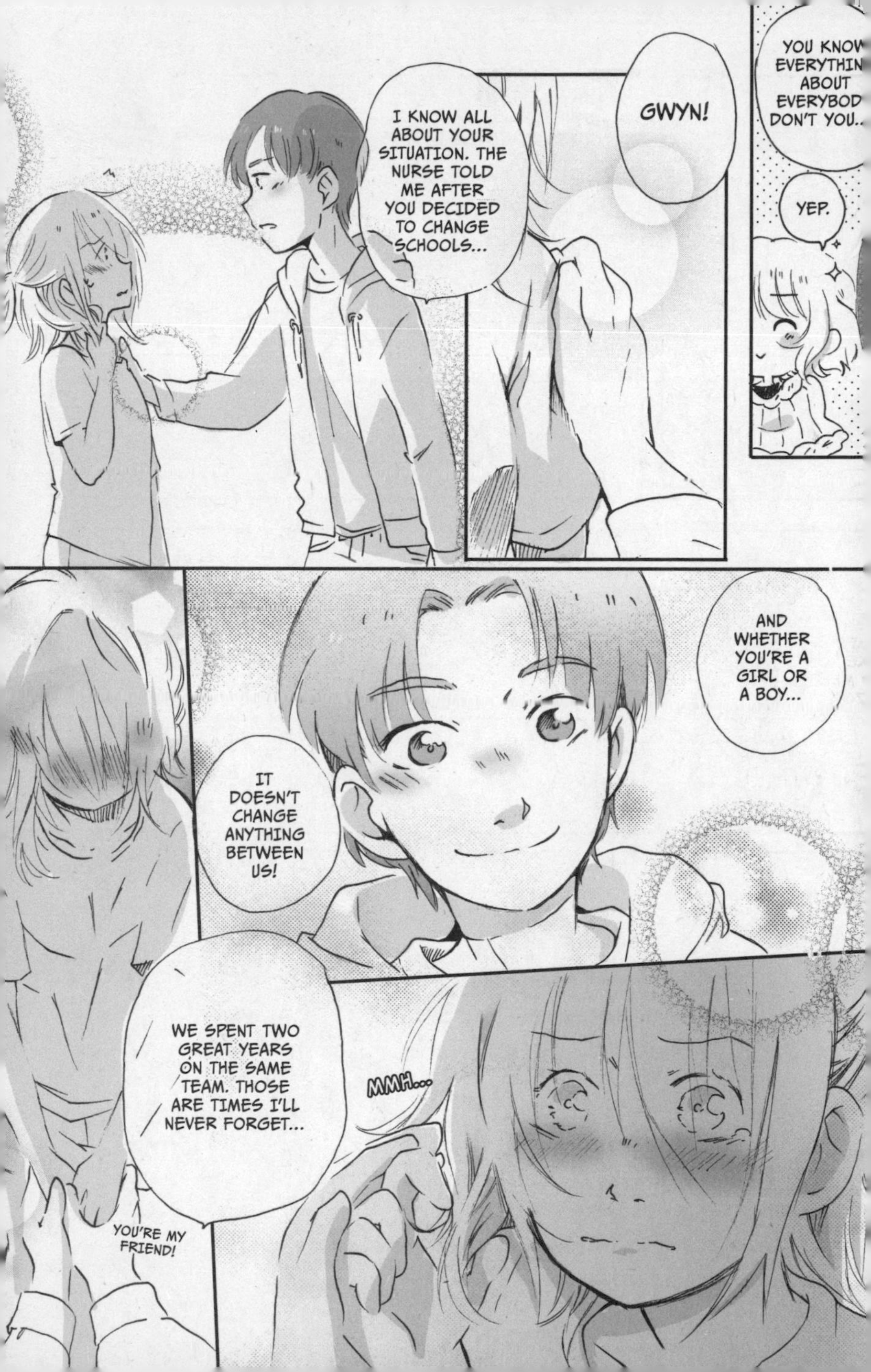
YOU KNOW EVERYTHIN ABOUT EVERYBOD DON'T YOU..
YEP.
GWYN!
I KNOW ALL ABOUT YOUR SITUATION. THE NURSE TOLD ME AFTER YOU DECIDED TO CHANGE SCHOOLS...
AND WHETHER YOU'RE A GIRL OR A BOY...
IT DOESN'T CHANGE ANYTHING BETWEEN US!
WE SPENT TWO GREAT YEARS ON THE SAME TEAM. THOSE ARE TIMES I'LL NEVER FORGET...
MMH...
YOU'RE MY FRIEND!

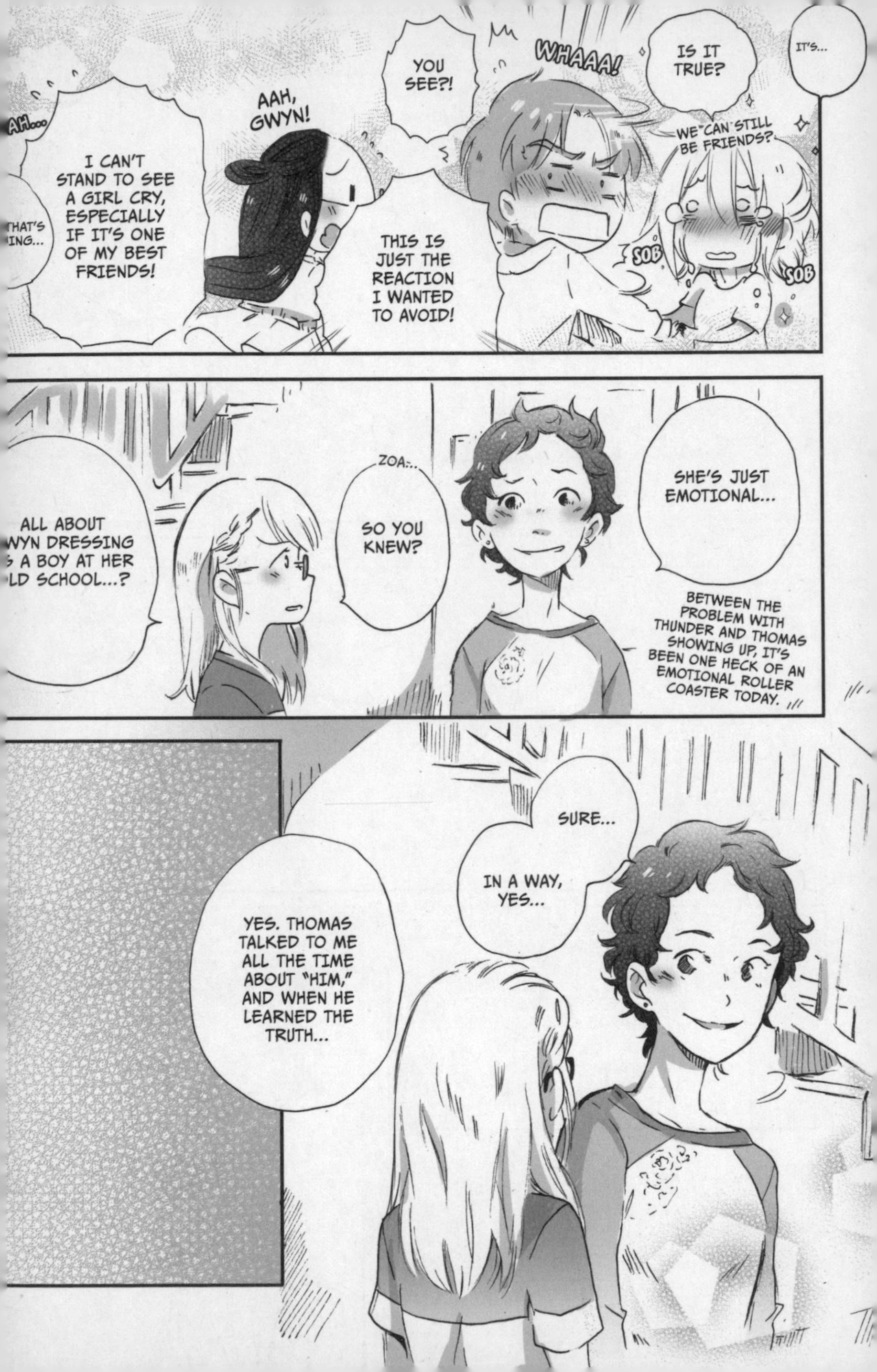
IT'S...
IS IT TRUE?
WE CAN STILL BE FRIENDS?
WHAAAA!
SOB
SOB
YOU SEE?!
THIS IS JUST THE REACTION I WANTED TO AVOID!
AAH, GWYN!
I CAN'T STAND TO SEE A GIRL CRY, ESPECIALLY IF IT'S ONE OF MY BEST FRIENDS!
AH...
THAT'S
SHE'S JUST EMOTIONAL...
BETWEEN THE PROBLEM WITH THUNDER AND THOMAS SHOWING UP, IT'S BEEN ONE HECK OF AN EMOTIONAL ROLLER COASTER TODAY.
ZOA...
SO YOU KNEW?
ALL ABOUT WYN DRESSING A BOY AT HER LD SCHOOL...?
SURE...
IN A WAY, YES...
YES. THOMAS TALKED TO ME ALL THE TIME ABOUT "HIM," AND WHEN HE LEARNED THE TRUTH...

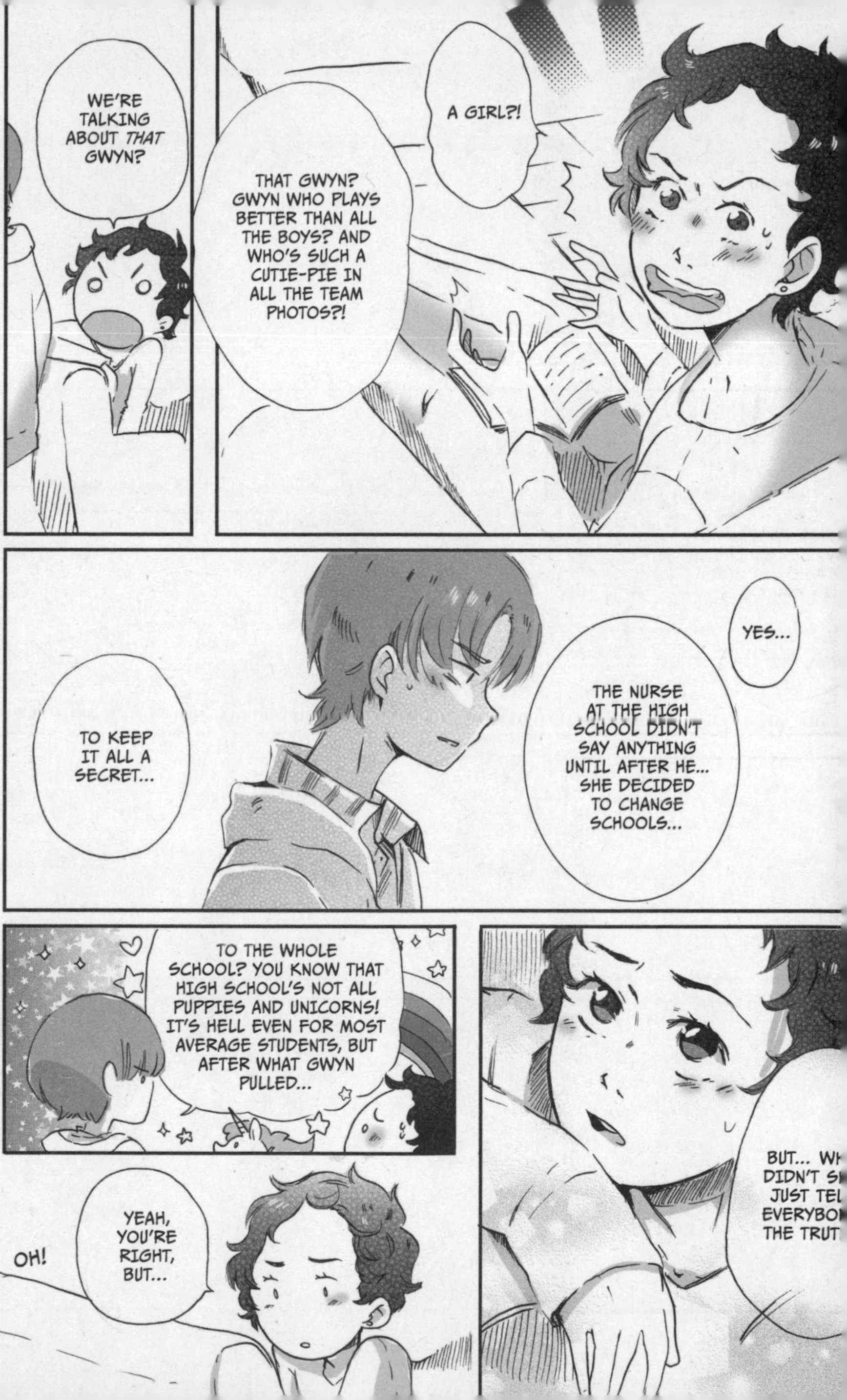
A GIRL?!
THAT GWYN? GWYN WHO PLAYS BETTER THAN ALL THE BOYS? AND WHO'S SUCH A CUTIE-PIE IN ALL THE TEAM PHOTOS?!
WE'RE TALKING ABOUT *THAT* GWYN?
YES...
THE NURSE AT THE HIGH SCHOOL DIDN'T SAY ANYTHING UNTIL AFTER HE... SHE DECIDED TO CHANGE SCHOOLS...
TO KEEP IT ALL A SECRET...
BUT... WH DIDN'T S JUST TEL EVERYBO THE TRUT
TO THE WHOLE SCHOOL? YOU KNOW THAT HIGH SCHOOL'S NOT ALL PUPPIES AND UNICORNS! IT'S HELL EVEN FOR MOST AVERAGE STUDENTS, BUT AFTER WHAT GWYN PULLED...
YEAH, YOU'RE RIGHT, BUT...
OH!

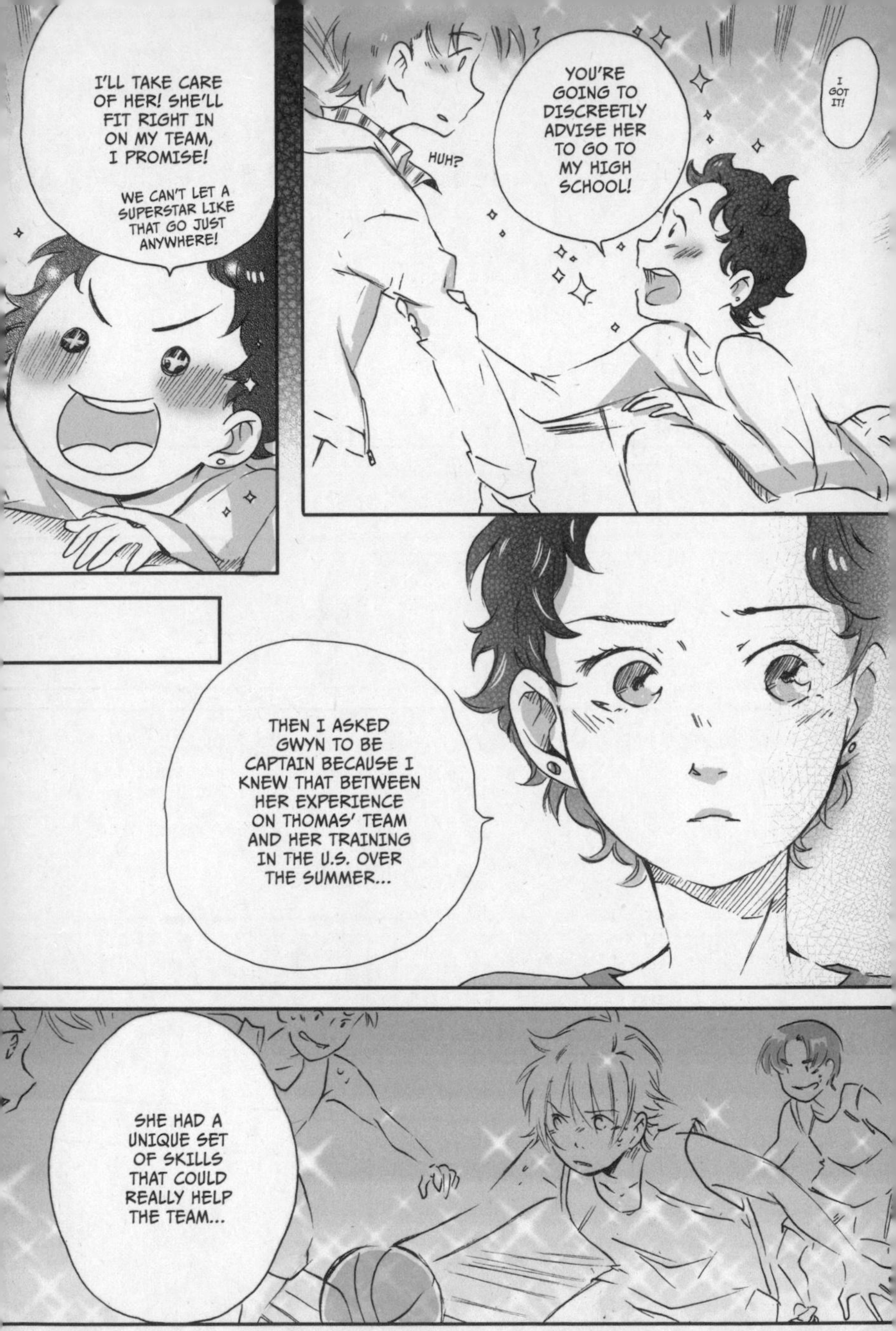
I GOT IT!
YOU'RE GOING TO DISCREETLY ADVISE HER TO GO TO MY HIGH SCHOOL!
HUH?
I'LL TAKE CARE OF HER! SHE'LL FIT RIGHT IN ON MY TEAM, I PROMISE!
WE CAN'T LET A SUPERSTAR LIKE THAT GO JUST ANYWHERE!
THEN I ASKED GWYN TO BE CAPTAIN BECAUSE I KNEW THAT BETWEEN HER EXPERIENCE ON THOMAS' TEAM AND HER TRAINING IN THE U.S. OVER THE SUMMER...
SHE HAD A UNIQUE SET OF SKILLS THAT COULD REALLY HELP THE TEAM...

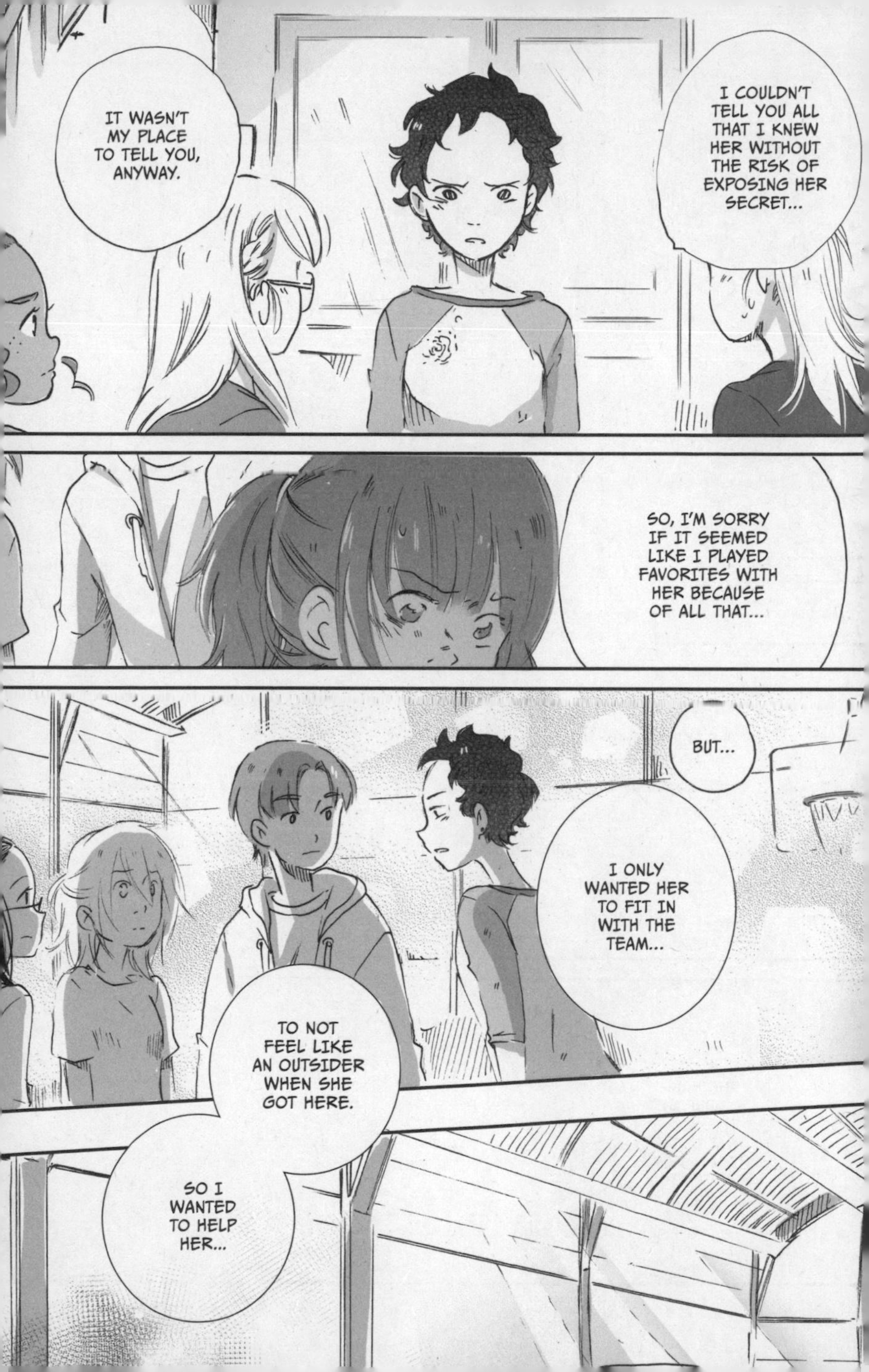
I COULDN'T TELL YOU ALL THAT I KNEW HER WITHOUT THE RISK OF EXPOSING HER SECRET...
IT WASN'T MY PLACE TO TELL YOU, ANYWAY.
SO, I'M SORRY IF IT SEEMED LIKE I PLAYED FAVORITES WITH HER BECAUSE OF ALL THAT...
BUT...
I ONLY WANTED HER TO FIT IN WITH THE TEAM...
TO NOT FEEL LIKE AN OUTSIDER WHEN SHE GOT HERE.
SO I WANTED TO HELP HER...

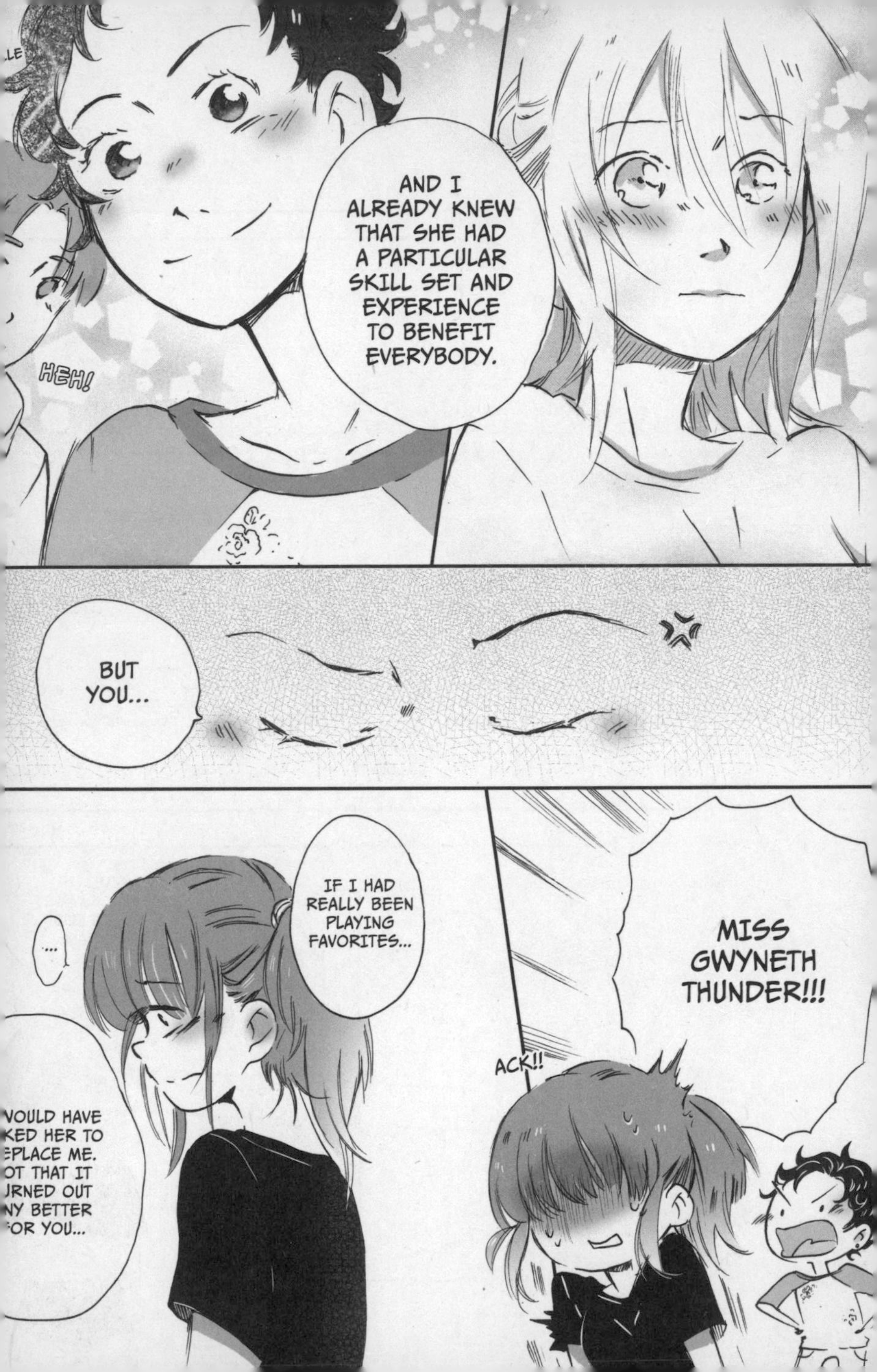
AND I ALREADY KNEW THAT SHE HAD A PARTICULAR SKILL SET AND EXPERIENCE TO BENEFIT EVERYBODY.
HEH!
BUT YOU...
MISS GWYNETH THUNDER!!!
ACK!!
IF I HAD REALLY BEEN PLAYING FAVORITES...
....
VOULD HAVE KED HER TO EPLACE ME. OT THAT IT URNED OUT NY BETTER FOR YOU...

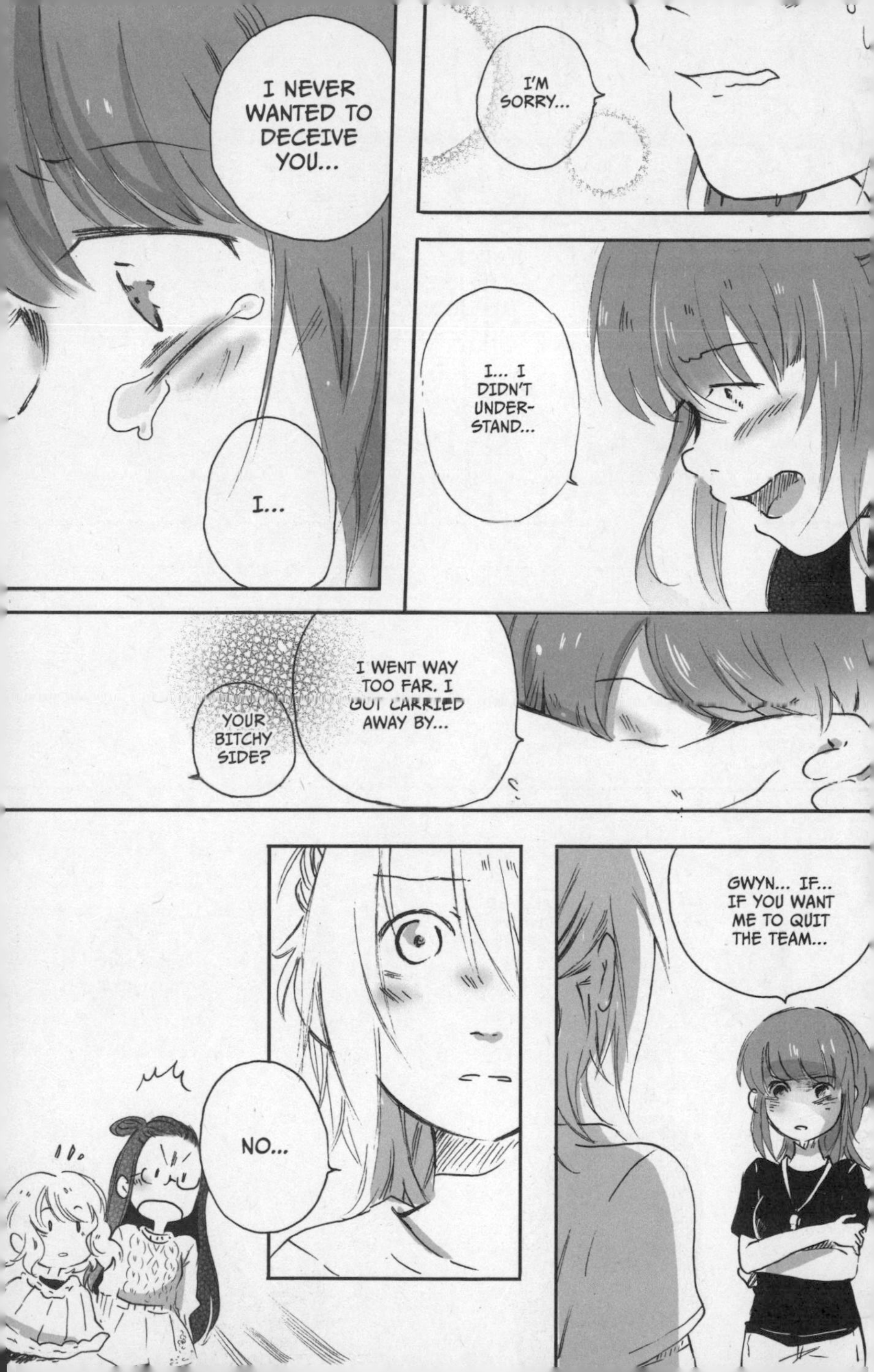
I'M SORRY...
I... I DIDN'T UNDERSTAND...
I NEVER WANTED TO DECEIVE YOU...
I...
I WENT WAY TOO FAR. I GOT CARRIED AWAY BY...
YOUR BITCHY SIDE?
GWYN... IF... IF YOU WANT ME TO QUIT THE TEAM...
NO...

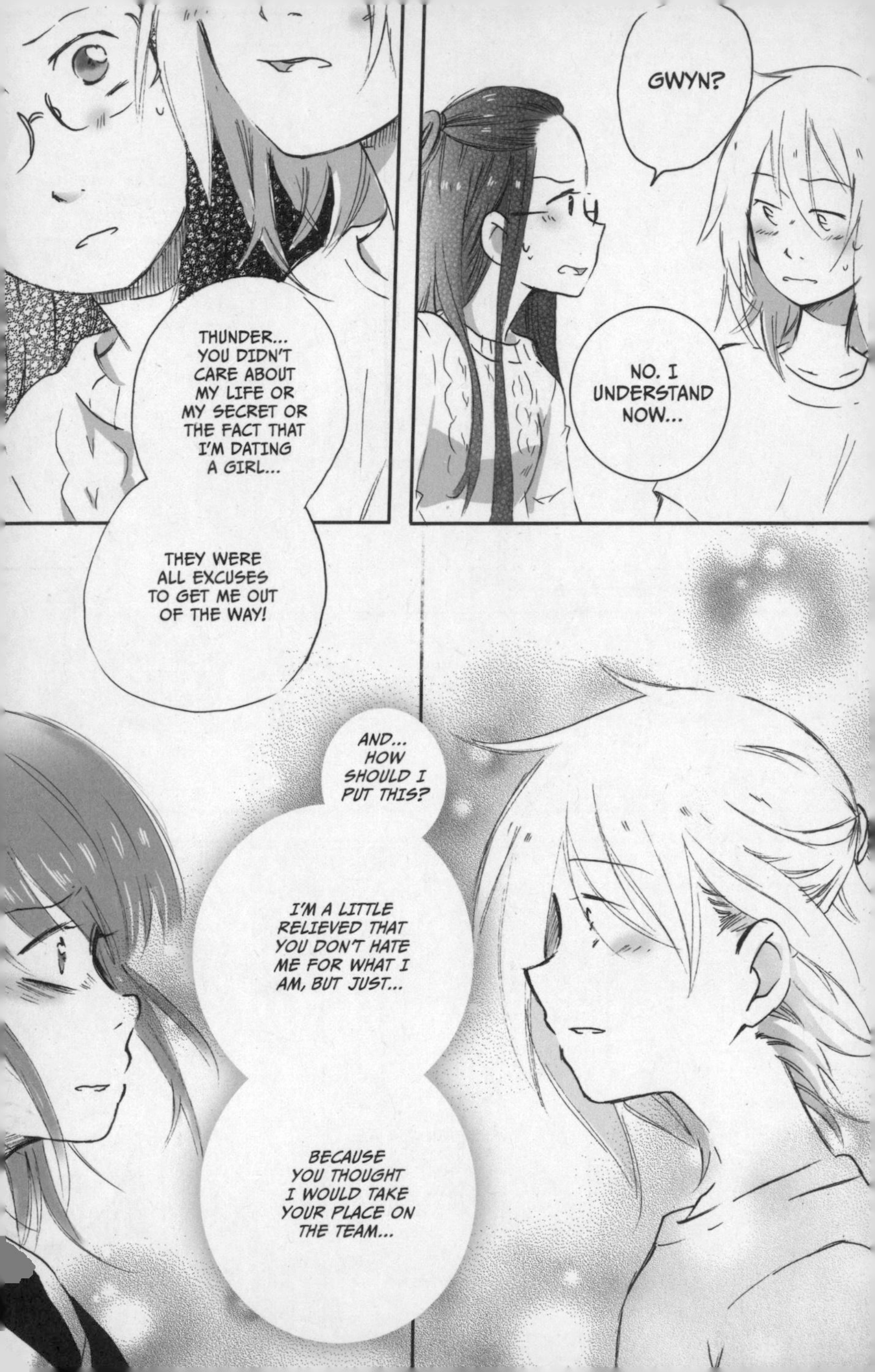
GWYN?
NO. I UNDERSTAND NOW...
THUNDER... YOU DIDN'T CARE ABOUT MY LIFE OR MY SECRET OR THE FACT THAT I'M DATING A GIRL...
THEY WERE ALL EXCUSES TO GET ME OUT OF THE WAY!
AND... HOW SHOULD I PUT THIS?
I'M A LITTLE RELIEVED THAT YOU DON'T HATE ME FOR WHAT I AM, BUT JUST...
BECAUSE YOU THOUGHT I WOULD TAKE YOUR PLACE ON THE TEAM...

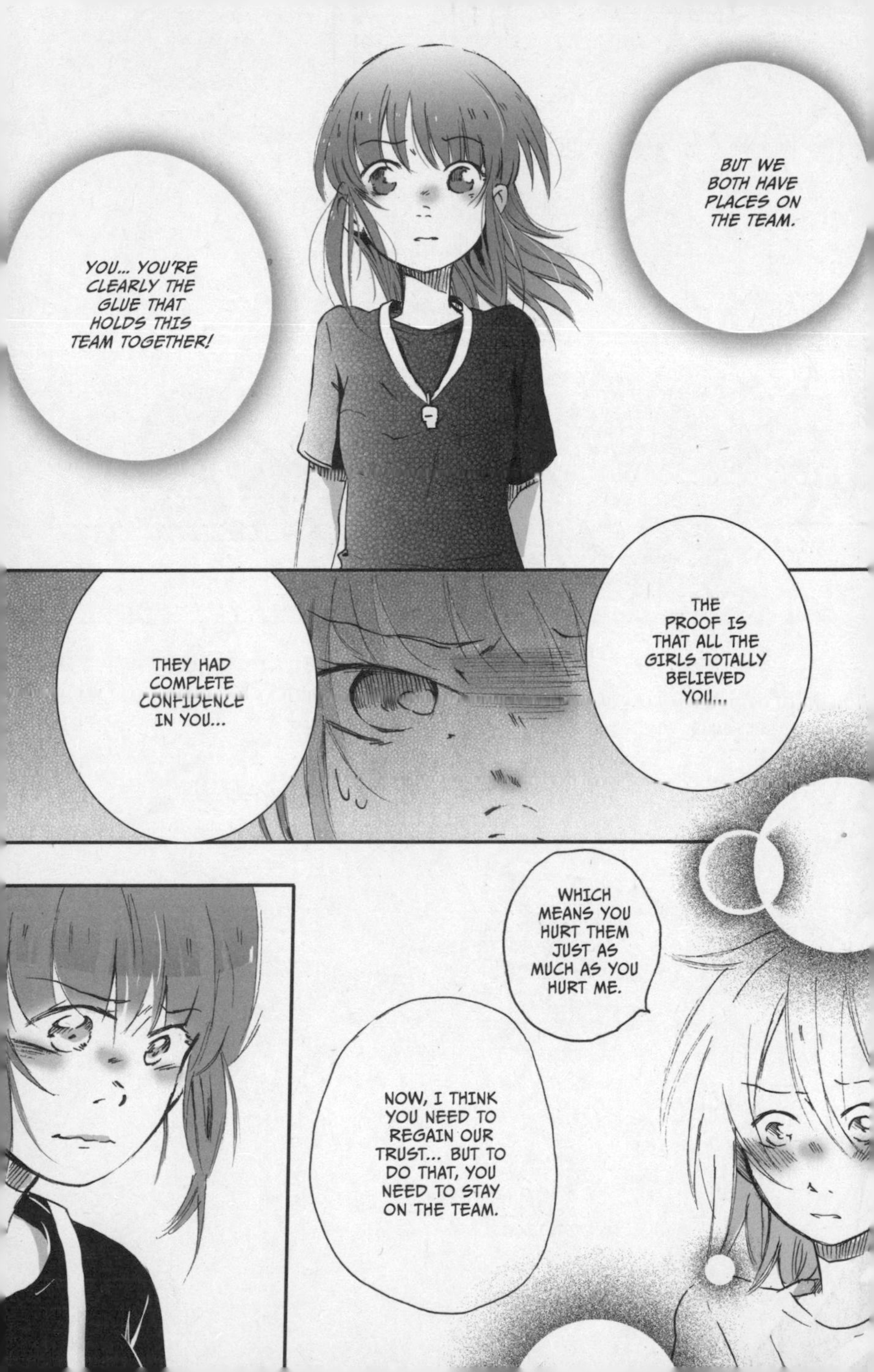
BUT WE BOTH HAVE PLACES ON THE TEAM.
YOU... YOU'RE CLEARLY THE GLUE THAT HOLDS THIS TEAM TOGETHER!
THE PROOF IS THAT ALL THE GIRLS TOTALLY BELIEVED YOU...
THEY HAD COMPLETE CONFIDENCE IN YOU...
WHICH MEANS YOU HURT THEM JUST AS MUCH AS YOU HURT ME.
NOW, I THINK YOU NEED TO REGAIN OUR TRUST... BUT TO DO THAT, YOU NEED TO STAY ON THE TEAM.

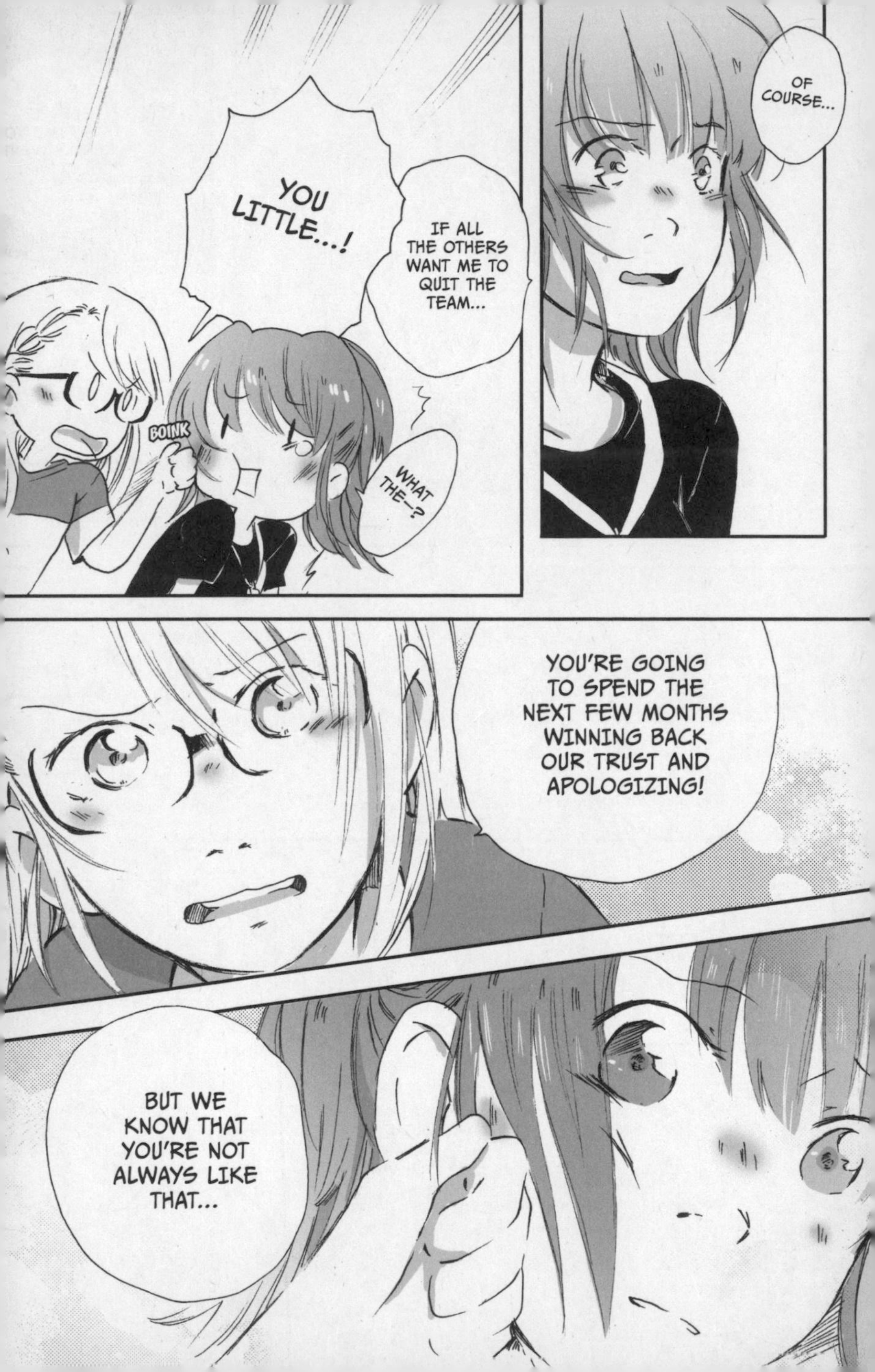
OF COURSE...
IF ALL THE OTHERS WANT ME TO QUIT THE TEAM...
YOU LITTLE...!
BOINK
WHAT THE--?
YOU'RE GOING TO SPEND THE NEXT FEW MONTHS WINNING BACK OUR TRUST AND APOLOGIZING!
BUT WE KNOW THAT YOU'RE NOT ALWAYS LIKE THAT...

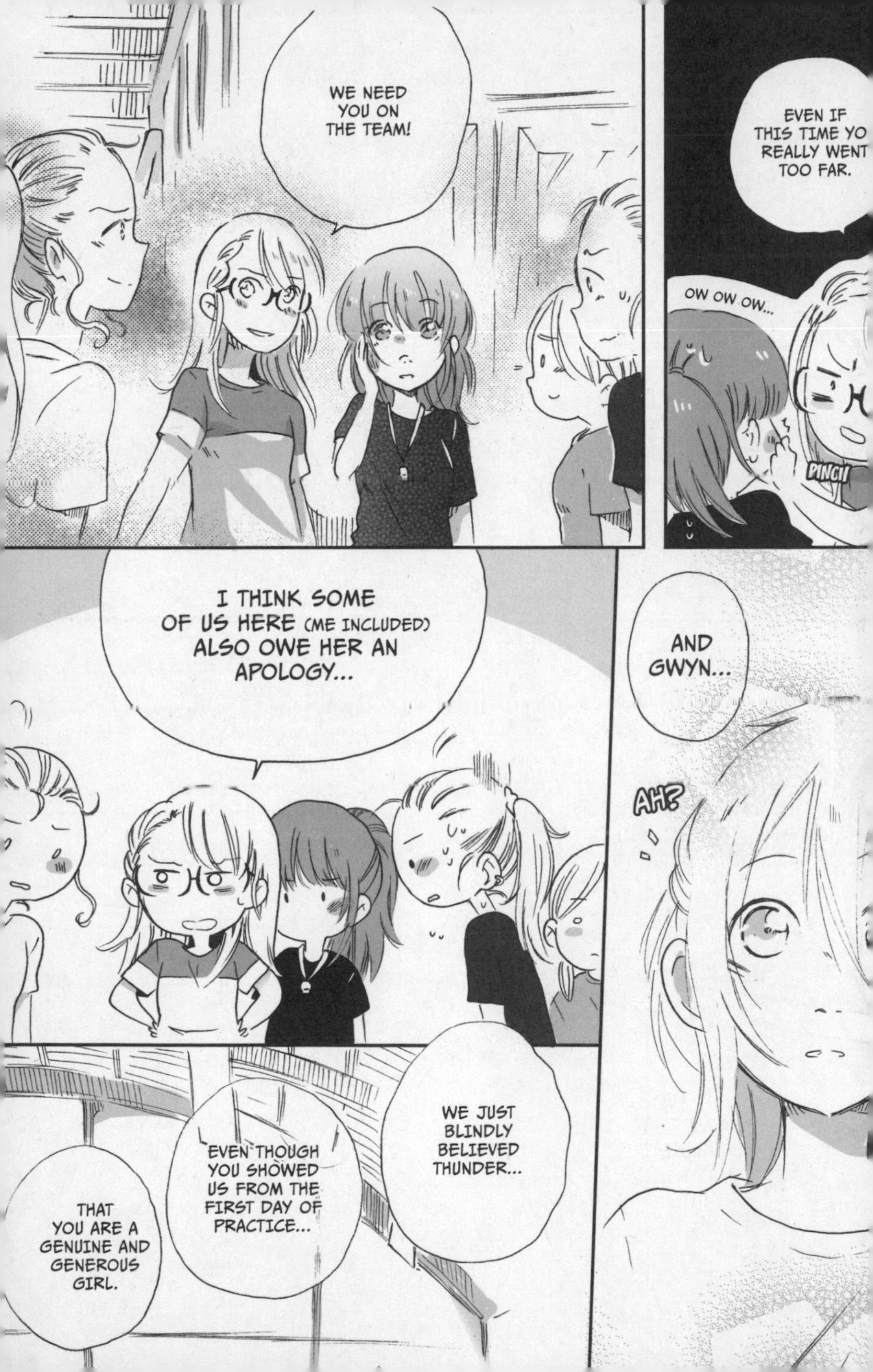
EVEN IF THIS TIME YO REALLY WENT TOO FAR.
OW OW OW...
PINCH
WE NEED YOU ON THE TEAM!
AND GWYN...
AH?
I THINK SOME OF US HERE (ME INCLUDED) ALSO OWE HER AN APOLOGY...
WE JUST BLINDLY BELIEVED THUNDER...
EVEN THOUGH YOU SHOWED US FROM THE FIRST DAY OF PRACTICE...
THAT YOU ARE A GENUINE AND GENEROUS GIRL.

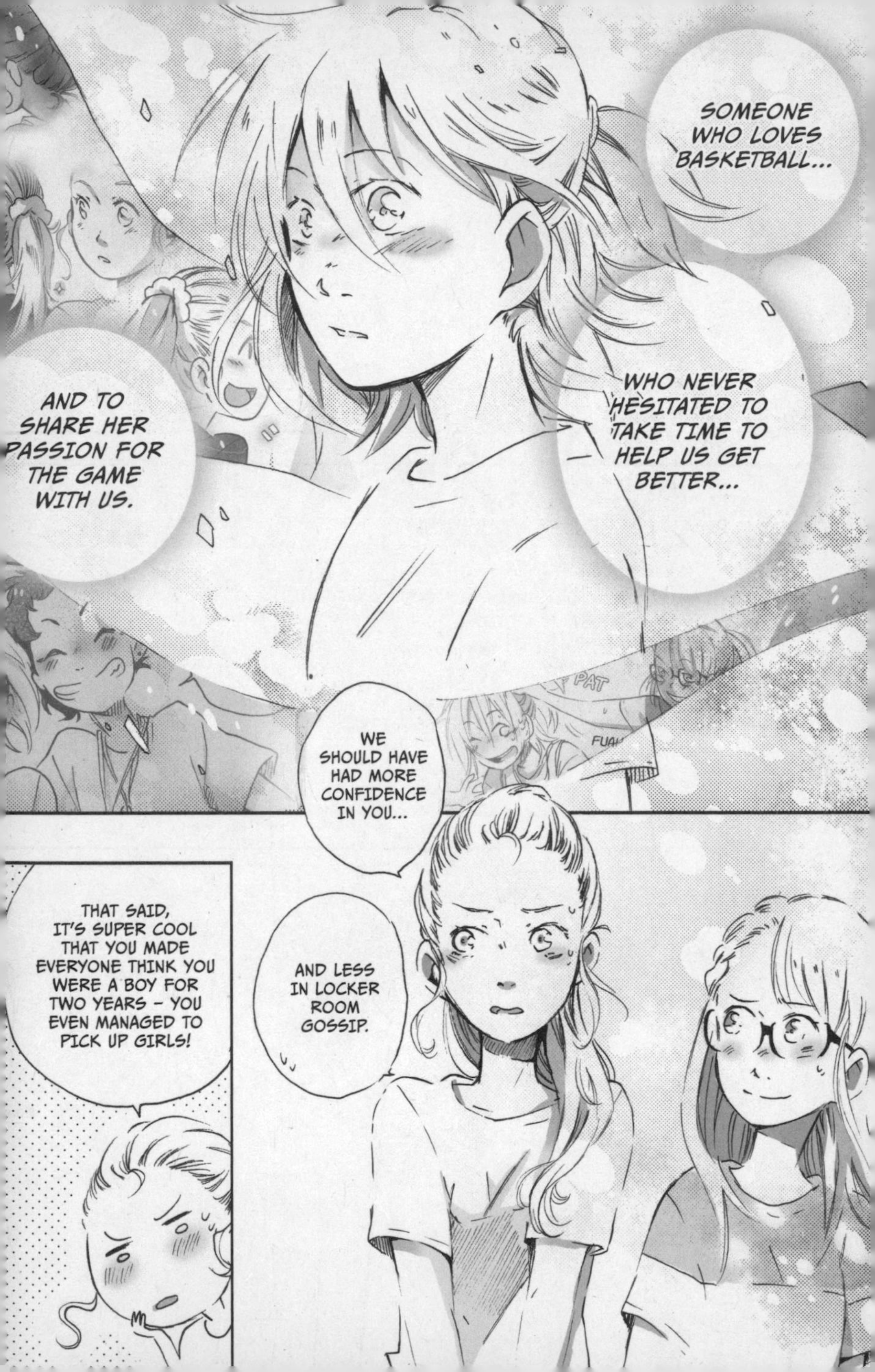
SOMEONE WHO LOVES BASKETBALL...
WHO NEVER HESITATED TO TAKE TIME TO HELP US GET BETTER...
AND TO SHARE HER PASSION FOR THE GAME WITH US.
PAT
WE SHOULD HAVE HAD MORE CONFIDENCE IN YOU...
AND LESS IN LOCKER ROOM GOSSIP.
THAT SAID, IT'S SUPER COOL THAT YOU MADE EVERYONE THINK YOU WERE A BOY FOR TWO YEARS – YOU EVEN MANAGED TO PICK UP GIRLS!

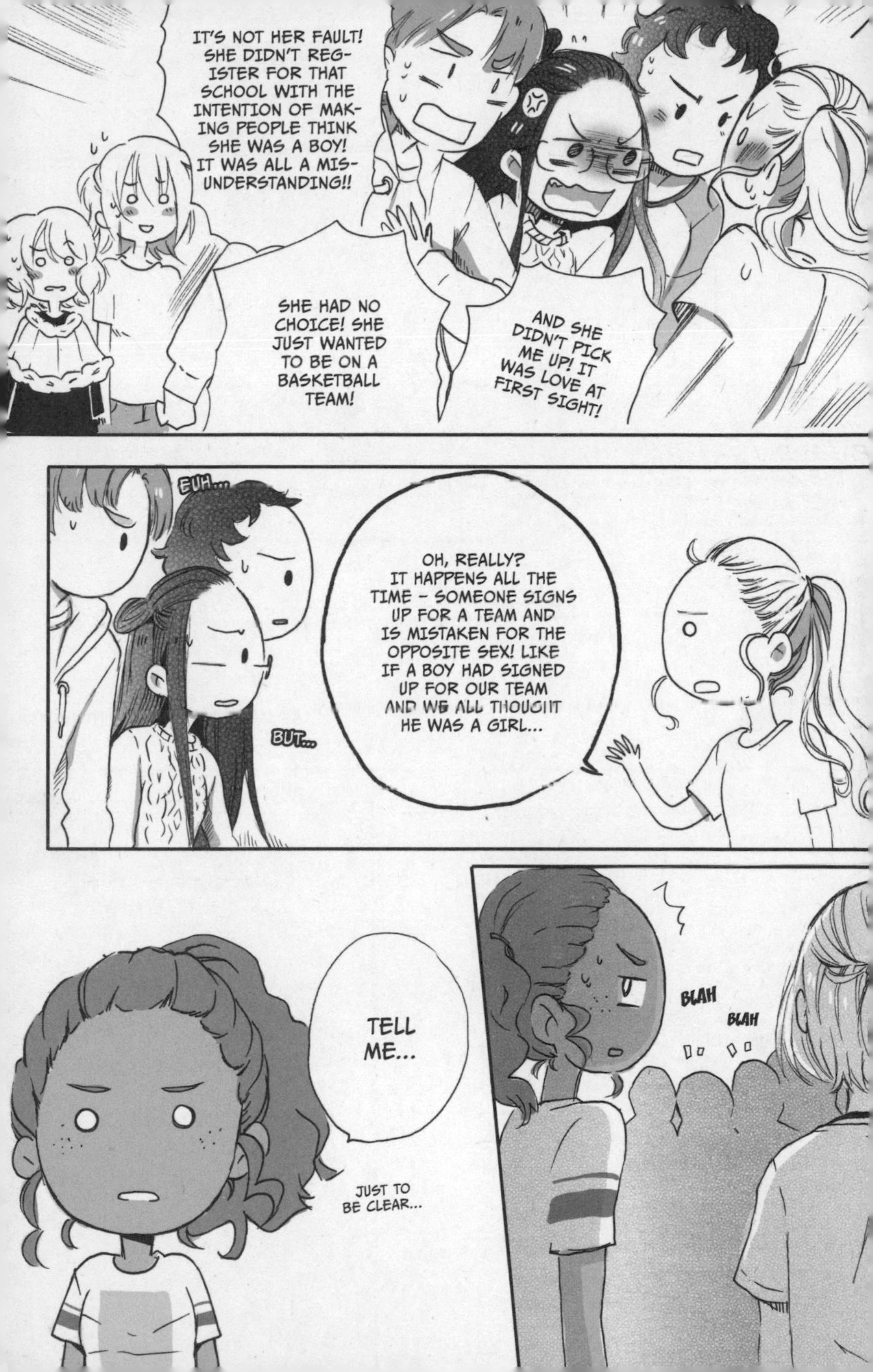
IT'S NOT HER FAULT! SHE DIDN'T REGISTER FOR THAT SCHOOL WITH THE INTENTION OF MAKING PEOPLE THINK SHE WAS A BOY! IT WAS ALL A MISUNDERSTANDING!!
AND SHE DIDN'T PICK ME UP! IT WAS LOVE AT FIRST SIGHT!
SHE HAD NO CHOICE! SHE JUST WANTED TO BE ON A BASKETBALL TEAM!
OH, REALLY? IT HAPPENS ALL THE TIME - SOMEONE SIGNS UP FOR A TEAM AND IS MISTAKEN FOR THE OPPOSITE SEX! LIKE IF A BOY HAD SIGNED UP FOR OUR TEAM AND WE ALL THOUGHT HE WAS A GIRL...
EUH...
BUT...
BLAH
BLAH
TELL ME...
JUST TO BE CLEAR...

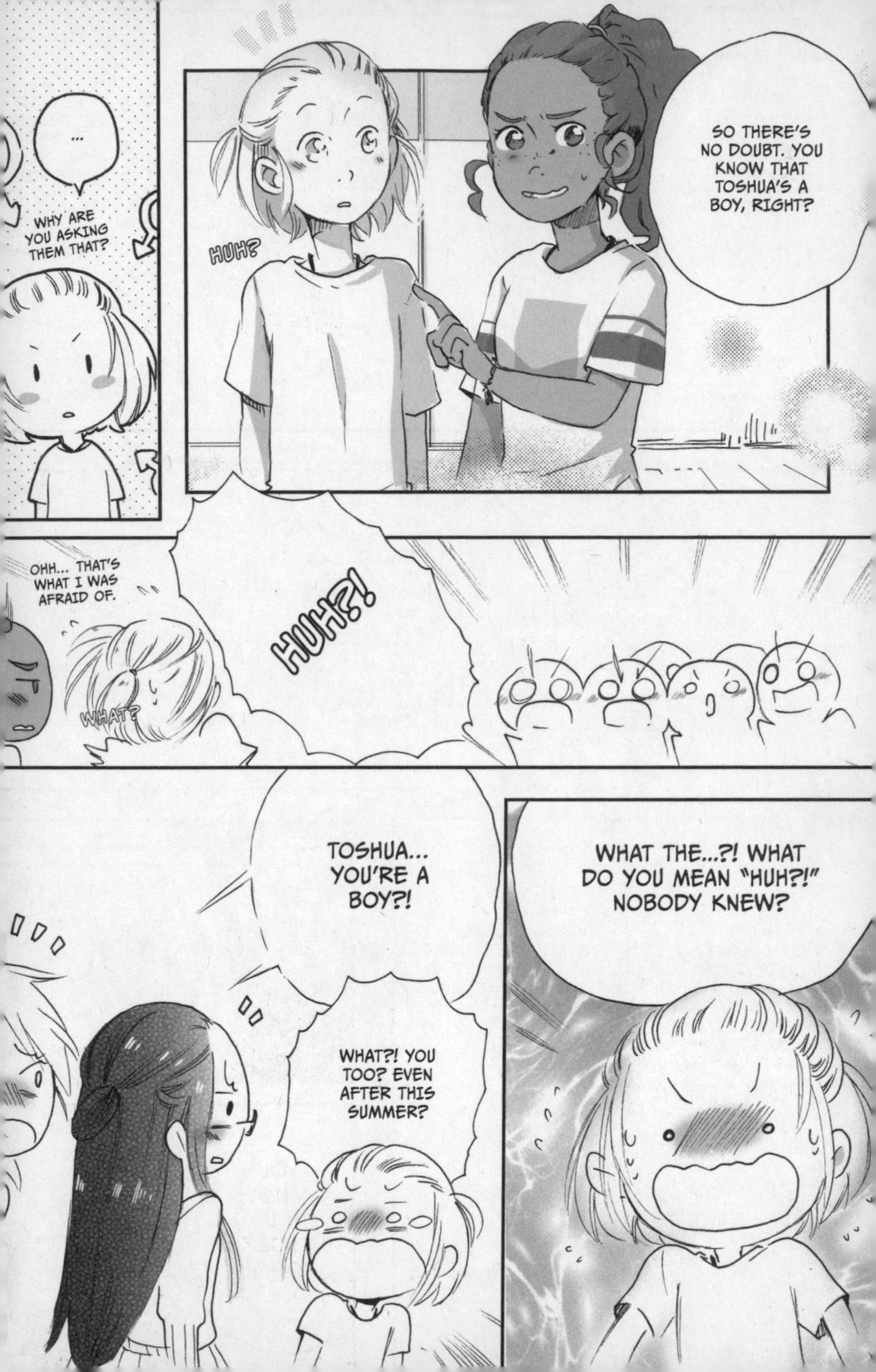
SO THERE'S NO DOUBT. YOU KNOW THAT TOSHUA'S A BOY, RIGHT?
HUH?
...
WHY ARE YOU ASKING THEM THAT?
HUH?!
OHH... THAT'S WHAT I WAS AFRAID OF.
WHAT?
WHAT THE...?! WHAT DO YOU MEAN "HUH?!" NOBODY KNEW?
TOSHUA... YOU'RE A BOY?!
WHAT?! YOU TOO? EVEN AFTER THIS SUMMER?

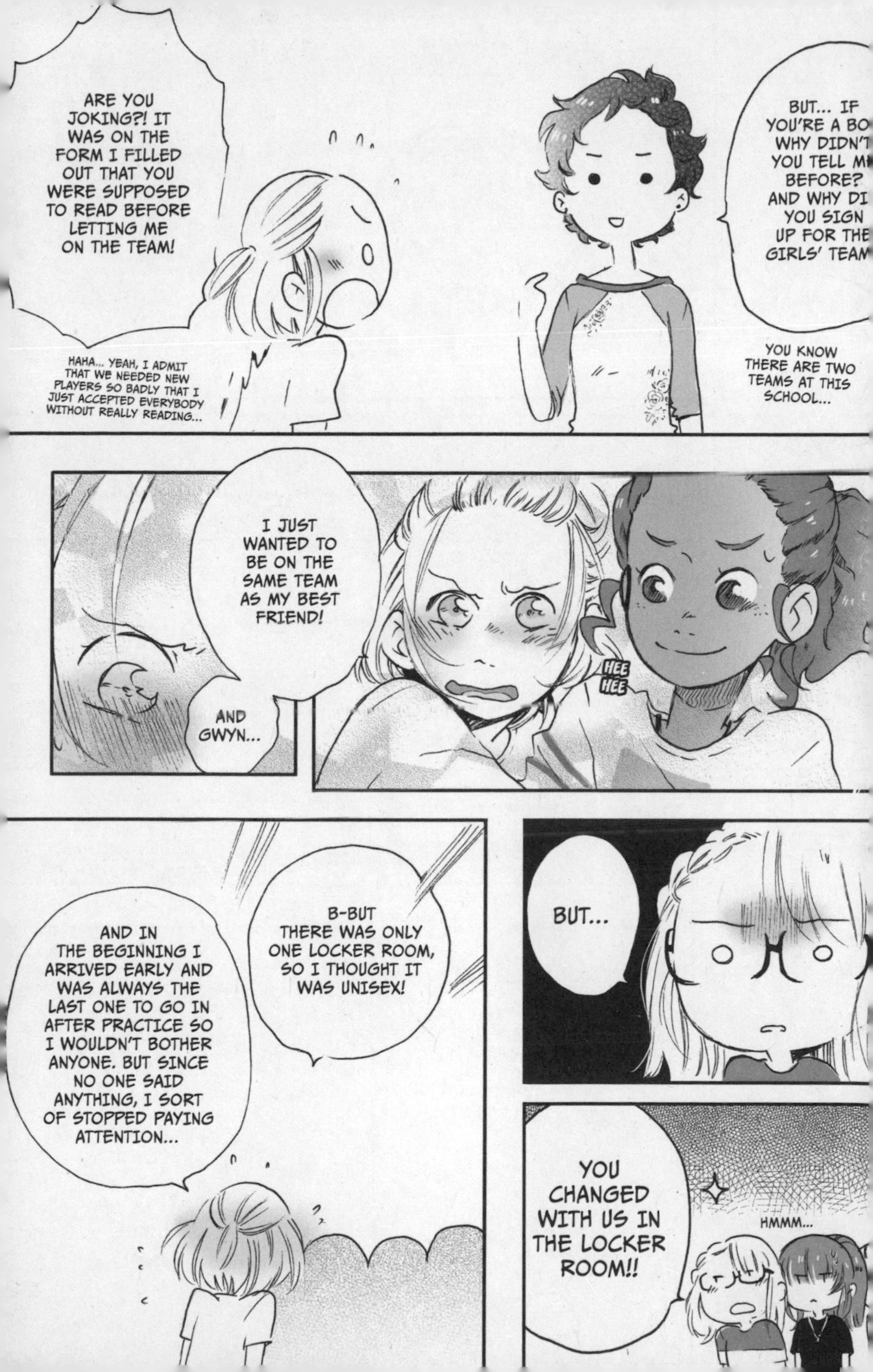
BUT... IF YOU'RE A BO WHY DIDN'T YOU TELL M BEFORE? AND WHY DI YOU SIGN UP FOR THE GIRLS' TEAM
YOU KNOW THERE ARE TWO TEAMS AT THIS SCHOOL...
ARE YOU JOKING?! IT WAS ON THE FORM I FILLED OUT THAT YOU WERE SUPPOSED TO READ BEFORE LETTING ME ON THE TEAM!
HAHA... YEAH, I ADMIT THAT WE NEEDED NEW PLAYERS SO BADLY THAT I JUST ACCEPTED EVERYBODY WITHOUT REALLY READING...
I JUST WANTED TO BE ON THE SAME TEAM AS MY BEST FRIEND!
HEE HEE
AND GWYN...
BUT...
YOU CHANGED WITH US IN THE LOCKER ROOM!!
HMMM...
B-BUT THERE WAS ONLY ONE LOCKER ROOM, SO I THOUGHT IT WAS UNISEX!
AND IN THE BEGINNING I ARRIVED EARLY AND WAS ALWAYS THE LAST ONE TO GO IN AFTER PRACTICE SO I WOULDN'T BOTHER ANYONE. BUT SINCE NO ONE SAID ANYTHING, I SORT OF STOPPED PAYING ATTENTION...

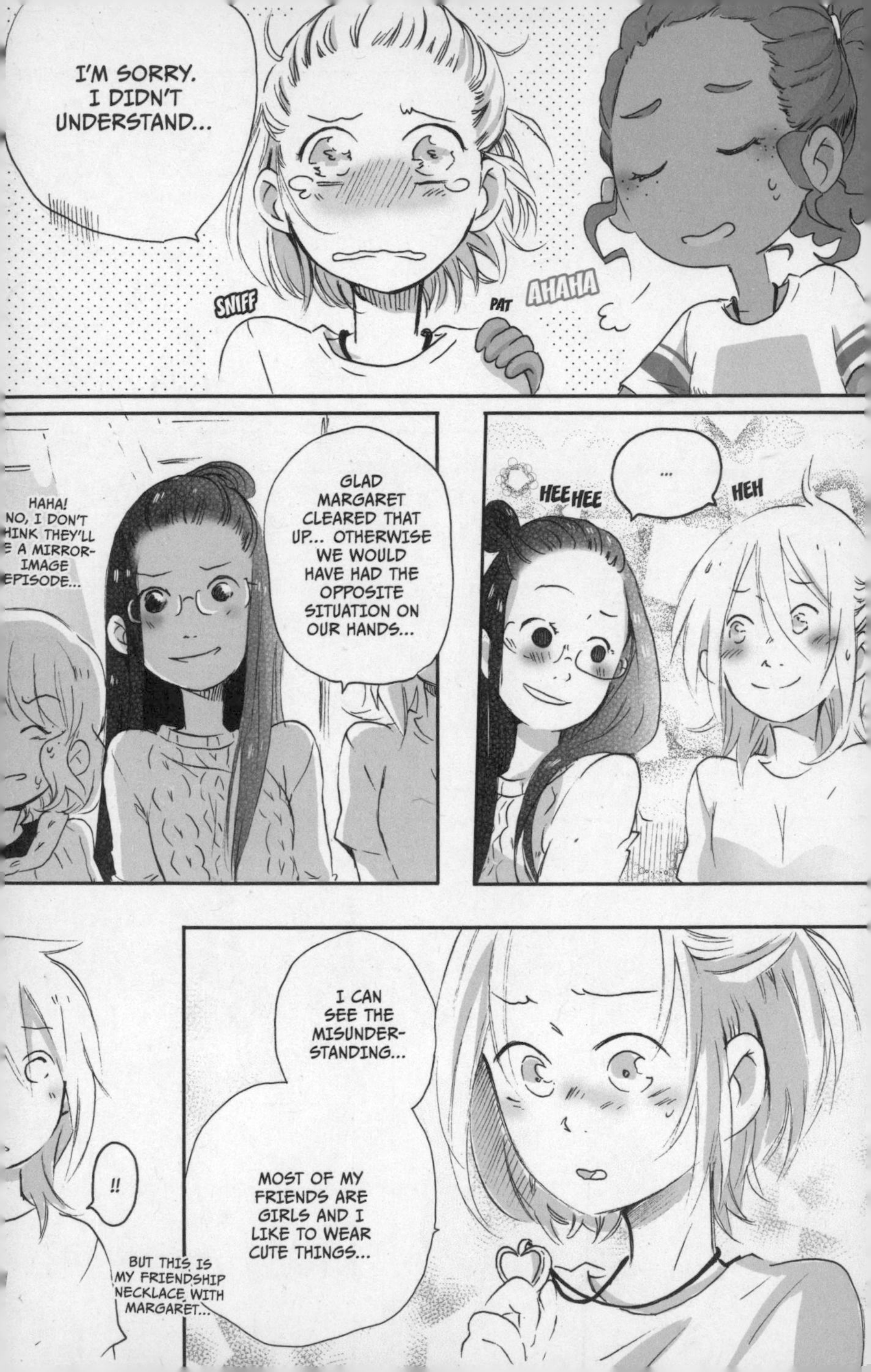
I'M SORRY. I DIDN'T UNDERSTAND...
AHAHA
PAT
SNIFF
HEH
...
HEE HEE
GLAD MARGARET CLEARED THAT UP... OTHERWISE WE WOULD HAVE HAD THE OPPOSITE SITUATION ON OUR HANDS...
HAHA! NO, I DON'T HINK THEY'LL E A MIRROR-IMAGE EPISODE...
I CAN SEE THE MISUNDER-STANDING...
MOST OF MY FRIENDS ARE GIRLS AND I LIKE TO WEAR CUTE THINGS...
BUT THIS IS MY FRIENDSHIP NECKLACE WITH MARGARET...
!!

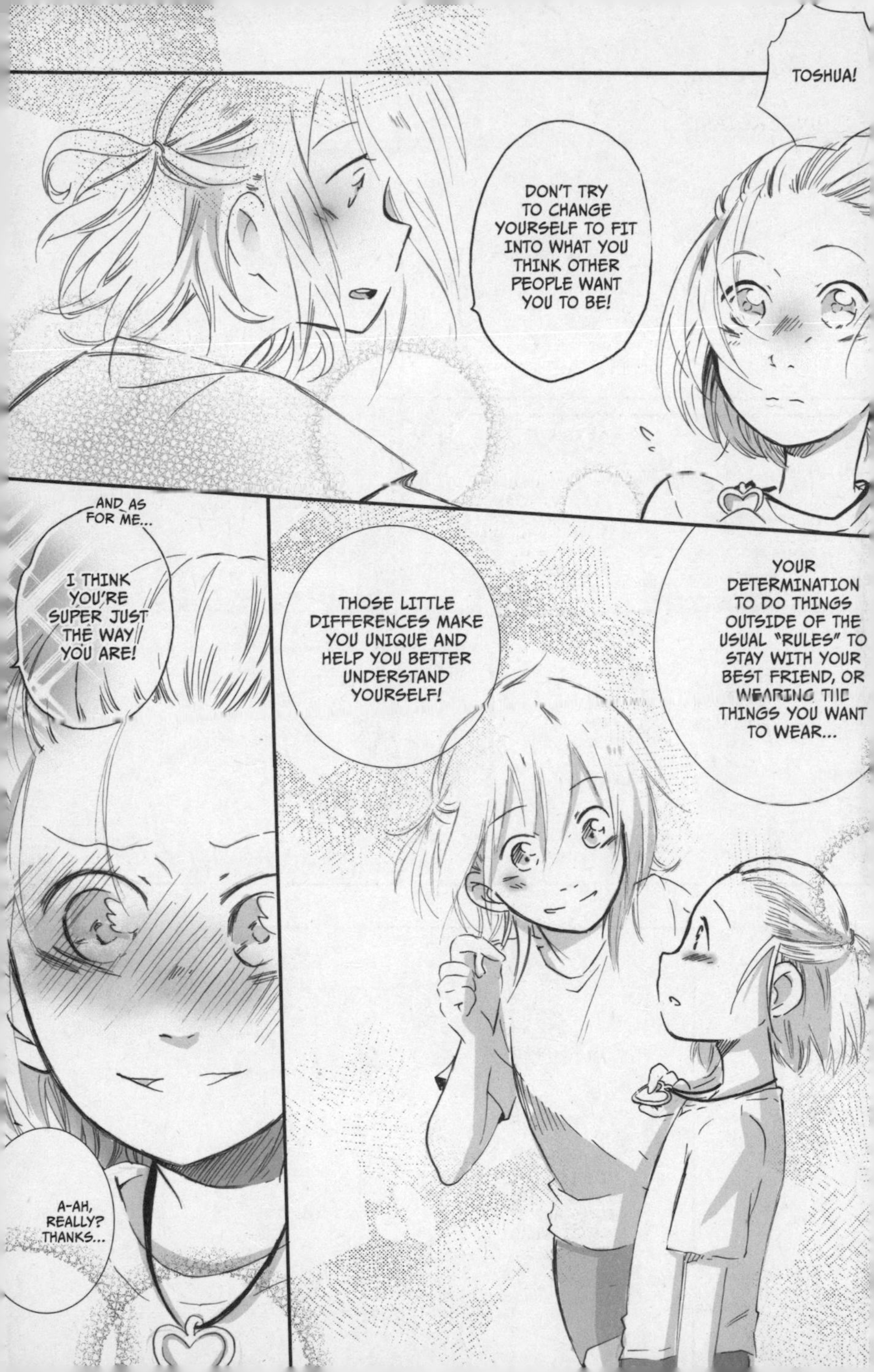
TOSHUA!
DON'T TRY TO CHANGE YOURSELF TO FIT INTO WHAT YOU THINK OTHER PEOPLE WANT YOU TO BE!
YOUR DETERMINATION TO DO THINGS OUTSIDE OF THE USUAL "RULES" TO STAY WITH YOUR BEST FRIEND, OR WEARING THE THINGS YOU WANT TO WEAR...
THOSE LITTLE DIFFERENCES MAKE YOU UNIQUE AND HELP YOU BETTER UNDERSTAND YOURSELF!
AND AS FOR ME...
I THINK YOU'RE SUPER JUST THE WAY YOU ARE!
A-AH, REALLY? THANKS...

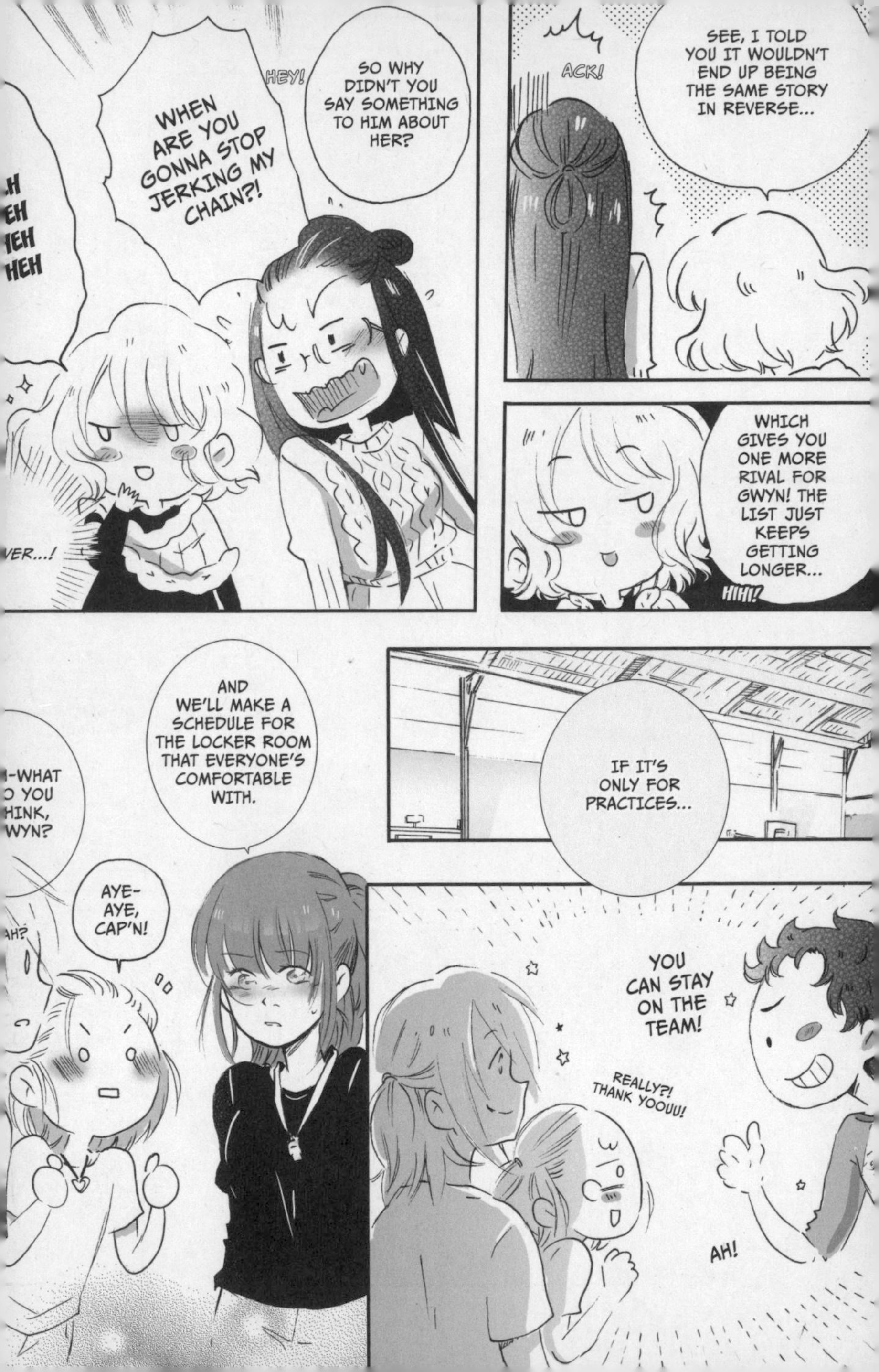

ACK!
SEE, I TOLD YOU IT WOULDN'T END UP BEING THE SAME STORY IN REVERSE...
WHICH GIVES YOU ONE MORE RIVAL FOR GWYN! THE LIST JUST KEEPS GETTING LONGER...
HIHI!
SO WHY DIDN'T YOU SAY SOMETHING TO HIM ABOUT HER?
HEY!
WHEN ARE YOU GONNA STOP JERKING MY CHAIN?!
IF IT'S ONLY FOR PRACTICES...
AND WE'LL MAKE A SCHEDULE FOR THE LOCKER ROOM THAT EVERYONE'S COMFORTABLE WITH.
YOU CAN STAY ON THE TEAM!
REALLY?! THANK YOOUU!
AH!
AYE-AYE, CAP'N!

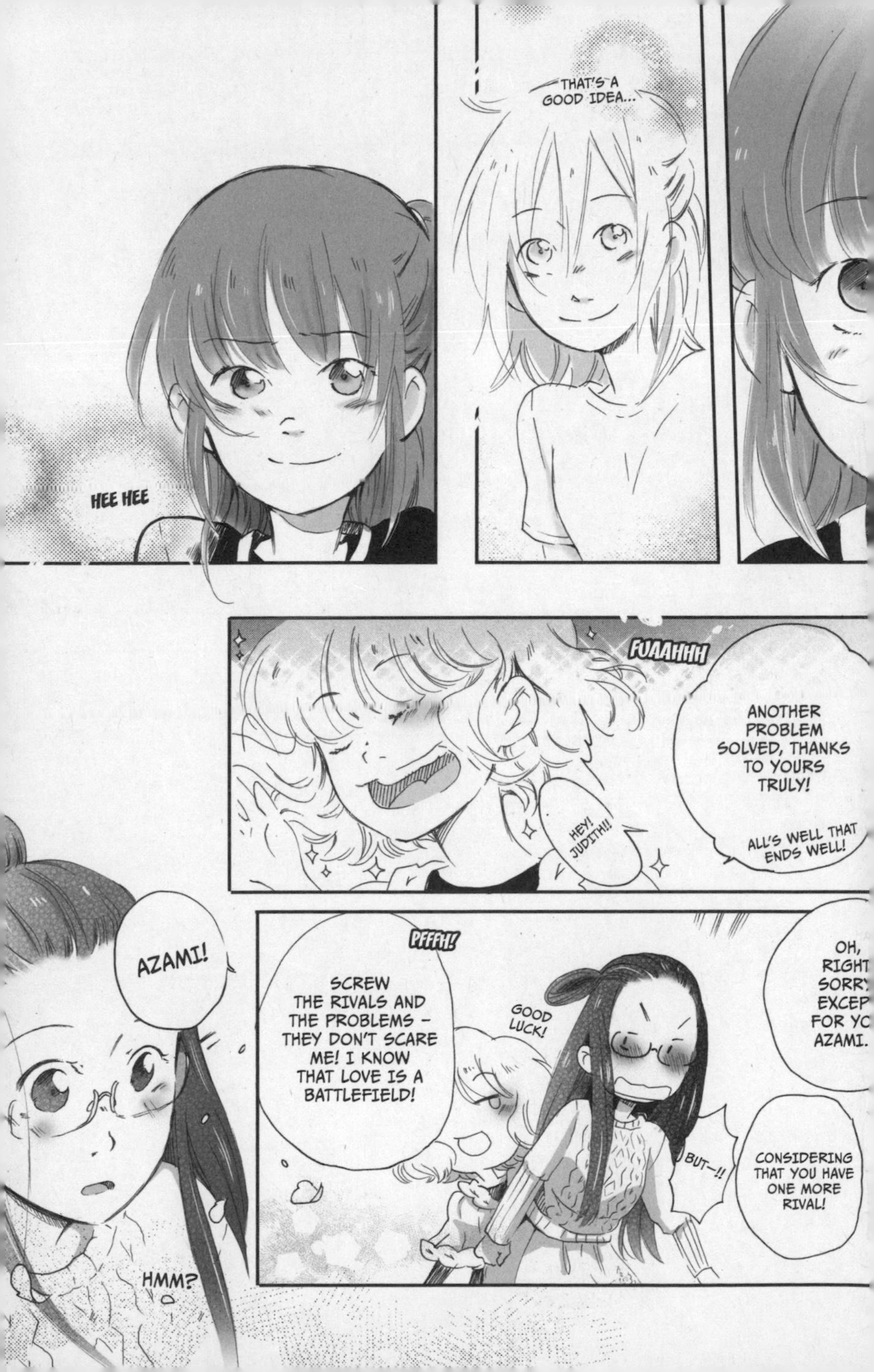
THAT'S A GOOD IDEA...
HEE HEE
FUAAHHH
ANOTHER PROBLEM SOLVED, THANKS TO YOURS TRULY!
ALL'S WELL THAT ENDS WELL!
HEY! JUDITH!!
PFFFH!
SCREW THE RIVALS AND THE PROBLEMS – THEY DON'T SCARE ME! I KNOW THAT LOVE IS A BATTLEFIELD!
GOOD LUCK!
OH, RIGHT SORRY EXCEP FOR YO AZAMI.
CONSIDERING THAT YOU HAVE ONE MORE RIVAL!
BUT–!!
AZAMI!
HMM?

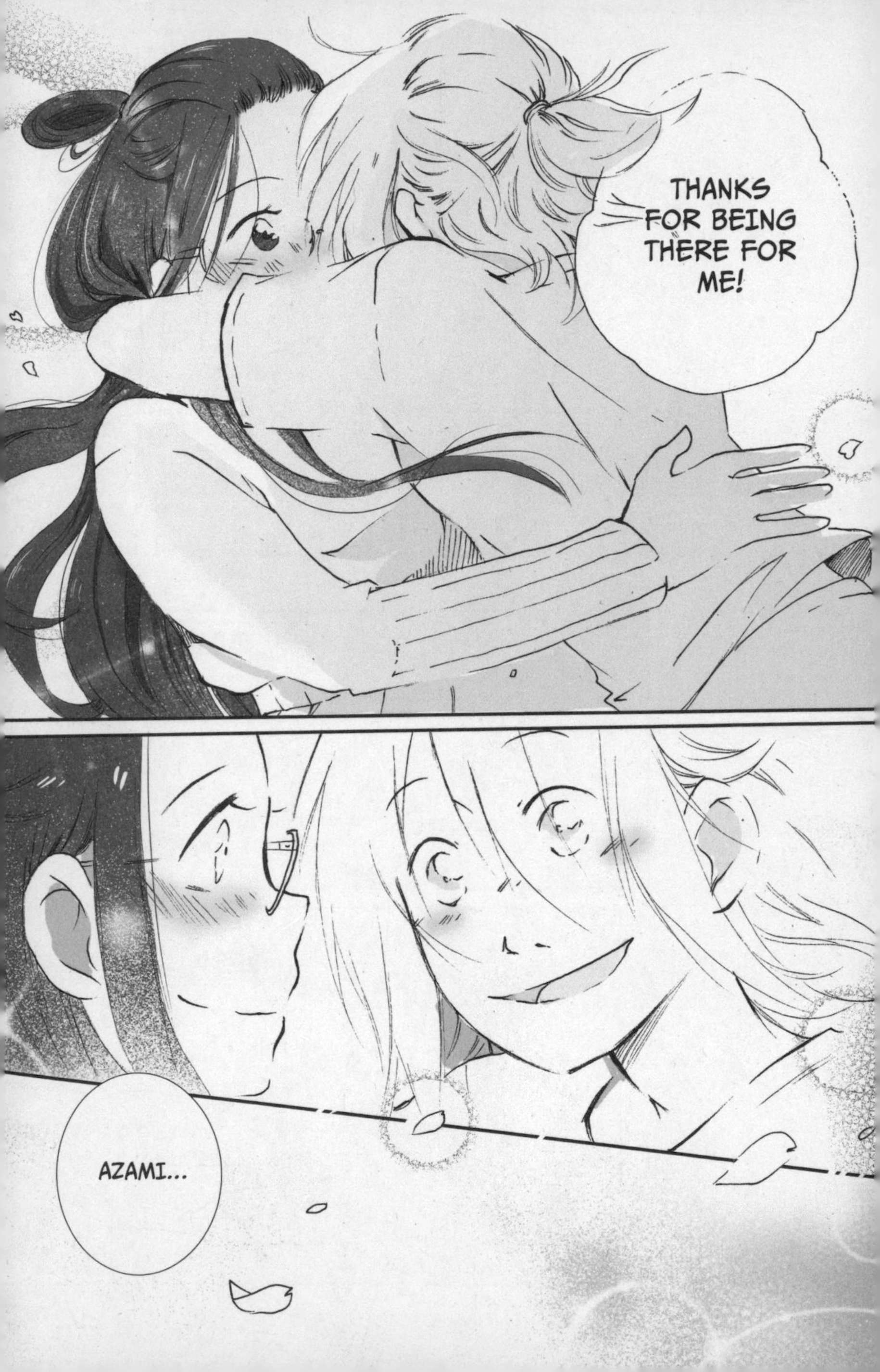
THANKS FOR BEING THERE FOR ME!
AZAMI...

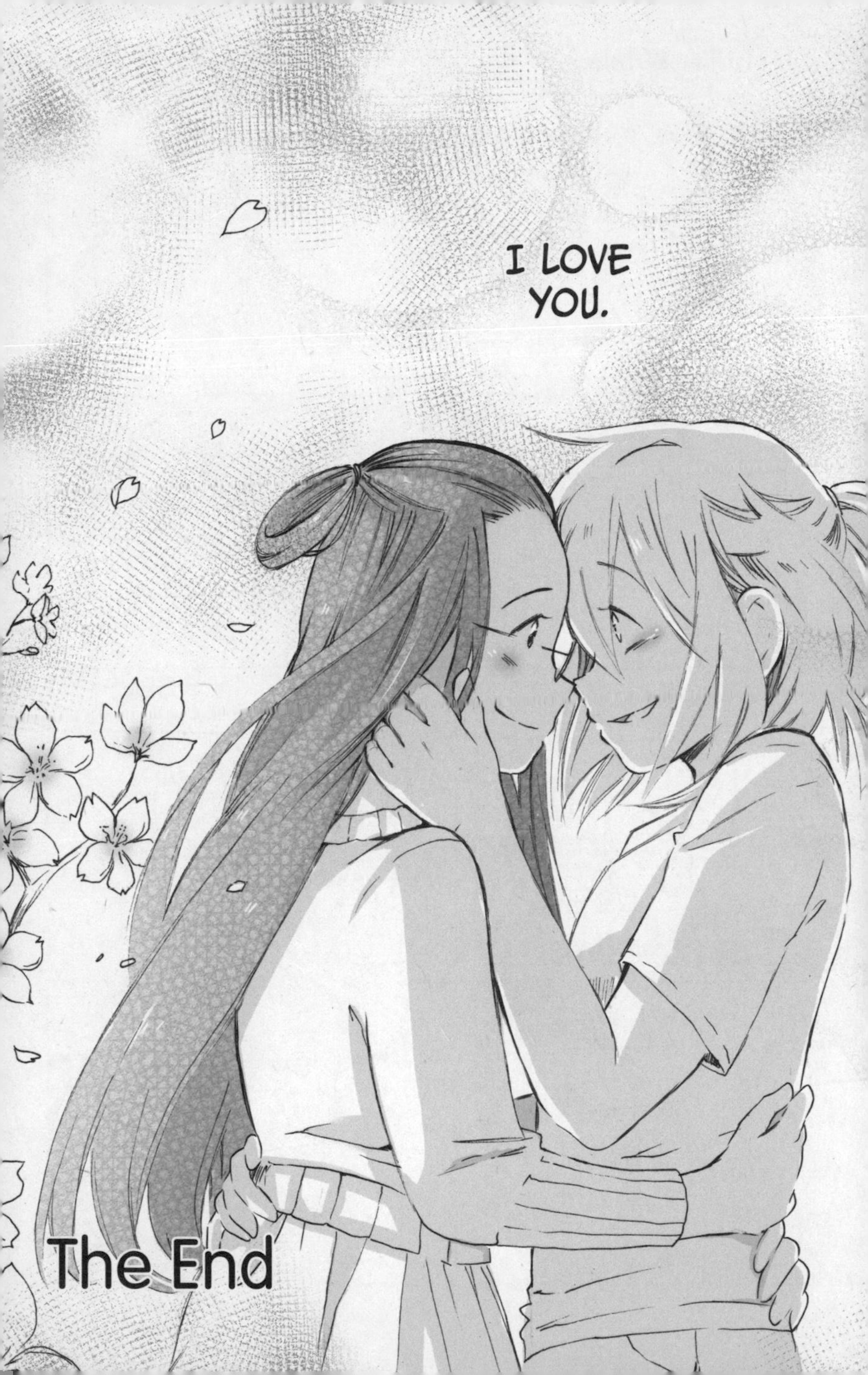
I LOVE YOU.
The End

MAGIC HAIR

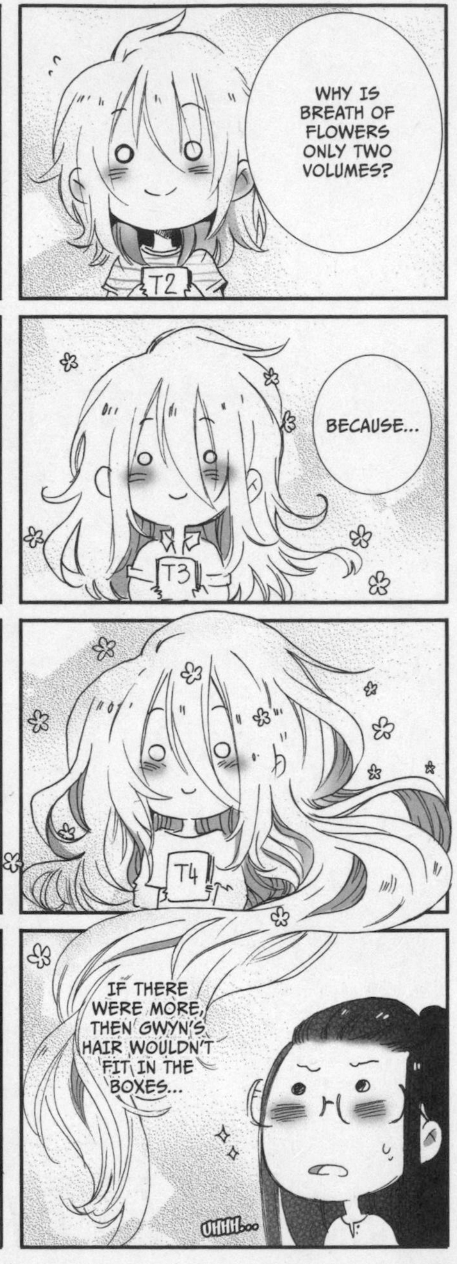
WHY IS BREATH OF FLOWERS ONLY TWO VOLUMES?
T2
BECAUSE...
T3
T4
IF THERE WERE MORE, THEN GWYN'S HAIR WOULDN'T FIT IN THE BOXES...
UHHH...

A FAMILY RESEMBLANCE

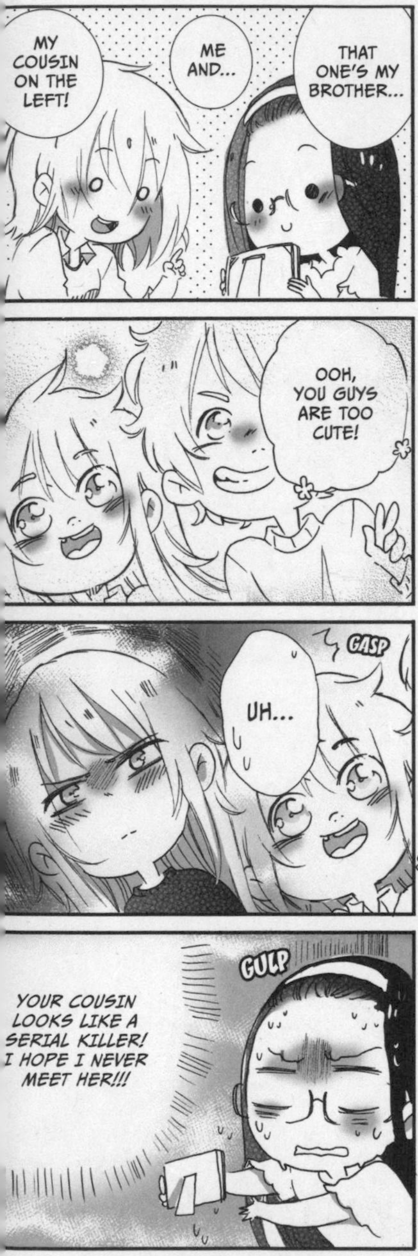
THAT ONE'S MY BROTHER...
ME AND...
MY COUSIN ON THE LEFT!
OOH, YOU GUYS ARE TOO CUTE!
GASP
UH...
GULP
YOUR COUSIN LOOKS LIKE A SERIAL KILLER! I HOPE I NEVER MEET HER!!!

BREATH OF FLOWERS

BREATH OF FLOWERS

And now we've reached the end of
BREATH OF FLOWERS, my first
published manga! It was a great first
experience in the publishing world!

I hope to be able to publish other stories
and continue to share adventures and
emotions with all of you!●

SPECIAL THANKS

- MY EDITORS, FOR EVERYTHING! (THE LIST WOULD BE TOO LONG...)

- MARION FOR HER ADVICE ON THE SCRIPT AND ROMANTIC ENTANGLEMENTS

- LUCILE FOR HER PIERCING LOOKS AND HER VALUABLE HELP WITH THE COVERS

- AYA WHO WAS ALWAYS AVAILABLE TO GIVE ME HER ADVICE ON THE DIALOGUE AND SCRIPTS

- KIRA FOR HER HELP WITH THE FRAMES (TEAM SHOJO FROM EDITIONS H2T)

- MY DEAR MOTHER FOR HER UNWAVERING SUPPORT!

AND YOU, THE READERS OF THIS MANGA! THANK YOU!

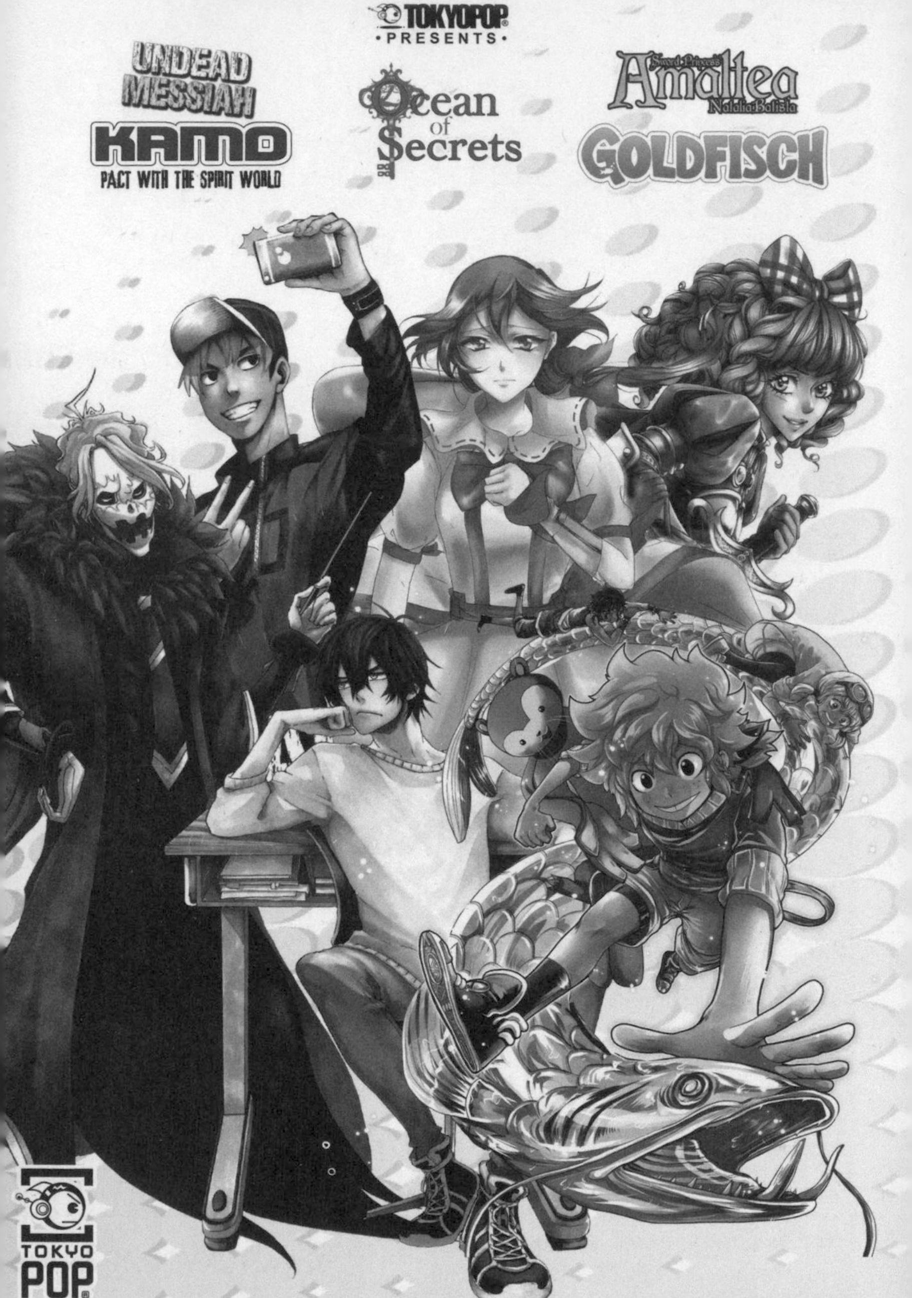

TOKYOPOP
PRESENTS
UNDEAD MESSIAH
KAMO
PACT WITH THE SPIRIT WORLD
Ocean of Secrets
Sword Princess Amaltea
Natalia Batista
GOLDFISCH
TOKYO POP

TOKYOPOP PRESENTS

INTERNATIONAL WOMEN of MANGA

Nana Yaa

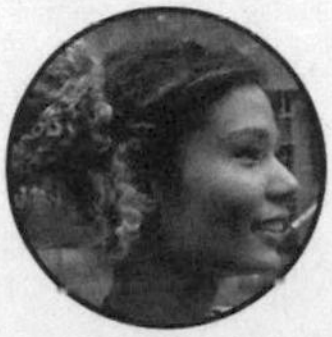

GOLDFISCH

An award-winning German manga artist with a large following for her free webcomic, ***CRUSHED!!***

Sophie-Char

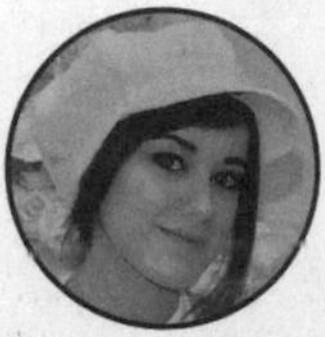

Ocean of Secrets

A self-taught manga artist from t Middle East, with a huge YouTu following!

Ban Zarbo

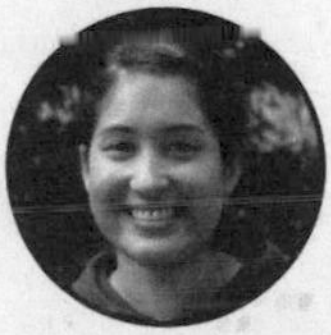

KAMO
PACT WITH THE SPIRIT WORLD

A lifelong manga fan from Switzerland, she and her twin sister take inspiration from their Dominican roots!

Gin Zarbo

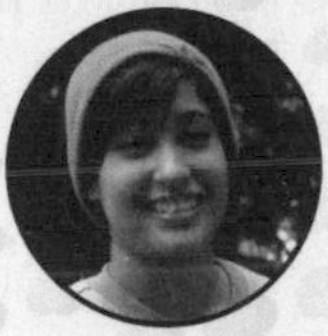

UNDEAD MESSIAH

An aspiring manga artist since she w a child, along with her twin sister sh releasing her debut title!

Natalia Batista

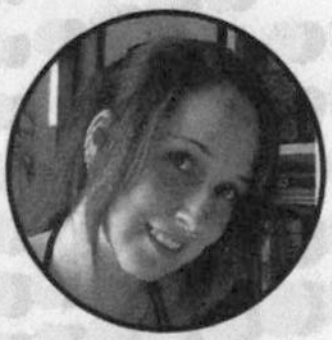

Sword Princess Amaltea
Natalia Batista

A Swedish creator whose popular manga has already been published in Sweden, Italy and the Czech Republic!

TO LEARN MORE PLEAS VISIT OUR WEBSITE

www.TOKYOPOP.com

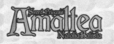

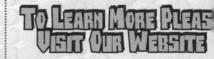

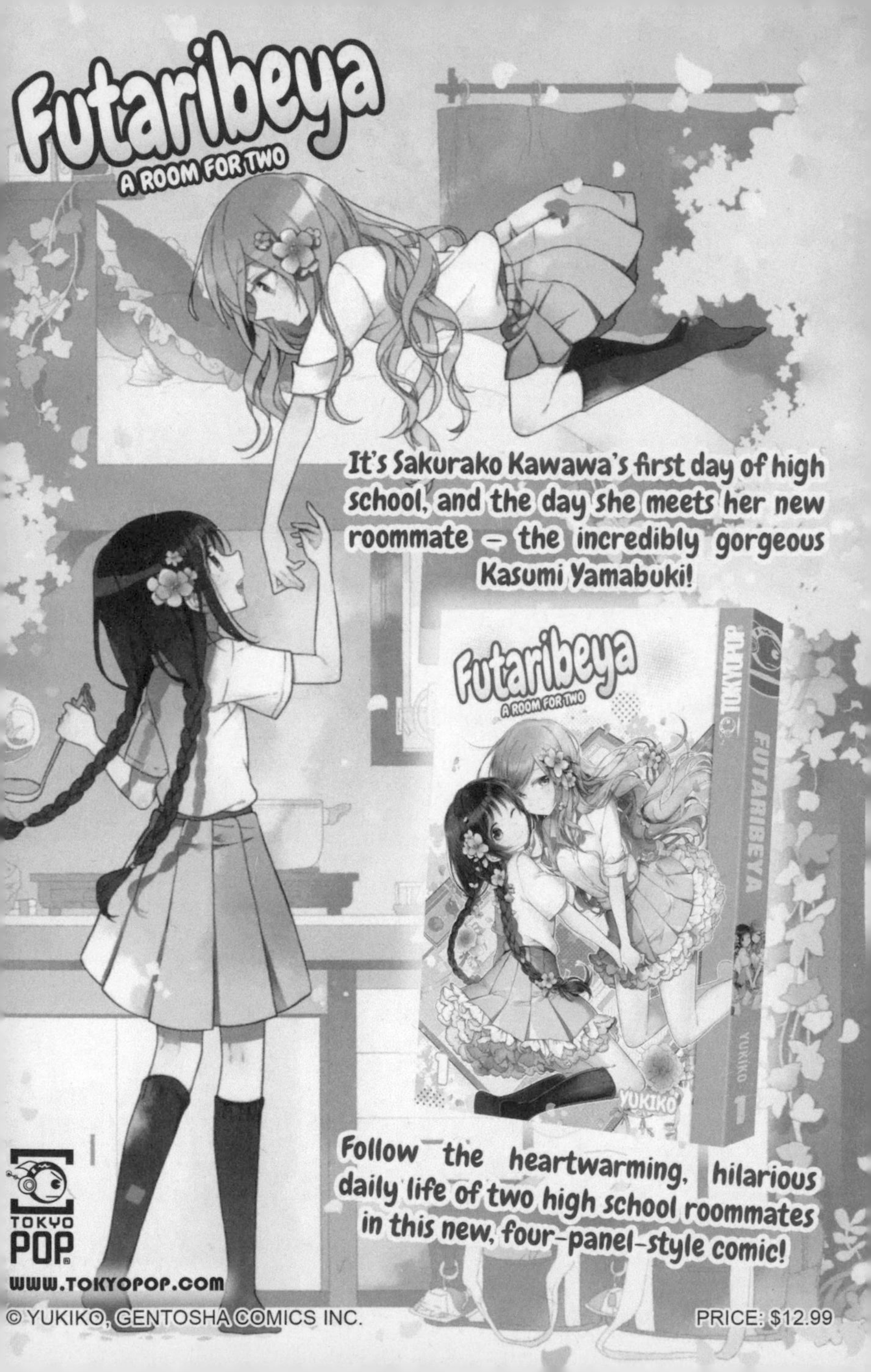
Futaribeya
A ROOM FOR TWO
It's Sakurako Kawawa's first day of high school, and the day she meets her new roommate – the incredibly gorgeous Kasumi Yamabuki!
Futaribeya
A ROOM FOR TWO
TOKYOPOP
FUTARIBEYA
YUKIKO
1
Follow the heartwarming, hilarious daily life of two high school roommates in this new, four-panel-style comic!
TOKYO POP
WWW.TOKYOPOP.COM
© YUKIKO, GENTOSHA COMICS INC.
PRICE: $12.99

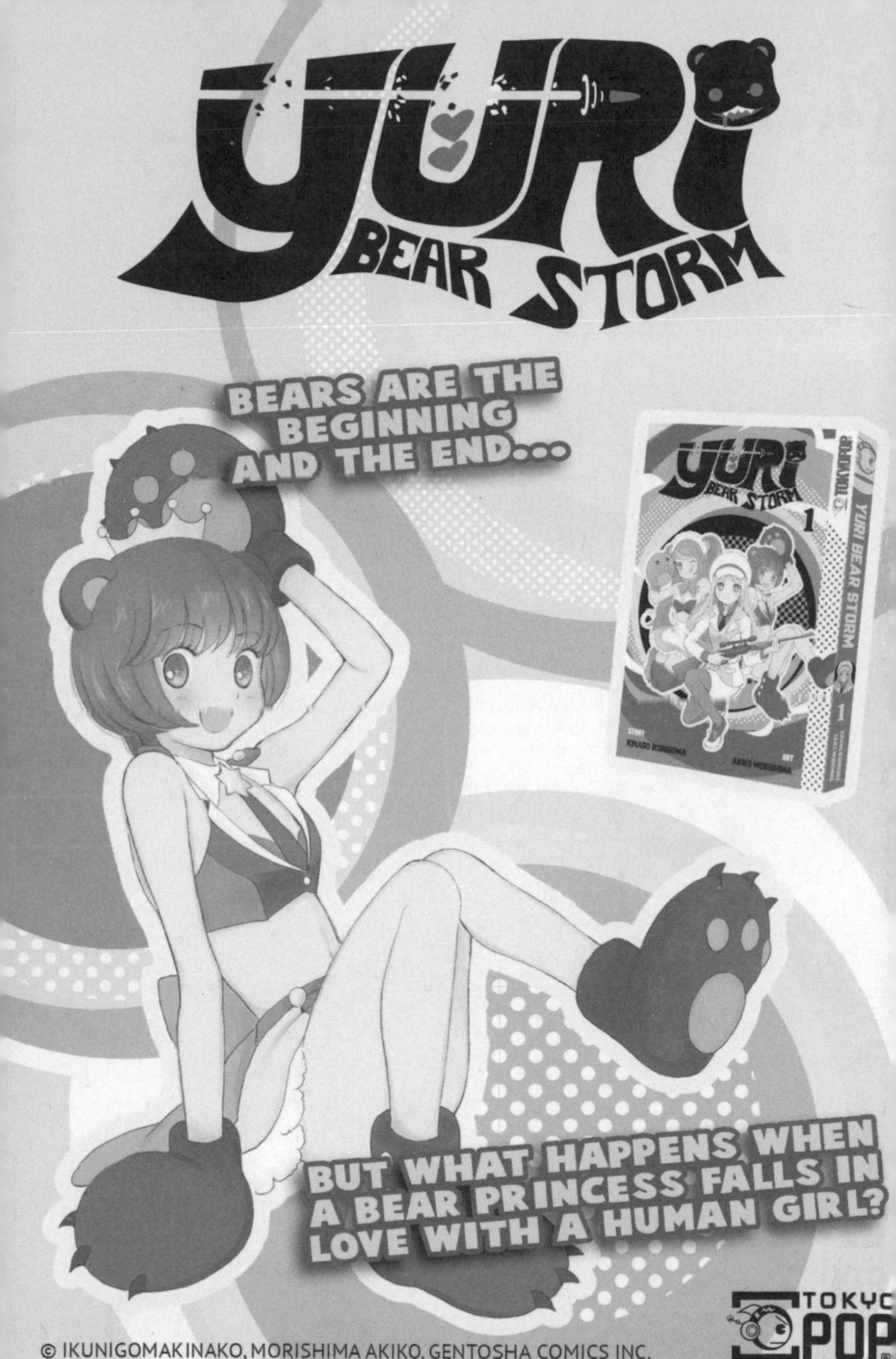
YURI BEAR STORM
BEARS ARE THE BEGINNING AND THE END...
BUT WHAT HAPPENS WHEN A BEAR PRINCESS FALLS IN LOVE WITH A HUMAN GIRL?

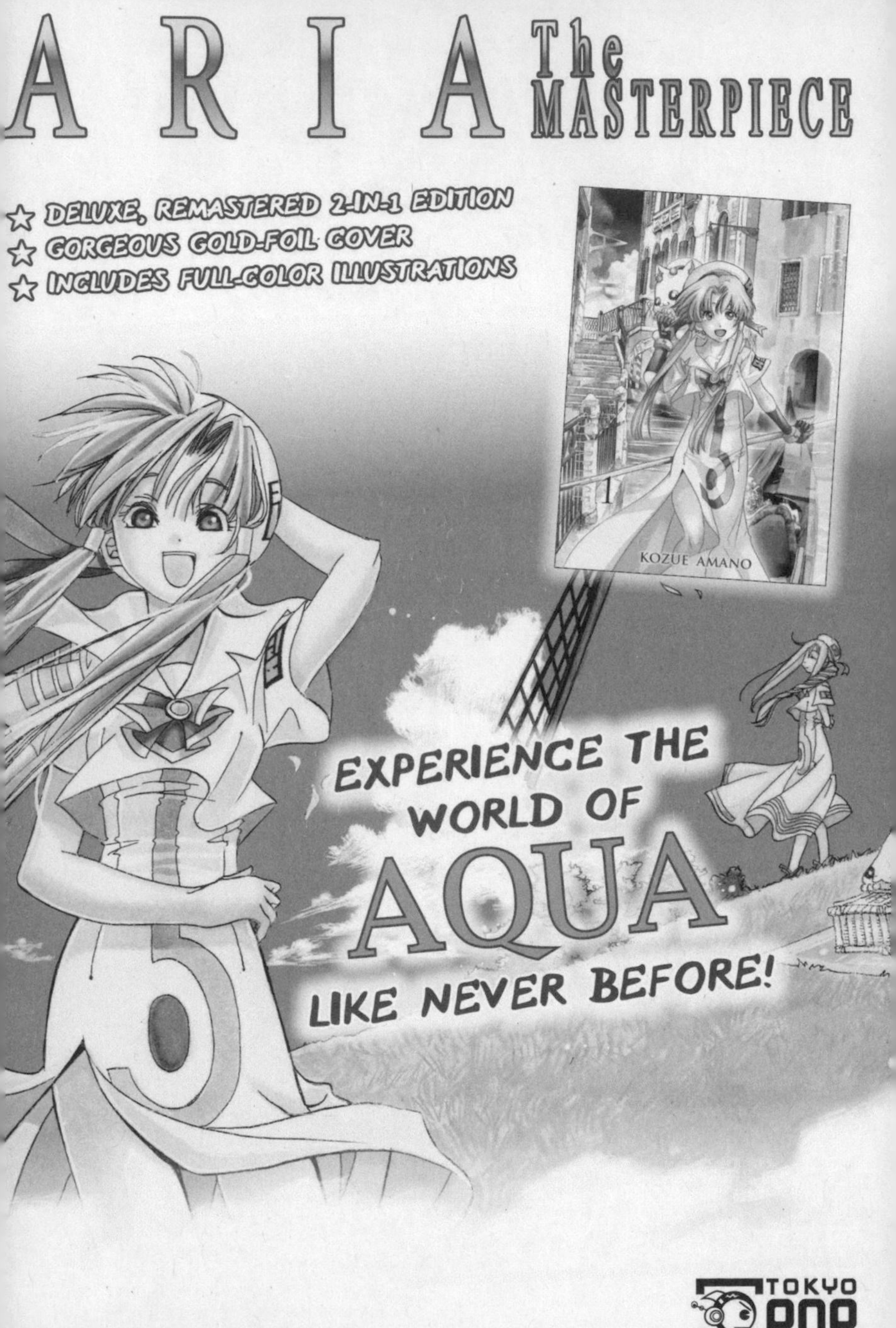
ARIA The MASTERPIECE
DELUXE, REMASTERED 2-IN-1 EDITION
GORGEOUS GOLD-FOIL COVER
INCLUDES FULL-COLOR ILLUSTRATIONS
1
KOZUE AMANO
EXPERIENCE THE WORLD OF
AQUA
LIKE NEVER BEFORE!
TOKYO POP
© KOZUE AMANO / MAG Garden

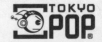

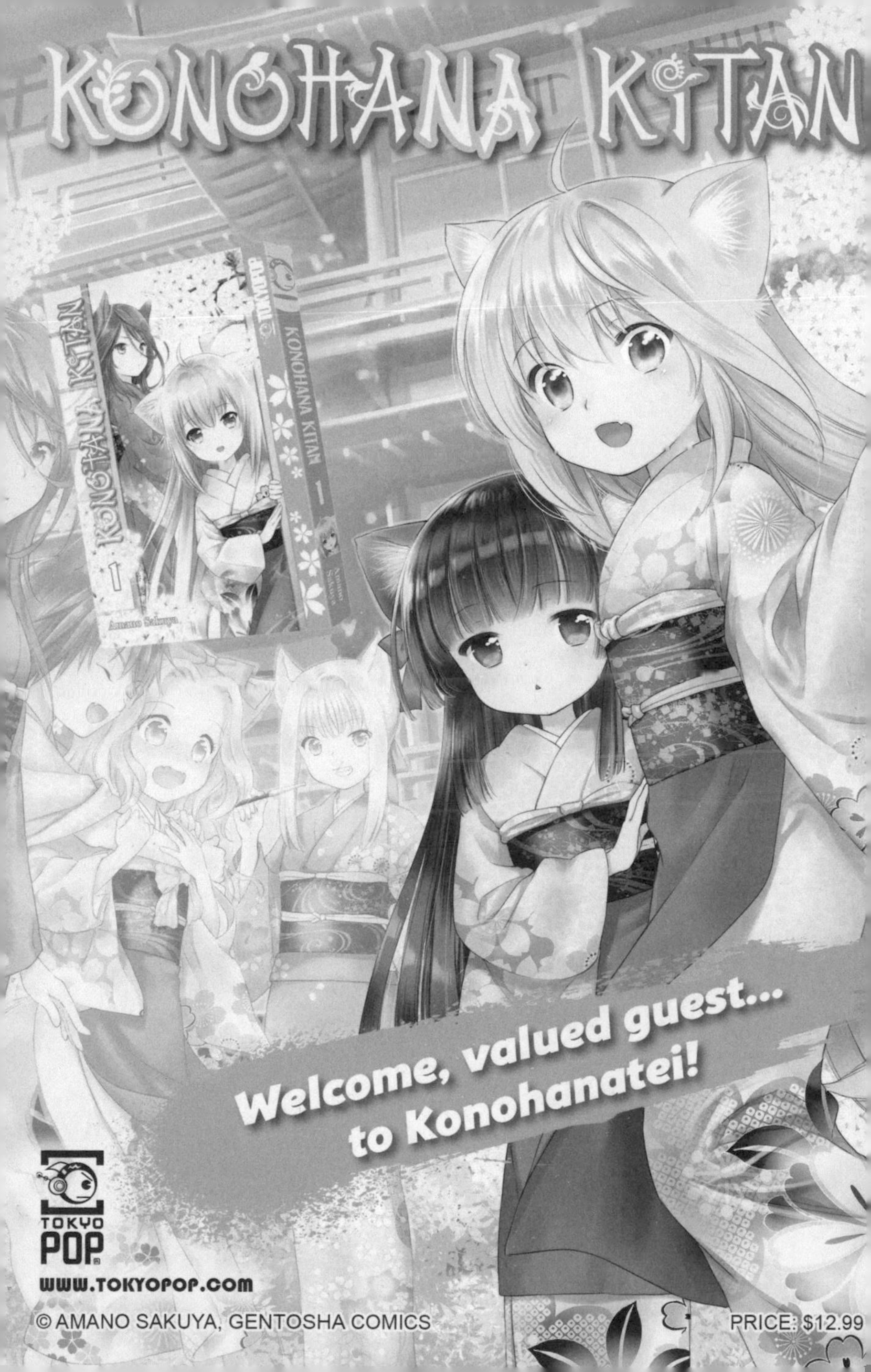

KONOHANA KITAN
KONOHANA KITAN
1
Amano Sakuya
KONOHANA KITAN
1
Welcome, valued guest...
to Konohanatei!
TOKYO POP
WWW.TOKYOPOP.COM
© AMANO SAKUYA, GENTOSHA COMICS
PRICE: $12.99

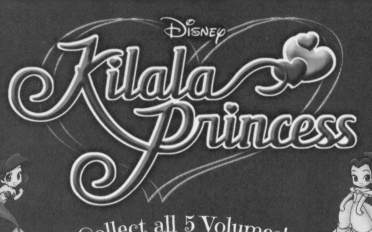

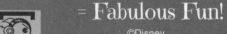

Disney Marie

MIRIYA & MARIE

☆ **Inspired by the characters from Disney's The Aristocats**

☆ **Learn facts about Paris and Japan!**

☆ **Adorable original shojo story**

☆ **Full color manga**

Even though the wealthy young girl Miriya has almost everything she could ever need, what she really wants is the one thing money can't buy: her missing parents. But this year, she gets an extra special birthday gift when Marie, a magical white kitten, appears and whisks her away to Paris! Learning the art of magic is one thing, but getting to eat the tastiest French pastries and wear the most beautiful fashion takes Miriya and Marie's journey to a whole new level!

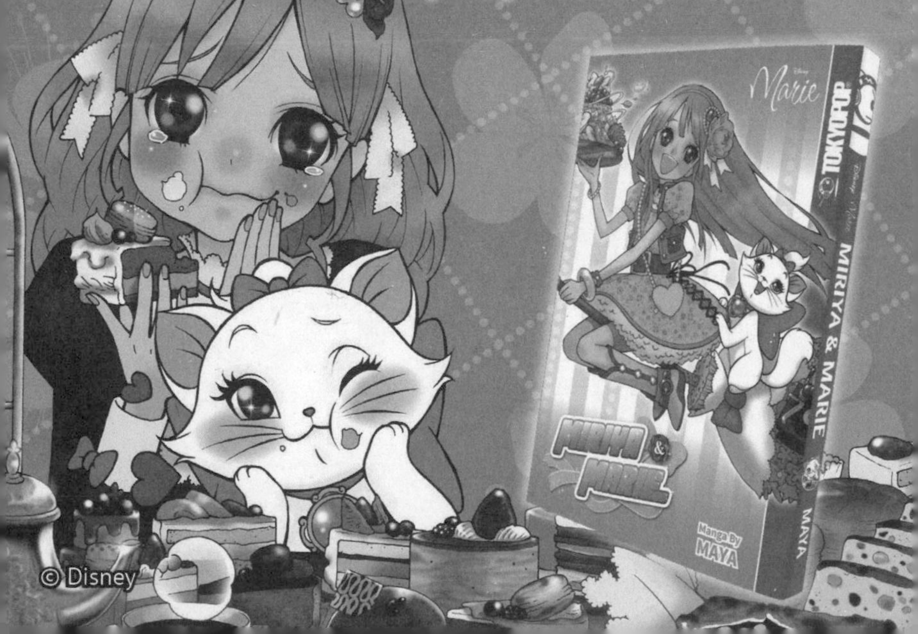
Marie
TOKYOPOP
MIRIYA & MARIE
Miriya & Marie
Manga By MAYA
MAYA

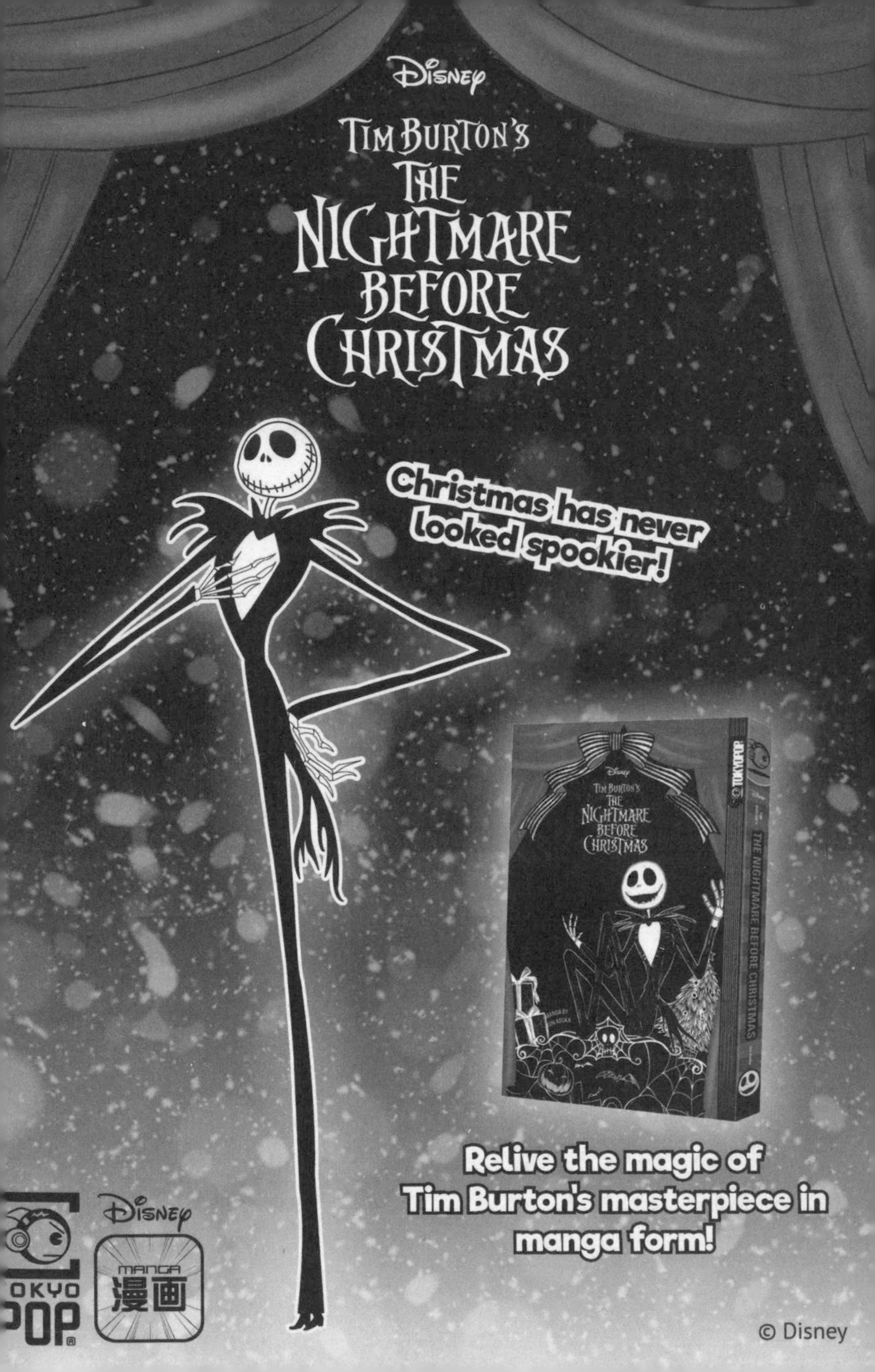
Disney
Tim Burton's
The Nightmare Before Christmas
Christmas has never looked spookier!
Disney
Tim Burton's
The Nightmare Before Christmas
TOKYOPOP
THE NIGHTMARE BEFORE CHRISTMAS
Relive the magic of Tim Burton's masterpiece in manga form!
TOKYOPOP
Disney
MANGA
漫画
© Disney

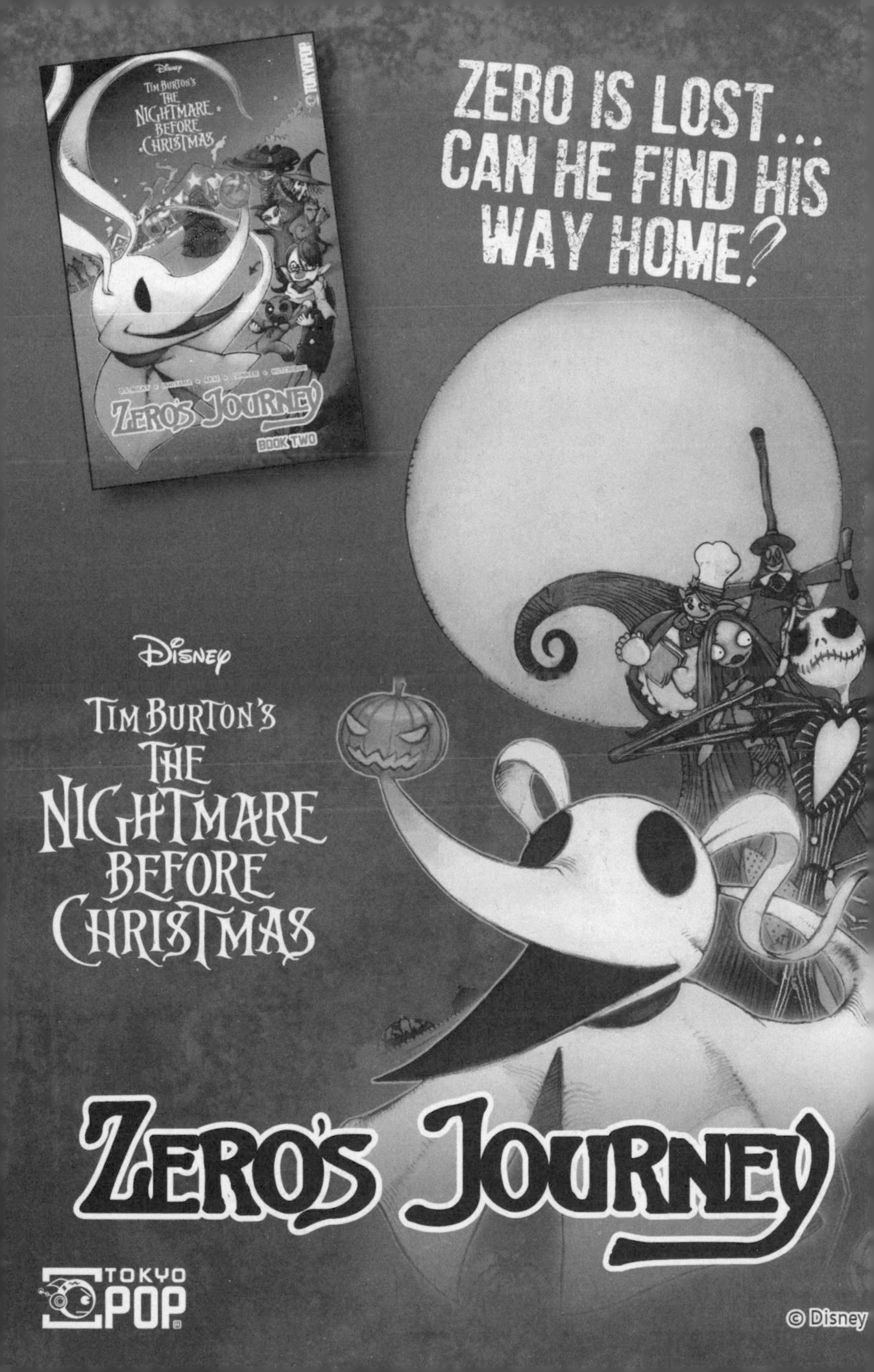
Disney
Tim Burton's The Nightmare Before Christmas
Zero's Journey
Book Two
ZERO IS LOST...
CAN HE FIND HIS
WAY HOME?
Disney
Tim Burton's
The Nightmare Before Christmas
Zero's Journey
TOKYO POP
© Disney